CHINA'S DEVELOPMENT
EXPERIENCE IN
COMPARATIVE PERSPECTIVE

Harvard East Asian Series 93

The Council on East Asian Studies at Harvard University, through the Fairbank Center for East Asian Research, administers research projects designed to further scholarly understanding of China, Japan, Korea, Vietnam, Inner Asia, and adjacent areas.

Sponsored by the

Subcommittee on Research on the Chinese Economy

of the

Joint Committee on Contemporary China

of the

American Council of Learned Societies

and the

Social Science Research Council

CONTRIBUTORS

ROBERT F. DERNBERGER
ALBERT FEUERWERKER
TEH-WEI HU
NICHOLAS LARDY
FRANÇOISE LE GALL
DWIGHT H. PERKINS
THOMAS G. RAWSKI
AMARTYA SEN
BENJAMIN WARD
THOMAS E. WEISSKOPF

CHINA'S DEVELOPMENT EXPERIENCE IN COMPARATIVE PERSPECTIVE

Edited by Robert F. Dernberger

Harvard University Press
Cambridge, Massachusetts
and London, England
1980

Library of Congress Cataloging in Publication Data
Main entry under title:

China's development experience in comparative perspective.

   (Harvard East Asian series; 93)
   Includes bibliographical references and index.
   1.   China—Economic conditions—1949–   —Addresses,
essays, lectures.   I.   Dernberger, Robert F.
II.   Joint Committee on Contemporary China. Sub-
committee on Research on the Chinese Economy.
III.   Series.
HC427.9.C56542   330.951'05   80-418
ISBN 0-674-11890-1

Preface

For far too long both China specialists and those engaged in research on problems of economic development have treated China's experience as a special case. One of the major objectives of the Subcommittee for Research on the Chinese Economy of the Joint Committee on Contemporary China of the Social Science Research Council has been to broaden research on China's contemporary economy and to increase its historical, interdisciplinary, and international perspectives. In 1976 the Subcommittee sponsored the three-day Research Conference on the Lessons of China's Development Experience for the Developing Countries. Attending the conference along with China specialists were economists who had studied other developing countries and had analyzed the process of economic development as a universal phenomenon. Although improving the validity of analyses of China's contemporary economy is an ample goal in itself, an equally important need is incorporating these analyses in the empirical evidence used by the student of general economic development. It was hoped that the participation of development economists would provide a basis for evaluating China's experience in the light of the problems and objectives of the other developing countries.

Since 1977 China has taken dramatic new directions in economic policy. A new leadership group, obviously advocates of less radical economic programs and policies than those of the 1960s and 1970s, has emerged and has successfully "purged" the more radical followers of Maoism. According to Chinese press reports, national conferences, the 11th National Congress of the Chinese Communist Party in 1977, and the 5th National People's Congress in 1978, the new leaders have questioned the success of the earlier economic model; they are determined to provide a more effective approach to the problems of eco nomic development.

It is still too early to predict what effect these new policies will have but nothing released in the Chinese press to this date reduces the va lidity of the evaluations in this volume of the economic model in the quarter-century after 1949. Much of the analysis is concerned with fundamental features of programs within that model, features that were advocated by both the radical and the moderate wings of the Chinese Communist leadership. Although the new leadership apparently advocates greater central control and planning of economic activity, greater reliance on foreign trade and borrowing of foreign technology, greater use of material incentives rather than normative appeals, and greater emphasis on tests of profitability and efficiency in production, these changes in emphasis appear to be within the context of the basic model analyzed here. In fact, to the dismay of more radical colleagues, the contributors to this volume did not devote much attention to the "two-line struggle." Moreover, their interpretations can be more closely identified with the arguments of the current leaders of China's socialist revolution than with those of the more radical followers of Mao.

Thus, developments in China during the past two years offer telling criticism of those Western analyses that interpreted the pronouncements of Mao's radical followers as valid descriptions of China's economic model. Those criticisms, however, do not contradict the arguments presented here or make them out of date.

We wish to thank those present at the conference for their critiques, comments, and suggestions. In addition to the authors in this volume, they included John Bresnan (Ford Foundation), Hollis B. Chenery (World Bank), Audrey Donnithorne (Australian National University), Alexander Eckstein (University of Michigan, deceased), John Gurley (Stanford University), Shigeru Ishikawa (Hitotsubashi University), Carl Riskin (Columbia University), Michael Roemer (Harvard University), Charles Robert Roll, Jr. (Rand Corporation), Peter Schran (University of Illinois), Dudley Seers (University of Sussex), Subramanian Swamy (Member of Parliament, India), Peter C. Timmer (Harvard University), and Kung-chia Yeh (Rand Corporation).

The Subcommittee is also indebted to Patrick Maddox for his assistance in organizing the conference, to James Kilpatrick, who ably served as rapporteur at the conference, to Françoise Le Gall, who assisted in editing the papers, and to Barbara Wimunc, who did most of the typing. We thank these people for their cooperative and active participation.

R. F. D.

Contents

CONTENTS

CHINA'S DEVELOPMENT EXPERIENCE IN COMPARATIVE PERSPECTIVE

Introduction

ROBERT F. DERNBERGER

There are four major reasons for using China's experience to test theories of economic development in the developing countries. Most important, because of the country's size, the Chinese account for one-third of the problem being studied. Second, if we include the social, political, and economic institutional environments as variables in the analysis, China's experience provides a considerably different environment from that found in most other developing countries. Third, although most Third World governments have explicitly adopted economic development as a policy objective, the Chinese government is both relatively stable and effective in carrying out economic policy decisions.[1] Finally, in the past three decades their efforts have been fruitful; China is a country that *is* developing.

Thus China's experience should have high priority on the agenda of economic development research. This volume is intended to provide a beginning for such research, but it is only a beginning. The chapters in this volume have been collected in the belief that combining the efforts of specialists on general economic development and of specialists on China's economy would lead to a more meaningful preliminary contribution than could be produced by a single researcher from either of these two groups. However, because of the conference format, with particular topics assigned to individual authors, there are many gaps.

The authors and their topics were chosen so that the detailed research on specific topics, when taken together, would provide an integrated analysis of the relevance of China's experience to that of the other developing countries. Since the treatment in each chapter obviously depends on the author's interests, the remainder of this introduction is devoted to a critical review of the individual chapters, emphasizing their relationship to the overall purpose of the volume.[2]

Amartya Sen (chapter 1) holds that the most common indicators of economic development in the developing countries—the level and rate of growth of per capita gross national product—not only fail to reflect the basic objectives of economic development but also have corrupted our view of the process. As a result we lose sight of the more important obstacles to achieving those objectives. Sen argues that indicators such as the size, distribution, and expected duration of per capita income; the prevalence of poverty; and the frequency of disasters are more relevant than gross national product to the interests and aspirations of people in the Third World. Sen defines common objectives of economic development for all the developing countries and suggests means for measuring the achievement of those objectives to facilitate comparisons among countries and within a single country over time. He isolates the sociopolitical structure as one of the most important variables in the development process. Furthermore, Sen's proposed success indicator draws attention to what he believes is the central obstacle to economic development in the Third World: the balance of power and conflicts among the interest groups in these societies. As Sen points out, each of these three modifications —objectives, measurement, and obstacles—facilitates comparison of China's experience with that of the other developing countries.

Sen suggests that a multidimensional quantitative measure of accomplishments would better reflect whether the developing countries have achieved their social and economic objectives. Few would disagree that such a measure would be more meaningful for comparison. Unfortunately, the assignment of weights to the components in the proposed index remains a problem. First we must determine the relative importance of growth, income distribution, avoidance of famines, life expectancy, and the like, to reflect the common interests and aspirations of people in the Third World. How is this to be done? Can the common interests and aspirations of different societies be given the same weights? Another problem is that of dynamic trade-offs among the objectives. For example, a short-run sacrifice of better health or more equitable income distribution may lead to more rapid growth and to an even higher level of health or more equitable distribution of income than would otherwise have been possible. These are obviously not simple problems. Nonetheless, Sen's chapter clearly points out the need for making our evaluations of the developing countries' efforts more comparable and suggests one method for doing so.

Thomas E. Weisskopf in chapter 2 attempts to determine the extent to which other countries have achieved their development objectives and why. He argues that India, Pakistan, and Indonesia are similar to China in terms of economic and historical environment, that they share characteristics that make them considerably different from China, especially politically. To explain the development experience of these "nonrevolutionary" Asian countries, Weisskopf divides each country's postwar growth experience into periods of a more democratic and a more authoritarian political regime. Finally, in a manner somewhat different from Sen's in chapter 1, Weisskopf selects several tests of economic development: growth of total, sectoral, and per capita output; food consumption and health and educational services; distribution of income and level of unemployment; extent of self-reliance; and success in extending democratic processes and individual civil liberties.

Although he recognizes that his sample is relatively small and that there may be alternative explanations, Weisskopf believes that his evidence leads to the following conclusion: compared with the more democratic regimes, the authoritarian regimes have achieved higher growth rates because they have assigned a higher priority to growth itself and because they prefer more liberal (free-market and free-trade) economic policies. But the growth record of the authoritarian nonrevolutionary regimes is favorable only when compared with that of the democratic regimes in the sample; it is significantly poorer than that of China. Furthermore, this relatively favorable record applies to growth rates alone; the authoritarian regimes do as poorly on the other success indicators as their democratic counterparts. Weisskopf therefore questions the long-run viability of democratic capitalism; on the basis of his sample, it appears that a revolutionary transformation of the social and political structures is a prerequisite for realizing many of the social objectives of economic development.

The countries in Weisskopf's sample and the time periods he adopts for grouping the empirical evidence support his claim that the social and political environment is an important variable in making comparisons among them and with China. However, Weisskopf's sample is seriously biased in favor of his conclusions. Although he recognizes these problems of methodology, an adequate test of his arguments requires defining the social and political variables more precisely so that they can be applied to the other developing countries and can include other explanatory variables.

More important, the dichotomous category of democratic versus authoritarian regimes may cause problems in interpreting the development of other non-Communist developing countries. Higher growth rates in these other countries appear to be associated with the effectiveness of the government's administration and control over the economy rather than with the extent of repression of individual rights. In Weisskopf's sample, of course, administrative efficiency and control are directly related to the extent of authoritarian rule, but this is not necessarily true in other Third World countries.

Finally, Weisskopf's emphasis on the political nature of the government may obscure the importance of nonpolitical variables. For example, he attributes the inequitable distribution of income to the social and political structure of the three countries he studies, but all three have labor surpluses. A larger sample of non-Communist developing countries would include some with a significantly better record of income redistribution, which might indicate that surplus labor has a considerable effect, independent of political and social structures.

These arguments are not presented to question Weisskopf's emphasis on social and political structures, nor to prejudge the results of future research. While few would disagree with the importance of social and political factors, as emphasized by both Sen and Weisskopf, a country's economic system is equally important. Any attempt to explain the differences between China's economic performance over the past twenty-five years and that of the other developing countries must begin with an account of China's unique economic institutions and policies. This is the purpose of chapter 3, by Benjamin Ward.

Recent research by Bruce Reynolds indicates that Chinese borrowing from the Soviet prototype in the 1950s can best be described as complete and slavish imitation.[3] Over time, however, increased Western interest in and Chinese publicity of innovations in their economic system led to a reinterpretation of developments in the 1950s, emphasizing the importance of deviations from the Soviet model. Ward believes that we should reconsider our judgments of those developments and argues that despite some important modifications, China's economic system and development policies continue to exemplify a Soviet-type economy. Ward believes that this categorization is appropriate for distinguishing the major differences between China's economic system and those of most other developing countries.

Ward concludes that there is a very strong interest in transferring the Soviet-type economic system to the other developing countries. More important, Ward believes that the Chinese variant may be of even greater interest to these countries because the Chinese have eliminated some of the model's most obvious and costly shortcomings and have modified it to meet needs that the other developing countries share. On the other hand, developments in the socialist economies over the past decade and in China during the past few years lead

Ward to question the long-run efficacy of the Soviet model in attaining the economic and social goals of socialism.

If Ward's reinterpretation is correct—that is, if China's economy can be classified as a Soviet type—then our objectives in this volume are considerably simplified.[4] While most would agree that China shares the four key determinants of the Soviet model, a crucial question remains. The level of abstraction required by Ward's use of only four key determinants leads him to regard as slight deviations some features of China's development experience that may well be fundamental to the system. These systemic features are necessary to explain how China's economic functioning and performance differ from those of the other developing countries and the other Soviet-type economies as well.

These problems are always present in attempts to abstract system categories from a large sample of countries. Nonetheless, Ward's reinterpretation draws attention to the many characteristics of a Soviet-type economy that China retained after the 1950s and provides, at one level of abstraction, a convenient description of the Chinese model in a terminology that can be used to integrate China's development experience into the context of existing studies. More important for our purposes, however, Ward's designation of China's economy as a Soviet type helps—at this same level of abstraction—to explain the results of China's development efforts and the difference between these results and those achieved by the other developing countries.

In chapter 4 Dwight H. Perkins presents and evaluates empirical estimates of China's development efforts since 1949. Before examining the empirical record, Perkins briefly surveys several aspects of China's economic system that differentiate it from those of the other developing countries, emphasizing several important adaptations of the Soviet model. Perkins uses data reported by the Chinese themselves to support his analysis of five major areas in which they have been significantly more successful than the other developing countries in achieving their economic development objectives.[5]

In the final section of his chapter, Perkins presents the factors that he believes are responsible for China's comparatively successful economic development. Perkins believes this success can be explained largely by the revolution's having "put the poor in command," by the Chinese historical tradition and accumulated experience with "efficient authoritarianism," and by the sheer size of the economy and its resource endowment. Thus the Chinese have been able to use their economic system to successfully promote economic development not because of attributes of the economic system itself, but because of special historical, political, and economic features that may be difficult to replicate in other countries.

It is very hard to disprove Perkins' well-reasoned arguments; by the same token, it is hard to disprove alternative explanations. Moreover, although he has ruled out "enthusiasm" because of the difficulty in measuring its effect, it is important; by emphasizing the three factors that he does present as the explanations for China's success, Perkins allows no role for ideology, except insofar as China's ideology is responsible for having put the poor in command. It would be somewhat surprising, however, if the many ideological campaigns had not created considerable enthusiasm, reinforced by self-interest, for the economic development programs of the past twenty-five years. In fact, Alexander Gerschenkron has argued that the role of ideology is to fool people into supporting development programs that are not in their best interests.[6] Belief in the ideology, the enthusiasm generated by that belief, and the tradition of efficient authoritarianism may have had significant effects on the cadre's implementation of the economic development programs.

These arguments are presented only to indicate the complexity of any attempt to identify and quantify all the ultimate "causes" of contemporary China's economic success. Perkins's explanatory factors, which are often overlooked in quantitative analyses of China's development, would remain important even if the list were expanded to cover the entire complex of interacting social, political, and economic forces since 1949.

The topics in part one are broad, and space limitations require that the discussion be restricted to broad generalizations and arguments. Part two examines in greater detail three aspects of China's development experience that have been widely acclaimed as indicators of success. These analyses should deepen our understanding of the Chinese experience and the reasons for its success. The topics in part two were chosen because these success indicators are important in an analysis of China's development, and because the objectives are qualitative rather than quantitative.

Each chapter in part one cites more equitable distribution of income as an important objective of economic development and refers, either implicitly or explicitly, to China's comparative success in achieving this objective. In fact, studies of development in the other countries have concluded that economic growth has not only failed to eliminate poverty but has led to growing inequality of personal incomes, at least until average per capita incomes reach relatively high levels.[7] The evidence for China's contrary record in this respect, however, is based on impressionistic judgments and reasoning; estimates for the size distribution of personal incomes are simply not available. In chapter 5 Nicholas R. Lardy argues that the indirect evidence supports Chinese claims that inequality of income distribution has been reduced. Since estimates for the provincial per capita net value of agricultural output were not available for the years after the 1950s, Lardy uses the available estimates for provincial per capita industrial production to show that regional inequality has been gradually but steadily reduced over the past two decades. In the other developing countries there is evidence of a direct correlation between growing regional inequality and growing inequality in the distribution of personal income, and Lardy believes that the evidence of increasing regional equality in China can be used as a first approximation of growing equality in distribution of personal income.

This more equitable distribution of regional income, according to Lardy, is the direct result of the leadership's active pursuit of this objective, and his evidence for the provincial allocation of investment and social services expenditures clearly supports that argument. He believes that China's central government was able to use its fiscal and planning systems to counteract the trend, found in other developing countries, of regional inequality resulting from economic growth. But Lardy argues that the fiscal systems of the other countries do not facilitate regional redistribution of investment funds and that it would therefore be difficult for them to replicate China's experience. Furthermore, because of the much higher incremental, capital-output ratios in the poorer regions of these countries (as well as in China), Lardy believes that they are unlikely to want to redistribute investment in order to achieve a more equitable distribution of income.

Lardy presents two major themes, both relating to important aspects of China's economic development: the increasing equity of regional levels of output and income, and the increasing equity in the size distribution of personal income. The evidence presented in support of the first conclusion is convincing but must be qualified. As Lardy shows, there was a large gap between the richer and the poorer provinces in both the levels of development and the incremental, capital-output ratios. China is moving steadily toward greater regional equity, in sharp contrast with the trend in other developing countries. But China still has a long way to go, and for the near future, at least, the economy will be characterized by rich and poor regions. It is also important to note that Lardy's analysis of the redistribution of social welfare expenditures is limited to those made through the state's unified budget. The state budget, however, excludes expenditures made by communes and by industrial enterprises, and these units are a major source for financing educational, health, and housing services and public consumption in China. Thus the distribution of social welfare expenditures outside the state budget favors the richer provinces; if Lardy included these expenditures, the pattern might be reversed.

Lardy's second conclusion—that the growing equity in regional, per capita production implies a growing equity in the size distribution of personal income—must be understood as a working hypothesis. He bases his argument on the observed simple long-run correlation in other (capitalist) countries between decreases in the equity of regional development with decreases in the equity of the size distribution of personal income. Because China's economic system gives the central government considerable control over prices, wages, employment, and migration, the results from capitalist countries need not hold for China. Furthermore, the trend toward regional equity is gradual, and the spillover effects of this trend do not appear to involve significant changes in the size distribution of personal incomes. Thus Lardy's arguments concerning increasing regional equality do not necessarily contradict the argument that the leadership's economic development policies in the past two decades have widened income differentials among local units of production.

What has happened to the size distribution of personal income in China since 1949 is a question that obviously deserves attention in future research. The Chinese have maintained an acceptable standard of living and have eliminated the worst extremes in the size distribution of income. On this we can all agree. Lardy's chapter also shows that they have been able to avoid the growing inequality in the relative distribution of regional incomes that is associated with economic growth in the other developing countries.

Whereas Lardy emphasizes the role of physical capital accumulation and redistribution in China's economic growth, Thomas G. Rawski (chapter 6) emphasizes China's inherited stock of technical skills and the development of those skills through learning by doing. Rawski defines technical skills broadly; he gives more importance to problem-solving, innovative, and management and administrative skills than to strictly engineering techniques. According to Rawski, both types of skills are acquired more by experience than by formal education or acts of investment. Thus Rawski's learning-by-doing model differs from the more traditional model, in which increases in technical skills acquired through learning by doing are attributed to new investment projects that embody new technology.[8]

Rawski's chapter, rich in examples from Chinese sources, first presents a chronological review of China's economic development since 1949 to show the importance and sources of technological skills during different periods. According to Rawski, the agricultural crises and withdrawal of Soviet technical assistance at the end of the 1950s forced the Chinese to adopt a self-sufficient industrial development policy. Despite the impact of the Cultural Revolution in the mid 1960s, Rawski believes that China's industrial growth after 1960 clearly shows that the accumulated stock and continued development of human technical skills has enabled China's industry to respond with remarkable flexibility to the demands of the sixties. Furthermore, the industrial and technological base that has now been established should provide for continued growth and development.

Rawski then analyzes the three types of industrial enterprises that make up China's industrial base and that will be the source of continued technological development: the Soviet-aid projects in the modern, large-scale sector; the medium- and small-scale plants in the traditional urban sector; and the small-scale plants in the rural sector. Rawski argues that no single technology is appropriate for successful industrial growth. Because of the economies of scale in production, the large-scale, capital-intensive industrial plants can significantly increase output at lower costs for standard items for which there is sufficient demand. On the other hand, these plants have diseconomies of scale when it comes to innovation or adaptation to unexpected changes. It is in this area that the small and medium-scale plants have the advantage, and their experience is an important source of human technical skills for sustained, long-run industrial development.

The rural, small-scale industries are of considerable importance to China's economic development, especially in agriculture, because of their low capital costs and short gestation period, their utilization of local resources, their limited pressure on the overburdened transportation network, and their ability to solve local supply bottlenecks. However, Rawski believes that in the long run the greatest contribution of the rural Chinese industries may be to the supply of human technical skills. These industries have introduced a process of skill acquisition and innovation based on learning by doing on a scale unparalleled in any other country in the Third World. According to Rawski, China's leadership is aware of the short-run costs of these trial-and-error methods of learning but is willing to accept the costs for the sake of the long-run benefits.

In his conclusion, Rawski takes issue with Alexander Gerschenkron's hypothesis that the latecomer can leapfrog many steps in economic development by borrowing the technology of the developed countries.[9] Rawski argues that the developing countries must expand their own human technical skills, not only to absorb the foreigners' technology effectively, but also to acquire technology that meets their own needs. Most developing countries have found it easier to accumulate physical capital than to develop human technical skills. Although Rawski does not pursue this line of reasoning, his analysis suggests that the methods used in China to develop these skills would appeal to the other developing countries.

However, two major considerations must be taken into account. Rawski frequently refers to the economic costs of China's policy of self-sufficient economic development and of the trial-and-error period in learning by doing, and he concludes that the Chinese leadership is willing to accept these costs for the sake of long-run expansion of industrial production. Inasmuch as the state has nationalized the means of industrial production and incorporated industrial profits and losses in the state's budget, the state not only pays these initial costs, it is also the direct recipient of the benefits. But in the other developing countries, industrial production often comes from private enterprises, and that output is sold at market prices. A nationwide program of learning by doing through trial and error and the creation of a mix of enterprises using different technologies with different costs would involve very large government subsidies and very high protective tariffs. And the benefits of these policies would accrue to private individuals. If properly identified and measured, these private benefits could be taxed to cover the state's costs; the many problems of carrying out such a program, however, would seem to greatly limit its political feasibility. China's large resource endowment, which makes self-sufficiency a feasible policy, is similarly unlikely to be replicated in many of the other developing countries. In the case of China, some may question whether acquiring these skills through trial-and-error learning while pursuing self-sufficient industrial development is the most effective procedure. To answer this question, it is necessary to determine how successful the Chinese have been in achieving self-sufficient industrial development. Rawski's implicit answers are optimistic ones and may be questioned. Most of his arguments concern the rate of change in China's technological capabilities and efficiency; they do not reveal much about China's capabilities and efficiency compared with those of other developing or developed countries. Rawski claims that China's industry is now more efficient than that of the industrial countries of the socialist bloc, but this conclusion must be compared with the impressions of knowledgeable visitors to Chinese factories, reports in the Chinese press, and the explicit statements of the new, post-Mao leadership. Whether China's industrial efficiency is greater or less than that of the other socialist industrial countries has yet to be empirically determined, but the evidence suggests that Chinese efficiency is far from ideal. Nonetheless, these are arguments over the absolute level of China's technical capabilities and efficiency; they do not deny Rawski's argument that the Chinese have made considerable progress since 1949.

An undeniable achievement is China's provision of health services to a large segment of the population. The Chinese widely publicize their accomplishments in this area, and Western visitors also emphasize public health services in China. Teh-wei Hu devotes a significant portion of chapter 7 to a detailed analysis of the health care delivery system and the distribution and financing of these services. As with redistribution of income and development of technological capabilities, it is difficult to estimate China's success in providing health care services. In fact, as Hu points out, it is very difficult to identify, let alone measure, the many contributions of improved health to China's economic growth and the costs of providing such services. From a small sample of reports in the Chinese press, Hu estimates that rural health care may have led to a net increase in the agricultural labor effort of as much as 5 million man-years or, according to Hu's calculations, 2% of China's total value of agricultural production. It is even more difficult to judge the increase in individual well-being, but Hu believes that the most important benefits are on the consumption side: the increased satisfaction of the peasants (no matter what the quality of the services) and the role of the health care system in the redistribution of income in favor of rural areas.

Hu argues that the possibility of transferring this system to the other developing countries is doubtful because many important elements of China's economic, political, and incentive systems are integral to its health care delivery system. In addition, Hu notes that the existing health care delivery systems of the other developing countries have many similarities to China's system. Although Hu does not analyze the efforts of the other developing countries or their results, he presents several lessons from China's experience. According to Hu, the Chinese experience has shown that any significant increase in rural health services requires training paramedics on the basis of local financing. These services are more effective if the paramedics are paid well compared with the average peasant, if there is a well-organized referral system to higher-level health facilities, and if there are monetary incentives to the individual to use the system efficiently. Services should not be free, and decentralization of both administration and financing induces more effective management and economy of operations. The central government can facilitate the redistribution of services by directing construction investment expenditures in the state budget away from urban hospitals in favor of rural hospitals and health stations.

11

Hu's chapter conveys the extent to which the Chinese leadership has attempted to expand public health services and make them readily available to the rural population. The sheer size of that effort and the significant reallocation of existing personnel in favor of the rural areas is unlikely to be duplicated in any other developing country, even in those with public health care systems similar to China's. As for the resulting improvement in health, even though it is impossible to measure empirically, China again appears to compare favorably with the other developing countries. It is very important to note, however, that Hu's analysis is restricted to the system of the 1960s. Thus the results—the comparatively favorable state of health in the Chinese population—are not necessarily attributable solely to the public health care delivery system described and analyzed by Hu. The current level of health in China must be attributed, in part at least, to the post-1949 and pre-1965 increase in and more equitable distribution of income and of food; the increase in the number, if not the equitable distribution, of medical personnel and supplies; improvements in sanitation and housing; the mass campaigns for disease prevention and inoculations, and the like. In other words, the Chinese people did not suddenly become healthier in 1965 with the introduction of the new health care system, with its reliance on paramedics. Nonetheless, a much greater portion of the rural population now has access to medical attention as the result of that system.

It would be possible, of course, to analyze several other success indicators, but the three analyses in part two reveal the importance of the contemporary economic and political system, the country's resource endowment, and the traditional social system in explaining China's comparatively successful economic growth after 1949. The relevance of China's experience to that of the other developing countries, therefore, appears to depend greatly on the extent to which that experience is explained by features of China's institutions, society, geography, and history that are not found in the other countries. The chapters in part three attempt to examine this question more thoroughly than the discussions in parts one and two.

Albert Feuerwerker (chapter 8) analyzes the "complementarities" between certain aspects of the Chinese economic model and underlying factors in the rest of China's social system over the past twenty-five years. Feuerwerker's analysis of the linkages between the economy and the social system is a broad, knowledgeable, and well-reasoned argument, rich in illustrations, concerning the extent to which China's development experience is embedded in the country's geographical, historical, cultural, social, and political environment. The specific linkages examined are the complementaries between China's development strategies and the natural environment, the political system, the value system, the social system (narrowly defined), and the external world.

Feuerwerker's analysis is not intended to be deterministic; the underlying factors do exert an impact on China's economic model, but they are not the sole determinants of that model. Nor is he interested in the origin of the underlying factors. Furthermore, although the linkages he identifies between the economy and other parts of the social system help explain China's distinctive economic growth, he does not attempt to evaluate their contribution, either positive or negative, to that growth. Finally, Feuerwerker does not relate his analysis of these linkages to the question of transferring the Chinese economic model. While he agrees that any of these linkages may exist in the other developing countries, he believes that the interrelationships among them are unique to China. Despite these self-imposed constraints, the robust nature of Feuerwerker's discussion strongly reinforces the implicit hypotheses of this volume. These conclusions/hypotheses can be stated as follows:

1. Since 1949, the Chinese have achieved a distinctive and comparatively favorable record of economic development.
2. That record is strongly influenced by and integrated with characteristics of the Chinese social and political system, geography, resource endowment, and historical evolution.
3. Because of this interdependence, direct transfer of China's development experience to the other developing countries is not possible.

The individual contributions to this volume present strong evidence and arguments in support of the first two of these hypotheses. None of the authors in parts one and two, of course, was directly concerned with investigating the third hypothesis; it emerged as an implicit result of their discussions or as an explicit comment or intuitive judgment in the course of those discussions.

Feuerwerker's analysis of the linkages between developments in China before and after 1949 concerns the second, not the third, of these hypotheses. Although the third hypothesis assumes the interdependence of characteristics peculiar to China and the economic results achieved in the post-1949 period, the acceptance of the second hypothesis—that these interdependencies exist—is neither a necessary nor a sufficient argument for the third hypothesis.

Quite simply, the contributors' arguments that these interdependencies exist and are important factors in explaining the pattern of economic institutions, policies, and results in the post-1949 period (the second hypothesis) do not enable us to discriminate between two alternative interpretations. On the one hand, the existence of these interdependencies might mean that the characteristics of the Chinese environment were consistent with the economic institutions and policies introduced after 1949 and that they facilitated the economic developments resulting from those institutions and policies. On the other hand, as is implied by the arguments in these chapters and by the way the third hypothesis emerges from those arguments, the particular characteristics of the Chinese environment may be the *critical* variables in explaining post-1949 policies and results. If the latter interpretation is correct, then the third hypothesis—that the direct transfer of China's development experience is not possible—appears to be the logical conclusion of the arguments presented in this volume.

The conference discussions indicated the need for a concluding chapter on the relevance of China's experience to the other developing countries. That question is addressed in chapter 9, beginning with a review of two important arguments that became evident during the discussions. As stated in the preface, a major purpose of the conference and this volume was to integrate analyses of China's development experience into the study of economic development throughout the Third World.

Most of the analyses presented here are primarily concerned with China's experience and are written by China "specialists." However, the discussions at the conference, which included general economic development specialists, clearly indicated the importance of devoting equal attention to the economic, social, and political characteristics of the other developing countries before trying to answer questions concerning transferability. Who are the agents of change in the other developing countries? What are their objectives? What programs have they adopted that are similar to those being implemented in China, and how successful have they been? In other words, the chapters in this volume provide only some of the arguments needed before one can attempt to answer questions concerning the transferability of the Chinese experience to other settings.

On the other hand, if the third hypothesis is correct, it appears to be sufficient by itself to preclude the possibility of transfer—unless, of course, China's development experience were transferred as an integrated package, including complete replication of the social, political, and economic, as well as physical, environment. Interpreted in this manner, the question becomes trivial and not very meaningful in the search for solutions to the economic development problems of the Third World. In the nonsocialist developing countries the major interest is not in the transfer of the complete package of economic, social, and political institutions and policies (including a Communist revolution) but in the transfer of programs and policies that address a particular problem.

Chapter 9 analyzes in detail several Chinese economic programs to determine the extent to which they are integrated into the institutions and policies of China's socialist revolution, its unique historical heritage, and its physical environment, as well as to determine the extent to which these programs, and their results, are separable from that environment. The programs selected are the collectivization of agricultural production; the small-scale industry program; and the mobilization, full employment, and allocation of labor.

Although these are only three of the large number and wide variety of Chinese economic programs, they are of major importance in explaining China's comparative success and are of significant interest to the other developing countries. Equally important, the analysis of specific reasons for the success of these programs should indicate how much that success depended on features peculiar to China. According to this analysis, these features of China's environment are not likely to be found in the other developing countries. In other words, the more detailed analysis of particular Chinese programs and policies strongly supports the conclusion presented either implicitly or explicitly by the other contributors to this volume. This conclusion, however, can serve only as a tentative hypothesis for further research. It is hoped that this volume will not only help stimulate that research but also serve as a useful beginning.

Notes

1. In China, as in any other developing country, the political administration of the economy and the local implementation of economic policies (the level at which the economic activities take place) must be analyzed to determine what happened and why and how it happened. On the other hand, as is not true for many of the other developing countries, there can be little doubt that China's political leaders are dedicated to economic development and are able and willing to direct the government's efforts and the economy's resources for that purpose.

2. A more detailed summary of the individual chapters in this volume is presented in Robert F. Dernberger, "The Relevance of China's Development Experience for Other Developing Countries," *Items,* 31, no. 3 (September 1977): 25–34. The chapters are summarized here only to show how they relate to the central question posed in this volume and to provide a critical review of the limitations of their argu-

ments concerning the relevance of China's development experience to that of the other developing countries. Many of these limits are explicitly recognized by the authors themselves, and they are not presented as criticism of the authors' contributions in discussing the topics that they were assigned.

3. See, for example, Bruce Reynolds, "Procurement Pressure in China: The Manager as Entrepreneur," paper presented to the Workshop on the Pursuit of Interest in the People's Republic of China, Ann Arbor, Michigan, August 1977, especially part 2 (mimeographed); and Bruce Reynolds, "The Adaptation of Russian Planning Practices in China's First Five-Year Plan," paper presented to the Conference on the Chinese Economy in a Comparative Context, Stanford, California, January 1977 (mimeographed).

4. Ward believes that only four fundamental economic institution and policy characteristics are essential for being classified as a Soviet-type economy: nationalization of the means of production in industry, the collectivization of agriculture, the mobilization of the state and population by means of a Leninist party, and a big-push industrialization effort as a central economic policy objective.

5. The Chinese have released only a limited amount of quantitative data for their economic performance since 1949, and the assumptions and methodologies that have been used to derive alternative quantitative estimates for that performance have created considerable disagreement and debate among specialists. Perkins, as well as the other contributors to another conference volume sponsored by the Subcommittee on Research on the Chinese Economy, have evaluated these methodological debates and conclude that the data released by the Chinese are relatively reliable or, at least, the best available. See Alexander Eckstein, ed., *Quantitative Measures of China's Economic Output* (Ann Arbor, Mich.: University of Michigan, forthcoming).

6. See Alexander Gerschenkron, "Ideology as a System Determinant," in Alexander Eckstein, ed., *Comparisons of Economic Systems* (Berkeley: University of California Press, 1971), pp. 269–289.

7. See Simon Kuznets, "Quantitative Aspects of the Economic Growth of Nations: Distribution of Income by Size," *Economic Development and Cultural Change* 11, no. 2, pt. 2 (January 1963); and Hollis Chenery, et al., *Redistribution with Growth* (London: Oxford, 1974).

8. Kenneth J. Arrow, "The Economic Implications of Learning by Doing," *Review of Economic Studies* 29 (1962): 155–173.

9. Alexander Gerschenkron, "Economic Backwardness in Historical Perspective," in Alexander Gerschenkron, *Economic Backwardness in Historical Perspective* (Cambridge, Mass.: Harvard University Press, 1962).

One

THE DEVELOPMENT PROBLEM

1

Economic Development: Objectives and Obstacles

AMARTYA SEN

The aim of this chapter is to identify the objectives of development in general and the obstacles to achieving these objectives. Although it is not concerned with China specifically, it provides a basis for evaluating China's development experience.

Underdevelopment is a bastard historical concept. The word hints that some desirable thing that is going to happen has not yet happened. Behind the concept there is clearly a historical vision, but it is not made clear which one that is. While this lack of specification gives the concept of development remarkable catholicity, it also makes the concept difficult to use in a consistent way. The recent preference for "developing" over "underdeveloped" as the appropriate adjective introduces a calculated element of euphemism and confusion between a handicap that can be overcome and a handicap that is currently being overcome. The vagueness of the historical vision of the future is now supplemented by blindness about the present. The hurrah takes place whether or not the game is being played.

One cannot get a clear idea of development objectives by looking at what the so-called developing countries are achieving or at what their governments are trying to achieve. It would be better to focus directly on the interests and aspirations of the people in question. But that approach leaves open at least two issues. First, whose aspirations and interests are at stake? Even within a given country, objectives vary from class to class, group to group, person to person. The assumption of homogeneity of interests and aspirations—however important for solidarity in an international forum—is peculiarly unrealistic. Second, aspirations are conditioned by ideas of feasibility, which change with actual experience, and a static view of aspirations when "the world is being turned upside down" is clearly not legitimate.

Conflicts, People, and Commodities

The commonest measure of development is the trend rate of growth of per capita real gross national product (or real national income). This measure of achievement is congruent with the interests and aspirations of some, but this congruence need not be guaranteed for all, not even for most of the people involved. The distribution-independent format of real national income prevents a systematic translation of this indicator into a measure of economic fulfillment for the persons making up the nation. Much of the theory of real national income proceeds as if the nation were one person, or at least represented by some kind of leviathan, "King of all the children of pride."

A second limitation arises from the concern with the trend rate of growth rather than with dips. A characteristic of preindustrial societies is a recurrence of disasters such as famines, and one of the least controversial aspirations of the people involved is to escape this fate. The trend rate of growth drowns crucial information on this in the noise of the averaging process—over groups and over time.

The formulation of development objectives requires a system of relative priorities and weights dealing with the interests and aspirations of the groups that constitute a nation. Frequently enough this formulation is not done explicitly; indeed it often suits ruling groups to leave this issue vague. The domestic production of air conditioners for private use may appear to fulfill the objectives of "industrialization," "self-reliance," "modernization," and "technological independence." The maximization of GNP would give an air conditioner a greater weight than one year's consumption of food by a person in a typical poor country. This modern version of commodity fetishism permits a planner, or an economist, or a politician, to discuss the choices without explicitly bringing in relative weights on the interests of different sections of the population. The implicit bias thus gets built into the seemingly neutral conception of development.

The reality of the conflict between the interests of different groups has to be recognized as a prerequisite to the assessment of development objectives. Making things explicit does not, of course, eliminate conflicts of interests, but it does make it more difficult to use priorities that would arouse widespread hostility if clearly understood. The tendency to formulate development objectives in abstract terms, focusing on commodities rather than on human beings, has strategic value in channeling the development process in directions that would otherwise be unacceptable. Vigilance, eternal or not, is certainly the price of equity.

This issue has a certain amount of technical statistical interest as well. The format of traditional national income statistics obscures the interest conflicts underlying social evaluation, through its commodity fetishism. Amounts of a given commodity going to different persons coming from widely different classes and income groups get aggregated in a national total, and the conflicts are obscured in this opaque vision of national income as merely a collection of commodities. Bringing in income distribution as an afterthought does not retrieve what has been lost, and the right way surely is simply to consider national income as a collection of person-good relations, a typical element of which will be the amount of commodity j going to person i. There are no insurmountable analytical or empirical difficulties in using this structure for national income evaluation,[1] which inherently links the problems of size and distribution of national income. The traditional national income format seems to start off on the wrong foot; and in view of the harm it has already done to discussions of development achievements in countries other than China, one must view with considerable concern attempts to apply the same format to China.

Changing Aspirations

One of the clichés of orthodox development economics is the so-called limited aspiration level of the traditional peasant. For articulated aspirations in a static social atmosphere, there is probably much truth in such a diagnosis, and minor changes in an otherwise frozen framework may not disturb the pattern of aspirations suddenly. But these is plenty of evidence that experience influences aspirations; and dramatic experience (for example, in taming a turbulent river through dams) may lead to dramatic readjustment of expectations.

Aspirations relevant to development objectives cover not merely freedom from hunger, removal of poverty, escape from disasters, and so forth, but also the abolition of the traditional pattern of exploitation and inequities. Although such inequities may have been tolerated for a long time, an assumption of inescapability frequently underlies this tolerance. When the contingent nature of such inequities is recognized, aspirations to eliminate them become a real force. The recent history of many countries bears witness to such transformation.

It is possible to have sophisticated debates as to whether an aspiration that is born in the process of fulfilling it can be used to justify the need for fulfilling it. It might be argued that to do so is like justifying the use of narcotics by noting the need of those who have already started using them. The similarity is superficial, and the fundamental difference can be seen by introducing the concept of preferences over preferences. It is legitimate to ask which preference a person would like to have and to consider his ranking over preference orderings. A narcotics user in his lucid moments may, in fact, "prefer" not to have had the preference for narcotics (I wish I didn't get hooked on it), but it is unlikely that this would be the case with the erstwhile all-suffering person who comes to hate the inequities in the process of their removal. What looks symmetrical in terms of preferences over states of the world turns out to be quite different when preferences over preference orderings of states are examined.[2]

This range of considerations requires us to take a broader view of development objectives, incorporating the dynamism of aspirations. This, in addition to the question of conflicts and weights, indicates the need for considerable structure in the formulation of development objectives.

I believe that the choice of development objectives discussed in this chapter is not too idiosyncratic, even though a few of the standard objectives have been doctored somewhat to take note of the issues already discussed. I should add, however, that Development is not the only goal worth considering, and virtues such as participation, fraternal feelings, liberty, and concern may be seen as having intrinsic values, in addition to whatever role they play in the development of an underdeveloped economy. A full evaluation of the lessons from China's experience would be impossible without going substantially beyond the development objectives even after they have been broadened to incorporate economic factors not captured by GNP. Obviously, there are different layers of broadening, and in this chapter the limits are taken to be given by the *economic* considerations.

The Standard of Living

The objective of improving the living standard is one of the most discussed development goals. The living standard is often seen as reflected by the per capita real national income, though its limitations are well known.[3] But there is also the question of interpersonal weighting. To concentrate on this issue exclusively, let y_i be the homogeneous income of person i, and $\mathbf{y}$ the vector of individual incomes. Let $\phi_i(\mathbf{y})$ be the weight on person i's income. Then the weighted average of income is given by

$$V = \frac{1}{n} \sum_i \phi_i(\mathbf{y}) y_i, \tag{1}$$

with n the number of people involved.

The usual national income procedure is to equate all the weights, that is, take the same ϕ_i for all i, say 1, which leads to the mean income y^*:

$$V = \frac{1}{n} \sum_i y_i = y^*. \tag{2}$$

But on grounds of equity, it may be decided to put a greater weight on the dollar of a poorer person than on that of a richer person, that is, if $y_i < y_j$, then $\phi_i > \phi_j$. A special case is the procedure of equating the weight of person i to the income rank of that person: a weight of 1 on the richest person's income, a weight of 2 on the second richest's income, and so on. If i is the person's income rank, then normalizing the weights as a proportion of the mean rank value gives

$$V = \frac{2}{n(n + 1)} \sum_i iy_i. \tag{3}$$

It is easily shown that this reduces to a simple function of the mean income y^* and the Gini coefficient G of the Lorenz distribution of incomes,

$$V = y^*(1 - G), \tag{3a}$$

for large n.

This procedure of adjustment for inequality can be applied to the case of many commodities, too, with a "named good" ij defined as commodity j going to person i. Real income analysis can be applied to vectors of named goods also, thereby incorporating distributional weighting as an integral part of the evaluation of real income. It can be made to take care of varying population composition and size. With rank-order weights, equation 3a holds for price-adjusted values as an index of distribution-inclusive per capita real national income in a multicommodity world. This illustrates one case of using a person-commodity discriminating approach in evaluating real national income, and the general approach can be used in a variety of ways.[4]

The person-commodity approach would not give results very different from those of the traditional real national income analysis if the relative distribution of commodities among persons were roughly the same between countries and over time. In fact, relative distributions vary widely. Furthermore, there is evidence that the Gini coefficient of income distribution increases at early stages of development and decreases only when a fairly high income has been reached.[5] In some intercountry pairwise comparisons, G may be the same, or G and y^* may move together, so that rankings of y^* are the same as those of V given in equation 3a, but this is very often not the case. The problem is important in examining real achievements in the light of development objectives.

Standard and Duration of Living

Should standard of living refer to the standard enjoyed at a point of time or the standard over a person's lifetime? It may be tempting to think that the two must come to the same thing when the entire time series of incomes is considered. This is not so. Contrast two countries with exactly the same time series of national income and the same time series of population (and therefore also the same time series of per capita income). But let everyone live for 70 years in country A and 35 years in country B, with birth and death rates differing between the two countries correspondingly. The standards of living in A and B are identical in the point sense but not in the period sense, and the difference in the latter sense cannot be detected by contrasts of the series of income per head or of population. Insofar as people might prefer being in country A rather than B, given a hypothetical choice, the standard of living in A should be taken to be higher.

A gross way of reflecting the expectation of life in national income figures is to concentrate, not on the per capita income this year, but on the per capita value of the expected lifetime income of someone born this year. This being difficult to estimate, even a grosser measure may be considered, namely, the product of the current mean income per head (y^*) and the mean expectation of life (e^*) today.

This correction would make a considerable difference, since some underdeveloped countries with relatively high per capita income in comparison with other underdeveloped countries, such as Senegal and Sierra Leone, do have exceptionally short expected lives. The contrasts in expanding life expectation add a dimension, even in judging development achievements, that is not subsumed by national income figures. For example, Kerala remains one of the poorest states in India in terms of income per head even after distributional adjustment using a person-commodity approach; but in terms of values of e^*y^*, or $e^*y^*(1-G)$, its achievements look remarkable. Since the genesis of this contrast in living standard seems closely related to public policy in health and education, the question is of serious practical interest and is of obvious relevance in evaluating China's experience.[6]

Minimal Standard and Poverty

In addition to the enhancement of the nation's overall standard of living, abolition of poverty is a frequently proposed development objective. There has been a great deal of discussion on this issue recently in both national and international contexts.[7] Poverty is usually identified by specifying a minimum acceptable level of income—the so-called poverty line—below which a person is classified as poor. The commonest measure of poverty is the proportion of the total population thus classified as poor. This may be called the head-count poverty measure H.

Complicated issues are involved in identifying a poverty line. Aside from complex biological considerations, social and cultural factors influence our conception of the minimum acceptable level of living. But even when the poverty line has been chosen and the "poor" have been identified, the measurement of "poverty" raises some additional issues. Identifying poverty with the proportion of the poor in the total population has the unfortunate property of being insensitive to the extent of the shortfall of the incomes of the poor from the poverty line. Indeed, according to this measure a transfer of income from the poorest person to someone who is richer can never increase poverty.

Rank-order weighting makes it possible to measure poverty in terms of a normalized weighted sum of the proportionate shortfalls of the incomes of all the poor from the poverty line. With appropriate axiomatization this approach yields the following measure of poverty:[8]

$$P = H[I + (1 - I)G_p],$$ (4)

where

H = the head-count poverty measure,

I = the mean shortfall of the incomes of the poor from the poverty line as a proportion of the poverty line,

G_p = the Gini coefficient of the Lorenz distribution of incomes among the poor.

Taking note of the distribution of shortfalls typically makes a difference to the poverty rankings. The following example shows how four Indian states in 1968–69 ranked respectively in terms of the head-count ratio H and the proposed measure P (in decreasing order of rural poverty), with the poverty line drawn at Rs 180 per year.[9]

H	P
Kerala	Maharashtra
Orissa	Mysore
Mysore	Orissa
Maharashtra	Kerala

The distinction is important for development policy, since the minimization of the head-count poverty measure H always makes it more worthwhile to concentrate on improving the lot of those poor who are close to the poverty line (those who are relatively richer). A little increase in their incomes may decrease the value of H while a small increase for groups that are much poorer will not decrease H. The concentration in India on the so-called potentially viable farmers (as opposed to "unviable" ones) in the recent rural development programs of the Small Farmers Development Agency and the Marginal Farmers and Agricultural Laborers seems to reflect the influence of this thinking.[10] Counting the heads of sufferers without regard to the extent of their sufferings permits peculiar distortions in the conception of development.

Temporal Minimality and Disasters

Disasters have plagued human society ever since its origin, and one of the most long-standing aspirations of mankind has been the freedom from these scourges. No list of development objectives can be regarded as even remotely complete without including the avoidance of famines and other disasters.

Long-run growth rates need not reflect such short-run disasters; a famine or two can come and go without deflecting the trend line. Even indicators such as the expectation of life need not catch the full impact of a famine, since the intense misery caused by a famine may get only a remote recognition in the national, or regional, life expectation. While some famines kill a high proportion of the population of a country or a province—the famine of 1970 was credited with slaying a third of the population of Bengal—many famines kill only a small fraction of the total national or provincial population but still cause overpowering agony. The elimination of famines and severe floods and droughts has to be given a place of its own in the formulation of development objectives. The focus on minimal levels has to be extended from intergroup variations to cover intertemporal fluctuations as well.[11]

Aside from their direct significance for welfare, disasters have many indirect influences on underdeveloped countries. Famines frequently kill more children than adults, causing a serious shift in the age composition of the communities affected.[12] They also make it more necessary to seek larger families as insurance against being left unsupported in old age, providing a rationale for the high birth rate that is characteristic of many underdeveloped countries.[13] Famines also disrupt the sense of security and confidence needed for development efforts. More important, perhaps, famines frequently change the distribution of assets, especially in the form of transferred land from the small landholder to the large landlord or the money lender.[14] Disasters can contribute quite generously to the long-run development of inequities.

Subjective Aspects of Objectives

Since any development objective can acquire that status only by virtue of being a part of the people's aspirations, all development objectives are in some sense subjective. Nevertheless, some of these goals can be easily stated in fairly objective terms. This applies to objectives formulated in terms of the expectation of life, per capita real national income with or without specified distributional corrections, frequency and intensity of famines and other disasters—indeed virtually all the variables to which I have referred.

Objective form may also be given to some of the more complex goals such as the removal of economic inequities. Given our conception of economic inequities, some of these goals may be definable in tangible terms—removal of bonded (or tied) labor, abolition of privileges related to hereditary positions or inherited assets, increase of social mobility as given by specific criteria. These goals may or may not be easy to achieve, but they can certainly be discussed in terms of very palpable magnitudes. The same applies to the provision of social services, such as hospital facilities, or educational opportunities, or the supply of drinkable water, or the availability of fast public transport.

There are, however, objectives that cannot be given such a tangible form despite their essentially economic nature and despite their popularity as goals; different people see their descriptive features differently. Examples of such concerns include economic self-confidence and technological independence. Notwithstanding their ambiguity as goals, their pursuit may play an important part in the development process; an exact coincidence of aims is not a precondition of joint action. These objectives are particularly hard to analyze and examine, but it is foolish to eliminate them on grounds of their imprecision. Indeed, aside from keeping track of them as ideas playing creative roles in development, one has to view them as potential sources of deflection from other development goals; romance can be both elevating and expensive.

Finally, it is clear that the determination of relative weights among objectives and the determination of relative weights incorporated within specific objectives involve noting conflicts between the interests of different classes or sections of the community and taking a position in the light of such conflicts. This is very largely a political process that must go beyond pure descriptions of aspirations. There is no escape from this process in the formulation of a development program.[15]

Obstacles

Obstacles to economic development can be viewed in the light of the analysis of objectives. Some of the obstacles are implicit in the objectives. Insofar as the interests of groups differ and conflict with one another, the translation of objectives into programs depends essentially on the balance of power among groups. Within the constraints imposed by the interfering (or threatening) ability of other groups, the groups established in power may formulate programs geared chiefly to their own aspirations. It is thus not mysterious that some of the objectives are never properly translated into programs of action. For example, inequalities of income distribution or asset distribution may remain as strong as ever or even be accentuated, the intensity of poverty may rise, and famine conditions may systematically recur, despite much progress in the achievement of other goals and objectives.

Not all obstacles to economic development arise from such conflicts, but many of them do, and an analysis of development obstacles is not likely to get very far if it proceeds on the assumption of a harmonious society united in seeking the universal ambrosia called development. The characteristics of ruling groups, the powers they enjoy, the constraints imposed by threats from other groups, the extent to which their respective interests coincide and conflict—these are central issues in analyzing obstacles to economic development.

The process of development can be viewed as a game with some common interests and some conflicts. The biggest breaks for groups not in power are typically made in areas in which the coincidence of interests is dominant. The incidence of epidemics of infectious diseases has been much reduced in recent years, bringing obvious gain to the poor but also to the infectable rich. In general, progress in communal health measures, while limited in most underdeveloped countries, has usually been more noticeable than progress in reducing the inequality of income distribution, and this is at least partly due to a broad coincidence of interests in matters of health and illness. For much the same reason the objective of stimulating overall growth tends to be more readily translated into development programs than the goal of inequality removal.

China's success in achieving the development objectives that are closely related to inequality removal has almost certainly been most strongly helped by the shifts in political power since the revolution. Prima facie, this makes it difficult to expect that the Chinese experience could be repeated, or even emulated, in countries with a more traditional power balance. However, it is also possible to argue that the development objectives for which conflicts are weaker (and positive interdependence stronger) provide greater scope of immediate emulation in other countries with a different power balance. The medical schemes and community health measures may, in this sense, be more easily emulated than, say, Chinese agrarian developments.

Obstacle Types

A well-established tradition in a substantial part of development economics is to define the objectives of development rather narrowly, essentially in terms of growth of GNP per head, and then to analyze the obstacles to achieving rapid development in that narrow sense. This, in view of what I have been discussing in this chapter, is a major distortion, and the limitations of that approach should be kept in view.

Within that relatively narrow framework, a variety of theories of barriers to development offer an array of diagnoses and hypotheses, beginning with a few, now classic, vicious circles and traps.[16] It is not easy to accept or reject these theories, partly because of intercountry variations of experience, partly because of lack of definitive empirical data, but also because of the vague formulation of most of these theories—a characteristic that has merits in terms of suggestiveness but not in devising empirical tests. Theories about obstacles to development are rarely pruned; they all seem to coexist in a vast cocktail party in which everyone is heard simultaneously.

This section does not contain a breakthrough that changes all this. Instead, it offers a few quick remarks on different types of obstacle theories. The more prevalent obstacle theories seem to be classifiable into the following types in terms of the nature of their foci: resource limitations; technology limitations; population barriers; and limitations of the economic system.

Theories of resource limitation focus on the inability of underdeveloped countries to expand their resource base. The most common theories within this broad type concentrate on low accumulation possibilities in underdeveloped countries for specified reasons such as poverty or on the international demonstration effects on consumption of modern goods.[17] While labor limitation theories typically emphasize utilization rather than availability, skill limitation approaches go into availability extensively.[18] In the presence of foreign exchange constraints, domestic production of machinery is also given a role of its own.[19]

Technology limitations are obvious characteristics of underdeveloped countries regarding knowledge since the industrial revolution. The question that arises is why this problem has not been resolved by international transfer of technology. Paul Streeten has distinguished between two aspects of the problem of transfer: the suitability gap (techniques used in rich economies may not be appropriate for the poor countries) and the communications gap (techniques are not communicated fast enough from rich to poor countries).[20] Streeten has also noted that trying to close one gap might widen the other. The suitability gap has been the subject of attention in the analysis of appropriate or intermediate technology,[21] while the communications gap has led to examinations of mechanisms of technology transfer and the underlying legal frame work (such as the patent system)[22] and of institutions like multinational corporations.[23]

Theories of technological dependence focus on these limitations as among the chief obstacles to development.[24] These theories are concerned not merely with the obstacles to transfer but also with systematic hindrances in evolving modern technology in underdeveloped countries exposed to the captivating influence, in more senses than one, of the richer countries. The literature of growth theory includes distressingly few attempts to deal with the endogenous evolution of techniques of production. Nicholas Kaldor and Kenneth Arrow are among the notable exceptions,[25] even though their models of learning are limited by the notion that only investment can result in learning.[26]

An extreme version of population barriers takes the view that the growth of total income is neutralized by a consequent growth of population (chiefly through a decline of the death rate), while a more moderate claim is that it is difficult to achieve a rate of overall growth in underdeveloped countries that is high enough to overcome population growth and raise the per capita income.[27] The latter is a less exciting but less controversial obstacle theory. There is some evidence that a rise in the living standard eventually brings down the birth rate, but the seriousness of the problem at earlier stages cannot be denied.

Resource availability and technology determine potential production; actual production depends substantially on the nature of the economic system. Aspects of the economic system that influence production *exclusively through* one of the factors already mentioned (for example, resource availability, or technology) need not be discussed separately, but other aspects work through different channels.

The modes of production and employment have a substantial influence on the use of production opportunities. This applies particularly to labor mobilization[28] but also to the utilization of capital resources.[29] Terms-of-trade and development obstacles arising from foreign exchange shortage are also problems due to the economic system in operation,[30] as is the ineptness of government policy leading to wasteful allocation of resources.[31] This category of problems includes the influence of political forces that impose feasibility constraints on government policy, such as ruling out interference with land holdings, or nationalization of capital, or even radical changes in tax rates.[32]

The purpose of a whirlwind tour of obstacle theories like this one is not, of course, the dispensation of undoubted wisdom. In the assessment of China's development experience, it may be useful to bear in mind the variety of directions in which development theorists have spotted enemy movements. The Chinese experience has been concerned with tackling all these limitations to a greater or less extent.

Pure Exchange Systems

An "obstacle" that has received less attention in the development literature than it deserves is the exchange system in operation, and it seems to me to be particularly relevant in contrasting China with other less developed countries, for example, India.

Define a pure exchange system as one in which all income is derived from some interpersonal exchange. The traditional precapitalist formations are not pure exchange systems in this sense; for example, in owner cultivation the output is received without any act of interpersonal exchange. Nor are advanced capitalist economies pure exchange systems, since social security payments (unemployment benefits, national pensions) are incomes without exchange. Socialist countries have such nonexchange incomes on an even larger scale. Indeed pure exchange systems are not observed anywhere.

Nevertheless, in the process of industrialization or colonial development a precapitalist economy typically seems to go through a phase in which its traditional sources of nonexchange income (cultivation of own land) contract sharply much before the modern sources of nonexchange income (social security) expand or even come into existence. There is, then, a much enhanced dependence on the exchange system for one's survival. As a stylized face, in the Kaldorian sense, I shall call this the phase of the pure exchange system transition; the name has the merit of being abbreviated PEST. The PEST phase does not imply that the pure exchange system fully holds but that the economy moves sharply *in that direction* for a while.

There are many consequences of the PEST phase. One of them is the greater exposure of the economy to the dangers of famines despite, as is the case in most areas of the world except parts of Africa, a growing availability of food per head on average. The group typically most affected consists of landless laborers. While a severe flood or a drought might reduce a peasant's income by cutting down his sowing, transplanting, or harvesting, it could wipe out a laborer's income if he is not needed because of the reduced level of activity.[33]

Several recent studies have dealt with possible world shortages of food, but the focus on the statistics of food availability per capita seems simplistic in developing a famine policy. I am unable to judge how important PEST is in increasing overall distributional inequality in such an intermediate phase,[34] but in terms of increasing the vulnerability of large groups of people to economic disasters, PEST has a clear importance, at least for many underdeveloped countries. And this relates closely to the development objective geared to temporal minimality. It is easy to see the advantages of the Chinese type of economic organization, which vastly extends the scope of nonexchange income and gears even the exchange activity of wage employment to objectives other than production for profit. The statistics of growth of GNP per head, or even of food consumption per capita, fail to catch this important aspect of development.

The contrast does not apply only to disaster avoidance. In the mobilization of labor the system of income generation is of considerable significance. If the absorption of the unemployed in public projects is confined rigidly to the system of paying an independently specified market wage, the possibility of curing unemployment becomes severely constrained by the ability of the economy to absorb additional effective demand.[35] Given the short-run inelasticity of the supply of food,[36] a large increase in effective demand in any part of the economy can drown people with low (and unresponsive) income below the starvation level.[37]

The magnitudes involved may be worth examining, and I do this in the specific context of India. Rural unemployment estimates for India vary substantially with the concept of unemployment used. For 1970–71 figures of 17.1 million and 42.4 million were tentatively arrived at respectively with the recognition and production approaches.[38] The government of India had already initiated a project called the Crash Scheme for Rural Employment (CSRE) in which people would be given jobs for ten months of the year at a wage of about Rs 100 per month. The scheme covered very few people. But suppose the intention were instead to cover the estimated unemployed population. What would it have cost? Take Rs 90 per month to avoid overstating the magnitude; then the figures involved are Rs 15,390 million and Rs 38,160 million respectively. As percentages of the net domestic product in agriculture that year, this would have been 10% and 24% respectively, and as percentages of net domestic savings (for the economy as a whole and not of agriculture only) 35% and 87% respectively.[39] This was not on the cards in the absence of a transformation of the pure exchange system of employment. The CSRE stayed minute, and the unemployed stayed where they were.

The system of labor and income prevalent in the PEST phase seems not merely to increase vulnerability to disasters; it also constrains dramatically the economy's ability to use the available resources. The inhumanity of the system competes with its equally distinguished inefficiency. China's attempts to evolve totally different systems of labor utilization are best viewed, it seems to me, in this specific context.

Notes

In revising this chapter I benefited from the seminar discussion on an earlier version, led by Dudley Sears.

1. For this more general person-commodity discriminating approach to national income evaluation, some basic theorems and one particular empirical application (dealing with interstate contrasts of rural national income in India) are presented in my "Real National Income," *Review of Economic Studies* 43 (1976).

2. See my "Choice, Orderings, and Morality," in S. Körner, ed., *Practical Reason* (Oxford: Basil Blackwell, 1974) and "Rational Fools: A Critique of the Behavioral Foundations of Economic Theory," *Philosophy and Public Affairs* 6 (1977).

3. See J. de V. Graaff, *Theoretical Welfare Economics* (Cambridge: Cambridge University Press, 1957), and P. Streeten, *The Frontiers of Development Studies* (London: Macmillan, 1972), especially chapter 3.

4. See my "Real National Income," and P. Hammond, "Economic Welfare with Rank Order Price Weighting," *Review of Economic Studies* 45 (1978).

5. See F. Paukert, "Income Distribution at Different Levels of Development: A Survey of Evidence," *International Labour Review* 108 (1973); also Hollis Chenery et al., eds., *Redistribution with Growth* (London: Oxford University Press, 1974).

6. See my "Poverty and Famines," prepared for the International Labor Organization (ILO) World Employment Program, forthcoming. See also United Nations, *Poverty, Unemployment, and Development Policy: A Case Study of Selected Issues with Reference to Kerala* (New York, 1975).

7. See, for example, Chenery et al., *Redistribution with Growth*. The discussion has been particularly vigorous in India; see P. Bardhan and T. N. Srinivasan, eds., *Poverty and Income Distribution in India* (Calcutta: Statistical Publishing Society, 1974). For an earlier contribution in the context of a developed economy, see A. B. Atkinson, *Poverty in Britain and the Reform of Social Security* (Cambridge: Cambridge University Press, 1969).

8. See my "Poverty, Inequality, and Unemployment," *Economic and Political Weekly* 8 (1973), and "Poverty: An Ordinal Approach to Measurement," *Econometrica* 44 (February 1976). Sudhir Anand has proposed altering this measure by taking I to be the weighted shortfall as a proportion of the mean income of the community as opposed to the poverty line; see his "Aspects of Poverty in Malaysia" (mimeographed), St. Catherine's College, Oxford, 1975. Anand presents a penetrating analysis of the profile of poverty in Malaysia including the intercommunity differences.

9. See I. Z. Bhatty, "Inequality and Poverty in Rural India," in Bardhan and Srinivasan, *Poverty and Income Distribution*. The concern with the exact pattern of poverty as used in the measure P also reveals some interesting intergroup patterns of the poverty problem; see F. Seastrand and R. Diwan, "Measurement and Comparison of Poverty and Inequality in the United States," presented to the Third World Econometric Congress, Toronto, 1975; N. C. Kakwani, "Measurement of Poverty and the Negative Income Tax," Development Research Center, International Bank for Reconstruction and Develop-

ment; Anand, "Aspects of Poverty in Malaysia"; M. Alamgir, "Poverty, Inequality, and Development Strategy in the Third World," First Congress of Third World Economists, Algiers, February 1976.

10. See my *Employment, Technology and Development* (Oxford: Clarendon Press, 1975), appendix B.

11. Recent contributions to the theory of justice by John Rawls — see his *Theory of Justice* (Cambridge, Mass.: Harvard University Press, 1971) — have been important in drawing attention to minimal levels of living as indicators of social welfare. See also E. S. Phelps, ed., *Economic Justice* (Harmondsworth: Penguin, 1972). The reasoning can also be extended to variations over time of the same group of people, requiring a special concern about periods of greatest distress.

12. While children under five formed around 16% of the population of Bengal at the time of the Bengal famine of 1943, perhaps the biggest famine of this century, the Department of Anthropology at Calcutta University found that a quarter of the "destitutes" were below the age of five, and of the deaths surveyed a third were of children under five.

13. See, for example, R. Cassen, "Economic-Demographic Interrelationships in Developing Countries," in H. B. Parry, ed., *Population and Its Problems* (London: Oxford University Press, 1974).

14. See P. C. Mahalanobis, R. Mukherjea, and Ambica Ghosh, "A Sample Survey of After Effects of the Bengal Famine of 1943," *Sankhya: Indian Journal of Statistics* 7 (1947), pt. 4.

15. These issues are of specific concern to the so-called social choice theory, pioneered by Kenneth Arrow. It is sometimes thought that social choice theory must eschew class analysis and be wedded to starting from tastes as opposed to interests; see Frances Stewart, "A Note on Social Cost-Benefit Analysis and Class Conflicts in LDCs," *World Development* 3 (1973). There is no reason that this should be the case, but this is not to deny that some treatments of collective choice give the impression of dealing with individuals as if they were ships passing at night — there is the hello and the goodbye, but no real contact.

16. For an excellent survey of many of the theories involved, see G. M. Meier, *Leading Issues in Economic Development*, 2d ed. (London: Oxford University Press, 1970).

17. See, for example, R. Nurkse, *Problems of Capital Formation in Underdeveloped Countries* (Oxford: Blackwell, 1953). Theories of colonialism, while many-sided in their diagnosis of underdevelopment, typically give a special role to accumulation problems; see S. Amin, *Accumulation on a World Scale* (New York: Monthly Review Press, 1974). On a very different vein, Alfred Marshall had also tried his hand at explaining poverty by accumulation failures in his discussion

of "poverty caused by ceremonial extravagance in spite of personal thrift" in "India, and to a less extent in Ireland." *Principles of Economics,* 8th ed. (London: Macmillan, 1949), p. 187.

18. See S. Bowles, *Planning Educational System for Economic Growth* (Cambridge, Mass.: Harvard University Press, 1969); M. Blaug, *Education and Employment Problems in Developing Countries* (Geneva: ILO, 1974).

19. See K. N. Raj and A. K. Sen, "Alternative Patterns of Growth under Conditions of Stagnant Export Earnings," *Oxford Economic Papers* 13 (1961); P. K. Bardhan, *Economic Growth: Development and Foreign Trade* (New York: Wiley, 1970).

20. "Technology Gaps between Rich and Poor Countries" in P. Streeten, *The Frontiers of Development Studies* (London: Macmillan, 1972).

21. The literature is vast; for some recent empirical work, see the collection of case studies in A. S. Bhalla, ed., *Technology and Employment in Industry: A Case Study Approach* (Geneva: ILO, 1974).

22. See *The Role of the Patent System in the Transfer of Technology to Developing Countries* (New York: United Nations, 1975), sales no. E.75.II.D.6.

23. See, for example, C. Vaitsos, *Transfer of Resources and Preservation of Monopoly Rents,* Economic Development Report No. 168, Center for International Affairs, Harvard University, 1970; O. Sunkel, "Transnational Capital and National Disintegration in Latin America," *Social and Economic Studies* (March 1973); Streeten, *Frontiers of Development Studies.*

24. See, for example, A. G. Frank, *Capitalism and Underdevelopment in Latin America* (New York: Monthly Review Press, 1967); T. dos Santos, "The Structure of Dependence," *American Economic Review,* Papers and Proceedings, 40 (1970); C. Furtado, *Economic Development in Latin America* (Cambridge: Cambridge University Press, 1970). See also the critical review by Sanjay Lall, "Is 'Dependence' a Useful Concept in Analysing Underdevelopment?" *World Development* 3 (1975).

25. N. Kaldor, "A Model of Economic Growth," *Economic Journal* 67 (1957); N. Kaldor and J. A. Mirrlees, "A New Model of Economic Growth," *Review of Economic Studies* 29 (1961–62); K. J. Arrow, "The Economic Implications of Learning by Doing," *Review of Economic Studies* 29 (1961–62).

26. While Kaldor and Mirrlees make learning a function of the percentage rate of growth of investment, Arrow makes technical capability grow with the sum of past gross investments. Aside from technical experiences arising from noninvestment activities, there is also the question of experience in producing modern machinery (as op-

posed to acquiring it from abroad for domestic investment); on the last, see A. Fishlow, "Empty Economic Stages?" *Economic Journal* 75 (1965).

27. See G. Ohlin, *Population Control and Economic Development* (Paris: Organization for Economic Cooperation and Development, 1967), for critical assessment of various population theories. See also Parry, *Population and Its Problems.*

28. See the ILO country mission reports on Colombia (led by Dudley Seers), Ceylon (led by Dudley Seers), Kenya (led by Richard Jolly and Hans Singer) and Philippines (led by Gus Ranis). I have tried to discuss this question in *Employment, Technology, and Development.* See also R. Jolly et al., eds., *Third World Employment: Problems and Strategy* (Harmondsworth: Penguin, 1973).

29. See, for example, G. C. Winston, "Capacity Utilisation in Economic Development," *Economic Journal* 81 (1971).

30. See, for example, R. Prebisch, *Towards a New Trade Policy for Development,* Report by the Secretary General of UNCTAD (New York: United Nations, 1964).

31. See, for example, I. Little, T. Scitovsky, and M. Scott, *Industry and Trade in Some Developing Countries* (London: Oxford University Press, 1970).

32. See my "Strategies of Economic Development: Feasibility Constraints and Planning," in E. A. G. Robinson and M. Kidron, eds., *Economic Development in South Asia* (London: Macmillan, 1970).

33. These and related issues are discussed in my "Poverty and Famines," and in my "Starvation and Exchange Entitlement: A General Approach and Its Application to the Great Bengal Famine," *Cambridge Journal of Economics* I (1977).

34. There is some evidence for such an increased inequality in an intermediate phase of development in terms of usual measures of inequality, for example, the Gini coefficient; see the cross-country study by Paukert, "Income Distribution at Different Levels of Development."

35. Cf. my *Choice of Techniques* (Oxford: Blackwell, 1960).

36. This does not contradict the role of demand—often neglected —in stimulating expansion in some other sectors of an underdeveloped economy; see L. Lefeber, "On the Paradigm of Economic Development," *World Development* 4 (1974); see also A. K. Bagchi, *Private Investment in India 1900–39* (Cambridge: Cambridge University Press, 1972).

37. There is considerable evidence that the Bengal famine of 1943 started with such a sudden rise of effective demand (partly due to war efforts) in late 1942, causing acute distress and starvation among

large groups of people who were surviving on income earned in the preceding seasonal peak; this led eventually to the dynamic phase of galloping famine as speculation activities based on reports of hunger turned everyone who could afford it into a hoarder of food. The overall food availability in per capita terms was not exceptionally low, despite the disruption of some supply from Burma. The government stuck inactively to its per capita availability statistics—thought to be wrong by its critics though probably not so—without examining the income and expenditure mechanism.

38. Cf. my "Dimensions of Unemployment in India," Convocation Address, Indian Statistical Institute, Calcutta, December 1973.

39. As proportions of net domestic capital formation, the percentages would have been 32% and 80% respectively. The figures of the unemployed do not include the urban jobless even though the savings and capital formation figures refer to the whole economy.

2

Patterns of Economic Development in India, Pakistan, and Indonesia

THOMAS E. WEISSKOPF

In recent years the development experience of the People's Republic of China has drawn increasing attention throughout the world. This may be attributed to reports of China's progress with respect to many important development objectives and to the unique character of the Chinese approach to economic development.

I intend to develop a useful perspective from which to consider the Chinese experience by examining development patterns in several other nations that are in significant respects comparable with China: independent India, Pakistan, and Indonesia.[1] At the beginning of the modern postwar period these three nations more closely resembled China in their basic economic characteristics than any other countries in the world. Yet since then, their political histories, their development strategies, and their development achievements have differentiated them sharply from China.

Initial Economic Conditions

At the beginning of the modern postwar period China, India, Pakistan, and Indonesia, in that order, were the four most populous underdeveloped countries of the world and the four largest countries in South and East Asia.[2] Compared with other underdeveloped countries, these four giants had relatively high densities of population per unit of cultivable land. In all of them the rate of growth of population was quite rapid during the 1950s, adding to the already high pressure of labor on land. Estimates of per capita GNP in 1950 place China,

India, Pakistan, and Indonesia among the poorest countries (and territories) in the world. Because of their large populations, however, they ranked among the top eight underdeveloped countries in total GNP.

Average levels of living in all four nations in the early 1950s were of course very low, given the low levels of per capita GNP. Estimates of calorie and protein consumption per capita per day for India, Pakistan, and Indonesia were significantly below the minimum required for adequate nutrition.[3] Comparable figures are not available for China, but indirect evidence suggests that China was not much better off in this respect.[4] In all four nations (including prerevolutionary China) the distribution of economic well-being was extremely unequal. A small minority of the people lived at the margin of subsistence, surviving on per capita incomes and nutrition levels well below the national average. Regional inequalities were also pronounced, with urban residents generally better off than their rural counterparts and average per capita income levels varying widely among different areas within each country.

Each of the major Asian nations entered the postwar era of development as a predominantly agrarian society. Estimates of the sectoral distribution of the labor force and of national product in the four nations in the early 1950s are strikingly similar.[5] In each of them roughly 70%–75% of the labor force was occupied in agriculture, and (except in India) less than 10% was engaged in industrial activities. Of the latter, the great majority were at work in small-scale enterprises; only in India was as much as 2% of the labor force employed in large-scale modern establishments.[6] Agriculture in each nation accounted for roughly half of total national output, and industry as a whole accounted for no more than 20%. The proportion of manufacturing output, large-scale manufacturing in particular, was substantially higher in China and India than in Pakistan or Indonesia. In each country agriculture accounted for a substantially smaller fraction of total output than of the total labor force, reflecting its relatively low sectoral productivity per worker.

The character of the agricultural economy was also very similar in the four countries. With high labor-to-land ratios, the average size of operational holdings was very small. Rights to land and claims on its produce were very unequally distributed; a preponderance of quasi-feudal tenurial arrangements limited incentives for capital formation or economic improvement. Most agricultural activity was undertaken by indigenous peasant farmers, producing for their own consumption or local markets and using traditional and relatively primitive techniques of production. Modern capitalist farming was relatively rare, although in India and Indonesia a limited amount of plantation agriculture was devoted to export crops and operated for the most part under foreign management. Agricultural output was highly dependent on the weather, as only a small fraction of the cultivated land was assured of water from irrigation facilities. Rural underemployment was widespread, and indebtedness was a chronic problem for a large fraction of small landholders and landless agricultural laborers.

Comparative data on agricultural production in China, India, Pakistan, and Indonesia in the early 1950s indicate that total crop output per person was similar among the four nations but that total crop output per unit of cultivated land was substantially greater in China and Indonesia than in India and Pakistan.[7] These figures reflect not only the greater proportionate significance of labor-intensive crops (such as rice) in China and Indonesia but also higher output per unit of land for some individual crops in these countries. China and Indonesia had reached higher yields than India and Pakistan in rice cultivation; India had the lowest yields in wheat, maize, and cotton as well as rice. Per capita production of all cereal crops combined was considerably higher in China and Pakistan than in India and Indonesia. Since cereals account for well over half of the average Asian diet, the evidence suggests that China and Pakistan were better able to feed their populations than the other two nations.

The initial conditions of industry in the four nations differed much more sharply than did the conditions of agriculture. With respect to natural resource endowment, China was probably most favored (with coal, oil, and many metallic minerals), India next (plentiful coal, limited oil, iron ore, but lacking in nonferrous metals), followed by Indonesia (oil, bauxite, and tin, but no usable coal or iron ore), and last Pakistan (virtually no mineral fuels or metal ores). All four nations produced a variety of agricultural inputs for light industry (cotton, other vegetable fibers), and Indonesia was particularly well endowed with forestry products (rubber, timber).

Industrial activity in each country was dominated in employment and output by small-scale and traditional forms of enterprise. But the development of industry as a whole, especially of modern industry, was considerably more advanced by the early 1950s in China and India than in Pakistan or Indonesia.[8] India had the longest history of modern enterprise, beginning with cotton textiles in the mid-nineteenth century and diversifying into many other industries—jute textiles, sugar, cement, steel—by the end of World War II. Pakistan, carved from undivided British India in 1947, inherited only a tiny fraction of the modern industry that had grown up on the subcontinent. Modern industry in China made significant progress in the twentieth century, but it remained somewhat less extensive and diverse than in India. Very little modern industry was initiated in Indonesia until World War II, as most of the available industrial raw materials were exported in unprocessed form.

In each nation foreign capital, management, and technology had played a dominant role in developing the modern sector of the economy—the relatively small cluster of large-scale enterprises involved in industry, trade, transport, communications, banking, and plantation agriculture. But the degree to which indigenous groups had gained control of the modern sector varied from one country to another. Indigenous capitalists were involved in Indian industrial development from the very beginning, although they were typically quite dependent on foreign management and technological expertise. As the modern sector of the Indian economy slowly grew in size and diversity, Indian capital played an increasingly important role; but even after World War II and the attainment of Indian independence, foreigners still held financial control of a substantial fraction of Indian corporate business, and foreigners played a significant role through management and technical contracts in many other enterprises as well.[9] In China the major role of foreigners in the modern sector diminished considerably by the end of World War II as a result of the disruptive effect of the war itself and the takeover by the Nationalist Government of (what remained of) the enterprises established or seized by the Japanese during their occupation of China. In Pakistan the foreign stake was relatively limited, largely because the inherited modern sector itself was very small; most of the lucrative foreign assets were located in Indian territory. In Indonesia the situation was complicated by the coexistence of two distinct alien groups— the Dutch colonialists and the Chinese community that immigrated to Indonesia during the period of Dutch rule. Both before and immediately after Indonesian independence the modern sector was almost exclusively under the control of Western (primarily Dutch) and Chinese businessmen.[10]

Each of the four Asian giants entered the postwar period with a very low level of development of human resources. Literacy rates were very low, higher education confined to a tiny elite, and technical and managerial skills very scarce. However, differences in the educational heritage of the four nations were quite significant. Initial levels of literacy were higher in China, India, and Pakistan (roughly 20%) than in Indonesia (roughly 10%).[11] India inherited a large and competent indigenous civil service from the British colonial bureaucracy; China has a long tradition of relatively effective public administration; Pakistan's civil service legacy from the British period was much smaller than India's; while Dutch colonial policy allowed relatively little participation by indigenous Indonesians in government. India and China began the postwar period with an absolutely and proportionately much larger number of professionals and skilled technicians than did Pakistan or Indonesia. On the whole, India and China were probably most favored by their endowment of indigenous human resources; Indonesia was unquestionably the worst off because of the particularly restrictive nature of Dutch colonial rule.

Thus the broad economic structure and demographic characteristics of China, India, Pakistan, and Indonesia were quite similar as each nation entered the modern postwar period. Their great size—but not their degree of economic backwardness—differentiated them sharply from almost all other underdeveloped countries. Among the most significant differences in the initial economic conditions of the four giants were China's and Pakistan's relatively greater per capita productions of cereals, and China's and India's relatively greater development of industry and human resources.

The Social and Political Context

Economic development has taken place in independent India, Pakistan, and Indonesia in social and political settings that have much in common, especially when contrasted with the Chinese experience. Yet certain differences in the political trends and the overall approaches to development have characterized the three nations, and these differences have affected their relative progress.[12]

India, Pakistan, and Indonesia share the historical legacy of a long period of direct colonial rule. In each of the three countries independence was attained after a period of nationalist struggle, which triumphed when the European colonial powers were weakened by the devastation of World War II. The Indian nationalist movement was the oldest and the most broadly based of the three, the Pakistani movement was the youngest, and the Indonesian movement was the only one that had to resort to armed struggle against the ruling colonial power.

In all three nations the attainment of independence involved no revolutionary social upheaval but simply a transfer of power from the retreating colonial rulers to the dominant indigenous classes that had led the nationalist movements. Independence resulted in little change in the highly inegalitarian domestic class structure that had long characterized these countries. Most of the upper classes retained their social, political, and economic power in the postindependence period, with the exception of a very limited number of people most closely identified with the former colonial rulers. In all three nations urban and relatively Westernized elites tended to dominate politics and government at the national level, while rural and more traditional elites maintained predominant power at the local level.

The Western capitalist conception of property rights had been introduced into all three countries by their European colonial rulers, and after independence powerful landed classes and business interests sought successfully to assure the protection of private property. Although the rhetoric of the nationalist political leadership (especially in India and Indonesia) was replete with professions of socialist ideals, this rhetoric was aimed largely at generating support among the lower classes for nationalist elites and did not involve any major threat to the propertied classes or to the growth of capitalist institutions. In each nation the new rulers intended that the state play a very important role in promoting economic development, through various forms of economic planning, public enterprise, government taxes, subsidies, and controls. But this state role was clearly to be played in the context of a mixed capitalist economy in which private enterprise would remain the dominant economic force. The actual ability of government officials and economic planners to direct the economy was limited in all three nations, both by the continuing power of propertied classes and by the general lack of social discipline that Gunnar Myrdal has labeled "the soft state."[13]

Along with Western capitalist property rights, Western forms of bourgeois democracy were also transmitted in varying degrees to India, Pakistan, and Indonesia. Each nation began its independent existence with a constitutional political system in which there was competition for political offices among representatives of different parties. Elections were held and government administrations periodically changed in both Pakistan and Indonesia during the first decade after their independence; but parliamentary democracy was little more than a facade covering power struggles among the upper classes, and it soon gave way to direct authoritarian rule. In India the parliamentary democratic system was more deeply rooted and proved more durable, but in the absence of any change in the highly inegalitarian social structure it offered much greater opportunities for the stronger than for the weaker classes in the political arena.

All three nations have faced serious problems of national integration because of significant cultural, religious, and linguistic differences between regions or subgroups of the population. The Indian people are made up of more than a dozen major (and hundreds of minor) linguistic groups with separate cultural identities, and this ethnological heterogeneity is further complicated by religious divisions between the Hindu majority and Moslem, Christian, Sikh, and other religious minorities. Pakistan is overwhelmingly Moslem, but until the liberation of Bangladesh the Eastern and Western regions were sharply divided by linguistic and cultural differences. The Indonesian population consists of four broadly distinguishable ethnic groups: the majority inland community of Moslems with a cultural tradition strongly influenced by an earlier era of Hindu domination; the less numerous and strongly Islamic coastal peoples; the tribal groups of the mountainous interior regions (mainly in the Outer Islands); and several million persons of Chinese origin based in urban areas, most of whom were still considered aliens when Indonesia attained independence.

With respect to all these general characteristics—colonial history, class structure, basic political and economic institutions, ethnic heterogeneity—modern India, Pakistan, and Indonesia have much more in common with one another than any of them does with the People's Republic of China. Their dramatic social and political differentiation from China contrasts sharply with the broadly similar initial economic conditions.

The most important distinctions between India, Pakistan, and Indonesia involve differences in the continuity and nature of political rule, on the one hand, and the strategy of economic development, on the other. Of the three nations India has had the most stable political history. The Indian system of parliamentary democracy, modeled after the British, has survived to the present day; although it was suspended and severely shaken by Prime Minister Indira Gandhi's declaration of a national emergency in June 1975 and her highly authoritarian rule during the following nineteen months. At all times until the elections of 1977, the Congress party (encompassing a large part of the Indian nationalist movement) remained securely in power at the national level and dominated the formulation and execution of economic policy. Although certain policies varied from one period to another, there was substantial continuity in the Indian approach to development from independence to the mid 1970s.

The political history of Pakistan, up to the disruptions that led to the independence of Bangladesh, can be divided into two distinct periods. The first decade, the "democratic" period, was characterized by bitter power struggles and frequent changes of government in the context of a barely viable parliamentary system. The second period, from 1958 to 1969, was one of authoritarian rule by Field Marshal Ayub Khan, who put an end to the earlier instability and imposed his own version of law and order.

Indonesia has already experienced three sharply different periods of political rule, which have imparted to the Indonesian development experience an unusual degree of discontinuity. As in Pakistan, the first decade involved a "democratic" period during which political struggles led to increasing instability and ultimately to the collapse of the parliamentary system. In the Indonesian case the strong personality who intervened to establish a more authoritarian order came not from the conservative military establishment (as did Ayub Khan) but from the top of the civilian nationalist leadership. President Sukarno dominated the Indonesian political scene from 1958 to 1965, but because of the independent power of the Communist party of Indonesia (on the left) and the army (on the right), Sukarno's authority was never as firm as that of Ayub Khan. The third distinct period of political rule in Indonesia was ushered in by widespread armed struggle between left-wing and right-wing groups in 1965. In 1966 the army emerged in decisive control of the country and set about establishing a "New Order" under the authoritarian leadership of General Suharto, who has since remained in power.

The strategies of economic development pursued in India, Pakistan, and Indonesia have all reflected a belief in the importance of the role of the state; a certain distrust of private enterprise and the market system; a degree of economic nationalism, tempered by a pragmatic inclination to make use of foreign investment, aid, and technology; a strong desire to promote industrialization; and—at least at the rhetorical level—some commitment to greater social and economic equity. In practice, however, there have been fairly clear differences in the degree to which different regimes have pursued these lines of economic policy. In discussing these differences it is useful to distinguish between the single (more or less continuous) Indian regime, the two Pakistani regimes, and the three Indonesian regimes, each delimited by the periods noted before.

Of the six the Sukarno regime was the most interventionist, that is, the most inclined to expand the role of the state, the most hostile to private enterprise (especially foreign), and the most suspicious of the market mechanism. Sukarno also tended to be more nationalist in economic orientation, stressing greater self-reliance rather than an expansion of foreign trade and foreign capital inflows. At the other end of the spectrum, the Ayub Khan and the Suharto regimes have been the most liberal, that is, the most inclined to use the market mechanism rather than direct government controls and the most tolerant of (and helpful to) private enterprise. These two regimes were also more internationalist in their external economic relations, looking more favorably on the expansion of trade and capital inflows. In all these respects the Indian government pursued an intermediate policy, sometimes moving in a more interventionist and nationalist direction and at other times moving toward a more economically liberal and internationalist stance. The "democratic" regimes in both Pakistan and Indonesia also tended to occupy a middle ground, although the relative weakness of central government during those periods limited the scope for effective state intervention.

There is little to distinguish the three nations (and six regimes) in their relative emphasis on agricultural and industrial activity. In each case import-substituting industrialization was given high priority and agriculture was somewhat neglected in the first decade or so after independence. Subsequent difficulties in maintaining a sufficiently rapid rate of agricultural growth led to growing concern and some increase in resources and effort devoted to the agricultural sector. Differences in the sectoral emphases of the development strategies in India, Pakistan, and Indonesia are attributable largely to their differing initial conditions. With a head start in industry and a good base of industrial raw materials, India was in the best position to promote a more substantial and diversified industrial structure. With a less favorable resource endowment, Pakistan had to pursue a strategy of industrialization more oriented to agro-based light manufacturing, and Indonesia was bound to devote considerable attention to the development of her lucrative natural resources for export.

There was much talk of land reform programs as part of an overall agricultural development strategy in all three nations, but the degree of success in implementing such programs varied considerably with the degree of commitment shown by different regimes. In no case did enough redistribution of land take place to reduce significantly the great inequality in the distribution of holdings. The Indian government achieved a little more in this respect (primarily in the early years after independence) than the Pakistani government (in the early years of the Ayub Khan regime); in Indonesia, more or less spontaneous seizures of land by poor peasants in the latter period of the Sukarno regime were for the most part reversed with the subsequent accession to power of Suharto, who proceeded with a limited and more carefully controlled program of land reform under the New Order. By the mid to late 1960s, government decision makers in all three countries had clearly opted for an agricultural growth policy based primarily on technological rather than institutional change.

On the whole, the commitment of the political leadership to policies designed to promote social and economic equity was stronger in India than in Pakistan or Indonesia under any of the alternative regimes.[14] India's five-year plans have all stressed the desirability of an equitable pattern of growth. In contrast, the Ayub Khan regime was quite explicit in conveying its view that issues of equity were secondary to the prime objective of economic growth; indeed, Pakistani economic policy was for a long time predicated on the assumption that substantial inequality was functional for economic growth. Although less explicitly so, the Suharto regime has shown an attitude toward equity very similar to that of Ayub Khan. Sukarno recognized a multiplicity of development objectives, but he was generally much more concerned with promoting Indonesian nationalism than with reducing social and economic inequalities among indigenous Indonesians. Finally, the "democratic" regimes in Pakistan and Indonesia were for the most part too preoccupied with immediate political struggles and short-run economic policy to be able to articulate effectively any long-term development goals.

In summary, economic development in modern India, Pakistan, and Indonesia has taken place within a highly inegalitarian socioeconomic framework and a set of basic political and economic institutions favoring an essentially capitalist form of development. The degree of political and economic stability and continuity has been highest in India and lowest in Indonesia. The strategies of economic development pursued in all three nations have involved significant roles for both the state and private enterprise, but the economic policies of the Ayub Khan regime in Pakistan and the Suharto regime in Indonesia have been more liberal and internationalist in orientation than those pursued under other regimes.

Development Progress

It is now widely recognized that economic development involves a variety of objectives whose relative importance is a matter of ethical judgment. For the purpose of comparing the development progress of modern India, Pakistan, and Indonesia, I shall distinguish six types of development objectives and seek to determine, as far as the available information permits, how much has been achieved in each country with respect to each objective.

Growth in Value Aggregates

Table 2–1 presents data on aggregate and sectoral economic growth in India, Pakistan, and Indonesia, compiled in a way that facilitates comparative analysis. Although the underlying data no doubt have considerable margins of possible error, the relatively long term growth rates shown in the table can be presumed to be reasonably ac-

TABLE 2-1 Growth rates (in average annual percentages)

Variable	India			Pakistan			Indonesia		
	1951^a–72	1951^a–61	1961–72	1951^a–69	1951^a–58	1958–69	1959^a–72	1959^a–66	1966–72
1. Real total output	3.5	3.7	3.3	4.0	2.5	4.9	3.8	1.8	6.1
2. Population	2.1	2.0	2.3	2.5	2.3	2.6	2.7	2.3	3.1
3. Real per capita output	1.4	1.7	1.0	1.5	0.2	2.3	1.1	–0.5	2.9
4. Agricultural output^b	2.1	2.7	1.5	2.9	1.3	4.0	2.7	1.6	3.9
5. Industrial output^c	4.5	4.4	4.6	9.0	8.1	9.6	6.7	1.7	12.8
6. Mining output	3.2	3.3	3.1	7.9	6.5	8.8	9.4	3.0	17.5
7. Manufacturing output	4.2	4.3	4.1	8.4	7.7	8.9	4.5	1.2	8.4
8. Food output	2.3	3.0	1.8	3.7	2.1	4.5	2.5	1.7	4.2
9. Per capita food output	0.2	1.0	–0.5	1.2	–0.2	1.9	–0.2	–0.6	1.1

Sources: (1)–(7) Calculated from population and constant price national accounts data given in OECD, Development Center, *National Accounts of Less Developed Countries, 1950–1966* (Paris: OECD, July 1968) and subsequent reports no. 5 (February 1971) and no. 8 (July 1974). (8)–(9) Calculated from production figures given in FAO, *Production Yearbook, 1968, 1972,* and population figures from UN, *Demographic Yearbook, 1963, 1972.*

Note: The initial and terminal years of each period are the middle years of the three-year averages used to calculate the growth rates (see note 15).
a. 1953 for items 8 and 9.
b. Includes output in agriculture, animal husbandry, forestry, and fishing.
c. Includes output in mining, manufacturing, construction, and utilities.

curate.[15] Growth rates are shown for each country for as long a period between 1950 and 1975 as the available data permitted.[16] Two subperiods are also distinguished for each country: in Pakistan the Ayub Khan period (1958–1969) is separated from the "democratic" period (1951–1958), and in Indonesia the New Order–Suharto period (1966–1972) is separated from the Sukarno period (1959–1966).

Over the full periods spanned by the available data, there was little difference among the three countries in the average annual rates of growth of real total output (3.5%–4.0%) or real per capita output (1.1%–1.5%). In different subperiods, however, there was a much greater degree of variation. The highest rates of aggregate economic growth (total and per capita) were achieved in Indonesia under the New Order (6.1%, 2.9%) and in Pakistan under Ayub Khan (4.9%, 2.3%). India fared somewhat better in the first decade of development (3.7%, 1.7%) than in the second (3.3%, 1.0%). The least successful growth experiences were in Pakistan before Ayub Khan (2.5%, 0.2%) and in Indonesia under Sukarno (1.8%, −0.5%).

In all three countries the long-run growth rate of agricultural output was between 2% and 3% per year. Except in Pakistan, food production barely kept pace with the growth of population. As with aggregate output, however, there was considerable variation in the growth of agricultural output during different periods. Agricultural growth was most rapid during the Ayub Khan and the Suharto subperiods in Pakistan and Indonesia. During the earlier subperiods in those countries, and during the later subperiod in India, the growth of agricultural output and food output lagged behind the growth of population. Table 2–2 casts further light on the differential agricultural growth performances by comparing changes in the average yields of the principal cereal crops in each country. In Pakistan and Indonesia there were no significant increases in yields in the first subperiod but substantial increases in the second subperiod. Yields in India increased at a moderate rate during both subperiods; the faster rate of growth of output in the first subperiod was apparently attributable to a faster rate of expansion of agricultural acreage.

Industrial growth rates have been consistently more rapid than agricultural growth rates. Again, the highest rates were recorded under Suharto in Indonesia (12.8%) and Ayub Khan in Pakistan (9.6%), but even during the "democratic" period in Pakistan industrial growth was rapid (8.1%). India showed a steady rate of industrial growth averaging roughly $4\frac{1}{2}$% per year throughout the whole period.

These figures are somewhat misleading when used to compare industrial progress in the three countries. The recent high rate of industrial growth in Indonesia reflects an extremely rapid rise in the

TABLE 2-2   Changes in agricultural yields (in hundreds of kilograms per hectare)

Period	Rice	Wheat	Maize	All cereals	Cotton
India					
1948–1952	11.1	6.6	6.5	7.2	0.9
1960–1962	14.9	8.4	9.5	7.4	1.2
1970–1972	16.8	13.0	10.1	11.3	1.2[a]
Pakistan					
1948–1952	13.8	8.7	9.8	11.3	2.0
1958–1959	14.0	7.9	10.3	11.2	2.2
1968–1970	17.4	11.0	10.6	14.4	3.1[a]
Indonesia					
1948–1952	16.1	—	7.6	13.9	—
1958–1960	17.4	—	9.5	15.3	—
1965–1967	17.7	—	9.5	15.4	—
1970–1972	24.0	—	9.9	20.6	—

Sources: FAO, *Production Yearbook, 1961, 1968, 1970, 1972.*

a. Figure for 1968–69.

output of the extractive industries (mainly petroleum) combined with a rate of growth of manufacturing output no greater than in Pakistan. More important, both Pakistan and Indonesia started from a much smaller base of manufacturing industry than did India, and this undoubtedly made it easier to achieve impressive rates of growth for some time. Table 2–3 displays the sectoral composition of output (measured at constant prices) in each country in selected years from 1950 to 1972. In the early 1950s the manufacturing sector accounted for roughly 13% of India's net domestic product, while the corresponding figure was only 6% in Pakistan. At the beginning of Indonesia's rapid industrial growth in 1966, the manufacturing sector accounted for only 8% of net domestic product. In absolute size the gap between India's manufacturing base and that of Pakistan and Indonesia was even greater, since India's national product is some four or five times larger than that of the other two countries.

According to table 2–3, the share of the manufacturing sector as a whole in total output in the early 1970s was still largest in India (17%), second in Pakistan (13%), and smallest in Indonesia (9%). The figures show in all three countries a declining trend in the share of agriculture and a rising trend in the share of industry in total output (in the Indonesian case, these trends begin to emerge only after 1966). Simi-

TABLE 2–3 Sectoral distribution of output and the labor force (in percentages)

Variable/Sector	India			Pakistan			Indonesia		
Output[a]	1950	1961	1972	1950	1958	1970	1960	1966	1972
1. Agriculture[b]	51	50	40	60	54	46	54	53	44
2. Industry[c]	18	21	25	7	12	18	14	14	20
a. Mining	1	1	1	*	*	*	4	3	6
b. Manufacturing	13	15	17	6	9	13	9	8	9
3. Services[d]	31	29	35	33	34	36	32	33	36
Labor force	1950	1961	1971	1950	1961	1968	1961		1971
4. Agriculture[b]	72	74	72	77	75	70	73	—	66
5. Industry[c]	11	12	13	7	9	12	8	—	10
a. Mining	na	1	1	*	*	*	*	—	*
b. Manufacturing	na	10	10	6	8	10	6	—	8
6. Services[d]	17	14	15	16	16	18	19	—	24

Sources: (1)–(3). OECD, Development Center. *National Accounts of Less Developed Countries, 1950–1966* (Paris: OECD, July 1968) and subsequent reports no. 5 (February 1971) and no. 8 (July 1974). (4)–(6) India, 1950: K. N. Raj, *India, Pakistan and China: Economic Growth and Outlook* (Bombay: Allied Publishers, 1967), table 8. Pakistan, 1950: IBRD, *World Tables*, 1971, table 2. Others: ILO, *Yearbook of Labor Statistics, 1966, 1971, 1974*; figures corrected to exclude unemployed and unaccounted for.

a. Net domestic product at factor cost, constant prices (Pakistan: 1959 prices; India, Indonesia: 1960 prices).
b. Includes agriculture, animal husbandry, forestry, and fishing.
c. Includes mining, manufacturing, construction, and utilities.
d. Includes all sectors other than those listed in notes b and c.
* Less than 0.5%.
na = not available.

lar but slower trends are apparent in the (less reliable) figures on the sectoral distribution of the work force shown in table 2–3. Hence in all three countries sectoral productivity per worker remains substantially higher in industry than in agriculture, and these differentials in sectoral productivity appear to be growing.

Growth in Welfare Indicators

Perhaps the best single indicator of the average standard of living in a country is GNP per capita, but it suffers from well-known deficiencies as a measure of society's economic well-being. Because all goods and services (however wasteful or luxurious) are aggregated together, and because prevailing (or imputed) market prices are used as the measure of value, growth in GNP does not necessarily reflect growth in the extent to which a society is producing goods and services that meet certain basic social and economic needs of the people. Among the most essential of these needs are food, shelter, and clothing, as well as an adequate level of health and education. To assess progress with respect to the satisfaction of such needs, it is necessary to examine the growth in certain specific indicators of nutritional levels, living standards, health care availability, and the like.[17]

Time series data on such welfare indicators in India, Pakistan, and Indonesia are scanty and of questionable reliability. Comparable figures for the three countries are limited to certain societywide averages relating to standards of nutrition, health care, and education. The available data of this kind are presented in tables 2–4 and 2–5.

The per capita daily consumption levels of cereals, calories, and protein shown in table 2–4 are all very low by international standards, as one would expect for countries as poor as India, Pakistan, and Indonesia.[18] The figures show an increase in average nutritional standards in India in the 1950s, followed by a slight decline in the 1960s, stagnation in Pakistan in the 1950s followed by steady improvement in the 1960s, and a significant decline in Indonesia from the late 1950s to the mid 1960s. These trends correspond precisely to the overall trends in per capita food production shown in table 2–1. By the end of the 1960s only Pakistan showed an average level of per capita calorie consumption above the estimated minimal nutritional requirement.[19] Given the highly unequal distribution of income in all three countries, this suggests that a large majority of people in all three countries remain below the minimal requirement.

The health care indicators shown in table 2–4 present a somewhat mixed picture. All three countries have apparently reduced the number of inhabitants per physician, and India and Pakistan have reduced the number of inhabitants per hospital bed. Infant mortality

TABLE 2–4 Nutrition and health indicators

Indicator	Years	India	Pakistan	Indonesia
1. Cereal consumption	1951–53	334	419	—
(grams/day/capita)	1954–56	370	411	342[a]
	1960–62	383	424	—
	1963–65	381	454	306
	1968–69	379	475	—
2. Calorie consumption	1951–54	1,750	2,000	—
(number/day/capita)	1957–60	1,910	1,980	2,125[b]
	1960–63	2,020	2,090	—
	1963–65	2,000	2,260	1,850
	1968–69	1,940	2,350	—
3. Protein consumption	1950	46	48	—
(grams/day/capita)	1957–59	50	47	48[b]
	1960–62	51	48	—
	1963–65	50	51	41
	1968–69	48	54	—
4. Inhabitants per physician	1950	6,000	20,000	66,000
	1960	5,800	11,000	41,000
	1970	4,800	6,000	26,000
5. Inhabitants per hospital bed	1957	2,600	3,600	1,300
	1964	1,700	3,800	1,400
	1970	1,500	2,600	1,500
6. Infant mortality	1950–54	185	107	150
(rate per thousand)	1960–62	139	142	125
	1970–71	130	128	135

Sources: (1)–(5) UN, *Statistical Yearbook, 1961, 1966, 1974,* except for figures cited in note a. (6) UN, *Demographic Yearbook, 1963;* IBRD, *World Tables, 1976,* table IV-1.

a. Figure for 1955–1957 given in Gunnar Myrdal, *Asian Drama* (New York: Pantheon, 1968), table 12-4.

b. Figures for 1958 given in ibid., table 12-2.

has apparently been reduced in India, and perhaps in Indonesia, but it may have increased in Pakistan. It is difficult to generalize about the three countries from these rather unreliable figures.

The estimates of literacy and school enrollment ratios in table 2–5 are probably somewhat more accurate than the health indicators. Indonesia, in spite of its poorer general economic performance, appears to have made the greatest progress in increasing literacy. India showed some improvement in the 1950s and more in the 1960s; Pakistan showed no improvement in the 1950s, and there is no evidence for the 1960s. School enrollment ratios, at all three levels, rose by a

TABLE 2–5 Education indicators

Indicator	Year	India	Pakistan	Indonesia
1. Literacy (percentage of persons 15 or older)	1951	19	19	10
	1961	24	16	39
	1971	36		56
2. School enrollment				
a. Primary level (percentage of school-age children)	1950	21	16	29
	1960	42	33	60
	1970	79	44	71
b. Secondary level (percentage of school-age children)	1950	8	9	3
	1960	10	11	6
	1970	28	16	12
c. Tertiary level (Students/ 100,000 population)	1950	118	91	8
	1960	253	149	113
	1970	469	350	187

Sources: (1) 1951: India, Pakistan: IBRD, *World Tables, 1971,* table 2; Indonesia: Myrdal, ibid., p. 1676; 1961, 1971: IBRD, *World Tables, 1976,* table IV-5. (2a, b) 1950: IBRD, *World Tables, 1971,* table 2. 1960, 1970: IBRD, *World Tables, 1976,* table IV-5. (2c) UN, *Economic Survey of Asia and the Far East,* 1973, table I-4-4.

a. Estimated by Gunnar Myrdal, *Asian Drama* (New York: Pantheon, 1968), p. 1676.

greater extent in India than in Pakistan or Indonesia. In all three countries enrollment ratios increased most rapidly at the tertiary level and least rapidly at the primary level. By 1970 India remained ahead of Pakistan and Indonesia at all levels of education, but all three countries fell far short of providing universal primary education to their people.

In sum, the progress of the three countries with respect to average nutritional levels has followed closely their relative success in raising agricultural output in general and food output in particular. In the fields of health and education the available evidence is mixed, but on the whole India has probably made greater progress (from a higher initial base) than Pakistan or Indonesia. This conclusion is consistent with evidence that expenditures on education and health have accounted for a substantially larger proportion of total government expenditure in India than in the other two countries.[20]

Economic Equity

The recent growth in concern about issues of economic equity in underdeveloped countries has unfortunately not yet been matched by any corresponding growth in the availability or reliability of empirical information on the distribution of income and wealth. Among the three countries under study here, data relating to the distribution of economic welfare are most plentiful in India, somewhat less plentiful in Pakistan, and very limited in Indonesia. But in all three countries the data are incomplete, sometimes contradictory, and of uncertain reliability. In the following pages I draw from relevant studies that have been carried out with the available data, in an effort to reach some conclusions about trends in the distribution of income by size class and by region in India, Pakistan, and Indonesia.

A great number of studies have been carried out in India seeking to determine the size distribution of income and its trend over time; the main problem is to evaluate the reliability of these studies and to reconcile differences among them.[21] There is little question that the degree of overall income inequality is high.[22] It is somewhat harder to determine whether there has been any change in the degree of inequality over time.

Most of the relevant studies have used the detailed information on consumer expenditure patterns collected annually by the Indian National Sample Survey; assumptions about savings patterns are then added to estimate distributions of income by income class. Some of these studies conclude unequivocally that income inequality worsened during various subperiods between 1951 and 1968; others show a decline in rural inequality but an increase in urban inequality, with little overall change.[23] Several of the studies have been (justly) criticized for failing to take account of differential price changes facing different income classes. For much of the period, and especially in the 1960s, price movements have been unfavorable to the poorer classes, with the result that current price estimates tend to understate the increase in income inequality. Another recurrent problem is the likely underestimation of consumption expenditure and income of high-income households; if this problem grows over time (as one might expect, in the context of generally rising incomes), it too leads to a downward bias in the measured trend of inequality.

Other evidence, independent of the expenditure surveys, tends to support the hypothesis of increasing inequality from the early 1950s to the late 1960s. During this period there has been a substantial increase in the share of asset income in total nonagricultural income;[24] there has been virtually no change in the highly unequal distribution of land ownership,[25] in a context where access to new agricultural inputs is highly correlated with size of holding; and the incidence of taxation and public expenditure has been on the whole quite regressive.[26] Moreover, the average real earnings of Indian factory workers, presumably a privileged elite within the working class, increased by only about 10% from 1951 to 1971, much less than the increase in average per capita income for the population as a whole.[27] There is also some evidence that the real wages of agricultural laborers have not increased at all.[28]

It is possible that between independence in 1947 and the beginning of planned economic development in 1951, some reduction in inequality resulted from the dispossession of the former rulers of the princely states and some of the largest absentee landlords. The impact of these initial moves on income distribution was considerably dampened, however, by the compensation provided by the Indian government. For the period since the late 1960s, beyond the range of evidence already cited, there is every indication that income inequality has worsened. Most observers of the "Green Revolution," which took root in parts of India in the 1960s, agree that whatever its effect on agricultural output it has had a disequalizing effect on agricultural incomes.[29] Moreover, the price of food in India has continued to rise more rapidly than the general price index.[30] As a result, the poorer classes have been suffering a larger erosion of their money incomes than the rich. All in all, one can conclude that income inequality has not been significantly reduced in India since independence; most probably it has increased.

In the case of Pakistan the available evidence suggests that the overall size distribution of income may have been a little less unequal than in India.[31] If this is so (the intercountry comparability of the data is questionable), it is most probably because East Pakistan was the only area of the subcontinent where any significant degree of land redistribution took place, and because a smaller proportion of the Pakistani population lives in urban areas where inequality is greater than in rural areas.

Most observers believe that the degree of inequality in Pakistan has increased since independence, in part because the Pakistani strategy of development so explicitly embraced the notion of "functional inequality."[32] But the available estimates of distribution of income by income class—based as in India on sample surveys of consumer expenditure patterns—do not support this view. The few studies that have been carried out (all with data from the 1960s only) suggest that inequalities of income have remained more or less constant in urban areas and have declined in rural areas, with overall inequality declining.[33] Critics have pointed out that the survey data on which these studies have been based tend systematically to underestimate the level and the growth of income among the highest income groups. Correcting the figures for such underestimation might well reverse the apparent trend and show increasing rather than decreasing inequality in the 1960s.

In the absence of clear results from studies of the overall size distribution of income, one may turn to studies providing partial pieces of information. Several studies have sought to trace the trend in the real wages of industrial workers:[34] the evidence points to a decline in the 1950s, some improvement in the early 1960s, a decline again in the mid 1960s, and improvement in the late 1960s. During the entire period there appears to have been a modest improvement in the economic welfare of industrial workers, largely attributable to an increase in real wages in the late 1960s. A study of the trend in real income of the rural poor in East Pakistan showed a significant decline in the 1950s and no significant increase in the 1960s.[35] These studies do not offer any conclusive evidence on overall trends in inequality, but they do suggest that some of the relatively poor classes in Pakistan were not sharing fully in the benefits of the growth of the economy as a whole.

Further bits of evidence tend to support the contention that the relatively well-to-do classes have benefited disproportionately from Pakistani economic growth. The very high degree of concentration in ownership of Pakistan's industrial assets has likewise concentrated the gains from rapid industrial growth.[36] Government subsidization of private business enterprise since the early 1950s has favored the new urban capitalist class. The perpetuation of a highly unequal distribution of land ownership in West Pakistan (where much of Pakistan's agricultural growth has taken place) put the largest landholders in the best position to take advantage of government programs to stimulate agriculture in the 1960s. The structure of taxation has become increasingly regressive, and the beneficiaries of public service expenditures have been primarily the urban upper- and middle-income classes.[37] All in all, it seems likely that income inequality has increased in Pakistan, but the empirical basis for drawing any conclusion is somewhat weaker than in India.

Information on the size distribution of income in Indonesia is limited to the island of Java (accounting for roughly 60% of the total population) and to the period beginning in 1963, when the first of a series of systematic surveys of household consumption expenditure was undertaken. No estimate of the size distribution of income in all of Indonesia has yet been published, so it is impossible to compare the overall degree of inequality with that of India or Pakistan. Although again the intercountry comparability of the data is highly questionable, estimates of rural and urban inequality in Java appear to be slightly lower than in India or Pakistan.[38] If accurate, this may be due to the relatively lower degree of general development in the Javanese economy.

A careful analysis of the consumer expenditure surveys carried out in Java from 1963 to 1970 leads to the following conclusions.[39] First, there was relatively little change in the distribution of income in rural areas. Second, there was a perceptible trend toward increasing inequality in urban areas. This was especially true of the largest cities, notably the capital city of Jakarta. Third, the overall size distribution of income in Java became more unequal. This finding of increased inequality is supported by independent evidence that the real level of living of the bottom 40% of the population actually deteriorated at a time when the overall per capita income increased substantially.[40] Although the evidence does not extend very far into the New Order period, it does suggest that the benefits of the recent surge of economic growth in Indonesia have been very unequally distributed.

For the study of trends in regional income distribution the relevant units in India are the separate states. Estimates of per capita product are available on a statewide basis for various time periods between 1955 and 1970.[41] In 1955 the richest state (West Bengal) had more than twice the per capita product of the poorest state (Bihar). Since that time, the trend in regional differentials has been somewhat mixed. The fastest-growing states include a couple of the richest as well as a couple of the poorest in initial per capita product; the slowest-growing states include one of the richest and several intermediate cases. In 1970 the disparity between the richest state (Punjab) and the poorest (Bihar) was still greater than two to one, but there had been quite a few changes in the rank ordering. An overall measure of dispersion would probably show little change in the period as a whole, with perhaps a very modest egalitarian trend.

In Pakistan the trend in the distribution of income between the two major regions of the country has been unmistakably and painfully clear.[42] In the immediate postindependence period per capita income was estimated to be only 17% higher in West Pakistan than in East Pakistan (a much smaller disparity than between many Indian states). But during the 1950s per capita income actually declined in the East while it rose in the West; the estimated differential reached 32% by 1959. In the 1960s per capita income increased in both regions but much more rapidly in the West; by 1969 the differential was estimated at 60%. These percentage differentials understate the true disparities in regional standards of living because of (unaccounted-for) price differentials favorable to the West.

The very substantial difference between the rates of economic growth in East and West Pakistan is attributable in considerable measure to deliberate policies of the central government (located in the West and dominated by West Pakistanis), which favored the West over the East in the allocation of public expenditure and of scarce resources such as foreign exchange. But the West also enjoyed certain natural advantages, such as a better initial infrastructure, a larger pool of entrepreneurs, less population pressure on the land, and crops that were favored by more rapid technical progress. These advantages combined with government favoritism to produce an environment much more conducive to the growth of capitalist industry and agriculture in West than in East Pakistan.

As with the size distribution of income, data relating to regional distribution of income in Indonesia go back only to the mid 1960s. There is strong evidence from consumer expenditure surveys that income growth in the city of Jakarta was much more rapid than anywhere else in urban or rural Java.[43] Estimates of regional gross domestic product in the twenty-six separate provinces of Indonesia from 1968 to 1972 shed further light on trends in the regional distribution of income.[44] There are enormous differences in regional per capita product in Indonesia. The richest regions are the oil and timber provinces of the Outer Islands, the city of Jakarta, and parts of Sumatra; the poorest regions are the rest of Java and most of the islands of Eastern Indonesia. Economic growth between 1968 and 1972 sharply increased these regional disparities because much of the growth was based on the extraction of natural resources in the Outer Islands and (to a lesser extent) the growth of manufacturing industry in the Jakarta area. Much of the income produced in the Outer Islands is not received or spent there; instead it accrues to foreign companies and to the Indonesian government (through state-owned enterprises or taxation of private firms). Since a large proportion of central government expenditures is incurred in Java, there is a secondary redistribution of income from the richest of the Outer Islands to the city of Jakarta and (progressively) to the much poorer remainder of the island of Java.

Employment

Formidable difficulties are involved in both the theoretical conceptualization and the empirical measurement of employment and unemployment in poor and largely agrarian societies. As a consequence, any effort to measure trends in employment conditions in India, Pakistan, and Indonesia is bound to be rather impressionistic and of very uncertain reliability. All three countries faced serious problems of unemployment and underemployment at the time of independence. Only fragmentary information on subsequent employment trends is available.

In India there is some evidence that employment conditions have worsened in the last few decades. The Indian National Planning Commission made a practice of issuing figures for the "backlog of unemployment" at the beginning of each Five-Year Plan period. These estimates began at 3.3 million unemployed in 1951 and rose steadily to 9.6 million in 1966; a later estimate by the Reserve Bank of India put the total at 12.6 million in 1969.[45] Although these estimates have been seriously criticized on methodological grounds, [46] they at least suggest an increasingly serious unemployment problem. The same impression is conveyed by the steadily rising number of job applicants registered at the National Employment Exchanges set up in urban areas by the Indian Ministry of Labor and Employment.[47] Such figures undoubtedly overstate the rate of growth of urban unemployment, but they have increased too rapidly to be discounted altogether. Further indirect evidence for a worsening employment situation in India is proved by the relatively slow rate of labor absorption into the industrial sector. Industrial employment rose at an average rate of only 2.2% per year between 1951 and 1971, while the rate of growth of industrial output was several percentage points higher.[48]

After independence, Pakistan faced problems of unemployment and underemployment very similar to those of India—perhaps more serious in the densely populated East and less serious in the more sparsely populated West. Once again, the available empirical evidence is very weak and is confined to the 1960s. For what they are worth, estimates of the overall rate of unemployment in Pakistan show a decline from approximately 25% in 1960 to approximately 20% in 1964 and 1969.[49] This apparent modest improvement in the employment situation in the 1960s gains credence from the relatively rapid rate of growth of industrial employment (over 6%) between 1961 and 1969.[50]

In Indonesia the available information on employment and unemployment does not permit any firm conclusions on trends over time. The overall deterioration of the economy in the years prior to 1965 could only have made a bad employment situation even worse. But what is of greatest interest is to determine the employment effects of the development strategy carried out under the New Order since 1966. There is a widespread impression that the initial stabilization policies hurt employment by driving many (relatively labor intensive) domestic industries out of business, and that subsequent policies designed to attract foreign investment imparted a capital-using and labor-saving bias to the growth process.[51] But data from the national censuses of 1961 and 1971 point to a very considerable increase in manufacturing employment during the period as a whole, comparable to the corresponding increase in real manufacturing output.[52] This suggests that the overall employment situation may have improved since 1966, though there are no doubt still millions of unemployed and underemployed today.[53] Most careful observers conclude that it is impossible to determine whether the rate of unemployment has changed in either direction since the establishment of the New Order.[54]

Economic Self-Reliance

The concept of economic self-reliance is an elusive one, despite the emphasis it has been given as a development objective. Broadly speaking, a nation is more self-reliant the more its own nationals can influence the nature and purpose of economic activity within its borders. The opposite of economic self-reliance is economic dependence. A nation is more dependent the more its economic activity is outside the control of its own nationals. The concepts of economic self-reliance and economic dependence can be applied at the regional and local as well as the national level; but for the purposes of this chapter I confine myself to the national level, where the distribution of power and influence over economic activity among nationals is not at issue.

A nation's economic self-reliance can be limited, on the one hand, by its vulnerability to external market forces which affect the terms of its economic relations with the outside world. It may be limited, on the other hand, by the ability of foreigners rather than nationals to influence economic decisions that affect economic activity within the nation. Neither of these two aspects of economic self-reliance lends itself to direct and precise measurement; in seeking to measure the extent of self-reliance achieved by any given nation, we must fall back on certain rough indicators that appear on theoretical grounds to be correlated with one or the other aspect of self-reliance.

Other things being equal, a nation is less vulnerable to external market forces the smaller its ratio of foreign trade to total economic activity, the more diversified its pattern of exports and imports (both in composition and in countries of destination and origin), and the more diversified its own structure of productive activity. Some of the more readily available data of this kind for India, Pakistan, and Indonesia are presented in table 2–6.

Of the three nations, Indonesia has been most heavily involved in foreign trade and India least so. Moreover, the proportion of exports and imports to total economic activity has been growing sharply in Indonesia since the beginning of the New Order in 1966, while it has changed relatively little in India and Pakistan. The commodity concentration of exports (as measured by the share in total export earnings of the top three export commodities) has been much higher in Indonesia than in India and Pakistan; it has remained close to 75% in

TABLE 2-6 Self-reliance indicators

Indicator	Year	India	Pakistan	Indonesia
1. Exports as percentage of GDP	1955	7.2	—	—
	1960	5.3	9.2	13.3
	1965	'3.9	9.0	5.3
	1970	4.2	7.9	12.8
	1973	4.4	—	18.2
2. Imports as percentage of GDP	1955	7.9	—	—
	1960	8.0	12.4	12.6
	1965	6.3	15.3	5.7
	1970	4.9	11.2	15.8
	1975	5.5	—	21.2
3. Earnings from three major exports as percentage of total export earnings	1960	26.4	33.6	79.7
	1965	22.2	30.1	75.5
	1970	18.5	23.5	77.5
	1973	19.1	—	75.1
4. Per capita production of electric power (millions of kwh)	1951	20.6	2.9	6.5
	1962	58.3	26.4	14.2
	1973	126.7	60.7[a]	23.2
5. Per capita production of steel (kg)	1951	4.2	0.0	0.0
	1962	11.3	0.0	0.0
	1973	12.0	1.3[a]	0.0
6. Per capita production of cement (kg)	1951	8.9	6.3	1.7
	1962	19.1	13.2	3.9
	1973	26.1	20.2[a]	5.8
7. Per capita production of nitrogenous fertilizers (kg N)	1951	0.0	0.0	0.0
	1962	0.4	0.4	0.0
	1973	1.9	1.6[a]	0.7

Sources: (1)–(2) IBRD, *World Tables, 1976*, table III-3 (for India and Indonesia) and table I (for Pakistan combined with Bangladesh). (3) IBRD, *World Tables, 1976*, table III-11. (4)–(7) Production levels from UN, *Statistical Yearbook, 1960, 1966, 1975*, divided by population levels from UN, *Demographic Yearbook, 1963, 1974*.

a. Figures for 1970.

Indonesia since 1960 while declining slowly from initially lower levels in the latter two countries. Finally, the figures in table 2–6 on per cappita production of electric power, steel, cement, and fertilizer suggests that India is substantially ahead of Pakistan and Indonesia in its degree of development of a diversified industrial base of production.

That India should be relatively more self-reliant than Pakistan or Indonesia in the first of the two aspects of self-reliance is hardly surprising, given its larger size (both geographically and economically) and its head start in industrialization. Smaller countries are almost certain to be more dependent on foreign trade than larger countries, and the development of a diversified production structure takes time. The second aspect of self-reliance, however, is to a greater extent amenable to policy decisions and hence more subject to change by deliberate government action.

The ability of nationals rather than foreigners to control economic activity within a nation is likely to be correlated with the following indicators: the extent to which a nation relies on internal rather than external sources of finance for investment; the extent to which a nation maintains a favorable balance of payments; the extent to which a nation is able to limit its international debt; and the extent to which a nation's productive enterprises are owned by nationals rather than foreigners. There are, of course, other important indicators of national capacity to control economic activity—for example, the extent to which indigenous technological skills and resources have been developed—but the indicators listed here are the ones that lend themselves most readily to comparative measurement.

Table 2–7 presents evidence on the rate of investment and the sources of investment finance for each of the three countries at various points of time. The figures, calculated from standard national income accounts, are subject to a considerable margin of error, but they should permit some broad comparisons to be drawn. If there is any systematic bias in the data, it is an underestimation of the significance of foreign capital inflows because these have been converted to local prices at prevailing official exchange rates. The official rates (except for the last few years in Indonesia) have generally undervalued foreign currency by a substantial margin.[55]

According to table 2–7, rates of investment reached similar peaks of about 17% (gross) or 12% (net) in all three countries. India and Pakistan attained these peak levels in the mid 1960s, while Indonesia reached them only in the most recent years of the New Order. The rate of net capital inflow into India was relatively low in the 1950s, increased to a little over 3% in the early and mid 1960s, and dropped off again by the end of the decade. The rate of net capital inflow into Pakistan in the Ayub Khan period (1958–1969) was somewhat higher than in India, averaging about 4% and going over 5% in the mid 1960s. In Indonesia under the New Order it has been even greater, averaging over 6% from 1967 through 1973.

The evidence suggests that India has done somewhat better than Pakistan or Indonesia in financing investment from internal sources. The net domestic savings rate (calculated by subtracting net capital inflow from net investment and hence probably overestimated) rose in

TABLE 2-7   Investment, savings, and capital inflow (in percentages)

Period	$\dfrac{GCF}{GDP}$	$\dfrac{NCF}{NNP}$	$\dfrac{NCI}{NNP}$	$\dfrac{NDS}{NNP}$	$\dfrac{NCI}{NCF}$
India					
1950–1952	10.2	5.7	0.6	5.1	11
1954–1956	14.8	10.6	1.4	9.2	13
1960–1962	16.0	11.6	3.1	8.5	27
1964–1966	17.5	13.2	3.4	9.8	26
1968–1970	15.7	11.1	1.4	9.7	13
1971–1973	16.4	12.1	1.2	10.9	10
Pakistan					
1949	4.7	−2.0	1.8	−3.8	—
1954	8.9	2.6	0.4	2.2	15
1959–1961	13.1	7.2	3.1	4.1	43
1963–1965	17.4	11.4	4.9	6.5	43
1967–1969	14.6	8.7	3.3	5.4	38
Indonesia					
1960–1962	7.9	3.0	2.2	0.8	73
1963–1965	9.0	3.1	1.9	1.2	61
1967–1969	9.5	3.4	8.1	−4.7	238
1971–1973	17.4	12.0	4.6	7.4	38

Sources: India, 1950s: Thomas Weisskopf, "Dependence," in Selden, *Remaking Asia*, table 6; capital consumption assumed to be 5% of GDP. India, 1970s: IBRD *World Tables, 1976*, table 1; capital consumption assumed to be 5% of GDP. Pakistan, 1949, 1954: Gustav Papanek, *Pakistan's Development: Social Goals and Private Incentives* (Cambridge, Mass.: Harvard University Press, 1967), appendix tables 2A, 2C; adjusted by assuming capital consumption and net factor income to abroad in same proportion to GDP as in 1960s. Indonesia, 1970s: Indonesia, *Monthly Statistical Bulletin* (May 1975). All others: OECD, Development Center, *National Accounts of Less Developed Countries, 1950–1966* (Paris: OECD, 1968) and subsequent reports no. 5 (February 1971) and no. 8 (July 1974).

Note: GCF = gross capital formation; GDP = gross domestic product; NCF = net capital formation; NNP = net national product; NCI = net capital inflow; NDS = net domestic saving; all ratios are calculated from current price values.

India from about 5% in the early 1950s to just over 10% in the early 1970s; in Pakistan this rate reached a peak around 7% in the mid 1960s; and in Indonesia it was very low or actually negative for most of the 1960s and only very recently began to mount toward 10%. The (underestimated) proportion of net investment accounted for by net capital inflow rose in India to a maximum of about 25% in the 1960s; in Pakistan it averaged about 40% during the Ayub Khan period as a whole; and in Indonesia it was around 70% from 1960 to 1965 (under Sukarno), rose dramatically in the late 1960s, and was still around 40% in the early 1970s (under Suharto).

Information on the balance-of-payments positions of India, Pakistan, and Indonesia is provided in table 2–8 for selected years since 1950. To make the data for the countries comparable, all figures have been standardized by total population. Total real product per capita has been of the same order of magnitude in each of the three countries throughout the period under review, rising slowly to about $100 in the early 1970s (according to World Bank estimates).[56] Therefore the figures in table 2–8 convey an appropriate impression of relative magnitudes on both a per capita and a per GNP basis.

All three countries have experienced balance-of-payments problems during much of the postwar period. The most relevant indicator of foreign exchange shortage is the foreign exchange gap, measured

TABLE 2–8 Trends in the balance of payments (in dollars per capita)

Item	1950	1955	1960	1965	1968	1970	1972
India							
Merchandise exports	3.25	3.54	3.07	3.41	3.49	3.49	3.90
Merchandise imports	3.15	4.05	5.27	6.18	4.73	4.15	4.22
Foreign exchange gap[a]	0.06	0.38	2.18	3.52	2.16	1.69	1.38
Foreign aid inflow[b]	0.07	0.21	1.26	2.58	2.33	1.73	1.23
Foreign investment inflow[c]	0.06	0.02	0.18	0.09	0.06	0.07	0.11
Investment income outflow	0.14	0.02	0.21	0.54	0.60	0.67	0.58
Pakistan							
Merchandise exports	4.61	4.12	3.91	4.62	5.21	5.17	—
Merchandise imports	4.80	5.76	5.97	9.12	7.88	9.31	—
Foreign exchange gap[a]	0.45	1.89	2.65	5.93	4.59	6.89	—
Foreign aid inflow[b]	0.00	1.29	1.96	4.66	4.36	3.68	—
Foreign investment inflow[c]	0.01	0.03	0.38	0.47	0.45	0.66	—
Investment income outflow	0.06	0.07	0.16	0.39	0.61	0.92	—
Indonesia							
Merchandise exports	11.11	11.15	10.01	6.39	8.07	10.29	13.37
Merchandise imports	6.28	7.01	8.51	6.15	7.69	9.79	11.00
Foreign exchange gap[a]	−2.21	−0.91	1.02	3.08	2.81	4.05	3.91
Foreign aid inflow[b]	0.58	0.03	2.00	0.89	2.45	3.57	3.32
Foreign investment inflow[c]	−0.04	0.05	0.23	0.18	0.26	0.73	1.85
Investment income outflow	0.33	1.37	0.76	0.95	0.72	1.17	2.65

Sources: Balance of payments figures from IBRD, *World Tables, 1971,* table 8, and IMF, *Balance of Payments Yearbook, 1974,* divided by population figures from UN, *Demographic Yearbook, 1963, 1974.*

a. Current deficit on goods and services plus long-term debt amortization.
b. Net transfers received by government plus government long-term borrowing.
c. Net private direct investment plus private long-term borrowing.

by the current deficit on goods and services plus long-term debt amortization.[57] The greatest gaps were experienced by Pakistan in the latter part of the Ayub Khan period (averaging $6 per capita) followed by Indonesia in the early 1970s (roughly $4 per capita) and India in the 1960s ($2.00–$3.50 per capita). Such a foreign exchange gap can be offset by inflows of foreign aid (grants or loans), private transfers, long-term private capital, or short-term private capital. The data in table 2–8 shows that in all three countries the gaps have been filled primarily by inflows of foreign aid and to a much lesser extent by inflows of long-term foreign private capital. Pakistan under Ayub Khan and Indonesia under Suharto have received substantially higher levels of per capita aid and long-term private capital inflow than India. Only in Indonesia in recent years has the inflow of private capital begun to assume significant proportions relative to the inflow of foreign aid.

As foreign aid has increasingly taken the form of long-term loans repayable in hard currencies, the aid-receiving countries have witnessed a steady growth in their external public debt. Table 2–9 presents recent estimates of outstanding public debt and debt service payments for India, Pakistan, and Indonesia. To help in assessing the relative significance of these debt estimates, they have also been calculated on a per capita basis and as a proportion of annual (goods and service) export earnings in each country. On a per capita basis the outstanding debt of Pakistan and Indonesia was roughly twice that of India by the early 1970s. But measured against the level of export earnings, Indonesia's debt position was the most favorable. In India and Pakistan debt service payments accounted for 20%–25% of export earnings and a substantially larger fraction of gross aid inflows. Thanks largely to the ample petroleum reserves of the Outer Islands, Indonesia's exports have risen much more rapidly than those of India or Pakistan since 1965 and debt service payments have remained below 10% of export earnings.[58]

This analysis of the balance-of-payments and debt positions of the three countries must be qualitatively extended to take into account the effects of the dramatic increase in the world price of oil since 1973. As a major petroleum exporter, Indonesia has been a prime beneficiary of the price increase and is now less vulnerable to balance-of-payments problems and more capable of handling the outstanding public debt. On the other hand, India and Pakistan, as major oil importers, are now correspondingly worse off and more dependent on foreign creditors.

The last of the self-reliance indicators to be considered here, the extent of national versus foreign ownership of productive enterprise,

TABLE 2-9   External public debt

Item		Millions of Dollars	Dollars per Capita	Percentage of Exports[a]
India				
Outstanding debt	1965	5,831	12.07	290
	1973	12,396	21.56	404
Debt service payments	1965	303	0.63	15
	1973	636	1.11	21
Pakistan				
Outstanding debt	1965	2,091	18.34	331
	1970	4,544	34.95	583
Debt service payments	1965	70	0.61	11
	1970	189	1.45	24
Indonesia				
Outstanding debt	1965	2,100	21.21	309
	1973	5,595	44.69	189
Debt service payments	1965	71	0.72	11
	1973	211	1.69	7

Sources: 1965, 1970: Debt figures from IBRD, *World Debt Tables, 1973*, table 1, divided by population figures from UN, *Demographic Yearbook, 1974*, and export figures from IBRD, *World Tables, 1971*, table 8. 1973: Debt figures from IBRD, *World Tables, 1976*, table II; divided by population and export figures from ibid., table 1.

a. Percentage of annual earnings from export of goods and services.

is the most difficult to measure. Some indication of the changing relative significance of foreign economic assets in India, Pakistan, and Indonesia can be gleaned from the data on the outflow of investment income shown in table 2-8. The level of foreign investment income (per capita) was broadly similar in India and Pakistan for most of the period from 1950 to 1970, rising especially rapidly after 1960. In Indonesia investment income fluctuated during most of the 1950s and 1960s; starting in 1968 at a level comparable to that in India and Pakistan, it rose rapidly to a much higher level under the New Order.

Detailed and comparable statistics on direct foreign private investment assets in underdeveloped countries are available only for the end of the year 1967; some of the relevant data for India, Pakistan, and Indonesia are presented in table 2-10. India had by far the largest total value of foreign investment assets, but the per capita levels were similar in all three countries in 1967. These levels represented a small proportion of total assets in each economy, including the traditional agricultural and small-scale industrial and service activities

TABLE 2–10 Direct foreign private investment assets

Measure	India	Pakistan	Indonesia
1. Total assets in 1967			
Millions of dollars	1,309	346	254
Dollars per capita	2.59	2.88	2.40
2. Percentage of assets in 1967			
Petroleum	16	35	65
Other primary products	17	10	19
Manufacturing	49	34	13
All other sectors	18	21	3
3. Total assets in 1970[a]			
Millions of dollars	1,329	415	369
Dollars per capita	2.47	3.19	3.24
4. Total assets in 1972[a]			
Millions of dollars	1,333	—	732
Dollars per capita	2.36	—	6.05

Sources: (1), (2) Investment figures from OECD, Development Assistance Directorate, *Stock of Private Direct Investments by D.A.C. Countries in Developing Countries, End 1967* (Paris: OECD, 1972), divided by population figures from UN, *Demographic Yearbook 1974.* (3), (4) Investment asset figures from line 1 supplemented by investment inflow figures from IMF, *Balance of Payments Yearbook, 1974;* divided by population figures from UN, *Demographic Yearbook, 1974.*

a. Estimated by adding to 1967 values the annual net inflows of direct private investment in subsequent years.

which still account for the bulk of economic activity and which are entirely under indigenous ownership. But regarded as a proportion of modern sector assets, a more appropriate yardstick, the share of foreign investment assets was much more substantial. No precise figures are available, but the share of corporate business (roughly equivalent to modern sector) assets owned by foreigners has been estimated at roughly 25% in India and 20% in Pakistan in the mid 1960s.[59] Given the smaller size of the Indonesian modern sector, the corresponding figure for Indonesia in 1967 might well have been close to 50%. Such figures on foreign ownership tend to understate the degree of foreign control because they fail to include the cases where control is exercised through the technological dependence of indigenous firms on foreign collaborators.

Table 2–10 also presents information on the sectoral distribution of foreign investment in 1967, as well as rough estimates of the total value of foreign investment assets in 1970 and 1972. Foreign investment was strongly oriented to the manufacturing sector in India, somewhat less so in Pakistan, and least in Indonesia. Most of the investment in Indonesia was in primary product extraction (especially oil), and this has continued to be true of new investment after 1967.[60] The estimates of total investment for later years confirm the rapid rise in foreign involvement in the Indonesian economy; by 1972 the per capita level was roughly twice that of Pakistan and $2\frac{1}{2}$ times as great as that of India. There can be little doubt that a large proportion— probably more than half—of Indonesia's modern sector enterprise is under foreign ownership or control.

The available evidence suggests that India is the most self-reliant and Indonesia the least self-reliant of the three nations with respect to the second aspect of self-reliance as well as the first. However, India's advantage is not so clear-cut in this case as before. And the differences among the three nations under consideration should not obscure the fact that by international standards all three remain quite dependent in important respects: foreign nationals continue to play an important role in their respective economies; they are heavily in debt to the outside world; and they continue to depend on the import of goods, capital, and technology in key sectors of economic activity.

Political Trends

On the objectives of promoting more extensive political rights and enhanced civil liberties, the record in India, Pakistan, and Indonesia has been uniformly disappointing. Although there have been significant variations in the experiences of the three countries, all are further from the democratic ideals in the late 1970s than they were in the early 1950s.

All three nations began their independent political existence in the early 1950s with nominally democratic political institutions and a constitutional guarantee of civil liberties. In each case, however, the actual extent of popular control over decision making was severely circumscribed by a highly stratified social structure that had undergone little change during the transition from colonial rule to independence. Political power and influence over governmental decision making was in effect concentrated in the hands of a small economically and educationally privileged minority.

Only in India did the formally democratic framework survive the first decade of independence and contribute in some modest degree to the extension of popular influence on political affairs.[61] The rural and urban poor, who constitute the majority of India's population, were socially and economically too weak to utilize the democratic institutions as a means of gaining some political influence. But it seems clear that some of India's "middle" classes—including organized urban workers, independent proprietors and professionals, and relatively well-to-do peasants—were able to mobilize some strength in the political arena and to prevent the upper business and landed classes from monopolizing political power. Throughout the 1950s and most of the 1960s India maintained a degree of civil liberties and freedom of the press that, though far from complete, was clearly greater than in almost any other poor country in the world. The beneficiaries of this state of affairs were again primarily the middle classes and not the majority of the people, whose very limited social and economic opportunities were the dominant facts of life.

In Pakistan and Indonesia the facade of democratic institutions gave way to more openly authoritarian political structures within the first decade after independence.[62] Ayub Khan instituted a military dictatorship in Pakistan in 1958 whose responsiveness to the popular will and respect for civil liberties was scarcely enhanced by efforts to develop an indirect form of "basic democracy" in the 1960s. Until 1970, effective power remained concentrated in a handful of military, business, and landed elites, while virtually the entire population was denied any significant degree of control over decision making or any freedom to dissent. In Indonesia President Sukarno's "guided democracy," introduced in the late 1950s, concentrated power in the hands of the state bureaucracy, but the governing elites were too divided and weak to impose their will on everyone else as successfully as did Ayub Khan in Pakistan. Until 1965 a number of groups, including even elements of the downtrodden peasantry linked to the well-organized Communist party, were able to have some influence on political and economic affairs. Following the holocaust of 1965, however, the New Order that emerged under Suharto and his military entourage proved to be even more authoritarian than the Ayub Khan regime. Civil liberties, already precarious under Sukarno, were summarily denied to any suspected opponents of the regime and govermental decision making was to depend solely on the will of the new political elite.

Events in the late 1960s and early 1970s proved to be extremely unsettling for political life in all three countries. In India the emergence of a revolutionary peasant movement, beginning with the Naxalbari uprising in 1967, led in subsequent years to government responses of an increasingly repressive nature. Civil liberties were set aside as large numbers of suspected left agitators and sympathizers were detained, imprisoned, or killed. Expenditures for police and security forces were sharply accelerated and the military power under the control of the central government was increased. In 1974 popular discontent with growing economic difficulties and widespread government corruption crystallized into a large, loosely organized opposition movement under the titular leadership of Jaya Prakash Narayan. Frustrated by the difficulty of bringing about change in national and state assemblies dominated by Indira Gandhi's Congress party, this movement increasingly resorted to extra-parliamentary tactics in trying to gain power and influence over political affairs. Responding to an immediate legal threat to her own continuation in office, Prime Minister Gandhi declared a national emergency in June 1975 and suspended the operation of India's democratic political institutions and constitutional guarantees of civil liberties. Mrs. Gandhi subsequently surprised everyone by abandoning her explicitly authoritarian form of rule in January 1977 and allowing free (albeit delayed) national elections to be held in March 1977. The Congress party was decisively defeated in these elections by a hastily united coalition of opposition parties, and a new administration headed by Morarji Desai, a prominent former Congress party minister, took office. Despite this reassertion of democratic order, the ease with which Mrs. Gandhi had been able to paralyze India's democratic framework raised serious doubts about its long-run viability.

As in India, political and economic discontent began to erupt into rebellious activity in Pakistan in the late 1960s. Widespread rioting in the major cities of both West and East Pakistan in 1968 drove Ayub Khan out of office in 1969 and forced his military successor, General Yahya Khan, to arrange for popular elections in 1970. Under these conditions of political flux the Bengalis of East Pakistan, increasingly resentful of the growth in economic disparities between East and West and chafing at their politically subordinate position, were encouraged to intensify their demands for greater regional autonomy. Several political and economic concessions by Western leaders proved to be too few and too late to prevent the growth of nationalism in the East. After a brutal effort by the Western authorities to retain the East by military might, Bangladesh was liberated in December 1971 with the indispensable military assistance of the Indian army.

The new Pakistan was governed until 1977 by Zulfikar Ali Bhutto and his People's party which had emerged as the dominant political force in West Pakistan in the 1970 elections. In an effort to legitimize his increasingly authoritarian rule and to head off growing political opposition, Bhutto held national elections in March 1977 and won by a large margin. This move proved counterproductive, however, for widespread evidence of election fraud exacerbated popular hostility to Bhutto's administration and ultimately led to his removal from office in July 1977 by a military coup. The new military leaders promised to hold fair elections and to restore civilian rule soon thereafter, but the prospects for a stable democratic system in Pakistan remained very poor.

In Indonesia the political climate ever since 1966 has been even more bleak than on the Indian subcontinent. Formal nationwide elections were carried out under the Suharto regime in 1971, but the conditions precluded any meaningful opposition from effectively participating. The ruling military clique has shown virtually no tolerance for dissent and was still holding (by its own undoubtedly low estimate) some fifty thousand political prisoners in 1976, most of them arrested ten years earlier during the bitter struggle for power.

The authoritarianism of the New Order has not failed to generate its own contradictions. Violent demonstrations broke out in the city of Jakarta in January 1974 on the occasion of a visit by Japanese Prime Minister Kakuei Tanaka; the rioting followed months of increasing unrest, especially among university students. In the most immediate sense the eruption was motivated by a strong nationalist reaction against the overwhelming influx of foreign capital into Indonesia (the Japanese being the most visible of the foreign capitalists). More generally, popular discontent had been growing because of the tremendous wealth and power that had accrued to a privileged elite in and around the Suharto administration (made all the more offensive by periodic revelations of massive corruption in high places), and the failure of the government to deal adequately with the continuing serious problems of poverty and unemployment. Shaken by the events of 1974, the Indonesian authorities moved to intensify their political repression and at the same time promised a better economic deal for the poor of Indonesia in the context of the Second Five-Year Plan (1974–1979).

Thus in each of the three nations—India, Pakistan, Indonesia— political rights and civil liberties were more precarious in the late 1970s than they had been at an earlier stage in their independent existence. As of 1977 Indonesia was still ruled by a repressive military regime and Pakistan had entered a period of renewed political instability. Although the Indian people had regained many of the political rights and civil liberties denied them under Mrs. Gandhi's emergency rule, the authoritarian example that she set appeared likely to grow in appeal to the new rulers as they struggled with the same problems that beset earlier democratic regimes.[63] In all three nations the long-run political trend since independence has been in the direction of more authoritarian forms of rule.

The Development Record: A Summary

The experiences of India, Pakistan, and Indonesia show a mixed pattern of successes and failures in the achievement of development objectives. In the first quarter-century of their independence, India,

Pakistan, and Indonesia each recorded long-run average rates of growth of per capita output between 1% and 1½% per year. Such rates represent a definite improvement over their growth performance under colonial rule, but they fall well below the average rate for Third World countries as a whole since 1950.[64] The industrial sector in each country has grown considerably more rapidly than the agricultural sector, and the share of industry in total output has grown accordingly. However, the share of industry in total employment has grown much more slowly, reflecting the relatively more rapid growth of per worker productivity in industry than in agriculture.

Economic growth in the three nations showed considerable variation across different subperiods. The most rapid growth rates were recorded under the Suharto regime in Indonesia (1966–) and the Ayub Khan regime in Pakistan (1958–1969). Economic growth in India was moderate throughout the full period but slower in the second than in the first part. The slowest growth occurred under Sukarno in Indonesia (1959–1966) and in the pre–Ayub Khan period in Pakistan (1951–1958).

The available evidence on nonmarket indicators of economic welfare suggests that India, Pakistan, and Indonesia are still unable to meet the basic nutritional requirements of a majority of their people, that infant mortality remains high by international standards, and that illiteracy remains widespread. However, each nation has made progress in expanding the availability of medical care and educational facilities. The data do not permit precise comparisons of progress in these respects, but Pakistan appears to have done somewhat better in raising average nutritional levels than India or Indonesia; and India, starting from a higher base, has achieved higher levels of medical care and educational opportunity.

None of the three nations has shown much progress in achieving greater economic equity. The limited data available suggest that the initially unequal size distribution of income in each nation has not changed markedly for the better or worse. Regional income disparities may have declined modestly, except in Pakistan where a growing economic differential between the richer West and the poorer East was a major factor contributing to the partition of the country in 1971.

The meager evidence on employment trends in India, Pakistan, and Indonesia shows that all three nations have far to go before they reach a position resembling full employment. If anything, rapid population growth—together with a pattern of economic development that has not been oriented toward maximizing employment—has exacerbated problems of unemployment and underemployment in each nation.

Progress toward greater economic self-reliance has been slow in India, Pakistan, and Indonesia. All three nations still depend in many ways on foreign help, and none has developed a fully indigenous capacity to operate and transform the domestic economy in response to changing conditions. India, again starting from a higher base, has reached a higher level of self-reliance, having achieved a greater degree of industrial diversity (and presumably technological capacity), a higher domestic savings rate, and a greater degree of national ownership and control of the corporate sector of the economy than Pakistan or Indonesia. But India still faces serious balance-of-payments problems in light of the relatively slow growth in food production and the more recent sharp rise in the cost of imported petroleum products.

Neither in India, nor in Pakistan, nor in Indonesia has the majority had much of a say in political and economic decision making. The distribution of economic power has remained so unequal, and the material basis of life for the majority so insecure, that it has been easy for the economically privileged to dominate even the most formally democratic of political systems. Within the limits imposed by a fundamentally inegalitarian society, the extent of both political rights and civil liberties has on the whole been broadest in India and narrowest in Indonesia. Only in India did a form of bourgeois parliamentary democracy prove viable for an extended period of time; in Pakistan and Indonesia it gave way within a decade after independence to various forms of authoritarian rule, as typified by the military regimes of Field Marshal Ayub Khan and General Suharto. In all three nations there has been an unmistakable long-term trend toward restriction rather than expansion of political rights and civil liberties.

Some Tentative Hypotheses

With so many different factors interacting in complicated ways, it is difficult to identify the sources of success and the causes of failure in the development progress of India, Pakistan, and Indonesia. Moreover, it is questionable whether any inferences drawn from the experiences of these three nations are applicable to other nations in the Third World. The historical and cultural backgrounds of nations in Latin America, sub-Saharan Africa, and East Asia differ greatly from those of India, Pakistan, and Indonesia. Even other nations in North Africa and the western, southern, and southeastern parts of Asia, which have a greater degree of historical and cultural affinity with India, Pakistan, and Indonesia, differ significantly from these three in important economic characteristics such as size and heterogeneity. Nonetheless, it may be of interest to suggest some tentative hypotheses based on the experiences of India, Pakistan, and Indonesia; these hypotheses may then be tested in future research with a larger sample of nations drawn from different parts of the Third World.

The long-run rates of growth of per capita output in all three nations have been somewhat disappointing, when measured against the needs of the people, the expressed goals of political leaders, or the performance of other Third World nations. These relatively slow rates of growth may have something to do with cultural differences between the three nations and other, faster-growing Third World nations such as the East Asian nations;[65] and the huge size and ethnic heterogeneity of India, Pakistan, and Indonesia may have rendered more difficult the task of administering policies designed to promote economic growth.

Yet if one examines the different subperiods distinguished according to the nature of political rule, one finds significant variations in the growth rates recorded by the three nations. The rates of economic growth recorded under the Suharto regime in Indonesia and the Ayub Khan regime in Pakistan were rapid by any standard; the rate of growth in India was relatively slow and the rates of growth under the Sukarno regime in Indonesia and during the pre–Ayub Khan subperiod in Pakistan were unusually low. Several factors correlate well with these differences in growth performance and may have some explanatory significance.

First, the most rapid rates of growth were achieved under strong authoritarian governments that gave high priority to promoting economic growth. Prior to Ayub Khan there was no strong governmental authority in Pakistan, nor was the commitment to promoting economic growth so clearly articulated. Sukarno in Indonesia wielded considerable power, but his authority was always under challenge and his priorities were often political rather than economic. India presents the most interesting alternative. Indian political leaders always placed high priority on achieving rapid economic growth, and indeed they set up the most elaborate institutional apparatus for economic planning. However, the Indian government (at least until the events of 1975) did not have the kind of concentrated authoritarian political control enjoyed by Ayub Khan and Suharto. It seems plausible to argue that India's more open political environment obliged the governing elites to respond to a greater extent to middle-class demands —for social services, for greater regional equity, for more government interference with private enterprise—with the result that the government was not in a position to devote itself wholeheartedly to the promotion of economic growth within what remained a basically capitalist economic framework.

A second factor that is correlated with the different growth experiences is the inflow of foreign capital. The rate of inflow of both foreign aid and foreign private investment was highest (in relative terms) in Indonesia under Suharto and in Pakistan under Ayub Khan. It is hard to assess the quantitative impact of foreign capital inflows on economic growth, but it seems plausible that differential rates of inflow have had some effect on the differential rates of growth experienced at different times by India, Pakistan, and Indonesia.

A third factor of some possible significance is the endowment of natural resources. While all three countries are broadly similar in agricultural conditions, Indonesia has a distinct advantage in its endowment of exportable primary products (oil and forestry products) and India has some advantage in its endowment of industrial raw materials (coal and iron ore). This differential in natural resource endowment no doubt helps explain the relatively greater development of industry in India and the much slower development of industry in Indonesia. With respect to economic growth, Indonesia's resource base proved to be particularly advantageous in the early 1970s because of the boom in primary product prices in general and oil prices in particular. The high rate of growth recorded in Indonesia under Suharto can be explained in part by soaring earnings from the exploitation of Indonesia's petroleum resources.

Finally, economists might wish to stress the importance of differences in the economic policies carried out under the various political regimes in India, Pakistan, and Indonesia. On the whole, the Suharto and Ayub Khan governments favored somewhat more liberal and internationalist economic policies than did their predecessors or any government in India. These policies involved less nationalization or regulation of the private sector, fewer administrative controls, less restriction of trade and foreign investment, and, in general, greater freedom for private enterprise and the market mechanism. The degree of economic liberalism, like the other factors, correlates well with overall growth performance in different subperiods in India, Pakistan, and Indonesia.

Because the periods of relatively rapid growth under Suharto and Ayub Khan are distinct from other periods in terms of several factors, it is not possible (without further evidence) to isolate the relative importance of the different factors as explanatory variables. However, there are good theoretical grounds for expecting the four variables to be mutually interdependent. First, one would expect an abundance of exportable natural resources to attract an inflow of foreign private capital from the industrial nations. Foreign private capital inflow is also likely to be greater (whether or not there are exportable primary products) the more liberal and internationalist the economic policies of the host government. And an authoritarian government is likely to be attractive to foreign investors because it promises to provide greater political and economic stability than a government more responsive to (unpredictable) popular pressures. Foreign public aid inflows are likely to be associated with relatively liberal economic policies because national and international agencies tend to link aid to economic liberalization. There has also been a pronounced tendency for the major aid-giving nation, the United States, to favor conservative authoritarian governments valued as political and military allies. Finally, one might expect an authoritarian government to find it easier than a more democratic government to implement economically liberal and internationalist policies because it can more successfully resist populist or nationalist opposition to such policies likely to arise especially among adversely affected and politically active urban groups.

Because of such interdependencies, it would be difficult even with a much larger sample of countries to determine the relative importance of authoritarianism, foreign capital, economic liberalism, and the like, in promoting economic growth within a capitalist institutional framework. It seems plausible, however, to suggest that in the basically capitalist environment that characterized all three nations the combination of an authoritarian political framework with government policies favorable to domestic and foreign private enterprise—as evidenced under Suharto in Indonesia and Ayub Khan in Pakistan—has been more conducive to aggregate economic growth than the less authoritarian form of rule and the more ambivalent attitude of government policymakers toward private enterprise that has been true of modern India. Still very much open to question is whether the authoritarian capitalist model can remain politically viable over a long period of time. So far the evidence is mixed: the Ayub Khan regime came to an inglorious end while the Suharto regime is still in full control.

The common experience in India, Pakistan, and Indonesia with respect to development objectives other than growth in value aggregates is much more striking than any variations of the kind observed in economic growth. Each of the three nations has made at best limited progress in promoting higher average standards of welfare in nutrition, health, and education and in promoting greater economic self-reliance. None of the three nations has made much progress in reducing class and regional inequalities, in approaching full employment, or in fostering greater political rights and civil liberties; indeed, in some of these respects the situation has become worse.

The most pronounced failures in the development experiences of the three nations have clearly been in the nongrowth dimensions of development in general and in the equity-related dimensions in particular (income distribution, employment, and political democracy). Even where some progress has been made—for example, in average standards of welfare or in self-reliance—there is reason to believe that the gains have not been equitably shared. It follows that any effort to explain these development failures must seek to identify obstacles to a more equitable pattern of development in India, Pakistan, and Indonesia.

Among the common features that may help to explain the inequitable development patterns in India, Pakistan, and Indonesia are (1) the persistence of a very inegalitarian social order, such that a privileged combination of property-owning and Westernized elites has had predominant influence on economic policymaking; and (2) the (related) promotion of a basically capitalist institutional framework for development. In India, Pakistan, and Indonesia the dominant elites have successfully resisted revolutionary challenges from below, with the result that the inegalitarian social order has been preserved and any radical departure from a capitalist framework of economic development has been prevented. The failure to bring about a more equitable pattern of development under such circumstances is hardly surprising, for both theoretical and historical evidence suggests that (at least) the early stages of capitalist growth tend to involve a worsening distribution of income.[66]

The limited efforts to depart from a purely capitalist model of growth in India and Indonesia may not have resulted in correspondingly greater successes in achieving economic equity. Too little is known about the distribution of income in Indonesia under Sukarno to judge the effect of his economically nationalist policies on income inequality. But the modest efforts of the Indian government to limit and regulate domestic and foreign private enterprise and to promote the growth of public enterprise do not appear to have resulted in any more equitable distributional trends than in Pakistan under Ayub Khan. Indeed it seems possible that India's economic strategy has actually impeded the achievement of greater equity by slowing down the overall rate of economic growth (as compared with what might have been achieved in a setting more favorable to private enterprise) without at the same time stepping up deliberate and effective measures to increase equity.[67] Other things being equal, a relatively slow rate of growth is likely to be particularly disadvantageous to the poor insofar as it implies slow growth in food production and slow growth in employment opportunities. India's greater efforts to curtail the accumulation of private fortunes and to step up social services have redounded primarily to the benefit of the middle classes rather than the poor, thus doing little to increase overall equity. Measures to aid the poor directly—land redistribution, large-scale labor-intensive public works programs—have been conspicuously lacking.

The main reason that India's modified capitalist approach has not led to more equity than other, more purely capitalist patterns is surely political. The modest departures from a pure capitalist strategy that have been undertaken in India have been brought about primarily as a result of the political influence of the middle classes in India's relatively open political system. But because the basic social order in India has remained so inegalitarian, the masses of poor people have not had the political power, even in the context of parliamentary democracy, to force the radical changes in economic strategy that would truly contribute to greater equity. Thus the situation in India has been little better than in Pakistan or Indonesia.

The trend toward greater authoritarianism, toward more restriction rather than expansion of political rights and civil liberties, in India, Pakistan, and Indonesia seems to have emerged at least partly in response to failures in economic development broadly construed. In India the commitment to parliamentary democracy and to civil liberties remained relatively strong through the mid 1960s; economic growth was modest, but there was still some popular confidence in the ability of the political leadership to fulfill promises of economic and social improvement for all. After the mid 1960s a slowdown in economic growth and heightened popular concern over the failure of government to reduce inequalities led to more and more discontent and to growth in the strength of opposition movements. Had Mrs. Gandhi's administration been able to bring about more social and economic progress in a democratic context, it is doubtful that popular opposition would have risen to the point where an authoritarian response was deemed necessary. Moreover, adverse reaction to the imposition of authoritarian rule was cushioned (at least initially) by the argument of Mrs. Gandhi's supporters that a more powerful and less inhibited central government could be more effective in promoting economic development, especially for the benefit of the poor.

In Pakistan and Indonesia the demise of parliamentary democracy in the late 1950s was partly a consequence of the inability of the early governments to make much economic progress, if only because the political situation was too unstable for an effective economic strategy. Under Sukarno's "guided democracy" the political situation was never really stabilized enough to permit much economic development; political and economic affairs became increasingly turbulent in the 1960s. The accessions to power of both Ayub Khan and Suharto were motivated and facilitated largely by the prior periods of economic distress, and they both sought to justify their political authoritarianism as a necessary condition of economic progress.

The experiences of modern India, Pakistan, and Indonesia suggest that powerful forces at work in poor, inegalitarian, and basically capitalist societies push in the direction of greater political authoritarianism. Where democratic institutions exist in such a context, they come under great pressure because they tend to limit the possibilities for rapid economic growth without at the same time leading to significant progress with respect to other development objectives. Under certain circumstances the situation may develop to a point where a successful social revolution is possible, but such circumstances are relatively rare in a world where powerful nations oppose such an outcome. It is more likely that the result (at least initially) will be an assumption of power by representatives of the upper rather than the lower classes and the establishment of authoritarian rule without any fundamental change in the inegalitarian character of the social order or in the basically capitalist institutional framework of development. Such has clearly been the pattern in India, Pakistan, and Indonesia.

It appears that authoritarian rule in an inegalitarian and capitalist context may at best contribute to an acceleration of the overall rate of economic growth. However, the evidence suggests that such an environment is not conducive to progress with respect to the nongrowth dimensions of development. As a consequence it tends to arouse increasing popular resistance and to place the governing authorities on the defensive. Under such circumstances Ayub Khan and Bhutto were forced out of power in Pakistan, and Mrs. Gandhi felt obliged to give up her repressive tactics and to allow her administration to be voted out of office in India. Suharto has managed to avert a political upheaval in Indonesia (through 1977) only by tightening the repressive grip of his regime.

To conclude on a necessarily pessimistic note, the prospects for broad-based economic development in contemporary India, Pakistan, and Indonesia seem very poor, at least in the short-run, because of their common inegalitarian capitalist socioeconomic order. In spite of the recent revival of democracy in India, the prospects for political rights and civil liberties in these nations also seem dim because of the stress that is placed on democratic institutions in a poor country experiencing little broad-based economic development. In the long-run one may hope that the inherent political instability in each country can generate forces that will lead to a fundamental change in the present socioeconomic order. Such a revolutionary change appears to be a necessary, although by no means a sufficient, condition for progress with respect to all the development objectives.

Appendix

This appendix provides comparable data on the initial economic conditions characterizing the People's Republic of China, India, Pakistan, and Indonesia in the early 1950s.

Table 2–A1 presents some basic information on population, area, and output. The population and area figures are considerably more reliable than the output figures, which are characterized by the large margin of error inherent in all international comparisons of real output. The (average) figures on population density conceal substantial regional variations in each nation, especially in Pakistan and Indonesia: according to data presented in Gunnar Myrdal, *Asian Drama* (New York: Pantheon, 1968), table 10–2, population densities in East Pakistan and Java were roughly twice as great as those of West Pakistan and the Outer Islands of Indonesia, respectively. The differences in the per capita output of the four nations shown in table 2–A1 are probably within the overall margin of error of the estimates, but the figures clearly place the four Asian giants near the bottom of an international rank ordering.

Table 2–A2 presents estimates of the sectoral distribution of output and the labor force. Since there are no reliable data for the early 1950s in the case of Indonesia, the earliest available Indonesian figures are given in the table. These estimates for the early 1960s in Indonesia most probably show a slightly greater role for industry and a slightly lesser role for agriculture than was true of the early 1950s.

TABLE 2–A1   Initial conditions: population, area, and output

Variable	China	India	Pakistan	Indonesia
1. Population, 1950 (millions)	560	358	79	7
2. Land area, 1950 (m sq km)	9.700	3.268	0.947	1.490
3. Population density				
a. Per sq km total land, 1950	58	110	83	51
b. Per sq km cultivated land, 1955	560	240	325	470
4. Population growth, 1950–1960 (average annual percentage rate)	1.8	1.8	2.4	2.1
5. Gross domestic product, 1950 (U.S. $ billion at 1960 prices)	35.0	22.1	5.6	4.1
6. Per capita GDP, 1950 (U.S. $ billion at 1960 prices)	65	62	75	54

Sources: (1), (4) IBRD, *World Tables, 1971,* Table 2. (2) FAO, *Production Yearbook,* 1961. (3a) Calculated from (1), (2). (3b) Gunnar Myrdal, *Asian Drama* (New York: Pantheon, 1968), table 10–2. (5)–(6) Figures for 1960 from E. E. Hagen and O. Hawlyryshyn, "Analysis of World Income and Growth, 1955–1965," *Economic Development and Cultural Change* 18, no. 1, part 2 (October 1969), tables 4–A and 8–A; extrapolated back to 1950 using growth rates from IBRD, *World Tables, 1976,* table III.

TABLE 2–A2 Initial conditions: sectoral distribution of output and the labor force (in percentages)

Sector	China (1952)	India (1950)	Pakistan (1950)	Indonesia (1960)
Output[a]				
1. Agriculture[b]	48	51	60	54
2. Mining	2	1	*	4
3. Large-scale manufacturing and utilities	9	6	7	10
4. Small-scale manufacturing and construction	9	10		
5. Other sectors	32	32	32	32
Labor Force[c]				
6. Agriculture[b]	77	72	77	73
7. Industry[d]	7	11	7	8
8. Other sectors	16	17	16	19

Sources: (1)–(5) China and India: K. N. Raj, *India, Pakistan, and China: Economic Growth and Outlook* (Bombay: Allied Publishers, 1967), table 9. Pakistan: OECD, Development Center, *National Accounts of Less Developed Countries, 1950–1966* (Paris: OECD, 1968). Indonesia: OECD, Development Center, *Latest Information on National Accounts of Less Developed Countries,* no. 5 (Paris: OECD, 1971). (6)–(8) China and India: Raj, *India, Pakistan, and China,* table 8. Pakistan: IBRD, *World Tables, 1971,* table 2. Indonesia: ILO, *Yearbook of Labor Statistics,* 1966; figures corrected to exclude unemployed.

a. Net domestic product at factor cost, current prices.
b. Includes agriculture, animal husbandry, forestry, and fishing.
c. Figures for Indonesia start from 1961.
d. Includes mining, manufacturing, construction, and utilities.
* Less than 0.5%

Notes

I would like to acknowledge my gratitude to many of the participants in the conference on the Lessons of China's Development Experience for the Developing Countries and to several other colleagues for their constructive comments on the original version of the chapter; I am especially indebted to Michael Roemer, George Rosen, and Amartya Sen.

1. My discussion of the Pakistani experience is limited mainly to the period prior to the liberation of Bangladesh (in December 1971), for not enough data was available at the time of writing to permit a thorough analysis of the post-1971 period.

2. See appendix table 2–A1 for the basic data on which this paragraph is based. Comparable data on countries other than China, India, Pakistan, and Indonesia are available in standard United Nations and World Bank sources.

3. See table 2–4 for detailed estimates.

4. Barry M. Richman, *Industrial Society in Communist China* (New York: Random House, 1969), pp. 538–539, cites evidence that 1958 per capita calorie consumption was 2200 per day, which is close to the minimum nutritional requirement cited by Gunnar Myrdal, *Asian Drama* (New York: Pantheon, 1968), p. 544. But Chinese agricultural output rose quite rapidly from the early 1950s to 1958, and average calorie intake can also be presumed to have risen from a somewhat lower level around 1950.

5. See appendix table 2–A2 for documentation.

6. According to figures cited in K. N. Raj, *India, Pakistan, and China: Economic Growth and Outlook* (Bombay: Allied Publishers, 1967), table 8, 2.6% of the Indian labor force and 1.3% of the Chinese labor force were employed in large-scale factories and mines in the early 1950s. The corresponding figures are undoubtedly lower for Pakistan and Indonesia, where industry was generally less developed.

7. The comparative data on which this paragraph is based are drawn from Myrdal, *Asian Drama*, table 10–2, and the FAO *Production Yearbook, 1968*. Myrdal presents indexes of agricultural output per capita and per hectare in the early 1950s, while the FAO yearbook tabulates figures on average crop yields and cereals output from 1948 to 1952.

8. The differentials in industrial development and infrastructure in the four nations in the early 1950s are amply illustrated by comparative data on the production of various industrial commodities and on energy consumption and railway traffic, as tabulated by the United Nations, *Statistical Yearbook 1960*.

9. See Michael Kidron, *Foreign Investments in India* (London: Oxford University Press, 1965), chaps. 1, 2, for a description of the changing role of foreign capital in India from the colonial to the immediate postindependence period.

10. The larger and more export-oriented enterprises in Indonesia tended to be controlled by Western firms, while the Chinese were more heavily involved in medium-scale manufacturing, trade, and financial activities. Although after independence a large fraction of the Chinese community acquired Indonesian citizenship, most people of Chinese origin continued to be viewed in many ways as aliens by the indigenous Indonesians. See Ralph Anspach, "Indonesia," in Frank H. Golay et al., *Underdevelopment and Economic Nationalism in Southeast Asia*, chap. 3 (Ithaca, N.Y.: Cornell University Press, 1969), pp. 111–118, for an analysis of the ethnic distribution of economic power in Indonesia at the time of independence.

11. Illiteracy rates for India, Pakistan, and Indonesia in 1951 (as

well as 1961 and 1971) are shown in table 2–5. Dwight H. Perkins, "Introduction: The Persistence of the Past," in D. H. Perkins, ed., *China's Modern Economy in Historical Perspective* (Stanford, Calif.: Stanford University Press, 1975), p. 4, estimates that as much as 25%–30% of the male population in China was literate before the 1949 revolution; no figures are available on the overall literacy rate.

12. The discussion of the social and political context of development in this section of the essay is based on the following sources.

India: Charles Bettelheim, *India Independent* (New York: Monthly Review Press, 1968); Jagdish Bhagwati and Padma Desai, *India: Planning for Industrialization* (London: Oxford University Press, 1970); Angus Maddison, *Class Structure and Economic Growth: India and Pakistan since the Moghuls* (New York: W. W. Norton, 1971); Barrington Moore, Jr., *The Social Origins of Dictatorship and Democracy* (Boston: Beacon Press, 1966), chap. 6; George Rosen, *Democracy and Economic Change in India* (Berkeley: University of California Press, 1967); and Thomas E. Weisskopf, "Dependence and Imperialism in India," in Mark Selden, ed., *Remaking Asia: Essays on the American Uses of Power* (New York: Pantheon, 1974).

Pakistan: Stephen R. Lewis, Jr., *Pakistan: Industrialization and Trade Policies* (London: Oxford University Press, 1970); Arthur MacEwan, "Contradictions in Capitalist Development: The Case of Pakistan," *Review of Radical Political Economics* 3, no. 1 (Spring 1971); Maddison, *Class Structure and Economic Growth;* Richard Nations, "The Economic Structure of Pakistan: Class and Colony," *New Left Review,* no. 68 (July/August 1971); and Joseph J. Stern and Walter P. Falcon, "Growth and Development in Pakistan, 1955–1969," Occasional Papers in International Affairs, no. 23, Harvard University Center for International Affairs, 1970.

Indonesia: Anspach, "Indonesia"; Cheryl Payer, "The International Monetary Fund and Indonesian Debt Slavery," in Selden, *Remaking Aisa;* Hans O. Schmitt, "Foreign Capital and Social Conflict in Indonesia, 1950–1958," *Economic Development and Cultural Change* 10, no. 3 (April 1962); Allen M. Sievers, *The Mystical World of Indonesia* (Baltimore, Md.: Johns Hopkins University Press, 1974); Ernst Utrecht, "Land Reform and Bimas in Indonesia," *Journal of Contemporary Asia* 3, no. 2 (June 1967).

13. See Gunnar Myrdal, *The Challenge of World Poverty* (New York: Pantheon, 1971), chap. 7, for a description and analysis of the soft state.

14. A commitment to greater equity must be distinguished from the effective implementation of policies to achieve greater equity. The differences in achievement with respect to the equity objectives were

far smaller than the differences in commitment displayed by Indian, Pakistani, and Indonesian political leaders.

15. To avoid the effects of short-term fluctuations, all the rates have been calculated using three-year averages around the initial and terminal years.

16. At the time of writing, national income and output data for each of the three countries were available up to and including the year 1973. The information provided here on Pakistan is deliberately limited to the period prior to the liberation of Bangladesh (1971).

17. To measure the extent to which a society is providing for the basic needs of all its people, it would be necessary to examine not only the total (or per capita) availability of essential goods and services but also their distribution among the people. Unfortunately, such distributional data, and especially changes in distribution over time, are extremely scarce in the countries under consideration here; the available information on economic equity in general is discussed later in this section.

18. Comparable figures for food consumption in other countries are available in the same sources cited in table 2–4.

19. The minimum calorie requirement for a person living in South Asian countries has been estimated to be roughly 2200–2300 per day; see Myrdal, *Asian Drama,* p. 544.

20. According to figures published in the United Nations, *Economic Survey of Asia and the Far East, 1972,* table I–38, expenditures on education and health as a proportion of total government expenditures in 1960 and 1969 amounted to roughly 20% in India and 10% in Pakistan. Comparable figures are not available for Indonesia, but according to the United Nations, *Statistical Yearbook, 1974,* table 206, public expenditure on education as a proportion of gross national product in 1970 was 2.9% in India, 1.7% in Pakistan, and 2.0% in Indonesia.

21. For an excellent survey of studies on income distribution in India, see Pranab K. Bardhan, "The Pattern of Income Distribution in India: A Review," in T. N. Srinivasan and P. K. Bardhan, eds., *Poverty and Income Distribution in India* (Calcutta: Statistical Publishing Society, 1974). Some of the points made in the following paragraph are based on Bardhan's critical review.

22. Estimates of the Gini coefficient of inequality of income distribution in India cited by Shail Jain and Arthur E. Tiemann, "Size Distribution of Income: Compilation of Data," Discussion Paper No. 4 of the Development Research Center, International Bank for Reconstruction and Development, 1973, range from 0.33 to 0.46.

23. Studies showing evidence of worsening inequality in India include Subramanian Swamy, "Structural Change and Distribution of

Income by Size: The Case of India," *Review of Income and Wealth,* Series 13, no. 2 (June 1967); M. Mukherjee and G. S. Chatterjee, "Trends in the Distribution of National Income, 1950–51 to 1965–66," *Economic and Political Weekly* (Bombay) 2, no. 29 (July 15, 1967); and V. M. Dandekar and N. Rath, "Poverty in India: Dimensions and Trends," *Economic and Political Weekly* (Bombay) 6, nos. 1–2 (January 2–9, 1971). Studies showing evidence of little overall change in inequality in India include M. Ahmed and N. Bhattacharya, "Size Distribution of Per Capita Personal Income in India," *Economic and Political Weekly* (Bombay) 7, special number (July 1972), and P. D. Ojha and V. V. Bhatt, "Pattern of Income Distribution in India: 1953–55 to 1961–64," in Srinivasan and Bardhan, *Poverty and Income Distribution in India.*

24. See Uma Roy Chowdhury, "Trends in Factor Shares in India Since the First Five-Year Plan," Government of India, Central Statistical Organization, 1972.

25. For a discussion of the ineffectiveness of various government programs for redistributing land ownership and agricultural incomes in India, see Dandekar and Rath, "Poverty in India," sect. 5.

26. See Maddison, *Class Structure and Economic Growth,* pp. 87–88, for a brief discussion of the negligible impact of taxation and the regressive impact of public expenditure on income distribution in India.

27. Index numbers for the real earnings of factory workers and for real per capita income in India from 1951 to 1971 are given in Thomas E. Weisskopf, "China and India: A Comparative Survey of Performance in Economic Development," *Economic and Political Weekly* (Bombay) 10, annual number (February 1975), table 4; according to those figures per capita income increased by almost three times as much as workers' earnings.

28. See, for example, Pranab Bardhan, "Green Revolution and Agricultural Laborers," *Economic and Political Weekly* (Bombay) 5, special number (July 1970), sect. 3.

29. See, for example, Francine R. Frankel, *India's Green Revolution* (Princeton, N.J.: Princeton University Press, 1971).

30. This has been true at least through the end of 1974, according to wholesale price indexes published by the Government of India, *Economic Survey* (annual).

31. See Maddison, *Class Structure and Economic Growth,* pp. 141–142.

32. The view that inequality has increased in Pakistan is expressed, for example, by Maddison, *Class Structure and Economic Growth,* pp. 140–141, and by Keith Griffin and Azizur Rahman Khan, *Growth and Inequality in Pakistan* (London: Macmillan, 1972), pp. 204–207.

33. The relevant studies are cited, briefly summarized, and criticized by S. M. Naseem, "Mass Poverty in Pakistan: Some Preliminary Findings," *Pakistan Development Review* 12, no. 4 (Winter 1973).

34. These studies include Azizur Rahman Khan, "What Has Been Happening to Real Wages in Pakistan?" *Pakistan Development Review* 7, no. 3 (Autumn 1967), updated by Griffin and Khan, *Growth and Inequality in Pakistan,* pp. 204–205; and Stephen Guisinger and Mohammad Irfan, "Real Wages of Industrial Workers in Pakistan: 1954 to 1970," *Pakistan Development Review* 13, no. 4 (Winter 1974).

35. See Swadesh R. Bose, "Trend of Real Income of the Rural Poor in East Pakistan," *Pakistan Development Review* 8, no. 3 (Autumn 1968).

36. According to Stern and Falcon, "Growth and Development in Pakistan, 1955–1969," p. 58, "less than two dozen families control two-thirds of all industrial assets and 70% of bank assets."

37. For evidence on the regressiveness of taxation and public expenditure in Pakistan, see Stern and Falcon, "Growth and Development in Pakistan, 1955–1969," pp. 58–60, and Maddison, *Class Structure and Economic Growth,* p. 142.

38. Five different estimates of rural and urban inequality in India are given in Jain and Tiemann, "Size Distribution of Income"; the average Gini coefficient for rural areas is 0.35 and for urban areas is 0.46. According to the estimates of Asbjorn Bergan, "Personal Income Distribution and Personal Savings in Pakistan," *Pakistan Development Review* 7, no. 2 (Summer 1967), the corresponding figures for Pakistan in 1963–64 were 0.35 and 0.44. Data presented by Dwight Y. King and Peter D. Weldon, "Income Distribution and Levels of Living in Java, 1963–1970," *Economic Development and Cultural Change* 25, no. 4 (July 1977), for Java during the mid and late 1960s show Gini coefficients for rural and urban inequality averaging 0.30 and 0.31, respectively, but the urban figure excludes the capital city of Jakarta and therefore certainly understates the level of inequality that would apply to all urban areas.

39. This paragraph is based entirely on the work of King and Weldon, "Income Distribution and Levels of Living in Java, 1963–1970," the most comprehensive analysis of income distribution in Indonesia currently available.

40. The precise proportion of the population whose real level of living has actually deteriorated under the New Order is a matter of dispute. H. W. Arndt, "Development and Equality: The Indonesian Case," *World Development* 3, nos. 2–3 (February–March 1975), is somewhat more optimistic than King and Weldon, "Income Distribution and Levels of Living in Java," suggesting that a considerable majority of the Indonesian people have benefited—albeit in unequal degree—from the rapid economic growth since 1966.

41. Indexes of per capita product by state from 1955 to 1970 are given in Weisskopf, "China and India," table 6; the discussion in this paragraph is based on those figures.

42. The empirical evidence in this paragraph on interregional income differentials in Pakistan is drawn from Griffin and Khan, *Growth and Inequality in Pakistan,* p. 3.

43. See King and Weldon, "Income Distribution and Levels of Living in Java, 1963–1970."

44. The source of the information in this paragraph on regional income disparities in Indonesia is a study by Hendra Esmara, "Regional Income Disparities," *Bulletin of Indonesian Studies* 11, no. 1 (March 1975).

45. For a tabulation of all the estimates of the "backlog of unemployment" in India, see the note on "Growth of Employment: 1950–51 to 1968–69" in the *Reserve Bank of India Bulletin* (Bombay) 23, no. 12 (December 1969).

46. A thorough analysis and critique of various methods of estimating unemployment in India is given in India, Planning Commission, *Report of the Committee of Experts on Unemployment Estimates* (New Delhi, 1970), chaps. 1–3.

47. According to figures published by India, Ministry of Labor and Rehabilitation, *Indian Labour Statistics* (annual), the number of registered job applicants rose from 330,000 in 1951 to more than 8 million by 1973.

48. See Weisskopf, "China and India," table 5.

49. These figures are given in Stern and Falcon, "Growth and Development in Pakistan, 1955–1969," table III–5.

50. According to the United Nations, *Economic Survey of Asia and the Far East, 1972,* table I–26, industrial employment in Pakistan grew at an average annual rate of 6.2% between 1961 and 1969.

51. This is suggested by Payer, "The International Monetary Fund and Indonesian Debt Slavery," and King and Weldon, "Income Distribution and Levels of Living in Java."

52. See R. M. Sundrum, "Manufacturing Employment in 1961–71," *Bulletin of Indonesian Economic Studies* 11, no. 1 (March 1975), for an analysis of the trends in manufacturing employment suggested by the 1961 and 1971 censuses in Indonesia.

53. Estimates of the total number of unemployed and underemployed persons in Indonesia range as high as one-third of the entire work force; see Rex Mortimer, "Indonesia: Growth or Development?" in Rex Mortimer, ed., *Showcase State* (Sydney: Angus and Robertson, 1973), p. 61.

54. See, for example, Arndt, "Development and Equality: The Indonesian Case," pp. 82–83.

55. The undervaluation of foreign currency is discussed in the Indian case by Bhagwati and Desai, *India: Planning for Industrialization;* in the Pakistani case by Lewis, *Pakistan: Industrialization and Trade Policies;* in the Indonesian case by Sievers, *Mystical World of Indonesia.*

56. See the annual issues of the *World Bank Atlas* published by the International Bank for Reconstruction and Development.

57. This is the indicator used in the International Bank for Reconstruction and Development, *World Tables 1971* to measure foreign exchange shortages.

58. According to figures drawn from the same sources as those cited in table 2–8, total export earnings increased at an average annual rate of 3.6% in India from 1960 to 1972, 4.8% in Pakistan from 1960 to 1970, and 13.6% in Indonesia from 1965 to 1972.

59. These estimates were made by Weisskopf, "Dependence and Imperialism in India," p. 213, for India, and by Shahid Amjad Chaudhry, "Private Foreign Investment in Pakistan," *Pakistan Development Review* 10, no. 1 (Spring 1970), p. 104, for Pakistan.

60. According to data given in Thomas W. Allen, "Policies of ASEAN Countries towards Direct Foreign Investment," SEADAG Paper on Problems of Development in Southeast Asia, no. 74-4, Asia Society–SEADAG, 1974, p. 77, roughly three-quarters of all foreign investment projects approved between 1967 and 1970 were in forestry and mining, and these data excluded the petroleum sector altogether.

61. The discussion of political trends in India here draws primarily on Maddison, *Class Structure and Economic Growth,* chap. 5; Myrdal, *Asian Drama,* chap. 7; Kuldip Nayar, *India: The Critical Years* (Delhi: Vikas Publications, 1971); and current reports in the *Economic and Political Weekly* (Bombay) and the *Far Eastern Economic Review* (Hong Kong).

62. Sources for the discussion of political trends in Pakistan include MacEwan, "Contradictions in Capitalist Development"; Maddison, *Class Structure and Economic Growth,* chap. 6; Myrdal, *Asian Drama,* chap. 8; *Nations;* and current reports in the *Far Eastern Economic Review* (Hong Kong). Sources for Indonesia include Gary Hansen, "Indonesia 1974: A Momentous Year," *Asian Survey* 15, no. 2 (February 1975); Sievers, *Mystical World of Indonesia,* chaps. 8, 11; and current reports in the *Far Eastern Economic Review* (Hong Kong).

63. In this regard the following passages from a report by William Borders to the *New York Times* (May 6, 1977) on the restoration of India's democratic institutions are significant: "Things are getting back to what they used to be in the area of law and order too, as the Desai government finds that without Mrs. Gandhi's sweeping emergency powers it is much more difficult to control smuggling, black

marketeering, strikes and near-violent social protests . . . 'Must there be an emergency for people to behave in a disciplined manner?' Prime Minister Desai asked in some exasperation the other day."

64. According to growth indexes published in the United Nations, *Statistical Yearbook* 1968, 1974, table 4, the average rate of growth of per capita output in all the "developing countries" was 2.6% per year between 1950 and 1973.

65. According to growth rates published in the International Bank for Reconstruction and Development, *World Tables 1976,* North Korea, South Korea, Taiwan, and the People's Republic of China are among the faster-growing nations of the Third World.

66. The existing theoretical and empirical literature on the relationship between economic growth and income distribution is briefly summarized and evaluated by Felix Paukert, "Income Distribution at Different Levels of Development: A Survey of Evidence," *International Labor Review* 108 (July–December 1973).

67. For a more thorough analysis of the nature and consequences of India's selectively modified strategy of economic development, see Thomas E. Weisskopf, "The Persistence of Poverty in India: A Political Economic Analysis," *Bulletin of Concerned Asia Scholars* 9, no. 1 (January-March 1977).

3

The Chinese Approach to Economic Development

BENJAMIN WARD

Two propositions describe the basic orientation of this chapter: (1) The Chinese have forced us to reconsider the fundamental problem of economic development. The key task for the next generation or so is not modernization but the stabilization of a humane agrarian regime. (2) The Chinese approach to economic development can reasonably be characterized as the achievement of a modernized socialist economy by using a Soviet-type economic system and growth strategy adapted to China's special conditions. Such an approach is transferable to a variety of environments.

The first assertion is not a Chinese formulation, nor does it imply that the Chinese have not been centrally concerned with modernization. Rather it suggests the dilemma that has been emerging with increasing clarity in recent Western accounts of the problems of economic development. Even optimistic estimates of the labor absorption to be achieved by continuing economic growth in developing countries suggest that by the year 2000 there may well be as many peasants in the world as there are today. The abysmal conditions in the countryside, the malnutrition and misery for hundreds of millions, may get worse rather than better. And the search for survival leads to excessive migration to cities, thus spreading the problem of the countryside over the entire society. The notable absence of such phenomena in land-poor and current-resource-poor China prompts the first assertion, which does not prejudge the question whether this result is the consequence of a unique set of values of the leadership.

The second assertion, aside from the issue of transferability, has a history in Chinese economic studies. The Chinese have self-consciously adopted many aspects of the Soviet Union's economic system since 1949: Soviet technology and training by Soviet engineers and technicians; the Soviet extensive growth strategy; the Soviet system of economic planning and control (which was often imitated in detail, at least superficially, down to the study of Soviet legal texts and training procedure). Western observers, with good reason, assumed that the Chinese were installing a Soviet-type economic system. But when the break with the Soviet Union came, shortly after the Great Leap Forward, divergences began to appear in Western interpretations of Chinese economic events, divergences that grew with the dramatic events of the sixties and have only recently begun to converge. Surely a central reason for this divergence was the drying up of information about what was really going on in China, which put China studies back to the situation faced by the student of the Soviet Union during Stalin's last years. Another reason no doubt was the nature of Chinese culture, still relatively impenetrable to the Western observer, and tended to open still further the range of behaviors and their interpretation that might qualify as plausible. And then there were the comments by the Chinese themselves. The straightforward interpretation was that they were simply telling the truth when they claimed to differ fundamentally from the social revisionists; but when those claims were couched in general language and accompanied by a news blackout, the skeptic too had an open field ahead. The resulting divergence of interpretations is to be expected when scholars are attempting to analyze the implications of a limited body of data. At such times there is no one truth.

The convergence that seems to have been occurring in the last few years is partly a product of increasing information, including a developing literature on the Cultural Revolution. Also, over the last fifteen years the slow process of developing cross-cultural understanding has continued. The third factor, the comments of the Chinese themselves about their economy, continues to offer mixed signals, but at least there are more of them, and they can now be added to a larger base of data and so perhaps interpreted with more confidence. It is in this context that I suggest that the dominant hypothesis of the fifties, that China is still basically a Soviet-type economy, be reconsidered. But the context for restudy is now quite different. China changed a good deal in these fifteen years, but so has the Soviet Union, and we have in addition the experience of a half dozen East European economies on which to draw. Chinese economic institutions can now be compared with a number of exemplars of the Soviet-type of economy and not just with the Soviet Union. The differing initial conditions provided by history, and the differing impact of the rest of the world on the domestic economies, can thus be appraised, and the tendencies, the "laws of motion," of such a system can be tentatively inferred.

The result is inevitably speculative. But, for what it is worth, my conclusion is that China is a close relative of the family of Soviet-type economies.

Transferability is a very complicated issue which is treated cursorily here. The question of revolution and its feasibility is ignored, nor is any attempt made to appraise the kinds of environments in which the Chinese pattern of institutions and policies, suitably adapted, are likely to flourish. Essentially the discussion is limited to the assertion that if China is a Soviet-type system then, because it has already proved viable in a variety of environments, extrapolation to still more environments is plausible. However, the assertion does imply something about learning. Not all the failures of Soviet-type economies, such as the collectivization fiasco in the Soviet Union itself, need be repeated in each new socialist transformation. Learning can and has occurred, and the ability to operate such a system presumably increases with the new information now being generated in a dozen or more national economies. So in dealing with transferability even in this limited context, some appraisal of what must be transferred, and what need not go, is in order.

The Soviet-Type Economy

Four traits have tended to distinguish the Soviet type of economy from others: (1) nationalization of the means of production, including at least all larger-scale production organizations and urban distribution organizations; (2) organization of agriculture into relatively large-scale collective and state farms; (3) mobilization of the state and the populace by means of a Leninist party; and (4) a rapid, catch-up industrialization effort as a central policy aim. Seven countries clearly meet all these tests, namely the Soviet Union, East Germany, Czechoslovakia, Hungary, Rumania, Bulgaria, and North Korea. Two others, Albania and North Vietnam, probably also do. Poland passes all the tests except the second; most of its agriculture is private. Yugoslavia also fails the second test, and some might have doubts about the "Leninism" of its Communist party. Cuba too may be a deviant on both these dimensions.[1]

China clearly passed all the tests by the end of the First Five-Year Plan. Its Leninist party was functioning effectively well before the revolution was victorious. Nationalization of large factories was completed early, and smaller factories inexorably came under state control. The First Five-Year Plan epitomized the Soviet type of extensive growth strategy. By 1957 collectivization of agriculture had been firmly installed.

Has there been any backsliding on any of these dimensions since 1957? Certainly not with respect to nationalization of industry. The history of the communes differs in a number of respects from the histories of collectivized agriculture elsewhere. There are similarities in some trends in collectivized agriculture in China and elsewhere, but clearly the basic notion of a large farm organized around joint production by some hundreds of peasants whose economic relationship with the state is governed by centrally fixed norms has survived into the mid seventies in China. As for the third trait, mobilization by a Leninist party, the Chinese Communist party was subject to a massive attack during the Cultural Revolution, an unprecedented phenomenon in socialist history, but events since 1968 suggest that there has been a strong tendency for the party to recover its central position in China's political and economic life. The continuity of economic policy in China is harder to appraise, given the paucity of data, but crude estimates suggest that the outcomes of economic activity, so far as they are known, remain roughly consistent with a continuation of the extensive growth strategy.

One of the most obvious differences between Soviet-type and capitalist economies is the Soviet type's relative use of structural instruments in support of their goals. Capitalist societies rely more centrally on indirect, financial instruments of control, and when they turn to structural instruments, they tend to involve, at least individually, relatively minor adjustments to the status quo. In socialist economies the direct controls of the plan are far more salient than the financial instruments, but more striking is the frequent resort to major structural change. Campaigns, reorganizations, revolutions—these are the distinguishing marks of the Soviet-type economy. Of course the application of these instruments varies widely over time and place, reflecting particular conditions as well as experience. But once again, China falls clearly into the Soviet-type box on this dimension. Furthermore, the specific features of such unique events as the Great Leap suggest patterns of similarity with events in other Soviet-type economies that have not always been noticed by observers.

Typically when Soviet-type and capitalist economies are being compared, the presence or absence of markets plays a central role in the discussion. That does not occur in this chapter, not because I think that the distinction is unimportant, but because it is difficult to analyze the actual behavior of the planning system in China on present information. I know of no substantial evidence with which to refute the claim that the Chinese planning system works, at both national and provincial levels, in ways essentially similar to socialist counterparts elsewhere. But I am aware of very little evidence of any kind on this topic, hence the emphasis on other topics. This gap in the argument renders the conclusion more speculative than even the student of other Soviet-type economies feels comfortable with.

The Extensive Growth Strategy

The picture of the economic growth process that has emerged over the last couple of decades, particularly in the United States, has considerable appeal. In broad outline it is based on the experience of the more advanced industrial nations, and its main thrust is that a similar path to modernity is open to, and in many cases is being followed by, a good many of the less developed countries. Countries developing along the main line have properties such as the following. (1) Once basic national institutions have been established, which assure the ability of the government to implement growth-oriented policies and the ability of other domestic institutions to respond to growth stimuli, countries can increase their per capita output at rates comparable to the developed countries. (2) Labor is transferred from agriculture to manufacturing, and the share of output originating in manufacturing grows, as has happened elsewhere. Indeed there are even similarities in sectoral structure change within manufacturing. (3) Technology is borrowed from the developed world, thus sharply constraining growth patterns. (4) The demand pattern of given income groups of consumers in the modern sector is strikingly similar from one country to another, tending to promote convergence in growth paths. (5) A country's volume of foreign trade, and often its trade ratio to national product as well, tends to increase with development, as does the national dispersion of its trade with its leading partners. Development thus tends to move a country from international economic dependence to economic interdependence.

These and some other trends tend to appear in countries undergoing economic development. Socialist countries following the Stalinist lead seem to have followed roughly the same pattern. However, there are differences; some of these stem from the intensity of the modernization effort, and some derive from the particular institutional features of the Soviet-type economy. Most notable perhaps among the former is the generally higher ratio of investment to national income that occurs in nearly all the socialist countries. This was especially striking in China during the First Five-Year Plan because of the relatively low level of per capita product from which the Chinese Communists began. There are no solid estimates of recent investment ratios, but indirect evidence suggests that this aspect of extensive growth has been continued in China.

A second aspect of the more intensive Soviet-type effort has been the relatively high priority assigned to heavy industry. Here again China in the fifties followed Soviet practice. Later policy pronouncements indicated a shift in emphasis toward agriculture, and a clear shift in emphasis toward smaller-scale industry; however, the extraordinarily rapid growth of Chinese steel output indicates that this shift was less than fundamental, and perhaps not more substantial than has occurred in other Soviet-type economies. The pattern of investment is of course influenced by factors such as effective consumer demand (including strike threats) for current goods, the availability of labor for further expansion of urban activities, and the margin over subsistence of both the rural and the urban populations. That China now has a steel output comparable to that of West Germany or Britain and a machinery industry of extremely broad capability when compared with other developing countries such as India may be the main indicator that the extensive growth strategy has remained a major influence on Chinese policy.

A defense of the extensive growth strategy as a variant of the general main-line strategy can be based on the gross evidence of success. Average growth rates of output and output per capita have been somewhat higher in socialist countries, but some of these countries have paid a heavy price in terms of consumption foregone; the Soviet Union's experiences in the thirties are the main case in point. This picture has recently been modified in three ways. The costs of main-line development under capitalist institutions, where the overwhelming majority of the world's hundreds of millions of malnourished now reside, have become clearer. Experience in other socialist countries indicates that collectivization of agriculture can be achieved without paying a price in human welfare anything like that forced on the Soviet citizenry forty years ago. Indeed, given the unquestionably less unequal distribution of income in socialist countries, compared with capitalist lands at a similar level of development, it appears that the socialist country has considerably more leeway in allocating resources both to investment and to the current consumption of the population as a whole. When these experiences are put into the development equation, the welfare aspects of development under the main line versus that under the extensive growth strategy appear in a very different light.

The extensive growth policy is usually discussed in socialist literature either in terms of unrevealing slogans, such as "the law of planned, proportional development of the economy" or in terms of crabbed and at times flawed analyses of the appropriate relative rates of growth of Departments I and II.[2] There is also a socialist literature on formal growth theory, but like its Western counterpart, it does not deal plausibly with the central policy issues faced by economic planners.[3] Perhaps the best defense of the policy of extensive growth has been offered by the Yugoslav economist, Branko Horvat.[4] It runs as follows: The major effective constraint to more rapid growth in most developing countries is a shortage of the means of production. Thus, given rational decision making by the planners, more rapid growth can be achieved by increasing the fraction of the national product allocated to investment. Studies of countries having varying investment ratios—as a proportion of national product—show that the productivity of increased investment, in terms of higher rates of growth, does not decline as the investment ratio increases. At least this is true up to relatively high investment ratios of 30% or so (in terms of gross concepts). However, a country cannot immediately expand its investment ratio by five or ten percentage points without paying some significant costs because of the relatively slow rate at which a nation's capacity to absorb new means of production expands; an annual increase of one or two percentage points until a figure of around 30% is reached turns out to be near the limits of absorptive capacity. A simple algebraic consequence of these facts is that the opportunity cost of the increased investment in terms of consumption foregone is just about zero; that is, the consumption increase from the more rapid growth of the economy at least balances the consumption loss from devoting a larger share of output to investment rather than consumption. In sum, a program of maximum growth is feasible without reducing consumption per capita below the levels that would have been achieved with a policy of slower growth. And of course as time goes on, consumption per capita becomes far higher than would otherwise have been the case.

This is a very striking theory, and to my knowledge it has not been refuted in the literature. Of course there are some qualifications. In particular, there is no appraisal of the role of foreign trade in the development process, and the ability of the planners to construct "rational" plans for such very rapid growth on present knowledge is certainly questionable.[5] Also, there has been a tendency for countries facing unexpected demands on their resources while attempting rapid growth to shift the burden of absorbing these demands onto the consumption sector, sometimes with disastrous consequences for the short-term welfare of the population. Nevertheless, it is probably the best available defense of the extensive growth strategy.

Chinese experience with extensive growth suggests that such a regime can operate with relative success. Collectivization itself was a far less bloody process in China (and in Eastern Europe) than it was in the

Soviet Union. And since that time, the Chinese seem to have developed the capacity to preserve real incomes at a surprisingly stable level while continuing rapid (if more volatile) industrial growth. The Chinese benefit from the size of their economy and its relative independence from external shocks, but they also have had an organizational task of formidable proportions. At any rate, the last twenty years of Chinese economic history not only are broadly consistent with the extensive growth strategy but also suggest that it has been implemented with a relatively high degree of effectiveness.

Autarky

The autarky policy comes in two varieties in China, international self-sufficiency and regional self-sufficiency. Both are related to defense policy, and trade-offs with extensive growth in that direction may be assumed without prejudicing the socialism-growth issue.[6] The international side of autarky is the most difficult to appraise because there may have been a substantial change in policy within the last few years. However, for much of China's history as a socialist country, its volume of trade has put it near the top of the list of developing countries. Its relatively low trade dependency can be attributed in large degree to its size and favorable resource endowment. For much of its history Communist China's dependency ratio has been above that of some other Soviet-type economies.[7]

China has obviously made strong efforts to insulate much of its economy from direct contacts with foreign traders, through the organization of the trading process, through unwillingness to permit direct foreign investment, and through limits on the contact of domestic production organizations with actual and potential traders.[8] Much of this merely repeats at least past practices of Soviet-type economies, though I believe the central role of the Canton fair has no direct ancestor in socialist history.[9] Under the pressure of the increased volume of trade in the seventies there has been some erosion of these controls, but it is probably too early to discern any medium-term trends.[10]

One of the major benefits to growth policy offered by the Soviet-type economy is the degree of control over imports that becomes feasible. In official statistics this is perhaps most clearly manifested in the virtual elimination of imports of consumer goods that have no direct impact on growth.[11] China's trade statistics certainly reflect application of this policy. A second and unmeasured benefit stems from the greater control of illegal trade that results from the very strict control of international flows by Soviet-type economies and from domestic sumptuary restrictions. Perhaps the most important device for controlling illegal activity lies in the financial system, which restricts far more substantially than other economies the usefulness of foreign currency and gold for the illegal trader. Here, too, China seems to fit the picture of Soviet-type policy very well. Also, if there are costs in terms of growth foregone to the restrictive trade policies, they may be more than compensated by gains in this second dimension.

The Chinese regional and local self-sufficiency policies have somewhat different rationales and have been carried well beyond comparable policies in Soviet-type economies. The most difficult one to appraise is the regionalization of industrial planning, since there seem to be no recent descriptions on which to base an appraisal. The pre–Great Leap regionalization seems to have been strongly influenced by its Soviet counterpart, the creation of *sovnarkhozy*, which occurred at about the same time.[12] However, the Chinese seem to have created a better design for this type of decentralization, and the approach has been developed further, while the Soviets soon abandoned their experiment. China's approach had two advantages over the Soviets'. First, their economy was substantially less developed; this usually means that there is less industrial interdependence, so that interregional flows, the principal elements that must continue to be controlled from the center, are substantially less diverse and voluminous. Second, the Chinese based their regionalization on provinces, of which there were about twenty, or a fifth of the number of *sovnarkhozy*. Even with some republican controls over groups of *sovnarkhozy* this proved far too unwieldy a number of regional control centers. An additional property of the Chinese economy that favored regionalization was the relatively backward transportation and information systems. If regionalization could reduce the burden on the transport system, it would not only improve current performance but also reduce the medium-term transport investment required to support future growth. The Soviet type of planning system has always made excessive burdens of information generation and processing on the central planners; a regionalization that reduced this burden could have a considerable impact on the rationality of the planned economy.[13]

There is very little one can say in appraisal of these hypotheses for the Chinese case. It cannot even be confidently asserted that the Chinese have retained regionalization for a substantial fraction of the large-scale industry that lies at the heart of Soviet-type planning.[14] What does seem to be the case is that there is a degree of regionalization for light industry and agriculture that has not been reached in any of the Soviet-type economies.

A prominent feature of Chinese policy, with obvious connections to regional autarky, is the small-scale industry program. Traditional crafts and services tend almost everywhere to decline with economic development. However, there is also a trend for modern service and small-scale industry to expand rapidly to satisfy certain demands of the growing modern sector. The processing of agricultural commodities often develops in the countryside; witness the Israeli kibbutz. But in Soviet-type economies there seems to have been a strong tendency for industrial activity to occur in towns that also support large-scale productive activities, rather than in small towns and the countryside as has occurred in China. Chinese defense of their policy has at times emphasized the contribution of small-scale industry to modernization rather than to socialist objectives.[15] Also small-scale industries do not replace large-scale industry; and, as the recent agreement for the purchase of large fertilizer factories attests, the policy does not preclude rapid development of large-scale production of products that have been favorites of the small-scale approach.[16] To some indeterminate extent the small-scale industry policy can be considered a rational adaptation to resource distribution, including a shortage of transport and a surplus of labor in the countryside.

Regional self-sufficiency also provides important support for the policy of migration control. This policy, also followed by Soviet-type economies but apparently executed with greater thoroughness in China, has undoubtedly offered substantial benefits to the growth policy. By restricting and even reversing migration to the cities, the authorities have reduced the costs of city maintenance and development, since almost everywhere it costs more in social resources to support a family in town than in the countryside, and real wages in China appear to continue to be higher in the towns. Presumably the authorities are not losing much in the way of urban production foregone by keeping the city population down, and presumably the productivity of would-be and erstwhile city dwellers in the countryside is positive. Whether there are unwanted side effects or whether the socialism side of the social welfare function is working effectively is not known; but it seems that, in principle, modernization and socialism are compatible on this dimension.

One final aspect of local self-sufficiency is that a relatively integrated small-scale economy may have substantial effects on incentives. The local citizenry is capable of perceiving both the costs and the benefits of the policy, since many—often most—of them must bear much of the cost and reap much of the benefit. This perception may make choices of scale and technique rational over some range and may inhibit waste in the direct production process. Furthermore, such benefits may not be restricted to production activities. Local provision of welfare benefits, such as health clinics and barefoot doctors, earlier levels of education, and even social security in the form of basic food guarantees, may all be administered more effectively at a local level, where corruption is likely to be visible and, again, costs and benefits internalized. All this is true only if the local citizens making the decisions understand their options (a task of considerable importance which is supposed to be performed by the party cadres) and influence policy (which also depends on the cadres). On this dimension, the Chinese look especially good to the superficial observer and have carried localization beyond that of Soviet-type economies. Probably localization is feasible in such an economy only if the Leninist party has successfully integrated itself into most of the rural communities.[17]

Egalitarianism

One of the major advantages of the Soviet-type economy for the purpose of economic development is the relatively wide range of options that it offers the leadership in designing an incentive system. Perhaps the single most important policy of this kind is nationalization. Eliminating private returns from property immediately reduces the skewness in the income distribution. Since developing capitalist countries tend to have even more skewed income distributions than affluent countries, with the wealthiest 5% of the population receiving over 30% of the income, this shift in the distribution tends to be substantial. And since the Leninist party tends to be at least as growth oriented as private capitalists, and often much more so, the resources saved can be shifted into the investment sector for a substantial increase in the investment ratio.

Another important range of options involves the design of a system of wage and salary payments that elicits the efforts needed for economic development at minimum cost, that is, the design of a maximum-growth incentive system. There has been considerable variation over time and country in the structure of material incentives in Soviet-type economies.[18] Horvat has suggested that wage scales tend to be relatively egalitarian when a country is poor, to tend toward increasing differentials as development proceeds up to a point, and then to turn back toward egalitarianism. Something like this seems to have happened in the Soviet Union, which may be a product, not of any fundamental underlying forces, but simply of relatively long postponed adaptations of ineffectively controlled trends in the wage system. At any rate, the Soviet Union introduced a major differential-reducing wage reform in the late fifties and continued the trend with a substantial increase in the minimum wage in 1968. This reform also substantially reduced the share of piecework and bonus payments in wage income, shifted away from piecework toward bonuses, and increased the relative importance of collective bonuses at the expense of individual incentive payments. Thus a trend began in the late fifties and proceeded through the sixties in the Soviet Union toward a more egalitarian, less individualistic, and more time-dependent (as opposed to productivity-dependent) incentive system.[19]

The structure of current Chinese wages and salaries is, like almost every other important aspect of the Chinese economy, discernible only from limited information supplied to visitors and bits and pieces available in the press. It appears, however, that the ratios of highest to lowest pay in Chinese factories are comparable to those in some Soviet-type economies. Ratios of 5 : 1 or 6 : 1 (not counting apprentices) are found in some Chinese factories and in a number of factories in Soviet-type economies. The major Chinese difference at present lies in the absence of bonus payments, but such payments have also been absent at times from Soviet-type economies.[20]

Group material incentives are common in China, most explicitly perhaps in the agricultural incentive system. The structure of payments there seems designed to ensure that increased productivity by a team or brigade will be reflected in higher incomes to the unit's members. Somewhat comparable arrangements may exist in industry as well.[21]

A notable difference between China and some other Soviet-type economies is the more limited extent to which differential payments seem to be used for labor allocation. This is most obvious in the case of rural-urban migration, where the economic signals point in one direction and the actual migration has apparently flowed strongly in the opposite direction. Within the towns there are some indications that turnover of factory labor is relatively low. This is in part a product of the mobility controls, which probably inhibit intercity migration, and in part a consequence of the high status and security of urban factory employment. It may also reflect relatively poorly developed horizontal communications networks, though this is impossible to appraise on current information.

Another prominent feature of China as well as of other Soviet-type economies is the strong indoctrination provided by schools, media, and party cadres which attempts to instill qualities that promote productivity. These efforts are not contradicted by public media, which may for a time enhance their value, and can plausibly hold out hopes for a better life for all as time goes by, if appropriate collective effort is expended. All societies make substantial use of indoctrination in the attempt to promote good work habits, and productivity of such efforts is difficult to appraise; but the socialist economies seem to devote relatively more resources to it.[22]

Is China different from Soviet-type economies in its application of this instrument? I think the answer is that there are a number of differences. The Chinese are starting from much farther back than did the Soviet-type economies, and the citizenry is well aware of this. Nationalism is a strong and positive force in promoting effort in China, while it is at best equivocal in most Soviet-type economies in Eastern Europe and for a large fraction of Soviet citizens. Dwight Perkins has noted the importance of values that a great many Chinese seemed to possess well before the Communists came to power and which appear to distinguish the Chinese from others by their acceptance of hard work and their willingness to work relatively selflessly for collective goals, whether those of the family or of some other social unit.[23]

Other differences may have other causes. There are conspicuous parallels between some of the Chinese programs, such as the "three-in-one" and the "two participations," and certain features of World War II shipyards in the United States, in which case a crash effort was made to produce very rapid increases in output with a relatively unskilled labor force recruited substantially from rural areas.[24] Prewar status barriers within the firm tended to be broken down as "responsible persons" were employed in a constant effort to teach workers skills or procedures or techniques. Limited consumer goods production under wartime constraints, and especially a housing shortage, reduced the direct incentive effects of the wage system; but the improvement for many such workers was still so vast that the basic incentive was really provided by the sense that a whole new world, a whole new way of life, was opening up, rather than by an increase in the relative availability of goods to individuals as their productivity increased. Soviet-type economies in several cases have been able to make good use of this pattern, and the Chinese, with their much more serious task, may be able to take advantage of it for longer than their predecessors. Once again China's twin goals of socialism and modernization seem to be having complementary rather than conflicting impacts.

Collectivized Agriculture

Collectivization has been the key to agricultural policy in Soviet-type economies. The form has certain important advantages. One of these is flexibility. The choice of farm size can be made a relatively easily administered policy variable, depending on local conditions, experience, and administrative skill. Collectivized farming can occur with apparent success under relatively traditional methods of cultivation or in a highly modernized, capital-intensive form. The variability in the mix of private and collectivized activity is also a policy variable.

The collective farming system also supports other policies of Soviet-type regimes. It enhances mobility control, especially by nationalizing or cooperativizing the distribution of inputs and outputs to and from collective farms. Perhaps most important, the extraction of surplus to support modernization of the general economy is partially divorced from short-run market forces. Taxes, price controls, and compulsory deliveries are the means of bringing the terms of trade between town and country more effectively under central control. In addition, a program of modernizing the countryside in less direct ways, such as education and public health, seems to be more easily implemented under collective farming than in small-scale peasant agriculture.[25]

Is collective farming a success? In one overwhelming sense the answer is an unequivocal yes. Most of the world's peasantry appears to suffer from serious material deprivation, of which malnutrition—in town as well as country—is the most visible manifestation. But few of the peasants living under collectivized agriculture appear hungry. This is a rather striking success against what may well be the fundamental problem faced by most developing countries over the next few decades.

On the other hand, it is not clear that collectivized agriculture is a more productive form of agriculture than peasant freehold or plantation farming. Agriculture tends not to be a growth leader in socialized countries, but then it is usually not given a leading share of investment resources. Studies of productivity, of output per unit of inputs and its change over time, though providing very incomplete coverage of the world's collectivized agriculture, do not suggest that performance has been especially high.[26] But performance is often judged by the standard of the Soviet Union while the situation in the other East European countries may be substantially more favorable.[27] Also comparisons with the United States are less useful than comparisons with developing countries facing comparable problems. The latter type of comparative study seems to be unavailable, but there is evidence to suggest that there tend to be massive misallocations of resources in less developed capitalist countries' agriculture and that a far less effective system of surplus mobilization and transfer exists from the point of view of further economic development.[28]

These remarks about collectivized agriculture in Soviet-type economies could also be made about Chinese agriculture, for the similarities in structure and policy both before and after the Great Leap are very striking. This is also true of the basic policy of town-country economic interaction and may even apply to the relative significance of agriculture and industry in the investment programs of the sixties, despite the special Chinese slogans. It applies not only to the general format of the collective farm but even to more detailed aspects of structure, such as the three-tiered organization of farms and the use of contracting for food supplies to nearby cities. It applies to many aspects of the incentive system for farmers, from the mix of private and collective production activity to emphasis on collective material incentives. It seems even to apply to basic attitudes of the leadership toward private plots, unfavorable in the long run, but willing to vary their material significance in response to medium-term needs and prospects. It also applies to attitudes toward farm size, with a revealed preference for larger units and for basic accounting to be carried out at a relatively high level; the regimes appear to share a long-term goal of converting collective farms into state farms, and some have already gone a long way in this direction.[29]

It is often argued that the major differences between the Chinese and the Soviet and East European agriculture stem from political causes. The Chinese, it is claimed, started from a strong peasant base with a leader whose background fitted him to be the "peasants' ombudsman" in high government circles and who was able to obtain both the consent of a substantial fraction of the peasantry for policies of structural reform and the trust of party cadres in the day-to-day operation of the commune system. This picture contrasts with that in the Soviet Union, where collectivization was imposed in a most brutal way, and where considerable numbers of the peasantry greeted the Nazi invaders of 1941 as liberators.[30] It is this basic political trust that has made feasible the domestic autarky policies, rural industrial development, and more flexible planning in agriculture.

Clearly the Chinese had a far stronger party organization in the countryside than was the case in the Soviet Union of the early plan era or in the East European countries during and for a while after collectivization. Equally clearly, collectivization was quite unpopular among the land-hungry peasants of the Ukraine in 1941, or Poland in 1956, or Yugoslavia in 1953, where the majority of peasants returned from collective farming to private agriculture when the chance was offered.[31] But the picture as always is cloudy for contemporary China and much less clear than these facts suggest even for Soviet-type economies; for example, the Czech peasants of 1968 had, de facto, an opportunity to decollectivize but remained organized in collectives. Minimum wages for collective farmers came relatively late to the Soviet Union but provide a far more secure material environment to the peasants than they had before.[32] And the shift from coercion administered with centralized inflexibility toward group material incentives encouraging productivity in the Soviet Union reflects changes that are hard to appraise but quite general in these economies. Finally, the party has certainly grown stronger in the countryside under the impact of improved organization, better communication, and higher levels of skills among the intelligentsia.[33]

In China problems of administration suggest less than perfect harmony between peasant and general policy. Income differentials between regions, between communes in different rings of relative affluence surrounding cities, and even among teams in the same commune, remain and are plausible sources of disincentive. The Cultural Revolution may not have penetrated as deeply into the countryside as accounts of that movement often claim, and informal extensions of private exchange may be much larger than they appear to the short-term visitor. The saving in infrastructure development that domestic autarky permits may in fact entail some cost in political control.

These are all maybe's that the available information about the Chinese countryside does not permit us to resolve. But it does seem that the similarities between the Chinese and Soviet-type economies in the countryside are far more pronounced than the differences and that some of the latter may be attributed either to China's particular material conditions or to differences in the nature of the revolution which may not persist in the long run.

Teleological Instruments

From the perspective of half a century of history, the Soviet October Revolution seems to have been a major turning point in the history of the industrial epoch. From it has grown a distinctive social form that governs social relations for a third of mankind and whose prospects for further expansion seem good. Associated with the social form is a world view that offers an interpretation of both man and history quite different from the conventional Western view. Its now-extensive history provides opportunities for learning and adaptation, so that newcomers have the opportunity to avoid some of the earlier mistakes of Soviet-type regimes.

This environment has posed a central and continuing intellectual dilemma for its leadership. On the one hand, most of the world's useful knowledge has been generated by nonsocialist experts, and this knowledge has undeniable value for builders of socialism. On the other hand, the new social form has opened up possibilities, has abrogated, so to speak, some of the laws of motion of capitalist society. But which laws? In the early days of a new system it is difficult to say. The leadership obviously wants to take advantage of the new situation, but it cannot distinguish the properties of the unexperienced alternatives and cannot wholly trust the experts whose training has steeped them in possibly uncongenial and, in a sense, traditional modes of thought.

This environment has brought forth the teleological instrument as a central ingredient in the Soviet-type policy mix. Its most spectacular exemplar is of course the revolution itself, the seizure of power by a group committed to the remaking of society. Revolutions are high-risk ventures, and conventional wisdom continues to hold that they have little chance of success;[34] certainly reasonably well informed observers agreed that for the Russia of 1915, the China of 1927, or the Cuba of 1957, the probability of a successful Communist revolution was in each case quite small. Success in such a venture must strongly reinforce one horn of the dilemma: Revolutionary will opens doors hardly perceived by conventional expertise.

In the great creative ferment of the Soviet Union of the twenties this question became central to policy debates over industrialization. Though the more extreme teleological views did not prevail, the First Five-Year Plan and its institutional supports constituted a veritable Soviet great leap. This leap started in concrete terms the process that was to establish the basic institutions of Soviet society, institutions that have now been functioning for about four decades. It also created, in combination with the Second Five-Year Plan, an industrial transformation of Soviet society, partly by very rapid growth of a number of sectors, but perhaps mostly by creating an integrated industrial base to support the relatively autonomous development of later decades.[35]

At the heart of a great leap lies the notion of dramatic increases in production achievable through the release of revolutionary energy, combined with effective organization of that energy. Yugoslavia's First Five-Year Plan was another manifestation of the great leap approach, as was the Cuban "ten million tons."[36] And of course there was the Great Leap itself. In Yugoslavia and Cuba, as in China, the leap was a failure in the sense that expectations far exceeded achievements. But in both Yugoslavia and China the leaps provided an orienting framework for the later trajectory of the economy that was to be substantially achieved within a more modest but still impressive time frame.

It is perhaps an exaggeration to suggest that the campaign is also a teleological instrument. But campaigns are similar (though over only a single dimension or two) in their attempt to extract greater performance from a social system than conventional practice suggests is feasible, and to do this partly by mobilizing energies voluntaristically. Campaign productivities are hard to appraise because they do not seem to have been carefully studied, and within these regimes distorting pressures on reporting systems are an almost inevitable accompaniment. But their frequent use is a fixed point of Soviet-type economies, and of China's economy as well. Many of them may serve more effectively as devices to capture the attention of cadres and rank and file than as means of generating an overall increase in human energy available for the economic process.[37]

A very common feature of hierarchic societies is the renewal process. Hierarchies seem to be strongly subject to long-run pressures toward corruption and substantial decline in their ability to implement the desires of the leadership. A renewal process represents an attempt to restructure values within the system in order to return to some earlier or at least some idealized period of commitment and effectiveness. Renewal processes have taken various forms, such as the founding of new monastic orders to replace ossified older forms, the renewal of commitment stimulated by a threat to the system's survival such as war, great leaps, and the emergence of reformist subsects within the hierarchy, as in the Protestant Revolution or the aviators and tankers of some interwar military establishments.[38]

World War II may well have served as a renewal process for the Soviet Union though it was swiftly aborted. The establishment of the New System in Yugoslavia after the Cominform break seems also to follow this pattern. Abortive renewals may have occurred in the East European revolutions of Poland, Hungary, and Czechoslovakia. The Chinese Cultural Revolution is a striking example of such a renewal process. Unfortunately, it is difficult from the current perspective and available data to evaluate its effects on the economy. Some changes, such as the abolition of bonuses within industry and the extension of the system of sending down cadres to engage in manual labor, certainly suggest that some renewal has occurred. Clearly a large number of people were affected by the renewal currents. But impacts in terms of overall economic performance are not easily perceived, partly perhaps because the Cultural Revolution was not tied to an economic great leap.[39]

Once again there seems to be a strong case for the argument that contemporary China is an example of a Soviet-type economy, whose deviations are attributable partly to learning from the past and partly to the special material conditions faced by the Chinese leadership. Teleological instruments are not specific to Soviet-type regimes, but the extent of their use in such systems is unparalleled in the rest of the world today. Fundamentally the Chinese resort to such instruments seems to reflect pressures and concerns similar to those of leaderships elsewhere in the Communist world.

Transferability

Diffusion is clearly a major process shaping the course of modern history. Given that the advanced countries are the fount from which technology has flowed, and given the apparent structure of wants of citizenry exposed to modernity in the media and elsewhere, this force is difficult to counter. Main-line development theory offers an optimistic interpretation of the potential of this process, suggesting that growth can be made to produce modernity in the developing world, given a domestic willingness to let the international interactions occur.

However, the costs of submitting to this approach are heavy. One major problem is that technology continues to change, and the newer processes have been unfavorable to the developing world, especially as a result of their more limited capacity to absorb labor. The higher growth rates of population have tended to increase the numbers of the miserable at the bottom of the pile and to enhance social disorganization in both town and country. Too often nowadays a developing capitalist country is one in which the enclave of modernity grows side by side with increasing economic deprivation for an ever-greater number of people.

The situation in the less developed of the Soviet-type economies, and particularly China, stands in sharp contrast. These regimes engage in a substantial effort to control the outside influence that is allowed to penetrate their societies as a part of their attempt to control growth and to control and shape the attitudes of their citizens. In China, in addition, an effort has been made to adapt technology to the special conditions of the semipermanent peasant economy. Small-scale and relatively labor intensive plants have in recent years demonstrated their usefulness to development. The policy of rapid modernization and development of industry has been retained while its social impact has been made more effective. The collectivization of agriculture has apparently been the key factor in virtually eliminating the more severe kinds of material deprivation. This is a strong recommendation for the basic policies followed in China and, for the most part, in other Soviet-type economies.

Can one expect diffusion to be extended from technology to social systems? If one were to match the economic condition of citizens in a Soviet-type economy with their counterparts in a developing capitalist economy of comparable per capita output, I think that it is plausible, though not established empirically, that a substantial majority of the citizens of the former country would be economically better off and more secure. Surely some strong diffusionist pressures are created by this crude fact.

China may be looked on as a sort of Mark III or improved Soviet-type economy, in which at least some of the lessons of past experience have been incorporated into the latest institutional design. The small-scale industry program is perhaps the most striking of these and offers the greatest contrast with Eastern Europe, but improved system design has probably had the greatest economic impact on agriculture. The incentive system, too, while a close relative of some past and current Soviet-type practices, appears to be an improved version, as has the system of control of town-country migration. Towering above all has been the magnitude of the task faced by the Chinese, in terms of both numbers of people to be organized and level of resource availability per capita at the start of the revolutionary venture. The Soviet-type economy has come a long way from the Soviet Union of the Stalinist thirties.

But this improved Soviet-type economy, as an alternative to more conventional approaches to economic development, is not without costs and risks. First, is there not a longer-run conflict between socialism and modernization entailed by the relative isolation of the Chinese economy from diffusionist currents? The Chinese can borrow modern technology and operate it reasonably effectively, but two questions remain. First, can they develop the creative potential in science and technology that resides in all the major advanced countries while preserving their isolation? One might interpret recent Soviet experience as suggesting that the answer is no, that the Soviets have discovered that the complexity and scope of modern developments require full international integration of the scientific-technical community if they are either to catch up or keep up. Second, is there an organizational imperative that derives from the technological imperative? That is, does the borrowed factory not have to be operated in ways that determine most important aspects of social relations, for example of specialization and relative status? The lives of factory workers seem very similar in various parts of the world; the most noticeable differences are not in work lives but in nonwork lives, which seem basically a product of different levels of real wages.[40] Perhaps there is too much jointness between these two imperatives for diffusion control to work. This is of course still an open question.

The old slogan "Trade brings freedom" was overdrawn, but it did point to the fact that some tolerance of strange ways was essential to the diversity that was unavoidable in trade centers. The peasant era saw its share of markets, and many of them prospered despite official disapproval. The first century of the industrial revolution seemed to be pointing toward the universalization of integrated market systems as the primary resource allocation mechanism of the new era; however, that trend has become much cloudier as the revolution's second century has worn on. The pioneer governments of the planned economy are in a position not unlike many of the peasant empires. They would like to eliminate domestic trade relations but find they must tolerate a certain amount as an essential complement to the planned economy. Beyond some point restriction of trade may not only conflict with the growth objective but also promote informal trading. Quasi-legal trading under the protection of officials is one of the oldest forms of trade. It is a problem in the most developed of the planned economies.[41] China is apparently less beset with the problem, but the tendency toward abuses of this kind seems built into the structure of the system. This clearly poses one of the central tests of the efficacy with which the goal of socialism can be pursued, especially since, to many of the participants, the tolerance of traders may well be an expedient means to efficient modernization. Perhaps the modernized version of the slogan should be "Trade erodes noncommercial values."[42]

The industrial revolution is sending out conflicting signals about the nature of class in the new epoch. In its first century the Marxian picture of a relatively small group monopolizing the means of production in order to extract the surplus from the wage-earning proletarian producers appeared to fit the emerging pattern. But in its second century the industrial revolution has tended to generate a substantial intermediate group of workers who do not own the means of production but have skills and knowledge that give them relatively high incomes and challenging jobs. They are by no means politically impotent and are able to pass on to their children a high probability of entry into similar status. At the same time, the real incomes of workers farther down the income hierarchy have risen substantially. All this has greatly complicated the issue of exploitation.

To the extent that the issue of class is interpreted as an issue of power and influence, Soviet-type regimes are clearly class societies— not in the Chinese sense of the existence of remnants of capitalism, but in the sense of the existence of a small elite that controls the means of production and makes the basic political and economic decisions in the society, including the basic decisions about the extraction of surplus and its allocation.[43] On the other hand, these societies have done astonishingly well in providing for the poorest members of their societies. Indeed one might say that the Chinese leaders behave toward less skilled workers and poorer peasants, not as the leading groups in most previous societies did, but rather as patrons to their clients. Increasing the living standards of the general population seems to be a far less equivocal goal in China and other Soviet-type economies than it is in developing capitalist societies. Perhaps this distinction is sharp enough that the same word, "class," should not be used to describe both phenomena. At any rate the tendencies in the development of class in the twentieth century do not suggest any emerging univocal pattern, beyond the "rise of the middle class."[44]

The collective farmer has often been likened to a serf. His mobility is restricted by higher, coercive authority, and he is obliged to perform certain labor services on the collective (demesne) land and to provide contributions in both money and kind to higher authority. And though given some return in money for his activity, the collective farmer's range of options is sharply restricted by the limited availability of goods and sales outlets.

The significance of this unfavorable contrast changes considerably when the current practical option, the situation of the peasant in developing capitalist economies, is contrasted with the collective farmer's lot. Nevertheless, the picture is striking enough to call into question the view of class structure just offered. Perhaps the best that one can say is that this contrast reflects a major tension in the structure and tendency of Chinese society. China is still a peasant society in the countryside, where dispersion and effective central control, combined with a recognition by the leadership of the basic needs and aims of the peasantry, have permitted a dramatic transfer of resources from country to town. Considerable efforts are made to preserve the mutual trust that seems to prevail, apparently at a higher level than in other developing countries. But the basic means of power, as with all the great peasant empires, lies with the central authorities and the army they control. The opportunities for abuse are built into the structure of the political economic system.

Rural income distribution is one of the areas in which the stability of the Chinese system will probably be given a stern test. Two underlying economic factors that universally influence rural distribution are differential fertility of the land and nearness to towns. An efficient investment policy calls for more resources to be devoted to the more fertile areas and to the areas closest to town. But because of the relative intangibility of these factors and the annual variability in the productivity of the land, it is difficult to design a system of differential charges that will preserve anything like equal pay for equal work without appearing to the producers to be an arbitrary and variable confiscation. And as long as there is a relative shortage of consumer goods, surpluses in the more successful farms are likely to be allocated in a greater degree to further investment, which could either skew the income distribution still further or weaken material incentives. Differentials of this kind create opportunities for the abuse of socialist social relations, including pressures for the development of informal trades. The Chinese have controlled these tendencies fairly effectively so far but still have a long way to go, perhaps longer than other societies using the Chinese way might have.

A long-run threat to the great peasant societies stemmed from the tendency for land to be appropriated by the service nobility and then used as a basis for developing independence from central control. What in the long run will preserve the loyalty of party cadres to the Chinese regime? Perhaps the best answer is mobility, the prospect that successful performance will lead to movement up the hierarchy. The appraisal of stability will then hinge on the ability of the leadership to maintain effective standards for promotion. But in addition there is the observed tendency, in China and elsewhere, for cadres to try to provide some special advantages for their own children. This, or the development of mobility barriers, is the device by which classes in the more conventional sense might emerge, breaking the patron-client tie between leadership and "masses" and diverting the surplus extraction process to serve other aims. The semipermanent dualism of the modernizing peasant society, nowhere sharper than in contemporary China, must be considered an important underlying tendency promoting developments of this kind.

The Cultural Revolution represented a major attempt by the Chinese to preserve the socialist goal in the face of such tendencies. The revolution seems generally to have been regarded in the West as at least a partial success. But it was, as the Chinese say, a "superstructure thing"; it did not alter the underlying tendencies that created the problem. Nor does the history of the Cultural Revolution suggest that it is a simple or predictable instrument to apply in the service of this goal.

If one were forced to summarize these comments in a single sentence, perhaps the following would serve: China offers an institutional pattern for economic development that appears to be substantially superior to its leading alternative, capitalism; however, the long-run stability of that pattern in the Chinese environment is not established, and a strong potential for deterioration of the distributive achievement continues to exist. Development of a more serious appraisal of the diffusionist potential of the Chinese pattern would seem to be a first priority in research.

Notes

I am very grateful to Paul Ivory for many informative and insightful comments on Chinese affairs, to Andrzej Brzeski, Gregory Grossman, K. C. Yeh, and various participants in the conference for their comments on the first draft, to John Burkett for research assistance, to Bojana Ristich for clerical and editorial assistance, and to the Institute of International Studies and the Center for Chinese Studies, Berkeley, for support.

1. Kenneth Jowitt, *Revolutionary Breakthrough and National Development* (Berkeley: University of California Press, 1971) discusses the developmental role of the party; Gregory Grossman, *Comparative Economic Systems,* 2d ed. (Englewood Cliffs, N.J.: Prentice-Hall, 1974), Peter Wiles, *Political Economy of Communism* (Cambridge, Mass.: Harvard University Press, 1962), and Robert Campbell, *Soviet Type Economies,* 4th ed. (New York: Houghton Mifflin, 1974), discuss the distinctive features of the Soviet-type economy.

2. The issues are analyzed in Wiles, *Political Economy of Communism,* chaps. 14–16.

3. Michal Kalecki's contributions in this vein are summarized in George Feiwel, *The Intellectual Capital of Michal Kalecki* (Nashville, Tenn.: Vanderbilt University Press, 1974). See also Oskar Lange, *Political Economy,* vol. 2 (1971).

4. Branko Horvat, *Toward a Theory of Planned Economy* (Belgrade, 1964).

5. A brief appraisal occurs in my "Marxism-Horvatism, a Yugoslav Theory of Socialism," *American Economic Review* 58 (June 1968).

6. This issue is discussed in the chapters by Sydney Jammes and Robert Dernberger in U.S. Congress, Joint Economic Committee, *China: A Reassessment of the Economy* (Washington, D.C.: U.S. Government Printing Office, 1975).

7. On Arthur Ashbrook's estimates (*Reassessment,* p. 25), China's foreign trade ratio has varied from roughly 2% to 5% during the years 1949–1973. Multiyear averages for the Soviet Union, 1928–1937 to 1955–1958, range from 3% to 6.5%, according to Simon Kuznets, "A Comparative Appraisal" in Simon Kuznets and Abram Bergson, eds., *Economic Trends in the Soviet Union* (Cambridge, Mass.: Harvard University Press, 1963), p. 365.

8. Part 5 of *China: A Reassessment* contains descriptions of various aspects of trade organization in China. As David Denny and Daniel Stein, "Recent Developments in Trade between the US and the PRC: A Legal and Economic Perspective," *Law and Contemporary Problems* 37 (Summer 1973): 260–273, point out, the restrictions are by no means all on the Chinese side.

9. Soviet trade organization and problems are surveyed in part 7 of the Joint Economic Committee Print, *Soviet Economic Prospects for the Seventies* (Washington, D.C., 1973). Some interesting comparative comments can be found in Alan Brown and Egon Neuberger, eds.,

International Trade and Central Planning (Berkeley: University of California Press, 1968), and in Peter Wiles, *Communist International Economics* (New York: Praeger, 1969).

10. Such as the acceptance of medium-term loans and of groups of foreign technicians in residence to set up turnkey plants.

11. An interesting discussion of autarky issues occurs in Wiles, *Communist International Economics,* chap. 15.

12. The 1957–58 reforms are described in Audrey Donnithorne, *China's Economic System* (London: Allen and Unwin, 1967), pp. 460–467, and in Dwight Perkins, *Market Control and Planning in Communist China* (Cambridge, Mass.: Harvard University Press, 1966), chaps. 5–6. One important difference between China and Eastern Europe, including the Soviet Union, today is the diversion of accounting profits to the state budget in China. This practice is not unknown in Soviet-type economies. It was used in several East European countries in the forties, including Yugoslavia, and de facto in the Soviet Union during World War II. Thus it is associated with highly centralized operations, whether because of inexperienced cadres or because of a volatile and primitive environment. Robinson and others have suggested that a different orientation among the Chinese makes such a scheme usable with more decentralized decision making, which is certainly conceivable, but this is not the only plausible interpretation. See also note 37.

13. See for example John Hardt et al., eds., *Mathematics and Computers in Soviet Economic Planning* (New Haven, Conn.: Yale University Press, 1967), especially the introduction by Herbert Levine, and chapter 1 by Richard Judy.

14. As argued by Nicholas Lardy, "Economic Planning in the PRC: Central-Provincial Fiscal Relations," *China: A Reassessment,* pp. 94–115.

15. Mao Tse-tung in the Wan Sui commentary on Soviet political economy: "We are developing a large number of medium and small sized enterprises under the guide of big enterprises and adopting extensively indigenous methods under the guide of foreign methods mainly for the sake of achieving a high rate of industrialization." "Miscellany of Mao Tse-Tung Thought," mimeographed (Washington, D.C., 1974), pt. II, p. 261). This was perhaps written in 1961. Of course this is not to suggest that Mao had no other goals, even during the Great Leap. Earlier in the same document we find: "The important element is the remolding of the people"; and, "Simultaneously with the development of productive forces, we must continue to carry out the transformation of relations of production and ideological remolding" (p. 259).

16. Such as the recent agreement to purchase a number of large

fertilizer plants. Estimates of outputs in the affected industries show simultaneous growth in large and small plants. See for example the CIA report, "China: Role of Small Plants in Economic Development" (Washington, D.C., 1974).

17. Individual reports on villages, such as Jan Myrdal, *Report from a Chinese Village* (New York: Pantheon, 1965), and Jack Chen, *A Year in Upper Felicity* (New York: Macmillan, 1973), portray the cadres as quite well integrated in the life of the brigade. Frederick Crook, "The Commune System in the PRC 1963–74," in *China: A Reassessment,* indicates the national availability of sufficient Party members to universalize this degree of penetration.

18. Maurice Dobb, *Soviet Economic Development since 1917,* rev. ed. (New York: International, 1966), describes the prewar incentive system's variations. See also Emily Brown, *Soviet Trade Unions and Labor Relations* (Cambridge, Mass.: Harvard University Press, 1966).

19. Leonard Joel Kirsch, *Soviet Wages* (Cambridge, Mass.: MIT Press, 1972); on recent Soviet developments and their significance see Janet Chapman's extremely useful "Soviet Wages under Socialism," mimeographed (University of Pittsburgh, 1974).

20. Christopher Howe, *Wage Patterns and Wage Policy in Modern China, 1919–1972* (Cambridge: University Press, 1973); Carl Riskin, "Mao and Motivation," mimeographed (Columbia University, 1972); Richard Baum, "Diabolus Ex Machina: Technological Development and Social Change in Chinese Industry," in Frederic J. Fleron, Jr., ed., *Technology and Communist China* (New York: Praeger, 1977).

21. Riskin, "Mao and Motivation."

22. Once again Riskin has some interesting comparative remarks on this subject. See also his essay in *China: A Reassessment.*

23. Introduction: "The Persistence of the Past" in *China's Modern Economy,* pp. 3–12.

24. These remarks are based mostly on personal recollections.

25. Keith Griffin, *Political Economy of Agrarian Change* (Cambridge, Mass.: Harvard University Press, 1974) offers a useful comparison of collectivization with other agrarian strategies. Some comparative accounts of agriculture in Soviet-type economies can be found in George Karcz, ed., *Soviet and East European Agriculture* (Berkeley: University of California Press, 1967).

26. For example, D. Gale Johnson's study of early plan era agricultural productivity in the Soviet Union (chapter 5 of Bergson and Kuznets, *Economic Trends,* p. 218) shows that outputs increased less rapidly than inputs between 1928 and 1938. During the fifties they increased around 20%–30% more rapidly than inputs. He also notes (pp. 225–

226) that Soviet grain yields in areas of comparable conditions in the two countries were 57% to 78% of U.S. yields for the first postwar decade but that yields in the late fifties in the Soviet Union "are at a reasonable level."

27. In the sense that collectivization was a far less violent disruptive process in these economies than it was in the Soviet Union. However, the collectivized regimes have not generated rapid increases in agricultural output. According to the recalculation of official data by Thad Alton and Associates, "Statistics on East European Economic Structure and Growth," Occasional Paper No. 48, mimeographed (1975), pp. 52–57, and Joint Economic Committee Print, *Economic Developments of Countries of Eastern Europe* (Washington, D.C., 1970), pp. 49–50, GNP generated in agriculture and forestry increased on the average by about one-third in the nineteen years from 1955 to 1974. Both Yugoslavia and Poland performed noticeably better during this period. (Official statistics show a more rapid rate of growth.)

28. See Griffin, *Political Economy of Agrarian Change,* and Bruce Johnston and Peter Kilby, *Agriculture and Structural Transformation* (New York: Oxford, 1975) for similar perspectives on the problems but different perspectives on appropriate policies for dealing with the peasant problem in developing countries.

29. On recent agricultural organization in China see Crook, "The Commune System in the PRC," and James Nickum, "A Collective Approach to Water Resource Development," (Ph.D. thesis, University of California, Berkeley, 1974). Chen's *Year in Upper Felicity* is also useful.

30. Alexander Dallin, *German Rule in Russia, 1941–45* (New York: St. Martins, 1957).

31. On Poland see Andrew Korbonski's article in Karcz, *Soviet and East European Agriculture;* on Yugoslavia see my account in Irma Adelman and Adam Pepelasis, eds., *Economic Development* (New York: Harper, 1961).

32. Bernice Madison, "Soviet Income Maintenance Programs for the 1970s," mimeographed, (San Francisco State University, 1972?).

33. For the history of Soviet party structure and organization see T. H. Rigby, *Communist Party Membership in the USSR, 1917–1967* (Princeton, N.J.: Princeton University Press, 1968).

34. Thomas Greene, *Comparative Revolutionary Movements* (Englewood Cliffs, N.J.: Prentice-Hall, 1974) surveys conventional liberal attitudes and research.

35. Two useful and complementary accounts of the early plan era are Dobb, *Soviet Economic Development since 1917,* and Alex Nove, *An Economic History of the Soviet Union* (London: Allen Lane, 1969).

36. Branko Horvat, "Yugoslav Economic Policy," *American Economic Review,* supplement, 61 (June 1971); Hugh Thomas, *Cuba:* The Pursuit of Freedom, 1762–1969 (New York: Harper and Row, 1971).

37. Taut planning is a sort of institutionalized campaigning, in which each year a production unit is expected in the plan targets to exert special efforts to uncover and exploit hidden reserves. The Chinese approach may be more efficient than its European counterpart—namely, the separation of the struggle for unexpected bonuses from the process of planning, by enhancing the forecasting power of the plan and by focusing energies more precisely.

38. See Benjamin Ward, *Socialist Economy* (New York: Random House, 1967), chaps. 5–6.

39. Jack Gray in his "The Two Roads: Alternative Strategies of Social Change in Economic Growth in China," in Stuart Schram, ed., *Authority Participation and Cultural Change in China* (Cambridge: University Press, 1973) presents a relatively strong version of the "two roads" interpretation of the Cultural Revolution as essentially a "conflict as to whether socialism should be based on popular power or on paternalistic administration" (p. 157). But to the extent that growth and socialism are compatible goals, the intensity of this "essential" contradiction is likely to be muted. The strong absolute and relative performance of the Chinese economy over a period that includes both the Great Leap aftermath and the Cultural Revolution (and that seems to have moved the economy up toward the mid range of the "mid-fifties main line") suggests that further pressures in the direction of socialist values can reasonably be expected to possess such compatibility.

40. An interesting case for this similarity in work lives as a product of the technological imperative is made by Baum, "Diabolus Ex Machina." The roles of consumer durables and of mobility in nonwork lives suggest the basis for distinguishing nonwork lives in this way.

41. Gregory Grossman informs me that discussions with recent emigré economists from the Soviet Union suggest that informal trading plays a substantially larger role there than had been previously believed by Western students. See also Dimitri Simes, "The Soviet Parallel Market," *Survey* (Summer 1975).

42. Oskar Lange's version was: "Beware the market, it is capitalism's secret weapon." In a recent exchange, Charles Bettelheim and Paul Sweezy, leading Marxist economists in France and the United States respectively, seem prepared to accept the market as an institution for the relatively long period of transition to socialism (after the seizure of political power by socialists). But they do not really appraise the central issue, namely, its compatibility with the emergence and de-

velopment of noncommercial values in economic behavior. See their *On the Transition to Socialism* (New York: Monthly Review, 1972).

43. These issues are discussed in Frank Parkin, *Class, Inequality and Political Order* (New York: Praeger, 1971).

44. I think it was M. M. Postan who pointed out that historians have been explaining European events since the twelfth century in terms of the rise of the middle class. The problem is that there is not really much of a theory that associates the "amount" of "rise" with the phenomena to be explained.

4

The Central Features of China's Economic Development

DWIGHT H. PERKINS

General appraisals of China's economic development experience usually begin with the quantitative record. An attempt is made to assess China's performance in terms of gross national product, industrial output, and some measure of income distribution and then to contrast that performance with similar data for another country. Depending on the data used and the nation chosen for comparison, China is then declared to have done well, fair, or rather poorly. India is the country usually chosen for such comparisons, but others are used as well. Over a decade ago, it was thought that the future of democracy in Asia, if not the entire less developed world, hung on the results of these comparisons. Since then it has become apparent that the present and future of democracy in the less developed world is indeed grim, but China's comparative growth performance appears to have had little to do with the creeping authoritarianism apparent in so many poor nations.

There is value in knowing that one nation's GNP grew at an average rate of 5% a year while that of another was rising at 3%. If the differences are due to real factors and not distorted price structures, it follows that the 5% country is leaving the ranks of the poor faster than the 3% country. But one learns little about why one nation is doing better than the other from one gross comparison. Finding out why one underdeveloped country moves ahead faster than another is necessary if one is to talk meaningfully of lessons to be drawn from the more (or less) successful nation's experience.

In attempting to explain the reasons for the special features of China's economic development, it is not very helpful to begin with the notion—and it is a standard one—that China's ability to carry out certain programs is the result of the leadership's ability to arouse the enthusiasm of the masses. The explanation may well be a valid one, and the Chinese may know what they are talking about; but the outsider, whether visiting China or writing in the comfort of his office 10,000 miles away, is in no position to measure the "enthusiasm" of the Chinese people.

The outsider must instead turn to explanations that, even if not the whole story, can show with some causal and provable detail why the Chinese have been able to accomplish certain changes. Three broad categories of reasons help explain why China has accomplished what it has. First, the Chinese Communist Revolution was fought in the name of and to a large extent by the poor. Revolutions, of course, have been fought in the name of many causes only to see the causes betrayed when the revolution succeeded. But in China a number of concrete steps were taken, particularly in rural areas, to ensure that the interests of the poor majority would dominate decision making in certain key areas. In most nations, in contrast, it is the rich or the more educated and organized "middle class" that dominates decision making, and it is reasonable to presume that giving the poor a major share of power would make a difference. In fact, several key features of the Chinese experience, in rural areas at least, can be understood only in these terms.

To say that the Chinese put the poor in command does not imply that all organizations in China were run by people of poor peasant origins. The key point is that cooperatives and communes were run by such people. The Politburo and other centers of power, in contrast, were manned by people of diverse origins. Even these higher-level power centers, however, saw the former poor as the main base of their political support.

Second, China has a particular authoritarian political system. Just being authoritarian does not distinguish China's politics from that of a few other less developed countries. But China is an authoritarian nation with a difference. The degree of political control over daily activities in China, whether economic or social, is far more thoroughgoing than in all but a handful of other less developed nations. The economic aspects of this phenomenon show how development is affected. China has been able to institute a system of centralized planning more complete than that in any other less developed nation except possibly North Korea. It is not that other nations have no interest in instituting a similar system; but most know that if they tried, they would bring their economies grinding to a halt. The Chinese economy has slowed down, but it has not ground to a halt, and it is worth attempting to understand why. Part of the reason, it appears, is that

China's people had acquired enough experience to make the new system work. They acquired this experience over decades and even centuries; it was not an instantaneous addition in 1949.

Third, like all nations, China has its own peculiar resource and factor endowment. Much of this endowment is a reflection of China's great size in land mass and people. Equally important is that crops can be grown on only a small proportion of China's surface. China, in a very fundamental way, is a land-short nation.

Elements other than these three, of course, have also played some role in shaping China's economic development. Marxist-Leninist ideology is an important example. But the term "putting the poor in command" covers some of the essential ground of that ideology and does so with a simple clarity that cannot be achieved by reference to the many works of Marx and Lenin, not to mention Mao Tse-tung.

There are many features of China's economy that distinguish that economy from others, but several stand out. To begin with, China's economy is socialist to a degree not found in many other nations in the less developed or non-Communist world. Private ownership is confined in the main to personal household effects, much rural housing (and a little urban housing), individual savings deposits, and the right to farm small private plots equivalent to about 5% to 7% of the total arable land. The land in these private plots is not privately owned; only the rights to farm some small piece of land can be said to be private.

Industry, even a firm with only a few workers, is owned by the state or collectively by rural communes and brigades. Much the same is true of commerce, banking, and transport. There are small private rural markets where farmers sometimes trade the produce of their private plots, and individuals may contract to do repairs on private homes in their spare time. But these activities are a tiny fraction of the total spectrum of industry and commerce in China. In agriculture the private sector is larger than in industry because it has so far proved impossible efficiently to collectivize much vegetable and hog raising, household handicrafts, and the like. Still, three-quarters or more of farm output is handled collectively.

Ownership is only one determinant of the degree of state control over the economy. Socialist economies can be run in a variety of ways, some relying extensively on decentralized decision making controlled by impersonal market forces, others on central plans expressed mainly in physical terms and backed by the force of law rather than the force of the market. Yugoslavia makes extensive use of the former techniques and the Soviet Union the latter. China is closest to the Soviet end of the spectrum but with significant differences.

Only a relatively small proportion of Chinese industry is controlled solely by central planners in Peking. Even large modern plants producing precision products for national markets are placed formally under provincial and city planning authorities or under joint province-central control. Smaller plants and those producing for more localized markets are placed under planning authorities at the district and county level. But one must be careful not to exaggerate the degree of decentralization achieved by these measures. The average province in China contains roughly 40 million people and tens of thousands of firms producing an average of around 15 to 20 billion yuan of gross industrial product. The task of the provincial planner, therefore, remains a formidable one.

The one industrial sector that appears to have achieved a high degree of decentralization is the rural small-scale industry program designed to serve agriculture. These enterprises, for the most part, are under county planners or communes, and the county appears to have a considerable control over their destiny, even to the extent of influencing whether these firms will be allowed to expand plant capacity. Investment in new plant capacity tends to be much more centralized at all levels than is control over daily operations, and this is true in the small-scale industry sector as well. Still, county planners have a great deal of influence over the decision to build and expand factories of the type designated to be in the small-scale category.

At all levels, county, province, and center, planner control is exercised directly and not through manipulation of the market. Each enterprise receives a series of targets (gross value output, cost, employment, profits, and so forth) from the planners at their level. The process involves three stages and negotiation between planners and enterprise managers. Initially the planners propose broad targets, and the factory replies with what it thinks it can do to meet these targets. The center (or province or county) then attempts to achieve consistency between what each enterprise can do and sends the final targets back to the enterprise. The enterprise is then expected to guide its actions to surpass those targets.

There is now a considerable body of literature on how a planning system of this nature works at both a theoretical and a practical level. In a word, it is complex. Making the system work at all involves the efforts of hundreds of thousands of people trained in planning, accounting, and statistical reporting. To coordinate the activities of so many enterprises, enormous amounts of information must flow both ways. Even if everyone at each level were completely selfless and passed on all relevant information whether or not it served his immediate interests, the task of obtaining accurate and timely information would be a formidable one. In practice, attempts are made to manipulate these flows of data for all kinds of purposes other than those required by the planning process itself. Skilled planners, therefore, must erect elaborate defenses against distortions of this kind.

Many nations rich and poor draw up formal plans, but these plans have a limited purpose. At most they have some influence over the public investment program, particularly the part that involves external assistance. At the least these plans deserve the name coined for Japanese five-year plans, "decorative." Almost never do formal plans outside Communist countries have much influence on the month-to-month operations of individual enterprises except in a very indirect way through general monetary and fiscal controls. In China, however, these plans are the principal means of controlling current enterprise operations. There is really no alternative. No market forces exist to govern the direction of factory production. Without effective implementation of central plans, as in fact occurred during the Great Leap Forward of 1958–1960, the result is chaos.

Agriculture is not subject to as rigorous control by plans as industry. Plans exist, of course, and they influence which crops are planted where. But the degree of control is much looser than in industry, and plans are often backed by general controls such as price manipulation rather than physical targets enforceable by law. Because agricultural production teams are cooperatives whose members divide their net income among themselves, prices have a significant influence on decisions. Planning in agriculture, as a result, is much less complex than that in industry.

A second key feature of China's economic development is that its highly complex system works reasonably well. We do not yet have enough data to say whether China's economic system is more or less efficient than that of, say, India, Japan, or the Soviet Union.[1] But we know that China's economy has grown and that the most complicated sector in both engineering and planning terms, namely the modern producer goods industry, has grown much more rapidly than the other sectors.

Estimates of Chinese GDP, the shares of agriculture, manufacturing, and services and growth rates are presented in tables 4–1 to 4–3. Different assumptions would lead to slightly different results; but all the data in these tables (except services) were derived from official Chinese publications or releases, and there is an increasing degree of consensus among people working on the Chinese economy that the official data, if used with care, are the best available.

Several distinguishing features of China's economy are immediately apparent from the estimates in tables 4–1 to 4–3. First, China's gross domestic product has grown at a rate of about 6% a year for over two decades. Different estimation procedures might bring this

TABLE 4–1   China's gross domestic product, selected years (in billions of 1957 yuan)

Year	Industrial value added (M+)	Agricultural value added (A)	Services (S)	GDP
1952	20.79	35.59	17.47	73.85
1957	38.16	44.72	21.80	104.68
1962	50.15	35.30	22.84	108.29
1965	72.60	49.10	28.94	150.64
1970	106.79	59.96	37.15	203.90
1974	152.80	67.09	46.35	266.24

Note: The estimates in tables 4–1 to 4–3 were derived mainly from official Chinese statements concerning the level of gross value output in industry and agriculture. There is some official data with which to estimate the service sector, but huge gaps have to be filled by assumption. Thus the service sector estimate is subject to a wider margin of potential error than the others. The estimates in these tables differ somewhat from my earlier estimates because of the addition of an explicit estimate of depreciation and the inclusion of a separately estimated series for construction in the industrial value added (M+) series and because of a correction of a computational error made in converting 1952 agricultural output into 1957 prices. Transportation is also in M+, not services. For a further discussion of these estimates, see D. H. Perkins, "Issues in the Estimation of China's National Product," Harvard Institute of Economic Research, Discussion Paper No. 471, to be published in Alexander Eckstein, ed., *Quantitative Measures of China's Economic Output* (Ann Arbor, Mich.: University of Michigan, forthcoming).

rate down to 5%, but in either case the rate is well above the percentage increase in China's population, which is about 2% and falling. Not many nations have done as well for such a sustained period. A number have grown at faster rates in recent years, but only a few have matched China's longevity. Others have grown rapidly for a time and then have faced a prolonged period of political instability and economic depression (Pakistan is only one of many examples). China's growth has not been steady and there have been periods of economic decline, notably in 1960–61 and 1967–68, but China's economy has

TABLE 4–2   Sectoral shares in GDP

Year	Industry (M+)	Agriculture (A)	Services (S)	GDP
1952	.282	.482	.237	1.000
1957	.365	.427	.208	1.000
1962	.463	.326	.211	1.000
1965	.482	.326	.192	1.000
1970	.524	.294	.182	1.000
1974	.574	.252	.174	1.000

Note: See note to table 4–1.

TABLE 4–3 Chinese growth rates, in 1957 prices (in percentages)

Period	Industry	Agriculture	GDP
1952–1957	12.9	4.7	7.2
1957–1965	8.4	1.2	4.7
1965–1970	8.0	4.1	6.2
1970–1974	9.4	2.8	6.9
1952–1974	9.5	3.4	6.2
1957–1974	8.5	2.4	5.6

Note: See note to table 4–1.

always bounced back into a renewed period of growth. China's GDP, as a result, has risen to nearly four times the level of 1952 when the post-1949 development effort began. Per capita GDP has more than doubled.

Another aspect of this development in China has been the degree to which growth has been concentrated in the industrial sector. The share of industry (and transport) has risen steadily from about a quarter of GDP to over half. Agriculture, in contrast, has managed to stay only a bit ahead of population growth, and its share has declined steadily as a result. In the course of economic growth the share of industry always rises and that of agriculture falls, but the pace at which these changes have occurred in China is more pronounced than in most other developing nations.[2] Within industry, the producer goods sector has grown more rapidly than the consumer goods sector.[3] Machine building, in particular, has increased at a very rapid rate.

A third distinguishing characteristic of Chinese development has been the ability of the nation to mobilize fully its resources for growth. The rising share of the producer goods sector is one aspect of this phenomenon. As national product has increased, China has succeeded in holding the rise in personal consumption to modest levels. Government consumption, mainly in the form of military expenditures necessitated by the 1960 break with the Soviet Union, rose sharply in the 1960s; despite this rise there is little doubt that China's investment rate (gross domestic capital formation as a precentage of GDP) has increased to a very high level. Precise estimates are not available, but indirect methods of estimation indicate that China's current rate of gross domestic capital formation has reached or passed 25% of GDP and is still rising.[4]

Even more dramatic has been China's ability to mobilize its labor force for development. Although there is a continuing debate in the economics literature whether "surplus labor" exists anywhere in the world, few would dispute that the adult population of most less developed nations is not fully employed throughout the year. Within most cities in the less developed world there are large numbers of overtly unemployed. In rural areas unemployment is disguised and seasonal, but extensive.

In China, in contrast, both urban and rural populations are hard at work throughout the entire year. Much of this activity is in occupations of very low productivity. Peasants carrying dirt from a nearby mountainside to build a dam or a small addition to the cultivated acreage are doing back-breaking labor in exchange for often only modest increases in farm output. Many rural people, one suspects, would choose leisure time if they were free to do so. Whether voluntarily or not, China has succeeded in mobilizing billions of man-days of labor from a labor pool that in most less developed nations would have remained idle.

China has also fully mobilized its agricultural land resources. There is no area in China comparable to parts of Latin America where land that could be used to grow crops is slated for low productivity activities such as grazing. The preferences of large landowners dominate decision making. In China there is virtually no fallow land or forestland that can be converted into cropland without large additional capital expenditures. All new land development, of course, requires some capital outlay, but in large parts of the developing world what is involved is clearing the land, building access roads, housing, schools, and so forth. In China these measures alone would be insufficient to open any significant amount of new land to cultivation. China's unutilized land is high on the mountainsides, in areas where there is no ready source of water, or in places where there are other natural barriers to turning it into good farmland.

A fourth characteristic of Chinese economic development, the one that currently receives the most attention, is the Chinese effort to narrow the inequalities in income in both urban and rural areas. Great attention, however, has not led to much effort to measure the degree of inequality that exists in China today. The one major work on the subject, on rural incomes only, is that of C. Robert Roll. His estimates, presented in table 4–4, reveal that the land reform of the early 1950s during which landlordism was effectively eliminated from rural China led to a substantial redistribution of income. The incomes of the top 20% of the population were reduced by nearly one-fifth, and those of the bottom 40% were raised by roughly 50%.[5]

The redistribution of Chinese income did not stop in 1952, but was given another boost in the cooperative movement of 1955–56. At that time all the peasants in a given co-op (which was frequently coterminus

TABLE 4–4   Changes in the distribution of rural income, 1930s to 1952

	Farm income			Total income		
	Percentage share		Change	Percentage share		Change
Income category	1930s	1952	in share	1930s	1952	in share
Top 10%	26.0	21.6	−4.4	24.4	21.6	−2.8
Top 20%	42.7	35.1	−7.6	42.0	35.0	−7.0
2nd 20%	23.8	21.3	−2.5	23.9	21.3	−2.6
3rd 20%	16.3	17.5	+1.2	14.9	17.4	+2.5
4th 20%	11.4	14.8	+3.4	13.2	15.0	+1.8
Bottom 20%	5.8	11.3	+5.5	6.0	11.3	+5.3
Bottom 10%	1.8	5.1	+3.3	2.5	5.1	+2.6

Source: C. Robert Roll, "The Distribution of Rural Income in China: A Comparison of the 1930's and the 1950's" (Doctoral dissertation, Harvard University, 1974), p. 76.

with a village) pooled their land, thus eliminating income inequalities due to differences in the size and quality of individual landholdings within the cooperative. In 1958–59 cooperatives were pooled into communes, thereby temporarily eliminating inequality caused by differences in landholdings between cooperatives within a single commune. The transfer down to the production team as the basic accounting unit, however, brought the situation back to that of 1957. In fact, the average production team today is much smaller than the old cooperative, but significant amounts of income are generated at the brigade and commune level as well.

There are two other major sources of inequality in rural areas. Income within the team is determined by the number of work points earned by family members; thus a family with more and better workers has a higher income. Far more important sources of inequality are the remaining differences between teams in the amount and the quality of their land. Land quality, of course, is determined not only by the properties of the soil but also by proximity to roads, electricity, urban markets, and the like.

How large are these remaining sources of inequality, and have they been reduced over the years? Unfortunately, only speculation is possible because no serious quantitative study of the subject has yet been made. As Roll demonstrates, there is little doubt that remaining between-region differences in income are substantial. If counties are grouped by average income per capita, the richest of six selected counties in 1952–53 had an average per capita income six times that of the poorest group.[6] Six times is less than the thirteenfold differential between rich peasants in the richest region and poor peasants in the poorest region, but it is still substantial. Cooperatives and communes eliminated the rich peasant–poor peasant differences but not the regional disparities. The latter could be abolished only through progressive taxes, by moving prople from poor to rich areas, or by directing state investment toward the poorer regions. The Chinese have never considered moving people to achieve greater equality, and there is little progressivity in the tax structure.

It is not altogether clear what rural investment policy has been. The Chinese emphasis on self-reliance seems to preclude large transfers of funds into poorer regions. Productivity considerations would lead investment planners to direct funds to areas where the gains will be greatest, and it is unlikely that the larger potential gains are on the average in the poorer regions. Chemical fertilizer, for example, is most effective when used on irrigated land, and irrigated land is not poor land.

In summary, there were large redistributions of rural income in the early 1950s through land reform and in 1955–56 through collectivization. Since then some areas have made major advances in output while others have lagged behind, but there is little evidence to suggest that this process has led to greater equality. Further research, however, could alter this conclusion.

The situation in urban areas is somewhat similar. A major redistribution of income and assets took place in the 1950s through the socialization of industry and commerce and the elimination of most property incomes. The closed nature of Chinese society, notably the lack of free emigration, meant that China could keep highly skilled personnel (other than those who had already fled) without paying salaries competitive with those in the West. The eight-grade wage system determined the incomes of most workers and employees. The eight-grade system was similar throughout the country and between regions except for minor variations due to cost of living differentials, hardship allowances, and the like.

There have been few changes in the nature of this system since 1956. The roughly three-to-one differential between grades 1 and 8 has been altered little if at all. Greater worker equality since 1956, therefore, could only have come about through promotions that significantly changed the distribution of workers in the grades, but we know next to nothing about any such changes. There has also been some rise in the free services provided to the workers (health, housing, and so forth), and these tend to be provided on the basis of need.

Technicians and cadres are paid according to scales other than the eight-grade system. Such wages can reach levels ten times that of the bottom of the eight-grade system. There is some evidence of creeping equality in these incomes, however. The wages of older technicians are not being lowered, but as they retire, they are replaced by younger people who are paid much lower salaries. If this process continues, one suspects that within a decade or two few people will be earning more than twice the top of the eight-grade system.

Finally, there is the difference in income between urban and rural areas. Work by Roll, however, suggests that this differential may not have been very great in the 1950s when allowance is made for differences in the cost of living. Whatever the precise magnitude of the disparity, rising farm purchase prices have contributed to an increase in average rural incomes while average wages have changed little. The greater provision of urban services, on the other hand, may tend to widen the gap, although recent efforts to promote rural health work in the opposite direction.

The fifth and final distinguishing characteristic of Chinese economic development to be discussed here is the Chinese effort to minimize the nation's dependence on external assistance and foreign trade. China's limited dependence on external financial assistance is the easiest to document. Estimates of China's balance of trade are presented in table 4–5. The balance of trade is an imperfect guide to capital flows into and out of a country, but in China's case a considerable body of additional information supports the view that China's balance of trade reflects in a rough way the direction and magnitude of Chinese external capital movements. The deficits of the early 1950s totaling over U.S. $1 billion were made possible by Soviet credits. After 1955 Soviet credits, particularly those of a long-term nature, dwindled to next to nothing. With the Sino-Soviet break in 1960, China began a major effort to repay these outstanding loans and had completed the process by 1965. Since then and until recently, China continued to maintain a balance-of-trade surplus. This surplus presumably provided in part for China's own foreign aid program in Africa and other parts of the Third World.

Beginning modestly in 1973 and in a major way in 1974, China borrowed abroad on an intermediate-term basis (up to five years) to finance a rapid expansion in imports of new plants in chemicals, steel, and other key sectors. Up to the mid 1970s it is fair to say that China depended on foreign financial aid on either concessionary or commercial terms to a lesser degree than any other less developed country that has achieved a sustained period of economic growth. Nations such as Burma may also have eschewed foreign assistance for long periods, but they have failed to grow as well. In per capita terms, aid

TABLE 4–5   China's foreign trade, 1950–1974 (in millions of U.S. dollars)

Year	Exports	Imports	Trade balance
1950	620	590	30
1951	780	1,120	−340
1952	875	1,015	−140
1953	1,040	1,255	−215
1954	1,060	1,290	−230
1955	1,375	1,660	−285
1956	1,635	1,485	150
1957	1,615	1,440	175
1958	1,940	1,825	115
1959	2,230	2,060	170
1960	1,960	2,030	−70
1961	1,525	1,490	35
1962	1,525	1,150	375
1963	1,570	1,200	370
1964	1,750	1,470	280
1965	2,035	1,845	190
1966	2,210	2,035	175
1967	1,945	1,950	−5
1968	1,945	1,820	125
1969	2,030	1,830	200
1970	2,050	2,240	−190
1971	2,415	2,305	110
1972	3,085	2,835	250
1973	4,895	4,975	−80
1974[a]	6,515	7,490	−975

Source: Nai-Ruenn Chen, "China's Foreign Trade, 1950–74," *China: A Reassessment of the Economy* (Washington, D.C.: U.S. Congress, Joint Economic Committee, 1975), p. 645. Trade balance figures were obtained by subtraction. The 1974 figure is from CIA, *People's Republic of China: International Handbook* (Washington, D.C., 1975), p. 9.

a. Preliminary.

to China never passed $2 in total and averaged under $0.50 a year throughout the early 1950s and zero thereafter.

An analysis of the degree of China's dependence on foreign trade is far more complex than an appraisal of the role of external financial assistance. The appropriate methodology would involve estimating China's GNP in the absence of foreign trade or some substantial part of that trade. Data limitations make such an analysis impossible. One is left, therefore, with the task of attempting to judge whether China's ratio of foreign trade to GNP is unusually low and whether Chinese imports appear to consist of items essential to the proper functioning of the economy. Even these inadequate measures can be dealt with only superficially here.

Estimating China's ratio of foreign trade (exports plus imports) to GDP is difficult because the Chinese trade data available outside China are calculated in U.S. dollars while Chinese GDP figures are in yuan. Either the former must be converted into yuan or the latter into dollars, but at what exchange rate? At the official 1974 exchange rate which floated around 1.95 yuan to the dollar, the 1974 trade ratio was 11%. Similar procedures for 1970 lead to an estimate for that year of only 6%. But it is unclear whether the higher percentage in 1974 reflects a real increase in the share of trade or simply a rise in the prices of traded goods that was more rapid than the revaluation of the yuan relative to the dollar.[7] Until an updated purchasing power parity comparison is made, we shall have to defer judgment. For purposes of this analysis a ratio of 10% is used as indicative of China's "typical" trade level.

Is 10% high or low? One of the basic findings of Simon Kuznets is that the foreign trade ratio tends to decline with the size of the country as measured by population increases. Ratios for other countries are presented in table 4–6. The question is, With which country should China be compared? There are no countries with populations as large as China's and the next three largest have ratios both above and below that of China. One could run a regression line through the

TABLE 4–6 Foreign trade ratios

Country	Population (millions)	Years	Ratio
Small average	1.9	1950–1954	.41
Large average	103.9	1950–1954	.21
United Kingdom	51.8	1953–1959	.32
Japan	91.5	1953–1959	.19
United States	174.9	1953–1959	.07
USSR	218.0	1953–1959	.06
India	413.3	1953–1959	.14
China	650	1953–1959	.10

Source: For China, see text. For other nations, Simon Kuznets, "A Comparative Appraisal," in Abram Bergson and Simon Kuznets, eds., *Economic Trends in the Soviet Union* (Cambridge, Mass.: Harvard University Press, 1963), p. 366. Population data are either from the same source or from United Nations yearbooks. The population estimates are for the year 1958 for all individual countries in the table except for the USSR, which is for 1961.

data for nations other than China and project it out to the 650 (or 800) million population point, but it is not clear what such an exercise would accomplish. All one can say is that China's foreign trade ratio is low, but not necessarily lower than what one would expect for a country the size of China that was not pursuing autarkic policies.

Have the commodities imported by China played a key role in China's economic development? Here the answer is a clear yes. From the beginning the People's Republic has cut all nonessentials from its import bill. In the 1950s over 90% of all imports were producer goods, and these provided much of the key equipment for the first and second five-year plans. In the 1960s the share of grain in imports rose to significant levels, but the purpose of these imports was to relieve pressure on and hence encourage the grain surplus areas to produce. In the 1970s, with the accelerated investment program in industry, there has been a renewed surge of complete plant imports.

There is no question that China in 1976 is far less dependent on imported producer goods than it was in the 1950s. China's machine-building capacity now provides most domestic requirements, whereas in the early 1950s virtually all machinery had to be imported. Yet it is equally clear that where certain types of advanced technology are involved (petro-chemicals, and so forth) China must still import to expand capacity. In many respects, therefore, China's current dependence on imports is more like that of nations with much higher per capita incomes than the "typical" less developed country. By rapidly expanding its producer goods sector, China can now continue to expand in many directions with domestic equipment. Few if any other nations with per capita incomes below $300 (or $1000) can make that statement. On the other hand, China is far more dependent on imports of high technology than the industrially most advanced nations: the United States, the Soviet Union, Japan, West Germany.

Thus it is incorrect to say that China's economic development has proceeded solely on the basis of China's own efforts. It is right to say that China has provided a far higher proportion of its own development investments (in both financial and physical terms) than most other less developed nations in the world today.

Putting the Poor in Command

The main features of economic development in the People's Republic of China reveal a program distinct from that followed by other less developed countries and in many important ways more successful than most. The remaining task is to attempt to explain the sources of both that distinctiveness and its comparative success. China's Communist revolution was built on peasants, but not every peasant was a revolutionary. The rural enemy of the revolution, the landlord, was readily identifiable, but the hard-core supporters of the revolution were not so easily identified. China's rural scene included, in addition to landlords, prosperous farmers tilling all the land they could handle, others who were neither prosperous nor poor, and millions more who tilled inadequate amounts of rented land or worked as laborers on the land of their neighbors. Most of these people had grievances against the Japanese invader, and a great many in all classes resented some aspects of landlordism and stood to gain from its abolition. Support for the Chinese Communist party and the Eighth Route Army in their role as leader of the battle against both landlords and the Japanese, therefore, potentially had a very wide base.

To a degree, the Chinese Communist party sought support from all classes of rural society oher than the declared landlord enemy. During the Yenan period, in particular, an effort was made to include almost all people who were willing to fight the Japanese regardless of their class. But the Party leadership never really veered from the view that their hard-core support lay in the poorest elements of rural society rather than among those who already owned enough land to escape abject poverty. This attitude of the Party was most apparent in the way that the land reform campaign of the late 1940s and early 1950s was carried out.

Once the people of a village were reasonably assured that military or police support for the landlords would not soon reappear, it was not difficult to persuade them to confiscate the landlords' land and redistribute it among themselves. It was difficult, however, to get these people to parcel out the land in a way that tended to equalize incomes within the village. With the elimination of the landlords, village power passed to the next most articulate and politically skilled elements in the village. For the most part these new holders of power were "middle" peasants who already owned some land and were among the more prosperous people of the village. These middle peasants were used to being in control of their own destinies and were experienced in managing their own farms and the relations of those farms with the outside world. Poor tenants and landless laborers, in contrast, were used to a life of dependency, to a master-servant relationship. Survival for the poor often depended on the goodwill of a richer neighbor who hired them to do menial labor or rented them a small piece of land. Hostility, or even indifference, from the landlord could be a threat to life. The poor, therefore, had only limited experience in managing their own affairs and were fearful of what would happen if the revolution failed and the status quo ante was restored.

Consequently, in the early stages of the land reform campaign, much of the redistributed land went to the more prosperous middle peasants because it was they who took charge of redistribution. As a method of building support for the Communists in the war against Japan and the Kuomintang, redistribution of this kind was perfectly adequate. It was not a method, however, that would move China toward the goal of a socialist agriculture—quite the opposite. Providing more land to middle peasants was a way of creating a large body of kulaks, of farmers well above minimum subsistence levels who could go on to build a strong capitalist agriculture. Giving land to the poorest peasants, in contrast, reduced these dangers. Landless laborers and tenants were far better off than before, but their farms were still too small to be viable or to give many of these peasants the resources with which to raise themselves to full membership in a kulak class.

Because of considerations such as these, the Communist party made vigorous and largely successful efforts to ensure that land went mainly to the poor and not to more prosperous villagers. In some cases the redistribution of land had to be redone. In each case great efforts were made to arouse the political consciousness of the poor and to get them actively involved in the reform campaign. By the end of land reform in the early 1950s, poor peasants dominated the organizations that conrolled rural political life.

To a significant degree people of poor peasant origins have continued to dominate rural politics. Over time, of course, the distinction between poor, middle, and rich peasants has become increasingly artificial since such distinctions have little economic meaning within the commune form of organization. The terms, in fact, have come to refer more to a state of mind than to one's class background in a literal sense. Rich peasant and landlord elements are those who work to restore "capitalist" agriculture by producing for profit and the market. Poor peasants are those who look after the interests of all their fellow villagers and the society as a whole. To encourage the development of poor peasant attitudes, massive nationwide education campaigns have periodically swept the countryside. Older poor peasants who remember how they were once exploited are encouraged to "speak bitterness," to tell their stories to the young.

The net result of all these activities is that local power in the countryside remains to an extent with those who were poor in the old society. Where power rests with those too young to know the old society well or who came from a more prosperous group, there is constant education designed to ensure that the ideology of the young will in certain key ways be similar to that of the former poor. Reality, of course, is more complex than this simplified rendition, but the Chinese have made great efforts to create a political power base in the countryside that is dominated by the former poor and not by kulaks or bureaucrats or any other group representing the more prosperous village members. During the crucial transition years of the 1950s these attempts achieved a considerable measure of success.

What difference did rural political dominance by the poor in the transition years of the 1950s make? The formation of cooperatives and later communes would have been difficult if not impossible without it. In the early stages of the cooperative movement voluntary association with cooperatives was stressed. But no one would join voluntarily unless he felt he would gain materially from the association, and for the most part richer peasants were less likely than poorer peasants to perceive gains in joining with others. If richer peasants did cooperate voluntarily with others, it was more than likely to be with other well-off peasants who would bring equivalent resources to the partnership. Thus during this voluntary period cooperatives tended to be collections of poor peasants who had little to lose. Some did well, others did not, but overall the program did not persuade the majority that they had a lot to gain by joining.

In the winter of 1955–56 a considerable degree of coercion was added to the cooperative membership drive. Technically, individuals could still join voluntarily, but cadres were allowed much more vigorous forms of "persuasion." Ample stress was laid on the fact that having most people in coops would leave little labor for hire by richer peasants. In the lower-level type of cooperative being formed, payment was to be on the basis of the amount of land as well as the amount of labor contributed to the coop. Much publicity was given to the immediate spurt in output that cooperatives would lead to, so that if all farmers in the nation joined, 90% would experience a higher standard of living within the first year or two of the movement. By the spring of 1956 virtually everyone in the Chinese countryside was in a cooperative.

Despite the reputed advantages of joining a coop and the disabilities that would ensue from failure to join, it is unlikely that many of the richer farmers joined voluntarily except in the sense that they could see the inevitable and hence went quietly. The land reform movement had demonstrated that it did not pay to arouse the "anger of the masses," of the majority of peasants who stood to gain in a direct material sense from the pooling of labor and land.

Of course there is no real proof that a certain percentage of the rural population joined the cooperatives only under great pressure.

No one ran an objective opinion poll in the Chinese countryside at the time. But it is possible to demonstrate that anyone whose income was substantially above the average of the village was significantly worse off after collectivization. Farm output grew by only a few percentage points in 1956 and 1957 whereas the top 20% or so of the population must have lost 30% and more of its income.[8] If the policy of payment according to land and labor contributed had been maintained, the loss in income of the upper-income groups would not have been so large, but the land payment was abolished before the first postcollectivization harvest was in the barn. The movement from lower-level to higher-level cooperatives, which entailed the abolition of payment for land, may or may not have been carried out by democratic means, but it could have been handled democratically. A substantial majority of cooperative members stood to gain from sharing equally the land of their more prosperous neighbors.

It is possible that the richer peasants were fooled by these procedures and did not realize that they were destined to lose materially, at least in the short run (and what peasant can plan ten or twenty years ahead?). If the richer peasants did hold such illusions, one can argue that China's collectivization could have been carried out even if those who were better off had dominated rural politics. It is far more likely that richer peasants listened to all the claims for cooperatives with a high degree of skepticism and few would have voluntarily joined an organization that clearly put their claims to better-than-average benefits at the mercy of their more numerous poor neighbors. It seems reasonable to argue, then, that China's cooperative movement would have been impossible in the form it took if it had not been preceded by a revolution that put poor peasants in command. The only alternative method would have been coops forced on the rural areas by an urban-based leadership more or less on the Soviet model, but then China would probably have suffered the kind of agricultural disruption that occurred in the Soviet Union, or worse.

In the move from higher-level cooperatives to communes in the summer of 1958, one can also see the effect of a rural political leadership dominated by people who were or at least thought like poor peasants. The immediate objective of the communes was to facilitate large-scale water conservancy projects, but once again it was presumably the poorer villages or coops that were more willing to experiment with an organizational form that involved sharing the resources of their richer neighbors. No one ever took a secret ballot to test true sentiment, but there is no reason to doubt that a majority of the rural population would have voted in favor of communes if given a chance. Communes in their 1958–59 form later ran into serious trouble and

had to be thoroughly restructured because their impact on farm productivity was strongly negative and everyone in rural China lost income as a result. There were, it turned out, significant limits on how
far rural China could be redesigned in the interests of redistributing
income to its poorest class.

Clearly this argument does not say that a majority of peasants actually voted in favor of joining communes or even that their entry into
the communes was purely voluntary. The argument does state that if
cadres had taken the time to explain the advantages of the commune
form to the poorer coops, a majority of all coops would have entered
on an essentially voluntary basis. Even under the hurried conditions
of 1958, when the communes were formed, one major reason for the
apparent lack of resistance to their formation was presumably that
many cooperative members saw the commune form as being in their
own best interests.

If one accepts this argument that China's cooperatives and communes were the product of a system dominated by the rural poor and
could only have been created in that form by such a system, then it
follows that much of what distinguishes Chinese economic development could have occurred only through a revolution that put the
poor in command. Labor mobilization to build water conservancy
projects is a good example. Nothing characterizes China's rural development more or distinguishes it better from rural development
elsewhere in the world than the hundreds of millions of people who
pick up hoes and shovels every winter to go out and dig ditches, move
rocks and dirt to level land, and the like. Many other less developed
countries have large numbers of underemployed or "surplus" workers, but none has succeeded to the same degree in putting these
people to work doing something useful.

The main barrier to effective mobilization of rural surplus labor is
that those mobilized are put to work on projects from which they receive few if any benefits. The construction of irrigation ditches and
roads leads to higher productivity on the land on either side of these
roads and ditches, but it is the owner of the land who captures this
increase in productivity. If the owner is an absentee landlord, he did
not share in the work. Even if the land is owned by those who till it,
the construction of an irrigation system for that land usually involves
far more work time than that available in the families of the direct
beneficiaries of the system. The village residents most likely to have
free time for local construction activities are precisely those who do
not have much of their own land to till—landless laborers and team
farmers with farms of below-average size. To get them to work on
projects that improve the land of others, they must be paid the going

rural wage, but the productivity gains from these rural projects are seldom great enough for the beneficiaries to pay these wages out of their own pockets. Rural works projects, as a result, usually depend on state subsidies, and the state in turn often gets the money for these subsidies from foreign aid donors who think that rural labor mobilization is a good idea. When the aid ends, these projects die.

Cooperatives and communes go a long way toward solving these problems. Land is collectively owned so that an irrigation or road project that benefits only a small percentage of the village's arable land still raises the income of all village members. Those who did most of the work on the project get paid in work points according to the amount of work expended, just as if they had put in an equivalent effort plowing or hoeing. The commune in one fundamental respect behaves like an individual family; all labor that contributes to an increase in the commune's total product can be mobilized without use of force. In capitalist agriculture, labor outside the family can be mobilized only where the marginal product of that labor is above the going rural wage.

Thus two of the most distinctive features of Chinese economic development, the cooperative-commune form of organization and the full mobilization of rural labor resources, were a direct product of a revolution that put the poor in command. The latter feature depended on the former, and the former would not have been carried out by a political system dominated by the upper end of the rural income scale even with the prior elimination of landlords.

Other distinctive features of Chinese development also owe something to this underlying change in the political system, although it is easier to conceive of these measures being undertaken by alternative kinds of political leadership. The decision to ration basic foods and clothing and effectively guarantee minimum needs to all, for example, might have been politically feasible in a state dominated by the rich or a middle class. The welfare systems of Western Europe and North America have achieved similar results without a revolution. But widespread resistance to further increases in welfare payments in the United States, with all its wealth, gives one a small taste of the resistance to being taxed to help others that one could expect to find in a much poorer country. One way this resistance can be reduced is to give the welfare recipients the power to tax the wealthier.

Socialization of industry and commerce was also facilitated by China's transfer of political leadership, but state ownership of the modern sector can clearly be achieved in societies that have not undergone revolutions as thoroughgoing as China's. The owners of major enterprises in any country are always a minute fraction of the total population. A political system dominated by a middle class, for example, can readily achieve socialization of industry if the middle class is persuaded that expropriating the very rich really serves their interests. The newly emerging elites of many less developed nations have no trouble being persuaded of the virtues of expropriation because expropriation means kicking out foreign managers and replacing them with members of the local elite.

Efficient Authoritarianism and a Heritage of Experience

Many other salient features of Chinese economic development cannot be understood as being directly and causally related to the fact that China's revolution gave the poor a large share of political power. China's system of planning and management, the high rate of investment and taxation, and the closed nature of the society, to take three important examples, must be understood as resulting from quite different sources.

In the early 1950s China introduced an only slightly modified version of the Soviet system of industrial planning and management. By any standards that system was one of the most centralized forms of economic control ever devised by man. In its original form, centralized planning and management had been devised by Soviet leaders to transform their country as rapidly as possible into a modern, militarily strong industrial state. Increased productivity, particularly productivity in the strategic producer goods sector, was the goal. A greater degree of equality for urban workers was consciously rejected as an immediate goal because it would interfere with these efforts to raise output. Nor was there much attention paid to raising the average standard of living of urban workers. In fact, during the first stages of the Russian industrialization there was a precipitous drop in real wages.

The Soviet type of planning and control recommended itself to China for many of the same reasons that it appealed to Stalin. China was a backward state perceived to be full of internal barriers to growth and under direct or threatened attack by hostile external forces. To survive, the People's Republic needed to be strong, but to be strong it had to create a machine tool and steel industry core for its economy, virtually from scratch and in a hurry. Survival, of course, was not the only goal of China's leaders. Like many other world leaders, they saw the Soviet model as the quickest way to rapid economic growth in general, not just in the military goods sectors. This perception turned out to be incorrect or at least oversimplified, but few observers in or out of China saw this in the early 1950s. China's leaders, like their Soviet counterparts, did not see this system as a way of rapidly achieving an equalized income distribution. Socialization eliminated high property and entrepreneurial incomes, but that plus the raising of apprentice wages and those of others at the bottom of the scale was as far as equalization was allowed to go. For the most part, workers were paid according to the highly differentiated Soviet-type eight-grade wage system. Technicians and cadres had their own differentiated scales, and their highest-paid members often received eight times and more the income of an unskilled worker.

Although this centralized system of planning and management has undergone significant modifications over time, it is still highly centralized and authoritarian in nature. Workers may be encouraged to criticize their managers, and managers have to spend periods of time working on the shop floor; still this system is a far cry from worker management on the Yugoslav model, where factories are effectively owned by their workers and operated in the direct material interests of those workers. In China final production orders come from higher levels and are expected to be obeyed. Profits, in turn, are not retained by the plant but passed to higher government bureaus. Worker criticism of management is designed mainly to limit managerial abuses and mistakes and to make planning more efficient; it is not used to shape the overall direction of the economy or the basic goals of a factory.

What is extraordinary about this economic system is that despite its complexity and the difficulty of operating it, the system works with a reasonable degree of efficiency in China. A market economy in a less developed economy may suffer from numerous distortions in the price structure, but it is simplicity itself in comparison with what is required by China's current system. Managers do what the economy requires in a market system because it is in their direct material interest to do so. An enforcement mechanism to ensure that they obey the plan is unnecessary. If there is a meaningful plan at all, it is enforced by manipulation of prices. A market system also does not require an elaborate planning structure staffed by tens and hundreds of thousands of skilled technical personnel.

How does China make such a system work? One must begin with the authoritarian nature of Chinese society. It is not just that China is ruled by a Politburo that is not democratically elected in the Western sense of the word "democracy." Authoritarianism in China did not begin in 1949, and it is not confined to a political elite. The Confucian system was itself highly authoritarian with its emphasis on obedience and respect by son to father, father to official, and official to emperor. Much of the effort in China over the past decade and more to criticize cadres for not listening to the masses can be understood only in light of this tradition. The Chinese are not trying to create anything even remotely approximating participatory democracy; they are trying to limit abuses of authoritarianism that are inherent in the society. When decisions made by higher-level authorities are clearly mistakes, the people may be encouraged to criticize, but since most decisions are presumed to be correct, obedience is the expected response most of the time.

Authoritarianism alone cannot explain why the Chinese economic control system works. Effective implementation of the plan is not simply a question of obedience; it is also a question of technique. Where in China did the government find the hundreds of thousands of people with the necessary technique? In the 1950s some of these positions were filled by Russians, but the Russians were always a small percentage of the total and, in any case, were withdrawn in 1960. Their withdrawal caused serious dislocations in Chinese industry in the early 1960s, but only traces of these problems remained by the mid 1960s. The Chinese replaced the Russians not with other foreigners but with Chinese. Since the early 1960s there have seldom if ever been more than a few hundred foreign technical advisors in China at any one time. All but a handful of these have been connected with the construction of new imported European, Japanese, and American plants, mainly in the chemical industry. When these plants have gone into operation, the foreigners have returned home.

Where did all these Chinese technicians come from only ten to fifteen years after the revolution? One cannot create a full-blown educational system capable of turning out hundreds of thousands of engineers, accountants, managers, and the like in such a short period of time. A nation must have a primary and secondary school system staffed by able teachers. If there is such a system, it is possible to send adequately trained students abroad for more advanced training or to universities at home, although in the latter case a way must be found to provide a qualified staff. If a nation has a fully developed educational system, there is no mystery in its ability to turn out well-trained graduates within fifteen or twenty years. But fully developed educational systems take a long time to create. Large numbers of good teachers cannot be trained any more quickly than technicians, nor can they get adequate training in a school system run by half-educated people. Creating and upgrading an educational system is therefore not a matter of a decade or two of effort, but of generations of such effort.

Yet by 1960 China had 625,000 university graduates, 500,000 of whom had graduated since the revolution.[9] The number of technical personnel at all levels was much larger. At the top of the pyramid were the several thousand scientists trained in graduate programs in the West, the Soviet Union, and China's own research institutes. The very best of these scientists and technicians proved able to run programs to develop nuclear weapons, missiles, fairly advanced computers, and other items of high technology. At less exalted levels, hundreds of thousands of these technical personnel were capable of running a complex system of central planning and management.

China was able to produce so many qualified people so quickly because even in the nineteenth century it had a cadre of highly educated personnel and a third of its male population was at least literate. During the first half of the twentieth century parts of the educational system that produced these people was gradually modernized. In addition, tens of thousands of students went abroad to the United States, Europe, and Japan for advanced training. Not all these students returned and many fled China in 1949, but even larger numbers did not flee. When the decision was made after 1949 to greatly expand the educational sysem at all levels, China had the people to staff that system. That staff, building on students already in the pipeline, was capable of turning out the required technicians. The quality of training may not have been up to the standards of more advanced countries, but it was a far cry from the situation in a country such as Indonesia, where the number of educated people at the time of independence was minuscule.

China's advantages over most other less developed nations in the area of economic management were not confined to its head start in building a formal educational system. There were also a great many people in the country who had relevant experience from their jobs. In the nineteenth century China already had a large urban population and the accompanying elaborate commercial network needed to supply that population with its basic needs. Whereas in many less developed countries the larger-scale commercial activities were run by Europeans and the smaller retail commerce by other foreigners (Chinese, Indians, Lebanese), in China these businesses were almost all in the hands of Chinese. Even foreign trade gradually passed into Chinese hands as foreigners in China lost the principal source of their advantage in that area, a greater knowledge of the foreign markets to which China was selling.

Beginning in the twentieth century Chinese technicians and managers also began to acquire experience in the operation of modern industrial enterprises. China's modern textile industry, for example, was already highly developed by the 1930s. Overall China's modern industry grew at an average rate of 9.4% a year between 1912 and 1936.[10] Some of these manufacturing enterprises were run by foreigners; the Japanese in Manchuria, for example, did not allow Chinese to acquire much experience in the operation of plants there. Some Chinese managers and technicians moved to Taiwan or Hong Kong in 1949 so that their experience was lost. But large numbers remained, and these supplied the initial core of people to run the post-1949 industrial economy. The advantages of experience are well illustrated by the role played by Shanghai in China's industrialization of the past twenty-five years. The government during the past twenty-five years and particularly during the first decade after 1949 discriminated against Shanghai in the allocation of funds and skilled personnel. Yet Shanghai's industry kept pace with that elsewhere, and Shanghai's lead in producing the most advanced precision products has yet to be challenged.[11]

Authoritarianism together with a heritage of relevant experience and training provides much of the explanation of China's ability to operate effectively a centralized system of economic planning and control over industry. Are there any other areas in which one or both of these characteristics explain the uniqueness of part of China's economic experience?

The ability to distribute basic foods and clothing to guarantee everyone their minimum requirements seems to be one case in point. Rationing systems are notoriously difficult to administer and are constantly being undermined by market forces even in advanced economies. China's apparent ability to keep the system in reasonable working order over a twenty-year period testifies to a skilled administration and a degree of control that makes corruption of the system difficult because of the likelihood of being caught.

China's ability to hold down the rate of increase in consumption and to raise taxes and the rate of investment is the product of several forces. In a labor-surplus economy, for example, there is little upward pressure on wages, and China is a labor-surplus economy in the sense that the marginal product of labor in agriculture is below the subsistence wage. But limits on rising consumption in China were reinforced up to the mid 1970s by the ability of China's leaders to close the society to outside influences through complete control over foreign travel, over the media, and over the movement of foreigners within China. Similarly, China's ability to raise taxes and thereby raise the rate of investment within a few years in the early 1950s from around 5% to over 15% of GDP can most easily be attributed to the enormous power of the Chinese state. It is unlikely that the population would have voted in a free and contested election for such a rapid increase in taxes. Even authoritarian governments tread carefully when contemplating a major tax increase.

China's efficient authoritarianism has also had costs, even when costs are reckoned in purely economic terms. The ability to implement programs has applied to poorly conceived programs as well as those that accelerated growth. In a less efficient and less authoritarian society, for example, a program modeled after the Great Leap Forward of 1958–59 would probably have done less damage to the economy. In a less disciplined society inertia and "corruption" would have undermined the efforts of the leadership to promote radical change quickly. In China in 1958–59 the problem was, if anything, the opposite. Lower-level cadres eager to demonstrate their loyalty and enthusiasm carried out central directives with greater thoroughness and consequently greater dislocation than the leadership had intended.

The means of achieving authoritarian control also tend to discourage the free flow of accurate information that is so crucial to successful implementation of plans. False reporting of performance and needs occurs in all societies but seems to reach particularly high levels in countries such as China where extreme secrecy, among other things, tends to remove many of the checks that exist in more open societies.

On balance, however, Chinese authoritarianism has combined with a heritage of relevant skills and experience to give China by less developed country standards a unique capacity to implement large complex economic programs.

Size and Factor Endowment

Many aspects of China's factor endowment have shaped the nation's economic development program. Two are China's great size and its shortage of cultivable land.

Much has been made of China's pursuit of autarky as a national goal. Chinese leaders have continually reiterated the theme that to become overly dependent on foreign trade is to weaken the nation's defense against its enemies. Mutually beneficial trade between countries is still encouraged, but much of the world's trade, it is argued, only serves the interests of capitalist nations. Borrowing from abroad in order to increase imports is regarded as a particularly dangerous method of expanding trade.

But for all the rhetoric on autarky and the evils of foreign aid with strings attached, has China traded or borrowed less than it would have under a more trade-oriented government? In 1933 China's total trade (net imports plus exports) was less than 7% of GDP and only slightly over 7% in 1914–1918.[12] During periods more favorable to international trade this percentage may have been slightly higher, but for no significant period of time was China's trade ratio much above 10% of GDP prior to 1949. The 1930s and 1910s, to be sure, are not the 1950s or the 1970s. China in the earlier periods was not in the midst of a major economic development program. To pay for the added imports required by its economic development program, China had either to cut back on less essential imports or to expand exports and other sources of foreign exchange. China chose the former course, but how much of a choice did China have?

China probably could have expanded exports more rapidly after 1949 than it actually did and could have relied more heavily on foreign aid if it had been available. But it is far from clear that such an expansion in exports and aid would have been large enough to greatly alter the basic patterns of China's foreign trade. Even if foreign aid had been available on a level comparable to that of say India, China's foreign trade ratio would have been increased by a few percentage points and only for a period of ten or fifteen years before interest and amortization payments fully offset new aid receipts.

China's rate of export expansion has been very uneven, with prolonged periods of stagnation; but if one takes the 1952–1972 period as a whole, China's rate of increase compares favorably with that of the rest of the world. In that twenty-year period Chinese exports rose by 253% (in 1952–72 prices) while exports of the world as a whole rose by 416% and of the less developed world by 247%.[13] However, China's export expansion might have been even more rapid if certain traditional exports (notably soybeans, tea, and silk) had not failed to recover to their pre–World War II levels. A detailed, commodity-by-commodity analysis would no doubt show that China could have increased exports more than it did, but then a comparable analysis of almost any other less developed country except possibly South Korea or Hong Kong would produce similar results.

A reasonable conclusion is that China's relatively low foreign trade ratio is a product of China's size more than of autarkic trade policies of the Chinese government. Given a low foreign trade ratio, the radical change in the composition of Chinese imports between the 1930s and the 1950s from consumer to producer goods can be explained by the major increase in China's rate of investment. Unable to produce many essential investment goods at home, China had to cut out purchases of nonessential foreign consumer goods to obtain the foreign exchange for imports of investment goods.

A low foreign trade ratio and a high investment rate also go a long way toward explaining China's overall development strategy. In brief, a nation that cannot rely heavily on imports is forced to follow something approximating a (supply-side) balanced growth strategy. To begin with, there must be balance between agriculture and industry. Single-minded pursuit of growth in one sector to the exclusion of the other quickly generates import requirements far beyond the nation's capacity to pay. Within industry as well there must be a degree of balance. If China obtained all its mid 1970s steel needs of 25 million plus tons from imports, that item alone would cost China around U.S. $6–$7 billion, an amount equal to its entire import bill in 1974.[14]

Thus the principal policy options open to Chinese planners were between a high and a low rate of investment and, within the consumption sector, between government (mainly military) and private consumer goods. Given these decisions and assuming some degree of consumer sovereignty over private consumption goods, the remaining options available to planners were severely limited. If one removes the assumption of consumer sovereignty over the consumer goods mix, the range of options increases slightly although much less so in a poor country than in a rich one. Chinese planners, for example, could raise the rate of growth in agriculture from say 2.5% to 3.5% a year, but they could not let it fall much below 2.5% for long without causing major economic and political difficulties.

Saying that Chinese planners' options are limited given a low trade ratio and a high rate of investment is not the same thing as saying that China's development strategy will be identical to that of any other nation with comparable trade and investment ratios. China's factor endowment also plays an important role, particularly in determining the relative performances of industry and agriculture. The most significant part of China's factor endowment is its shortage of cultivable land. China is a land-short nation in two basic ways. First, there has been little or no net expansion in China's cultivated acreage since the 1950s largely because the costs of developing currently uncultivated land are prohibitive. Second, Chinese grain yields per hectare, particularly in areas suitable for rice, are comparable to the highest yields achieved anywhere in the world, including Japan. Further breakthroughs depend crucially on scientific advances such as the development of new plant varieties and on large-scale investment in water conservancy in north China.[15] Food output can be expanded by increases in inputs of labor and items such as chemical fertilizer, but the return to these inputs is falling and in many cases is already very low. Expansion on a major scale will come instead through methods that take time (scientific breakthroughs) and are extremely expensive (for example, control of the Yellow River).

If the analysis that lies behind these statements is correct, then

China's rapid industrial development and much slower development in agriculture, one of the key characteristics of China's post-1949 economic performance, can be explained in part by China's factor endowment. In the absence of a severe shortage of land in both of the senses mentioned before, current high rates of investment in Chinese agriculture would have achieved much more dramatic results. Whether Chinese planners would have chosen to achieve higher agricultural growth rates or alternatively to shift investment funds in agriculture to other sectors cannot be known. But with a different factor endowment they would at least have had that chance.

China's revolution created political conditions that made possible major shifts in economic policy. With the poor in command in rural areas, cooperatives and communes could be formed with little disruption of the economy, and these collective units could in turn mobilize labor and resources to begin transforming the countryside. In the cities revolutionary political change also eased the processes of replacing privately controlled industry and commerce with state-owned firms and of introducing rationing of necessities.

But China's revolution was only part of the reason for the post-1949 government's ability to choose from a wide range of economic policy options. The political triumph of the poor had little to do with China's ability to introduce a centralized system of planning and management on the Soviet model. Of central importance was that China had the personnel to administer such a system. Those people were available because of a Chinese heritage of emphasis on education and experience with a complex commercial economy. China's authoritarian heritage, reinforced by the power of the Chinese Communist party, also opened key options to policymakers, notably in the area of increased taxes and the potential for a high rate of investment.

On the other hand, China's size and land-short factor endowment dictated certain strategies by limiting other kinds of options. A major shift in investment funds toward agriculture in the early 1960s managed to keep farm output growing faster than population, but not fast enough to alter sectoral development with a pronounced industrial producer goods emphasis. Similarly, limited dependence on foreign trade has been turned into a political virtue, but China's size has more to do with this degree of independence than any set of deliberate policies.

In dealing with the question of the transferability of China's economic development experience to other less developed countries, it is not enough to point to the fact that China has followed paths that are different or even unique. The reasons for China's ability or need to follow such policies are essential to any understanding of the transferability of those policies. Some of China's experience can be used by the handful of nations that have also gone through a revolution of the poor. Other aspects of that experience are transferable only to nations with the combination of authoritarianism, education, and experience with complex organizations necessary to make a centralized system of planning and management work. Certain policies make sense only for a nation similar in size or factor endowment to China. Autarky is seldom feasible for a small country; balanced growth between sectors is, as a result, neither necessary or likely to be desirable.

Failure to take these underlying causes of China's experience into account when discussing transferability of that experience is to negate the usefulness of the discussion. It is possible to debate what the underlying causes are, but not whether they are relevant to an analysis of the usefulness of China's economic experience for others.

Notes

1. Efficiency as used here refers to total factor productivity. For China we lack the data on capital and the size of the labor force needed to make such calculations for the 1960s and 1970s.

2. For a comparison of China's shares with those of other less developed countries, see my "Growth and Changing Structure of China's Economy," in D. H. Perkins, ed., *China's Modern Economy in Historical Perspective* (Stanford, Calif.: Stanford University Press, 1975), pp. 133–147.

3. This statement applies to the post-1957 period as well as before. The producer goods industry in 1973 was 4.8 times that in 1957, while the consumer goods industry in 1973 was 3.3 times that in 1957, according to estimates by R. M. Field, "Civilian Industrial Production in the People's Republic of China, 1949–74," in U.S. Congress, Joint Economic Committee, *China: A Reassessment of the Economy* (Washington, D.C.: U.S. Government Printing Office, 1975), p. 164.

4. For one estimate of the rate of investment for the early 1970s, see my "Growth and Changing Structure of China's Economy," pp. 163–165. In a more recent study ("Real Capital Formation in the People's Republic of China, 1952–1973," in Alexander Eckstein, ed., *Quantitative Measures of China's Economic Output* (Ann Arbor, Mich.: University of Michigan Press, 1980), R. M. Field estimates that GDCF as a percentage of GDP was 23.2% in 1965 and 24.5% in 1970.

5. Strictly speaking, one can estimate the decline in income from the changes in percentage shares only if one makes some assumption about the level of income in each period. I have assumed that average income in the two periods was the same.

6. C. Robert Roll, "The Distribution of Rural Incomes in China: A Comparison of the 1930's and the 1950's" (Ph.D thesis, Harvard University, 1974), p. 67.

7. According to estimates of N. R. Chen, China's trade turnover in real terms increased 58% between 1970 and 1974 while GDP was rising by only 33%. N. R. Chen, "China's Foreign Trade, 1950–74," in *China: A Reassessment,* p. 645.

8. The top 20% were not reduced to the national average income by the formation of cooperatives; they were reduced to the average income in their region. If they had been reduced to the national average, their income would have fallen by around 40% minus the increase in the average between 1955 and 1957.

9. Leo Orleans, *Professional Manpower and Education in Communist China* (Washington, D.C.: National Science Foundation, 1961), p. 128.

10. John K. Chang, *Industrial Development in Pre-Communist China* (Chicago: Aldine, 1969), p. 71.

11. In 1952 Shanghai accounted for 19% of China's gross value of industrial output. In 1973 this figure had fallen but only slightly, to 16%. R. M. Field, N. R. Lardy, and J. P. Emerson, *A Reconstruction of the Gross Value of Industrial Output by Province in the People's Republic of China: 1949–73* (Washington, D.C.: U.S. Department of Commerce, 1975), p. 9.

12. Trade data used in making these calculations were taken from L. L. Hsiao, *China's Foreign Trade Statistics, 1864–1949* (Cambridge, Mass.: East Asian Research Center, 1974), and the GDP figures are from my "Growth and Changing Structure of China's Economy," p. 117. The 1914–1918 figures were converted into 1933 prices to make them comparable to the GDP estimates.

13. See table 4–5 and UN, *Statistical Yearbook 1962* and *1973.*

14. In 1974 the unit price of steel imports by China from Japan was U.S. $315. This price probably overstates the price that China would pay if it imported all its steel requirements since current imports are weighted toward higher-priced varieties of steel.

15. I discuss these at greater length in, "Constraints Influencing China's Agricultural Performance," in *China: A Reassessment,* pp. 350–365.

Two

SELECTED FEATURES OF CHINA'S
DEVELOPMENT EXPERIENCE

5

Regional Growth and Income Distribution in China

NICHOLAS R. LARDY

Prior to the 1970s most development economists assumed that economic growth would lead to widely distributed improvements in economic welfare. Although there was some doubt about the rapidity of the process, it was generally believed that rapid growth of gross national product would lead to rising per capita personal income even among the poorer members of society. As a result, domestic development and international aid programs focused largely on the achievement of sustained and rapid economic growth. Much less attention was given to designing economic development programs specifically to alleviate the poverty of lower-income groups.

After more than two decades of rapid economic growth, which has not alleviated mass poverty in most less developed countries, this optimistic assessment is being challenged. It is now generally believed that rapid economic growth has frequently been accompanied by a rising inequality in the distribution of personal income. Although income distribution data in less developed countries are particularly weak, it appears that the benefits of rapid economic growth have not been broadly distributed but have accrued largely to the upper 40% of the population. This pessimistic assessment is not usually altered by considering the distribution of public services. These have also tended disproportionately to benefit upper-income groups.

In short, a growing body of empirical evidence supports the hypothesis first advanced by Simon Kuznets twenty years ago that the early stages of national growth are characterized by a deterioration in the distribution of personal income.[1] Both the later work of Kuznets and more recent studies suggest that the income share of the upper deciles of the population increases significantly in the initial stages of economic growth.[2] Although there is less consensus on intertemporal change in the share of the lowest decile,[3] recent cross-sectional investigation suggests that the income share of the poorest 40% of the population declines markedly in the early stages of economic growth—up to per capita income levels of about $300 U.S. (1971 prices). After a period of flattening out, the income share of the lowest 40% begins to rise, but only after per capita income has reached relatively high levels—about $1,000 U.S.[4] Thus there appears to be a U-shaped relationship between the level of economic development and the income share of the poorest 40% of the population.

In the postwar period only a few developing countries have been able to avoid this pattern and simultaneously achieve sustained growth of per capita national income and an improvement in the size distribution of income. Because of the prevalence of an inverted U-shaped relationship between level of development and the degree of income inequality, it is increasingly believed that without development programs that assign a higher priority to raising the incomes of poorest members of society, the distribution of income in most developing countries will become more unequal for a considerable time.

Although the regional distribution of output within countries has been less widely studied, empirical evidence suggests that it changes over time in a manner parallel to that of the size distribution of income. Jeffrey Williamson's investigation of the pattern of interregional inequality, based on both cross-sectional and time series data, showed that the early stages of economic growth are characterized by increasing interregional income disparity, while more mature stages of economic growth are marked by regional convergence.[5] In his sample of twenty-four nations, low-income countries exhibited relatively small interregional disparities. Middle-income countries had the most extreme interregional inequality, while highest-income nations revealed considerably less interregional disparity. These cross-sectional findings were corroborated by time series data. Williamson's analysis of interstate inequality within the United States from 1840 to 1960 showed a "classic pattern of regional inequality . . . during the early stages of growth, 1840–1880, regional inequality increased . . . from 1880 to 1920, the degree of inequality stabilized and even revealed a significant decline; the 1920–1960 experience has been varied, to be sure, but generally the evidence suggests a secular decline in the North-South problem, the rate of which has accelerated from the mid-1930's to the present."[6]

Less complete long-term data for Sweden, Italy, Brazil, and France also lend strong support to a similar pattern of regional development. Subsequent intensive investigations of Canadian and Japanese regional growth over periods including the early stages of industrialization also support the classic inverted-U-shaped pattern.[7]

Clearly the increase in regional income inequality is closely related to the growing inequality in the distribution of personal income in the early stages of national economic growth. Comparatively rapid economic growth in some regions primarily reflects a more rapid transfer of labor from low to high productivity sectors, principally from agriculture to industry.[8] Since at low income levels, product per worker in industry is considerably higher than in agriculture, and since a relatively small share of the national labor force is initially employed in the industrial sector,[9] over time such an intersectoral transfer leads to growing inequality in the size distribution of income. In effect, for given wage differences between sectors, initially increasing interregional income disparities that result from differentials in the regional rates of intersectoral labor transfer are necessarily accompanied by a lessening in the degree of equality in the personal distribution of income.

This early deterioration in the size distribution of income is further compounded if interregional wage differences in the same sector are correlated with the level of economic development. International cross-sectional studies suggest that substantial intrasectoral differentials in output per worker among countries are positively related to the differences in national economic development;[10] similarly, within-country studies suggest that interregional differentials in output per worker within the same sector are correlated with differences in regional development.[11] Thus the variation in per capita output in more and less developed regions is due both to the differing sectoral allocation of labor and to regional differences in output per worker within the same sector. Consequently, to the extent that the transfer of labor to the industrial sector in the early stages of development occurs primarily in more developed regions, where product per industrial worker and industry wages are relatively high, the growing interregional income disparities will exacerbate the trend toward greater inequality in the size distribution of income.

However, Williamson has shown that at higher levels of per capita national income, interregional output differentials are gradually reduced. As a result of the spread effects of modern economic growth and perhaps deliberate government efforts to achieve more balanced regional economic growth, the transfer of labor from agriculture to industry in less developed regions accelerates. This stage of economic development is generally associated with increasing equality in the size distribution of income. Accelerated intersectoral labor transfer in backward areas reduces interregional disparities in level of development; and because a relatively small portion of the national labor force remains employed in the agricultural sector, it also helps increase the income share of the poorer deciles. At the same time, the reduction in intersectoral productivity and in wage differences that accompanies higher levels of per capita national income contributes to an improvement in the personal distribution of income. To the extent that interregional differences in the sectoral distribution of the labor force remain, reduced productivity and wage differences contribute to convergence of regional output as well.

Income Distribution in China

Much of the appeal of the Chinese model originates in the apparently egalitarian nature of the developmental process since 1949. In the early post–Civil War period the government carried out a far-reaching redistribution of income and wealth which raised the living standards of the lower deciles of the population considerably compared with the pre-1949 period.[12] The most obvious components of this program were land reform and the transformation of private enterprises to state ownership. These programs largely eliminated concentrated property holdings as a source of continued inequality of income distribution. Other government policies have also had a direct bearing on the distribution of income. Extension of state control over the economy included central government determination of the level and structure of wages and salaries within the state sector. In industry, for example, the central government specified the structure of wages by industry, by skill level, and by geographic area. Through the relatively effective control of working capital by the state bank and administrative controls over the allocation of labor, wages in the industrial sector were not, as in the Soviet First Five-Year Plan period, rapidly bid up by labor competition between enterprises.

In addition to regulating the structure of wages within the state sector, the central government has controlled the level of industrial wages, farm purchase prices, and retail prices of industrial goods sold in rural areas to reduce the disparity between rural and urban incomes. Available evidence suggests that despite some growth of labor productivity, real wages in the industrial sector have not risen perceptibly since 1957.[13] In addition, between 1950 and 1974 the state has doubled agricultural purchase prices while the prices of industrial products sold in rural areas have been increased only 10%. The resulting improvement in the agricultural sector's terms of trade has actually added more to rural purchasing power than has the growth of agricultural output.[14]

Rationing of important consumer goods and the provision of subsidized medical care, education, and urban housing has also reduced interpersonal consumption differentials. Rationing of foodgrains, pork, cotton cloth, and edible oils, introduced in the early to mid 1950s, prevents higher-income groups from bidding up prices, which would reduce the ability of low-income groups to purchase these essential commodities.[15] Because these mechanisms for directly influencing the distribution of income have been available, the Chinese government, like other socialist states, has relied relatively little on the tax structure or transfer programs commonly used by Western countries to alter the distribution of earned income.

Western visitors to China in the past few years have usually been struck by the effectiveness of these policies in eliminating the extremes of wealth and poverty characteristic of many other less developed countries. Although the basic standard of living remains quite low, many observers believe that the Chinese government has succeeded in placing a floor under the incomes of most members of society.[16] Indeed it has been argued that a fundamental characteristic of development policy in China has been its explicit rejection of capitalist "trickle down" theories of growth and distribution and adoption of the view that economic development is not likely to occur unless the living standard of all segments of society is raised simultaneously.[17] This basic philosophy motivates Chinese efforts to limit income disparities between urban and rural areas and to minimize wage differentials in the state sector of the economy, particularly within industry.[18]

Evaluation of Chinese performance with regard to income distribution remains a largely impressionistic process. Until the Chinese begin to collect and release more detailed data, it will be difficult, if not impossible, to judge whether the distribution of income has become more or less equal since the mid 1950s, when the most significant institutional reforms were completed. The absence of adequate data for the agricultural sector is particularly critical because three-quarters of the population or more continue to be employed there. Many of the agricultural development policies pursued since the early to mid 1960s have probably increased inequality in distribution of income within the farm sector.

Keeping this caveat in mind, a study of trends in the regional distribution of output may provide another perspective from which to evaluate Chinese performance in achieving broader distributional goals

157

since 1949. Despite the interrelationship between the personal distribution of income and the regional distribution of output, the latter perspective provides only a very indirect measure of Chinese performance with regard to the former. The central government, through its control of the regional structure of wages, insures that large differentials between regions in value added per industrial worker are reflected primarily in transfers to the central government treasury rather than in substantial interregional variations in real income of factory workers. Similarly, there appears to be some effort to capture differential rents in agriculture through progressive taxes on agriculture and manipulation of the agricultural sector's terms of trade on a regional basis. Despite this partial severing of the link between regional and size distribution, the Chinese regional experience may still be relevant for other less developed countries where interregional variations in output per worker are more directly reflected in interregional disparities in real personal incomes. In particular, the Chinese case may provide an example of the benefits, in terms of regional convergence, that may be gained through a redistributive investment strategy.

A Comparative View of Regional Inequality

The Chinese have released virtually no information on the geographic distribution of national product. Thus it is difficult to compare the degree of regional inequality with other countries. Provincial statistical reports frequently provide a wealth of other economic data but only rarely report provincial national income.[19] Indeed, it is possible that the Chinese did not even undertake systematic compilation of provincial national income data until the 1960s.[20]

However, data that have been published by provincial authorities on the value of industrial and agricultural output can be used as the basis for a preliminary investigation of the degree of interprovincial income inequality. According to estimates based on Western national income concepts, in the mid 1950s about 70% of China's gross domestic product originated in industry and agriculture.[21] Thus differences in the sum of value added in these two sectors are a reasonable first approximation of differences in provincial national income.

The first column of table 5–1 shows the weighted sum of per capita value added in industry and agriculture by province in 1957 expressed as a proportion of the national average. These data reveal substantial interregional inequality. Shanghai, the leading industrial center, is almost six times as developed as the national average and more than eight times as developed as Honan, the poorest province. The northeastern provinces (Liaoning, Kirin, and Heilungkiang) and the municipalities of Peking and Tientsin are also considerably above the national average. Honan, Kwangsi, Kweichow, and Shantung, whose per capita value added is about three-fourths the national average, are the least developed regions of the country.

The pattern of interregional disparity appears somewhat different when industry and agriculture are examined separately, as shown in columns 2 and 3 of table 5–1. The most striking finding is the relatively even distribution of agricultural output. With the exception of the three municipalities of Shanghai, Tientsin, and Peking, whose suburban areas had only limited cultivated area prior to 1958, and the sparsely populated northwestern provinces of Tsinghai and Sinkiang, whose extensive pattern of agricultural development contrasts sharply with China proper, there is relatively little regional dispersion.[22] By contrast, disparity in the industrial sector is considerably more noticeable. The concentration of industrial output in the urban coastal centers of Shanghai, Peking, and Tientsin is particularly obvious. The strategic significance of the Northeast as a center of industrial output is also quite marked.

The greater interprovincial disparity in the industrial sector is reflected in the greater coefficient of variation (standard deviation divided by the mean) of provincial per capita output in industry compared with agriculture. As shown in the last line of table 5–1, the population-weighted coefficient of variation in industry is 0.92 while in agriculture it is 0.19. Thus the degree of interregional disparity in industry is several times greater than in agriculture.

There are several potential sources of bias in the measure of the overall degree of income inequality among provinces. On the one hand, provincial value-added data are estimated on the basis of national net output ratios for industry and agriculture. Because there are wide interbranch differences within industry in rates of value added and considerable regional variation in the structure of industrial output, this procedure may underestimate the degree of interprovincial inequality in the industrial sector. The rate of value added in the producer goods sector is about three-fourths greater than in the consumer goods sector.[23] The structure of industrial output in more developed provinces, particularly in the Northeast, is more heavily weighted in the direction of producer goods than the national average; thus the use of the national value-added ratio leads to an underestimation of the value added in industry in these provinces. Similarly, this procedure overestimates the value added in less developed provinces where the share of consumer goods in total output is rela-

tively high. As a result, the population-weighted coefficient of variation of provincial per capita value added in industry systematically
underestimates the overall degree of interprovincial income inequality. On the other hand, because livestock production is concentrated
in frontier regions, overvaluation of the animal husbandry component of agriculture appears to result in an upward biased measure of

TABLE 5–1 Per capita provincial output, 1957 (national average = 100)

Province	Industry and agriculture	Industry	Agriculture
Northeast			
Liaoning	200	401	81
Kirin	132	157	117
Heilungkiang	185	219	166
North			
Hopeh	93	56	115
Shantung	74	62	82
Honan	70	29	95
Shansi	97	95	98
Inner Mongolia	115	68	143
Peking	191	473	21
Tientsin	391	1,101	21
East			
Kiangsu	86	83	88
Anhui	80	37	105
Chekiang	93	78	103
Shanghai	587	1,550	12
Central			
Hupeh	104	75	122
Hunan	80	41	103
Kiangsi	90	52	111
South			
Kwangtung	95	82	102
Kwangsi	74	34	97
Fukien	79	69	85
Southwest			
Szechwan	77	56	90
Kweichow	75	30	102
Yunnan	82	48	103

TABLE 5–1   (*continued*)

Province	Industry and agriculture	Industry	Agriculture
Northwest			
Shensi	106	58	135
Kansu	89	36	119
Tsinghai	137	40	194
Sinkiang	132	65	171
Population-weighted coefficient of variation	0.29	0.92	0.19

Note: These figures were calculated on the basis of officially reported provincial gross value data for industry and agriculture (appendix tables 5–A1 and 5–A2). Gross value data were converted to net values by use of national value = added ratios in each sector. For agriculture the ratio used was 0.74. Lei Ch'i-ch'üan, "Kuan-yü wo kuo ti-i-ko wu-nien chi-hua shih-chi chi-lei ti jo-ch'ien wen-t'i" (Several problems of capital accumulation during the first five-year plan period in China), *Ts'ai-ching k'o-hsüeh* (Science of finance and economics), no. 2, August 31, 1957, p. 5. For industry the ratio used was 0.34. State Statistical Bureau, Comprehensive Statistics Office, "Kuan-yü tsung-ch'an-chih ho ching-ch'an chih ti yen-chiu" (Research on the gross and net value of output), *T'ung-chi yen-chiu* (Statistical Research), no. 2, 1958. Population data are officially reported figures for year-end 1957. State Statistical Bureau, *Ten Great Years* (Peking: Foreign Languages Press, 1960), p. 11. To facilitate the comparative analysis presented in the text the overall measure of inequality has been calculated based on the inclusion of municipalities (Shanghai, Peking, and Tientsin) within their adjacent provinces.

interregional inequality in the agricultural sector. Despite these two biases, the measure of inequality among provinces shown in table 5–1 provides a starting point for comparing the degree of regional inequality in China with other countries.

Finally the data in table 5–1 exclude the service sector, which in 1957 accounted for about 30% of gross domestic product. The distribution of services such as government administration and retail sales was determined largely by population. However, a significant portion of services is positively correlated with the level of provincial industrial output. This is particularly true for transportation and finance and to a lesser extent for wholesale trade as well. Thus the inclusion of services would tend to increase the overall degree of interregional inequality shown in the first column of table 5–1. In the absence of any provincial data on the service sector, I have assumed in the comparative analysis presented later that transportation, trade, and financial services are distributed in proportion to provincial industrial output while government administration, personal services, and residential rents are distributed in proportion to population.[24]

The degree of interregional inequality in China appears to be quite high by international standards. Table 5–2 shows the population-weighted coefficient of variation of per capita regional income for se-

TABLE 5-2   Interregional income inequality, selected countries, selected years

Country	Number of regional units	Years	Population-weighted coefficient of variation
Brazil	21	1950–1959	.70
China	24	1957	.39
India	18	1950–1956	.28
Italy	19	1951–1960	.36
Soviet Union	15	1960	.15
Yugoslavia	6	1956–1960	.34

Sources: Brazil, India, Italy, Yugoslavia: Jeffrey G. Williamson, "Regional Inequality and the Process of National Development: A Description of the Patterns," *Economic Development and Cultural Change* 13, no. 4, pt. 2 (July 1965):12. China: Table 5–1, with services included under the assumptions discussed in text. Because the provincial-level administrative status of Peking, Tientsin, and Shanghai creates problems of comparability with other nations in the sample where major municipalities do not have independent administrative status, the coefficient is calculated based on the inclusion of Shanghai in Kiangsu and Peking and Tientsin in Hopei. Soviet Union: Hans-Jürgen Wagener, "Les récents modèles de développement dans les régions économiques soviétiques," *Revue de l'Est* 4, no. 2 (1973):108.

lected countries. For all countries the dispersion of per capita regional income relative to the national average is weighted by each region's share of national population, a procedure that minimizes the effect of the particular division of administrative units within each country. Comparability within the sample is further enhanced because, with the exception of Yugoslavia, the number of political units does not vary markedly. Since more variation is absorbed within a larger region, countries with fewer divisions tend to have lower overall measured income inequality.

The degree of interregional income inequality in China substantially exceeds the inequality found in several countries that are treated in the economic development literature as classic cases of north-south dualism. For example, the disparities in China exceed both those found in Italy, with its well-known depressed Mezzogiorno, and those found in Yugoslavia, where interrepublican income disparities, exacerbated by differences in nationality and cultural heritage, have been an important element in economic planning. India, a country that is more directly comparable with China because of its similar level of development and continental size, has interregional disparities substantially less than those observed in China. Only in Brazil, where the Northeast has long been a depressed area, do interregional disparities appear to significantly exceed those found in China.

The Dynamics of Regional Growth

Few data on the value of provincial agricultural output and even less information on the distribution of services have been released since the late 1950s; thus it is not yet possible to trace the long-term growth of national income by region. However, reporting on provincial industrial growth has been relatively plentiful and appears to offer an empirically sound basis for assessing the dynamics of overall regional growth.[25]

There are two reasons for believing that trends in regional industrial output alone may be broadly representative of overall trends in regional national income. First, as was shown in table 5–1, interregional variation in the level of industrial output during the 1950s far exceeded that in agriculture. Second, China's annual industrial growth between 1952 and 1974 averaged 12% while agricultural growth was only about 3½% annually.[26] Since industry was the major initial source of interprovincial income inequality and has been by far the most rapidly growing sector, it is reasonable to assume initially that trends in regional income disparities have been determined largely by differences in provincial industrial growth. This assumption, however, is quite tentative, because interregional variation in the pace of agricultural development in the 1960s and 1970s may be quite significant and partially offset the trend of convergence of per capita industrial output discussed below. An investigation of this possibility will have to await the release of considerably more data on the value of provincial agricultural output for recent years.

Per capita industrial output by province in 1952, 1957, and 1974 expressed as a proportion of the national average is given in table 5–3. Arrangement of the provinces in descending order of industrialization in 1952 facilitates the intertemporal analysis that follows. As can be seen from table 5–3, there has been a modest trend toward equalization of per capita provincial industrial output, particularly in the upper and lower thirds of the provinces. Provinces whose industrial output was initially well above the national average, with few exceptions, have tended to converge toward the national average. This tendency has been particularly marked in the highly industrialized northeastern provinces of Liaoning, Heilungkiang, and Kirin. Shanghai and Tientsin have also grown comparatively slowly and as a result have tended to converge toward the national average. Only Peking, among the initially more industrialized areas, has enjoyed a markedly above-average rate of industrial growth.

On the other hand, the performance of the initially poorest prov-

TABLE 5–3 Per capita provincial industrial output, 1952, 1957, 1974 (national average = 100)

Province	1952	1957	1974
Shanghai	1,864	1,550	1,303
Tientsin	1,244	1,101	1,057
Peking	483	473	632
Liaoning	377	401	297
Heilungkiang	277	219	144
Kirin	166	157	138
Kiangsu	108	83	99
Chekiang	81	78	59
Kwangtung	80	82	88
Shansi	76	95	73
Shantung	73	62	70
Sinkiang	62	65	48
Hopei	60	56	101
Kiangsi	58	52	51
Hupeh	58	75	66
Fukien	53	69	57
Inner Mongolia	45	68	98
Szechwan	43	56	38
Shensi	42	58	63
Hunan	40	41	45
Tsinghai	38	40	59
Kansu	35	36	70
Anhui	35	37	36
Honan	33	29	41
Kwangsi	33	34	40
Yunnan	32	48	35
Kweichow	30	30	33

Notes: These figures were calculated on the basis of officially reported or estimated provincial gross value data for industry (appendix table 5–A1) and on population data from the following: For 1957 officially reported year-end population data are used for all regions. Municipal data for 1952 are based on official data in Morris B. Ullman, *Cities of Mainland China: 1953 and 1958*, International Population Reports, Series P-95, no. 59 (Washington, D.C.: U.S. Bureau of the Census, 1961). Municipal data for 1974 are from *Demographic Yearbook 1974* (New York: United Nations, 1975), p. 226. Provincial estimates for 1952 and 1974 are based on extrapolation forward from 1957 and backward from the officially reported 1953 provincial population data. Extrapolations are based on the individual provincial growth rates during 1953–1957 with the exception of Kwangtung, where I have used the adjusted growth rate suggested by John S. Aird, *Population Estimates for the Provinces of the People's Republic of China: 1953 to 1974*, International Population Reports, Series P-95, no. 73 (Washington, D.C.: U.S. Department of Commerce, 1974), pp. 12–13. Adjusting for the shift of population from Inner Mongolia to the northeastern provinces that occurred as a result of the boundary realignment in 1969 would further reduce the relative output values in Liaoning, Heilungkiang, and Kirin and raise the value for Inner Mongolia. This adjustment would marginally reinforce the rate of convergence discussed in the text.

inces has been generally above average. Very rapid rates of growth since 1952 are particularly apparent in Honan, Kansu, Tsinghai, and Shensi. With the exception of the remarkable growth performance of Hopei and Inner Mongolia, the middle range of provinces from Shansi to Szechwan has experienced average to slightly below-average industrial growth.

The long-term trend of slow but perceptible convergence is confirmed by summary measures of interregional income inequality. The population-weighted coefficient of variation declined between 1952 and 1957 (from 1.01 to 0.92) and between 1957 and 1974 (from 0.92 to 0.86). Similarly, the same underlying data can be used to construct Lorenz curves showing the cumulative share of output produced by the cumulative share of the population in 1952, 1957, and 1974. Since each curve lies wholly inside that of the preceding year, the Lorenz curve ranking shows an unambiguous improvement in the distribution of output.

Because of the nature of the underlying data, these summary findings can be regarded as only a tentative indicator of the direction of change of provincial income inequality during the first quarter-century of Communist rule. There are three possible sources of error: the limited sectoral coverage, uncertainties with regard to interprovincial variation in the rates of value added, and the 1974 provincial population data.

Most obviously the data are limited in their coverage; both agriculture and services are excluded. Since the share of industry was only about 25% of gross domestic product in 1957 and because of the relatively faster growth of industry, the use of provincial industrial output results in an overstatement of the rate of decline of aggregate income inequality. It may also give a somewhat biased picture of the particular regional pattern of reductions. The precise impact of the missing sectors is difficult to assess. The omission of services probably has relatively little effect on the direction of long-term change in the population-weighted coefficient of variation. That is, the growth of transportation, trade, and finance, which compose about 70% of services, is probably highly correlated with industrial growth. On the other hand, little information is available on the regional distribution of agricultural output in the 1970s. Because over half of gross national product originated in agriculture in 1957, a divergent path of growth since then could significantly affect overall inequality.

Second, the implicit assumption of constant rates of net to gross output within each province since 1957 probably results in an underestimate of the rate of convergence. Since the composition of output in provinces where industry is growing more quickly appears to be changing rapidly in favor of producer goods, which are characterized by higher rates of value added, the gross value data underlying the decline in the population-weighted coefficient of variation underestimate the rate of regional convergence.[27]

Perhaps most important, there is a considerable degree of uncertainty in the provincial population data used to calculate per capita output in 1974. Data used are based on an extrapolation from official 1957 provincial population figures using the growth rates experienced by individual provinces during 1953–1957. This procedure makes no allowance for changes in the relative pattern of natural rates of provincial population growth or for changes in internal migration patterns since 1957. Thus the estimated 1974 populations of several less developed interior regions where significant in-migration has occurred might be underrated. If this were true, the actual extent of convergence would be less than discussed above. However, the data is insufficient to estimate the influence of either migration or divergent trends in natural growth rates. Of course, to the extent that migration since 1957 represents a continuation of the 1953–1957 pattern, the acceptability of the projected 1974 provincial populations is enhanced. Since the 1953–1957 growth rates of the more remote regions, which may have been the primary recipients of interprovincial migration in more recent years, are already quite high, the projections may not be unreasonable. For example, the rates for Heilungkiang (5.1%), Kansu (2.8%), Tsinghai (4.6%), Inner Mongolia (5.1%), Shensi (3.0%), and Sinkiang (3.3%) are substantially above the national average rate of 2.3% during 1953–1957.[28]

In summary, a correction of these biases based on fresh information would probably reduce the rate but not change the direction of convergence discussed above. The assumption of constant rates of value added contributes to an underestimate of the rate of convergence, and the population growth rates used to project 1974 populations contain an implicit built-in allowance for migration that is probably large enough to accommodate a substantial portion of post-1957 interprovincial migration. However, the limited sectoral coverage of our income measure clearly leads to an overstatement of the rate of convergence.

Albert Hirschman, Gunnar Myrdal, John Hicks, and others have argued that the early stages of economic growth tend to be characterized by increasing regional disparities.[29] Locational advantages, historical accident, resource endowment, and other considerations may give certain regions within a country an initial advantage in modern economic growth. Hirschman hypothesized that when national growth accelerates, the greater importance of polarization effects as opposed to trickle-down effects would lead to more rapid growth in more developed areas and increasing interregional disparities. Capital would be attracted from backward areas to the more rapidly growing regions of the country and skilled labor would tend to migrate to advanced regions in response to greater employment opportunities. Government policies favoring maximal aggregate economic growth rather than balanced regional development might further compound growing regional disparities.

Only at substantially higher levels of per capita income, Hirschman suggested, would the trickle-down effects of growth become increasingly important and neutralize the polarization effects. Combined with increasing costs of growth in advanced areas and deliberate government policy to ensure more balanced regional growth, this would lead to a decline and eventually a reversal of the differential rates of growth between backward and advanced areas. Thus the interaction of these forces over time gives rise to the inverted-U-shaped pattern of economic growth.

Quantitative studies of Chinese economic growth suggest that the pattern of regional development conforms to this classic inverted-U shape. There is no evidence of a sustained increase in per capita income for the country as a whole in the first half of the twentieth century,[30] but there was considerable growth in Manchuria and in a few coastal cities. As a result, the fifty years prior to the formation of the People's Republic appear to have been marked by growing interregional inequality. However, the reduction of interregional income variation in China after 1952 seems to have begun at a substantially earlier stage of economic development than in other countries for which historical time series data are available.

Regional convergence in Japan, Canada, and the United States did not begin until after three to six decades of sustained per capita GNP growth. By contrast, in the Chinese pattern of development after 1949, the initiation of sustained growth of per capita GNP was accompanied by a simultaneous reduction of interregional income inequality. Furthermore, the levels of per capita income from which convergence began in Japan, Canada, and the United States were a severalfold multiple of the Chinese level in 1949. In short, although China conforms to the inverted-U-shaped pattern of regional development, the timing of the convergence phase appears to have been distinctly different from the historical experience of the developed countries.

The Chinese pattern also differs from Williamson's cross-sectional sample of countries in the post–World War II period shown in table

5–4. The Chinese case contrasts in particular with India, the other low-income country in table 5-4. At independence India was marked by considerable interregional income disparity, particularly between the former British provinces and the independent states. Although one of the goals of the federation has been to reduce these initial disparities, per capita state incomes have tended to diverge in recent years, both because of the extremely rapid agricultural growth in rich agricultural states such as Punjab, Haryana, and Gujarat and because of considerable divergence in industrial growth rates as well.[31] Al-

TABLE 5–4   Secular changes in interregional income inequality, postwar period

	Population-weighted coefficient of variation		
Kuznets income class	Rising	Stable	Falling
I	—	Australia United Kingdom	Canada United States Sweden
II	—	France	Finland West Germany Netherlands Norway
III	—	—	—
IV	—	Italy	Spain Brazil
V	Japan Yugoslavia[a]	—	—
VI	—	—	—
VII	India[b]	—	China[c]

Source: Jeffrey G. Williamson, "Regional Inequality and the Process of National Development: A Description of the Patterns," *Economic Development and Cultural Change* 12, no. 4, pt. 2 (July 1965): 17, table 2, for all countries except China. Williamson's data for most countries cover the decade from 1950 to 1960. Data for China are for the period 1952 to 1974.

a. Williamson's findings for Yugoslavia are based on data from the mid 1950s to 1960. More recent data show that the population-weighted coefficient of variation rose continuously from 1952 through 1971. See Vinod Dubey, *Yugoslavia: Development with Decentralization* (Baltimore, Md.: The Johns Hopkins University Press, 1975), p. 194.

b. Williamson's findings for India are based on data from 1950–51 to 1955–56. Calculations based on more recent data for the period 1960–61 to 1967–68 confirm that interregional inequality increased during the 1960s as well as during the 1950s. Indian Institute of Public Opinion, "The Course of State Incomes: 1960–1968," *Quarterly Economic Report* 15, no. 4 (April 1969): 22. Unfortunately, because of numerous changes in the number of states and frequent changes in individual state boundaries since 1956, it is not possible to compare directly the results of calculations based on these more recent data with Williamson's findings.

c. Tentative, based on data for the industrial sector only.

though some relatively developed states, such as West Bengal, have grown relatively slowly, overall disparities have actually tended to increase slightly.

Interestingly, China's pattern is also quite different from that of Yugoslavia and the Soviet Union, two countries in which the state could presumably avoid the classic pattern of regional growth through direct control of the interregional allocation of investment funds and skilled labor. Yugoslav economic growth over the last twenty-five years, however, has been characterized by increasing regional disparities. The Communist party in the late 1940s assigned a high priority to the rapid reduction of interregional income disparities, and each five-year plan since 1947 has provided special developmental assistance to specific underdeveloped republics; but the explicit plan goal of more rapid development in these backward regions has not been realized. Average per capita national income in less developed regions has fallen from two-thirds of that of developed regions in 1953 to about one-half in 1970.[32]

Although long-term data on the regional growth experience of the Soviet Union are limited, recent studies have shown that there is no trend toward regional equalization, even at the relatively high per capita income level attained in the post–World War II period.[33] In fact, the rate of interregional income divergence appears to have accelerated since 1960.[34] Particularly striking has been the long-term decline of per capita output relative to the national average for several southeastern republics. Between 1950 and 1971 the relative positions of Kazakhstan, Uzbekistan, Kirgizia, Tadzhikistan, and Turkmenia have fallen dramatically—in some cases by 50%. Studies of republican standards of living, as reflected in both personal and communal consumption, show wide interregional differences and suggest that they increased during the decade of the 1960s.[35] Apparently the overriding commitment of the Soviet leadership to maximal aggregate growth has militated against investment allocations that would be sufficiently redistributive to ensure more rapid growth in less developed regions.

This result was anticipated by Williamson: "It seems highly unlikely that the Communist nations have sacrificed rapid national growth for the 'secondary' Marxian goals of (1) introducing industrialization throughout the country in order to achieve the necessary conditions for socialism on a nationwide scale and (2) achieving idealistic equalitarianism implied by the socialist society."[36] The mechanisms by which the Chinese after 1949 were able to simultaneously initiate sustained per capita GNP growth and also reduce interregional inequality are the subject of the next section.

Central Control and Redistribution

In 1949 the Chinese Communists inherited three largely independent economic systems. By far the most advanced was that of the Northeast. Modern economic growth had begun there in the 1930s, largely as a result of large-scale Japanese capital investment. The advanced state of development, compared with the rest of China, was reflected in both the high level of per capita product and in the structure of gross domestic output.[37] Industry and services were far more important than in China as a whole; and within industry, producer goods were especially important. The major coastal cities, particularly Shanghai and Tientsin were also very advanced. Beneficiaries of decades of foreign investment, they produced primarily light industrial goods, largely for foreign markets. Finally, there was a vast hinterland where industrialization, with very few exceptions, had not begun. Industrial output in many interior provinces was less than twenty *yuan* per capita, and only 6%–7% or less of the inland population lived in urban areas. In short, by criteria such as the structure of output and employment, modern economic growth had not yet begun. In fact, the preconditions for modern growth were almost entirely lacking. Communications and transportation facilities were primitive or did not exist. China's limited railroad development was confined largely to the Northeast; vast, populous interior provinces such as Szechwan were not linked with the rest of the country. Most of the hinterland lacked other types of infrastructure as well, particularly hospitals and educational institutions.

These marked regional disparities in the level of economic development had enormously important implications for the new Communist government, which was committed to improving the personal distribution of income, to reducing regional inequality both in income and in the provision of public goods and services, to creating a more integrated national economy, as well as to sharply accelerating the overall pace of economic development. Although Western writers have usually focused on the last goal in their explanations of the profound institutional transformation carried out in post-1949 China, distributional goals have also been of prime concern to the leadership.

One of the most profound choices facing the leadership after 1949 was the degree to which industrialization should be based on further expansion of the existing industrial centers. These centers had considerable advantages due to their extensive infrastructure facilities, large numbers of highly skilled workers and experienced industrial managers, enormous economies of scale, and so on. Continued concentration of investment resources in these areas clearly offered the prospect of much more rapid growth of aggregate industrial output. On the other hand, this strategy had unfavorable implications for equity. Because existing interregional links were very weak, it was probable that such a strategy would have very few spillover effects and would lead to rapidly increasing interregional disparities. Thus the leaders faced a difficult trade-off between growth and regional equity.

Over the past twenty-five years the leadership has consciously chosen to sacrifice some economic growth in return for achieving improved regional economic balance. This choice has been reflected in an investment policy that by and large has favored poorer regions at the expense of the advanced. Equity goals have not been the only consideration in determining the regional allocation of investment; defense, the distribution of natural resources, and other factors have played an important role. Furthermore, the degree to which the Chinese have been willing to sacrifice growth in the pursuit of equity has not remained invariant over time. For example, in 1956 following a reappraisal of regional policy, the commitment to inland development was marginally reduced compared with the early years of the First Five-Year Plan. In the early 1960s the withdrawal of Soviet economic and technical assistance appears to have had a notably detrimental short-run effect on the achievement of improved regional balance since most Soviet-assisted projects were located inland. However, on the whole, the pattern of regional growth and the nature of economic planning in China suggests that regional equity has been prominent in the collective preference function of the Chinese leadership, especially when compared with other countries.

In the first few years after coming to power, the central government instituted policies that enabled them to exercise far-reaching direct control over the distribution of income. These policies included land reform, elimination of the private industrial and commercial sectors, regulation of wage differentials within the state sector, manipulation of the terms of trade between agriculture and industry, and rationing of the most important consumption goods.

In addition to these mechanisms for directly influencing the size distribution of income, the central government also began to systematically redistribute income and wealth in favor of less developed regions. The policies that the central government employed to increase the rate of capital formation from 5% in the 1930s to about 25% by the mid 1950s and to control the sectoral allocation of investment resources have also been used to transfer income and wealth to less developed regions.

The most important of these mechanisms is the annual state economic plan. The basic means of determining the overall allocation of resources within the economy, the national economic plan is intended to serve as a unified development program incorporating the plans of each of the provincial-level governments as well as the programs administered directly by the ministries of the central government. In the process of determining the national plan, the State Planning Commission simultaneously determines the broad outlines of the development plan for each province. These provincial plans set targets for the level of output of major industrial and agricultural products, the level and sectoral allocation of investment funds, increase in the industrial labor force and the level of average wages in the state sector, increases in school enrollments, number of hospital beds, volume of freight transport, value of retail sales, and the like. Within the framework of these centrally determined parameters, each province formulates a more detailed plan that includes the economic plans of municipal, district (*ti-ch'ü*) and county (*hsien*) governments as well as the programs managed directly by the provincial government. As a result, the national plan is designed as an integrated program that includes the plans of all levels of government.

The national budget, which is drawn up concurrently with the state plan, provides the financing for the economic plan. This includes not only funds for investment projects, but also funds for national defense, social programs, and government administration. The state budget is a unified fiscal plan that includes the revenues and expenditures of provincial and local governments as well as the central government. Thus provincial budgets are drawn up by the Ministry of Finance simultaneously with the elaboration of the national budget. These provincial budgets finance the programs included in provincial development plans. Part of the provincial budget, in turn, is allocated among subordinate municipalities and counties to finance local development plans.

Revenue Sharing

The concurrent determination of the national and provincial economic plans and financial budgets provides the central government with considerable control over the geographic distribution of resources. Although the bulk of tax sources are nominally designated as local revenues and are collected locally,[38] in the process of drawing up the unified national budget each level of government is assigned and allowed to retain only those revenues necessary to finance the programs contained in the economic plan and approved by its superior administrative level. In effect, collection of revenues does not imply freedom to determine expenditures. Excess revenues are remitted upward while shortfalls are financed from special subsidies. Because of the large interregional variations in fiscal capacity and the redistributive nature of the centrally directed economic planning process, revenue-sharing rates at each level of government are generally highly differentiated.[39] For example, extremely industrialized areas such as Shanghai, Peking, Tientsin, and the northeastern provinces annually remit to the central government from 50% to 90% of their revenues. That is, centrally approved local development plans in these areas are so limited that they can be financed with a relatively small portion of locally generated resources. The excess revenues are transferred to the central government for redistribution to other areas. On the other hand, less developed regions of the country have substantially lower remission rates. The least developed provinces generally retain all their revenues and receive additional direct subsidies from the central government amounting to 50% to 80% of their own local expenditure.

Redistribution is not limited to the top two layers of government but tends to extend to lower levels of administration. Provincial governments typically require their major municipalities to remit disproportionately high portions of their revenues, allowing a reduction in the burden on the less developed counties within each province.[40] Counties, in theory, finally redistribute resources among individual communes by establishing higher remission rates in the richer agricultural areas within each county.[41] Unfortunately, there are no data available that show the extent of redistribution within counties.

Because the coverage and specific rates for all important taxes are set nationally, provincial and local governments are limited in their ability to mobilize resources that are not subject to this system of revenue sharing and expenditure control.[42] Provincial and local governments cannot make major adjustments in tax rates or initiate new taxes as a means of mobilizing resources independent of central government control. Furthermore, they are prohibited from utilizing deficit spending to increase their expenditures above centrally determined levels. Only a few revenue sources, mainly the local agricultural surtax, are administered by local governments outside state budgetary channels. Similarly, enterprises have only limited access to funds for the self-financing of investment projects. Enterprises are required to remit most of their net income, including depreciation funds, to the state budget in the form of either industrial and commercial taxes or profits. They rely on nonreturnable budgetary grants for financing fixed investment and for most of their working capital. Only a small portion of working capital is financed through bank loans, and these are integrated into the state financial plan. Although these funds have occasionally been used for nonplan purposes, by and large they do not serve as an independent source of finance for enterprises.

Investment and Structural Change

Both qualitative evidence for China and empirical evidence for other countries suggests that incremental capital output ratios in less developed regions are well above their respective national averages and that substantially higher-than-average ratios of investment to output are required to systematically reduce per capita output differentials. However, the experience of Italy, Yugoslavia, Brazil, and other countries suggests that interregional income transfers alone may not be sufficient to eliminate the development gap between North and South.[43] In the long run, structural shifts in the pattern of output in backward areas are required to reduce disparities in the level of development.

The Chinese system of unified economic planning and financial planning has been notably effective both in carrying out interregional income transfers and in assuring rapid structural transformation of backward areas. The implementation of this policy since 1949 has been most conspicuous in the industrial and transportation sectors. Because of the pre-1949 concentration of investment resources in Manchuria and a few major coastal cities, 77% of industrial output originated in coastal areas in 1949.[44] For political as well as economic reasons, the new regime began systematically to build up industrial centers in inland areas.

Inland provinces, which in 1952 (the year prior to the beginning of the First Five-Year Plan) were the source of only 27% of industrial output, received 55% of national industrial investment during the first three years of the first plan.[45] However, this aggregate figure does not reflect the concentration of these resources in the few provinces selected by the center as special areas for intensive industrial development. For example, while the ratio of investment in 1953–1955 to initial output shares in inland provinces as a whole was about 2:1, Sinkiang, Inner Mongolia, Shensi, Tsinghai, and Kansu during the period 1953–1957 enjoyed ratios of from 3.4:1 up to 10.5:1.[46] It is, of course, precisely these provinces, all of which were relatively underdeveloped in 1952, that grew most rapidly during the First Five-Year Plan period.

During this period Peking singled out eighteen "key-point" (*chung-tien*) cities as recipients of enormous infusions of funds for both infrastructure and industrial development. As shown on the map in figure 5–1, most of these cities were located in inland areas. During the

FIGURE 5-1 Emerging industrial cities, 1953–1957

First Five-Year Plan period these cities, which in 1953 contained less than 20% of China's urban population, received almost 70% of all investment funds allocated for the construction of municipal public utilities, primarily for water supply, sewer, and public transportation systems.[47] Furthermore, the 200 complete plant projects supplied by the Soviet Union and Eastern European countries, which formed the core of the First Five-Year Plan, were heavily concentrated in key-point cities. Of 188 plants whose location has been identified, 110 were located in key-point cities.[48] The breadth of these plants, including extractive industries such as oil and coal; basic industries such as cement, iron and steel, and chemicals; fabrication of final goods such as locomotives, trucks, aircraft, electronic equipment, and machine tools, suggests that the development of inland regions was a balanced program that combined important infrastructure investment, the development of natural-resource-based extractive industries, and industrial complexes producing a broad range of finished goods.[49]

Thus—unlike Italy, where state support for regional development has been confined largely to infrastructure investment, or Brazil, where regional development has emphasized raw material–based extractive industries which generate limited additions to local income and employment—the development of backward areas in China has included the creation of major industrial complexes producing a broad range of manufactured goods for national markets. This deliberate development of regional linkages has been an important element of post-1949 economic planning.

Investment in backward areas is financed by a long-term outward transfer of income from more developed provinces. This is presented in its starkest form in Shanghai. During the period 1953–1957, for example, Shanghai produced almost 20% of industrial output but was allocated only about 2.5% of total national investment. This investment represented only about 7.25% of the revenues collected in the municipality. This outflow of resources has continued unabated since 1957. For the period 1949–1973 the ratio of industrial sector investment to total budgetary revenue in Shanghai was only 6.7%, a small fraction of the national rate.[50] Revenue-sharing data indicate that other advanced regions have also experienced substantial long-term outward flows of revenues. Liaoning and Kiangsu, which in the mid 1970s ranked second and third in terms of total industrial output, remit about three-fourths of their revenues to the central government each year.

Parallel and complementary to this redistribution of financial resources is the systematic transfer of skilled labor and technical and managerial manpower from more developed regions, particularly

Shanghai, to less developed areas. This program, like the redistribution of income, began as early as 1950. Between 1950 and 1956 the central government, through its direct control over labor allocation, transferred over 270,000 workers out of Shanghai. Of this number 28,000 were specifically identified as technicians and 170,000 as skilled workers.[51] This program, unlike later rustication campaigns whose objective was to send unemployed youths to the countryside, assigned skilled workers to specific industrial projects, usually in the key-point cities in less developed regions. This transfer of enormous human resources from Shanghai has continued since the 1950s. By the early 1970s Shanghai had supplied over half a million skilled workers to inland industry.[52]

As a result of this wholesale transfer of investment resources and skilled labor out of Shanghai and, to a lesser extent, the other advanced regions, many less developed regions have been growing relatively rapidly, and the differentials in per capita industrial output, shown in table 5–3, have tended to diminish. However, the trend of convergence has not been uniform, and the relative degree of industrialization of several of China's poorest provinces, notably Kweichow, Yunnan, and Anhui, has not risen significantly. A more complete understanding of the causes of differential provincial economic growth will have to await detailed examinations of the development of individual provinces.

Social Services

The system of revenue sharing and central government control of the economic development plans of provincial governments has also been used to ensure a more equitable regional distribution of social services. This process was facilitated by the expansion in the early 1950s of the scope of social programs financed by the state budget. Before 1953 rural primary school education and rural cultural and health programs were not financed by the state budget but were supported by revenues derived from the local agricultural surtax.[53] Considerable regional variation in the level of per capita agricultural output meant that there were wide regional variations in the ability of local governments to provide social services. Because the state budget did not yet include village (*hsiang*) expenditures, the center had no means for systematically redistributing funds to improve the distribution of these locally provided services.

Beginning in 1953, county-level (*hsien*) government budgets were incorporated into the unified state fiscal system, and most village-level revenues and expenditures were included in the county budget.[54] County revenues were expanded to facilitate the financing of village expenditures. Following this broadening of the scope of the state budget, expenditures for local education and other social programs were no longer financed from revenues that were closely tied to the level of agricultural development in each village. Instead they were financed from the county budget, and provinces began to redistribute revenues among counties to enable them, in turn, to redistribute revenues at the village level.[55]

The expansion of the scope of the state budget facilitated a reduction of regional differentials in the provision of some social services.[56] From 1949 to 1957 considerable progress was made toward reducing extreme inequality in provincial primary school enrollment rates. Nationally the proportion of the population enrolled in primary schools more than doubled, but provinces that ranked low in 1949 were able to expand their enrollments relatively more rapidly. This pattern continued into the 1960s and 1970s, although disparities have not been eliminated, and the provinces that performed least well in the 1950s still lag somewhat behind. Evidence on the regional distribution of hospital beds is less complete but seems to show no similar trend of marked reduction in interregional differentials, at least in the 1950s. Data for more recent years have not been released.

Planning for Regional Balance in Other Systems

Planning and finance in China give the central government considerable control of the level and sectoral allocation of investment resources within each province and allow the redistribution of revenues to finance local social programs. The unified nature of China's system contrasts sharply with the federal fiscal systems of Yugoslavia and India.

In Yugoslavia the decentralization of economic planning since the mid 1950s has systematically undermined the ability of the central government to subsidize less developed areas. Although the center was able to redistribute a significant volume of funds to poor areas until the mid 1950s, the growth of these areas was comparatively slow. Richer republics increasingly objected to the center's redistribution of investment funds, since they believed it lowered the rate of.national economic growth.[57] As decentralized decision making was introduced and the criteria of profitability increasingly determined the allocation of investment funds, the investment share of less developed areas fell dramatically—from about 34% in 1950–1955 to 24% in 1955–1959.[58] After the mid 1950s, when the role of republican governments and enterprises in determining the allocation of investment was expanded, the portion of investment funds controlled by the national government declined precipitously.[59] Since 1965 the Fund for the Accelerated Development of Underdeveloped Regions has been the major mechanism for central redistribution of investment resources. However, the financial resources available to this fund are rather limited, and the investment share of backward areas remains substantially below that of the 1950–1955 period.[60] Although the goal of the Social Development Plan for 1971–1975 is again the more rapid development of backward areas, the relatively slow growth of these areas in the first two years of the plan indicates that the goal will not be reached.[61]

The sectoral allocation of investment within backward areas in Yugoslavia has also been unfavorable to rapid growth. Regional development in the 1950s, in particular, tended to focus on raw-material-based extractive industries with little investment in infrastructure and manufacturing. The high capital output ratios and limited employment generated by these projects and the failure to develop complementary manufacturing facilities resulted in comparatively slow growth despite a centrally administered redistributive investment policy. Decentralization of investment planning since the mid 1950s not only reduced the investment shares of backward areas but also gave republican governments greater control of the sectoral allocation of the special development funds provided by the federal government. However, this has allowed the development of autarkic investment programs with frequent wasteful duplication of existing production facilities.[62] Thus both because of the limited redistribution of investment funds and the unfavorable sectoral allocation of investment within backward areas, it appears that regional disparities will continue to grow.

The prospects for reducing interregional income disparities in India are equally discouraging. Redistributive programs are carried out through a complex system of tax sharing, grants-in-aid, and special development plans. However, in striking contrast with Chinese coordination of central and local developmental and financial plans, in India there is little coordination either between federal and state development plans or between the plan grants administered by the Planning Commission and the tax-sharing and grants-in-aid program administered by the Finance Commission.[63] Funds administered by the latter tend to be allocated proportionately to state population rather than on the basis of the level of state per capita income. Although the redistributive character of plan grants is potentially greater, they have not favored backward states. One study of all transfers, including plan grants and fiscal transfers, shows that they are at best neutral in their redistributive effect.[64] This assessment must, however, be modified to reflect considerable interstate inequity in the mobilization of funds in India. The large degree of tax authority given to state governments has allowed considerable regional disparity in tax effort, with many of the wealthier states exercising very little tax effort.[65] Again this is in sharp contrast to China, where the unified tax system minimizes variations in tax burden among provinces.

In view of the institutional arrangements it is not surprising that the pattern of growth in India has been one of regional divergence. Data from the 1950s and 1960s show that interstate disparities in the level of development have been increasing. A recent study suggests that these growing disparities have resulted in substantial interregional variation in the per capita availability of calories, proteins, and other important nutrients.[66]

In 1949 the Chinese Communists inherited an economy whose regional structure, particularly in industry, was quite imbalanced by international standards. The gap in per capita output, primarily between the developed northeast and eastern coastal municipalities and the rest of the country, appears to have been greater than the north-south income gap in Italy and Yugoslavia, as well as in most other less developed countries. Since 1950 the Chinese leadership has systematically structured economic policy instruments to achieve a relatively high degree of central control over resource allocation. A leadership that appears to have placed considerable value on regional integration of the entire economy has, in turn, used these policy instruments to transfer resources to less developed regions to assure their comparatively rapid economic growth or at least to prevent their relative decline, as might be expected in a more market-oriented system of resource allocation.

The most important of these policy instruments have been the system of revenue sharing, the unified tax and fiscal system, and the requirement that enterprises deposit most of their profits in the state budget. These instruments have given the central government the ability to systematically influence both the intersectoral and interregional flows of resources throughout the economy. By extending the scope of the unified state budget to the lowest level of government administration, the center gained the ability to redistribute resources for financing local social programs and for investment purposes. Most significantly, however, unlike other countries where limited redistributive programs have been grafted onto institutional arrangements that encourage basically diverging growth paths, in China interregional redistribution has been an inherent dimension of the planning process from 1950 to the present.

Although there has been considerable decentralization of economic management authority to lower levels of government since the First Five-Year Plan, the basic policy instruments through which the center controls investment and influences the distribution of personal income, have remained relatively centralized. There is, nonetheless, continuing dispute among Western economists concerning the willingness of the leadership to sacrifice economic growth in pursuit of improvements in social welfare. For example, the policy of local self-sufficiency, which has been repeatedly asserted by the Chinese as a central tenet of development policy, is usually interpreted in the West as an endorsement of growing regional disparity in the quest for more rapid growth. However, I would argue that the operative primacy of distributional goals, especially the reduction of intersectoral and interregional inequality, is reflected in the relative stability of real wages in the industrial sector, the slow but continuous improvement in the terms of trade between agriculture and industry, and the gradual convergence of regional per capita output.

Despite the success of the Chinese in reducing interregional inequality, both the absence of adequate redistributive mechanisms in most other less developed countries and the comparatively high cost of the Chinese strategy suggest that it may not provide a model for other countries that wish to distribute more broadly the benefits of economic growth. Although a substantial portion of total investment resources in other countries is sometimes state controlled, the geographic mobility of these funds is frequently fundamentally constrained either by decentralized decision making that places resource allocation decisions at subnational levels of government or by a central government investment policy that favors maximal aggregate growth rather than regional balance. The absence of adequate redistributive mechanisms in most other less developed countries is symptomatic of the lack of an underlying political consensus in support of distributive objectives.

Even if adequate redistributive mechanisms were available, the relatively high cost of the Chinese pattern of regional development would discourage many less developed countries from pursuing the Chinese model. Although a precise assessment cannot be made with available data, the cost of rapid development of backward areas, in terms of national growth foregone, appears to have been quite high. Incremental capital output ratios in China's backward regions appear to have been substantially higher than in advanced regions. Achievement of rapid growth in less developed regions seems to be justified primarily in terms of social welfare and national economic integration. Many other low-income countries are likely to prefer more direct and less costly means of improving social welfare.

TABLE 5–A1   Industrial output by province, 1952, 1957, 1974 (millions of yuan, 1952 constant prices)

Province	1952	1957	1974
National	34,330	78,390	387,247
Northeast			
Liaoning	4,523	11,710	48,951
Kirin	1,102	2,378	10,296
Heilungkiang	1,889	3,930	17,038
North			
Hopeh	1,342	2,805	25,220
Shantung	2,091	4,068	22,775
Honan	881	1,705	11,582
Shansi	643	1,832	6,976
Inner Mongolia	192	757	7,219
Peking	825	2,300	20,400
Tientsin	1,836	4,300	19,266
East			
Kiangsu	2,584	4,553	25,874
Anhui	628	1,501	6,808
Chekiang	1,099	2,374	8,664
Shanghai	6,510	12,969	60,066
Central			
Hupeh	955	2,799	11,870
Hunan	770	1,819	9,222
Kiangsi	575	1,173	5,590
South			
Kwangtung	1,745	3,812	18,684
Kwangsi	343	798	5,044
Fukien	414	1,224	4,969
Southwest			
Szechwan	1,649	4,873	15,750
Kweichow	269	605	3,400
Yunnan	333	1,101	3,780
Northwest			
Shensi	381	1,263	7,259
Kansu	230	560	5,670
Tsinghai	37	101	874
Sinkiang	175	446	1,785

Source: Robert M. Field, Nicholas R. Lardy, and John P. Emerson, *Industrial Output by Province in the People's Republic of China: 1949–1975* Foreign Economic Report No. 12 (Washington, D.C.: U.S. Department of Commerce, 1976).

TABLE 5–A2 Gross value of agricultural output by province, 1957 (millions of yuan, constant 1952 prices)

Province	Output
Northeast	
Liaoning	1,817
Kirin	1,373[a]
Heilungkiang	2,300
North	
Hopeh	4,450
Shantung	4,125
Honan	4,298
Shansi	1,455[a]
Inner Mongolia	1,225[a]
Peking[b]	80
Tientsin[c]	64
East	
Kiangsu	3,716
Anhui	3,028[a]
Chekiang	2,424
Shanghai	76
Central	
Hupeh	3,500[a]
Hunan	3,481
Kiangsi	1,937
South	
Kwangtung	3,620
Kwangsi	1,754
Fukien	1,160[a]
Southwest	
Szechwan	6,040
Kweichow	1,608
Yunnan	1,839

TABLE 5–A2 *(continued)*

Province	Output
Northwest	
Shensi	2,282
Kansu	1,423
Tsinghai	372[a]
Sinkiang	901

Sources: In order of provinces: *Liaoning shih-nien* (Ten years of Liaoning), (Shenyang: Liaoning People's Publishing House, 1960); *Kirin Daily*, 18 March 1959; *Heilungkiang Daily*, 19 September 1958; *Hopei Daily*, 10 January 1958; *Tsingtao Daily*, 5 October 1959; *Honan Daily*, 1 January 1959; *Shansi Daily*, 10 October 1959; Inner Mongolia Statistical Bureau, *Statistics on the Economic and Cultural Achievements of the Inner Mongolia Autonomous Region* (Huhehot, 1960), p. 39; *Peking Daily*, 9 August 1956, (for Peking; for Tientsin see note c); *Hsin-hua Daily*, 10 January 1958; *Anhui Daily*, 12 February 1959; *Chekiang Workers Daily*, 3 January 1958; *Liberation Daily*, 30 August 1957, 20 January 1958; *Yangtse River Daily*, 11 March 1958; *New Hunan Daily*, 4 May 1958; *Kiangsi Daily*, 3 July 1958; *New China Semi-Monthly*, No. 5, 1958; *Kwangsi Daily*, 5 October 1955, 27 January 1960; *Fukien Daily*, 30 September 1959; *Impartial Daily*, 21 August 1957; *Kweichow Daily*, 8 April 1960; *Yunnan Daily*, 3 January 1958; *Shensi Daily*, 4 February 1958; *Kansu Daily*, 26 September 1957; *Tsinghai Daily*, 4 July 1958; *Sinkiang Daily*, 30 January 1959.

a. 1957 prices.

b. *Peking Daily*, 9 August 1956, gives the value of agricultural output in 1955 as 73.6 million yuan. I assumed that the total growth between 1955 and 1957 was 10%.

c. Based on the assumption that the value of per capita agricultural output is the same as that of Peking.

Notes

1. Simon Kuznets, "Economic Growth and Income Inequality," *American Economic Review* 45, no. 1 (March 1955): 1–28.

2. Simon Kuznets, "Quantitative Aspects of the Economic Growth of Nations: Distribution of Income by Size," *Economic Development and Cultural Change* 11, no. 2, pt. 2 (January 1963): 1–80. Montek S. Ahluwalia, "Income Inequality: Some Dimensons of the Problem," in *Redistribution with Growth*, ed. Hollis Chenery *et al.* (London: Oxford University Press, 1974), pp. 3–37.

3. Kuznets, in "Quantitative Aspects," had originally hypothesized that the deterioration in the size distribution of income as economic growth began was due to the rising share of the middle-income groups. He found that the share of the lowest-income groups in less developed countries was not significantly less than in developed countries. Ahluwalia's study, "Income Inequality," based on a larger sam-

ple, suggests that the income share of the poorest deciles in less developed countries is considerably below that of more developed countries.

4. Ahluwalia, "Income Inequality," pp. 16–17.

5. Jeffrey G. Williamson, "Regional Inequality and the Process of National Development: A Description of Patterns," *Economic Development and Cultural Change* 13, no. 4, pt. 2 (July 1965): 3–84.

6. Ibid., p. 23.

7. Alan A. Green, "Regional Inequality, Structural Change, and Economic Growth in Canada, 1890–1956," *Economic Development and Cultural Change* 17, no. 4 (July 1961): pp. 567–583. Thomas W. Cleaver, "Regional Income Differentials in Japanese Economic Growth," (Ph.D. dissertation, Harvard University, 1971).

8. Williamson ("Regional Inequality," p. 32) found for all countries for which data were available a highly significant inverse correlation within countries between regional per capita income and the regional share of agriculture employment in the labor force.

9. Simon Kuznets, *Economic Growth of Nations: Total Output and Production Structure* (Cambridge, Mass.: Harvard University Press, 1971), pp. 199–211.

10. Ibid., pp. 236–238.

11. In Yugoslavia within the modern sector, output per worker in backward regions is only about three-fourths of that of the developed regions. Vinod Dubey, *Yugoslavia: Development with Decentralization* (Baltimore, Md.: Johns Hopkins University Press, 1975), pp. 195–196.

12. See Chapter 4 for a more detailed discussion of the distributive effects of the land reform program.

13. Nicholas R. Lardy, "Economic Planning and Income Distribution in China," *Current Scene* (Hong Kong) 14, no. 11 (November 1976): 1–12.

14. Ibid., p. 5.

15. Dwight H. Perkins, *Market Control and Planning in Communist China* (Cambridge, Mass.: Harvard University Press, 1966), pp. 192–193.

16. Alexander Eckstein, *China's Economic Development: The Interplay of Scarcity and Ideology* (Ann Arbor, Mich.: The University of Michigan Press, 1975), pp. 346–347. Lloyd G. Reynolds, "China as a Less Developed Economy," *American Economic Review* 65, no. 3 (June 1975): 426. A. Doak Barnett, *Uncertain Passage: China's Transition to the Post-Mao Era* (Washington, D.C.: The Brookings Institution, 1974), pp. 324–356.

17. The most explicit statement of this view is contained in John G. Gurley, "Capitalist and Maoist Economic Development," in Edward

Friedman and Mark Selden, eds., *America's Asia: Dissenting Essays on Asian-American Relations,* (New York: Vintage Books, 1971), pp. 324–356.

18. On wage differentials in the industrial sector see Carl Riskin, "Workers' Incentives in Chinese Industry," in U.S. Congress, Joint Economic Committee, *China: A Reassessment of the Economy* (Washington, D.C.: U.S. Government Printing Office, 1975), pp. 199–224.

19. In the course of looking at dozens of provincial economic reports I have seen data on provincial national income only for Heilungkiang, Kirin, and Kansu.

20. Fang Ping-chu, "On the Role of Regional National Income Statistics and Some Problems in Regional Comprehensive Balances," *Ching-chi yen-chiu* (Economic Research), no. 4 (April 17, 1963): 1–15.

21. Dwight H. Perkins, "Growth and Changing Structure of China's Twentieth Century Economy" in Dwight H. Perkins, ed., *China's Modern Economy in Historical Perspective* (Stanford, Calif.: Stanford University Press, 1975), pp. 117, 161.

22. The high value of agricultural output in these regions may be due largely to shortcomings in the statistical methods used to value the output of animal husbandry. Wang Keng-chin, "Wo tui nung-yeh tsung ch'an-chih chi-suan fang-fa ti chi-tien i-chien," (My views on the method of calculating the gross value of agricultural output), *T'ung-chi kung-tso* (Statistical Work), no. 4 (1957): 4.

23. Shigeru Ishikawa, *National Income and Capital Formation in Mainland China: An Examination of Official Statistics* (Tokyo: The Institute of Asian Affairs, 1965), p. 66.

24. The net value of services in 1957 used is that estimated by Ta-chung Liu and Kung-chia Yeh, *The Economy of the Chinese Mainland: National Income and Economic Development, 1933–1959* (Princeton, N.J.: Princeton University Press, 1965), p. 66.

25. Most important, provincial reports appear to be the product of a unified system of accounting and are consistent with the few statements of national industrial growth that have been released. Robert M. Field, Nicholas R. Lardy, and John P. Emerson, *A Reconstruction of the Gross Value of Industrial Output by Province in the People's Republic of China: 1949–1973,* Foreign Economic Report No. 7 (Washington, D.C.: U.S. Department of Commerce, 1975).

26. Industrial growth rate based on official data in Robert M. Field, Nicholas R. Lardy, and John P. Emerson, *Provincial Industrial Output in the People's Republic of China: 1949–1975,* Foreign Economic Report No. 12 (Washington, D.C.: U.S. Department of Commerce, 1976), p. 14. Agricultural growth rate based on official data in Perkins, "Growth and Changing Structure," p. 117.

27. Scattered quantitative evidence suggests that structural transformation has been particularly rapid in comparatively fast growing provinces. For example, in Kwangsi, a relatively rapidly growing province, the portion of producer goods in total industrial output rose from 0.1% in 1950 to almost 23% in 1974. The comparable increase for the nation as a whole was from 29.6% to 61.7%. On the other hand, in Kwangtung, where the growth rate has been roughly equal to the national average rate over the period 1949–1973, the rate of structural change has been slightly below the national average. The output of consumer goods grew fifteenfold between 1949 and 1974 compared with thirteenfold growth for the nation as a whole. New China News Agency (NCNA), 24 March 1975, in *Survey of the People's Republic of China Press* (*SPRCP*), 31 March–4 April 1975. NCNA, 11 May 1975 in *SPRCP,* 19–23 May, 1975. State Statistical Bureau, *Ten Great Years* (Peking: Foreign Languages Press, 1960), p. 87. Robert Michael Field, "Civilian Industrial Production in the People's Republic of China: 1949–1974," in *China: A Reassessment,* p. 170.

28. John S. Aird, *Population Estimates for the Provinces of the People's Republic of China: 1953–1974,* International Population Reports, Series P-95, no. 73 (Washington, D.C.: U.S. Department of Commerce, 1974), p. 95.

29. Albert O. Hirschman, *The Strategy of Economic Development* (New Haven, Conn.: Yale University Press, 1958), pp. 187–190; Gunnar Myrdal, *Economic Theory and Underdeveloped Regions* (London: Duckworth, 1957); John R. Hicks, *Essays in World Economics* (Oxford: Clarendon Press, 1959), pp. 162–166.

30. Perkins, "Growth and Changing Structure," pp. 122–123.

31. Indian Institute of Public Opinion, "The Course of State Incomes: 1960–1968, Unequal Growth in India's States," *Quarterly Economic Report* 15, no. 4 (April 1969): 15–28.

32. Dubey, *Yugoslavia,* p. 72.

33. Abram Bergson estimates 1955 per capita gross domestic product in the Soviet Union to be about $920. Abram Bergson, "The Comparison of National Income of the USSR and the United States," in D. J. Daly, ed., *International Comparisons of Prices and Output* (New York: National Bureau of Economic Research, 1972), p. 149. This would place the Soviet Union roughly in category IV in table 5–4.

34. Hans-Jürgen Wagener, "Les récents modèles de développement dans les régions économiques soviétiques," *Revue de l'Est* 4, no. 2 (1973): 107–135.

35. Gertrude E. Schroeder, "Regional Differences in Incomes and Levels of Living in the USSR," in V. M. Bandera and Z. L. Melynk,

eds., *Soviet Economy in Regional Perspective* (New York: Praeger, 1973), p. 190.

36. Williamson, "Regional Inequality," p. 31.

37. Alexander Eckstein, Kang Chao, and John Chang, "The Economic Development of Manchuria: The Rise of a Frontier Economy," *Journal of Economic History* 34, no. 1 (March 1974): 239–264.

38. During the First Five-Year Plan period provincial and local governments collected about 60% of total national revenues. Li Hsien-nien, "Report on the State's 1955 final account and the State's 1956 budget," *Hsin-hua pan-yueh-k'an* (New China Semi-Monthly), no. 14, 1956, p. 8. Since 1957 provincial and local governments have collected about 80% of total government revenues. Ko Ling, "Leap Forward, Leap Forward Again—Study Vice-Premier Li Hsien-nien's Report on the State's 1958 Final Accounts and the 1959 Draft State Budget," *Ts'ai-cheng* (Finance), no. 9, (1959): 20; and Joan Robinson, *Economic Management in China* (London: Anglo-Chinese Educational Institute, 1975), p. 29.

39. Central-provincial revenue sharing is examined in some detail in Nicholas R. Lardy, "Economic Planning in the People's Republic of China: Central-Provincial Fiscal Relations," in *China: A Reassessment*, pp. 94–115.

40. For example, during 1955–1957 Canton municipality annually remitted 74%–79% of its revenues to Kwangtung Province. Provincial remissions to the central government ranged from 66% to 56% of total provincial revenues inclusive of the revenues of subordinate levels of government. The revenues remitted by the municipality actually supplied the province with 24%–40% of its total remissions. *Kuang-chou jih-pao* (Canton Daily), 23 November 1956, 26 April 1957; *Nan-fang jih-pao* (Southern Daily), 5 August 1956, 27 July 1957.

41. Ch'en Ch'i, "Financial Administration Following the Establishment of People's Communes in Honan," *Ts'ai-cheng*, no. 11, 1958, p. 9, Wang Sheng-min, "Several Problems in Carrying Out the Contract System in People's Communes," *Ts'ai-cheng* (Finance), no. 14, 1958, p. 14.

42. The unified nature of the tax system was first promulgated in January 1950. Government Administrative Council, "Regulations on the Administration of National Taxation," in *Compendium of Laws and Regulations on Financial and Economic Policies of the Central Government*, vol. 1, pp. 181–184 (Peking: New China Book Store, 1950). The provisions of this regulation have been reiterated repeatedly since that time. See, for example, Wei Min, "China's Tax Policy," *Peking Review*, no. 37, 1975 (12 September), pp. 23–25.

43. Hollis B. Chenery, "Development Policies for Southern Italy," *Quarterly Journal of Economics* 76, no. 4 (November 1962): 539. Dubey,

Yugoslavia, pp. 205–207. Werner Baer, "Regional Inequality and Economic Growth in Brazil," *Economic Development and Cultural Change* 21, no. 3 (April 1964): 268–285.

44. Liu Tsai-hsing and Chang Hsüeh-ch'in, "The Great Change in China's Industrial Map for the Past Decade," *Ti-li chih-chih* (Geographical Knowledge), no. 11, 1959, translated in *Extracts from China Mainland Magazines* (*ECMM*), no. 64, p. 10.

45. Liu Tsai-hsing and Chang Hsüeh-ch'in, "Several Problems in the Socialist Industrialization of Our Country," *T'ung-chi kung-tso t'ung-hsün* (Statistical Work Bulletin), no. 21, 1956, translated in *ECMM,* no. 69, p. 6.

46. Calculated on investment data in Nicholas R. Lardy, "Centralization and Decentralization in China's Fiscal Management," *China Quarterly* 61 (March 1975): 40, and industrial output data in appendix table 5–A1.

47. Municipal population data are from Morris B. Ullman, *Cities of Mainland China: 1953 and 1958,* International Population Reports, Series P-95, no. 59 (Washington, D.C.: U.S. Department of Commerce, 1961), pp. 35–36. Share of investment in public utilities from Chang Yen-hsing, "The Arrangement of Urban Construction Work Must Be According to the National Policy of Economy in Construction," *Chihua ching-chi* (Planned Economy), no. 12, 1957, p. 4.

48. Robert F. Dernberger, "The Transfer of Technology to the PRC," unpublished manuscript (May 1975), appendix table 3.

49. In terms of the Chenery-Taylor analysis of the large country's development pattern, the industries developed in backward regions include early, middle, and late industries but tend to be concentrated in the latter two categories. This is particularly favorable for continued convergence, since these two categories typically account for a substantial portion of the increase in the industrial share of GNP once growth proceeds beyond the relatively low levels of per capita national income already achieved by the Chinese. Hollis B. Chenery and Lance Taylor, "Development Patterns: Among Countries and over Time," *Review of Economics and Statistics* 50, no. 4 (November 1968): 409–412.

50. Investment data for 1953–1957 from Lardy, "Centralization and Decentralization," p. 40. Industrial output data in appendix table 5–A1. The ratio of investment to accumulation for the period 1949–1973 was reported by New China News Agency, 28 September 1974, *SPRCP,* 7–11, October 1974, p. 266.

51. Liu Chih-ch'ung, "On the Situation in Shanghai's Industry and Several Problems," *Ts'ai-ching yen-chiu* (Financial and economic research), no. 1, 1958, p. 61.

52. Eckstein, *China's Economic Development,* p. 364.

53. Government Administrative Council, "Decision on Unified Management of 1950 Financial Revenue and Expenditure," in *Shih-nien lai ts'ai-cheng tzu-liao hui-pien* (Collection of materials on finance during the last ten years, *TCTLHP*), (Peking: Finance Publishing House, 1959), vol. 2, pp. 35–40.

54. Government Administrative Council, "Directive on the Method of Compiling Each Level's 1953 Draft Budget," *TCTLHP*, vol. 2, pp. 47–52.

55. The regulation cited in note 54 specifies that provincial authorities were expected to redistribute revenues among counties to enable them, in turn, to carry out redistribution.

56. David Michael Lampton, "The Performance of the Chinese Political System: A Preliminary Assessment of Education and Health Policies," forthcoming.

57. Deborah D. Milenkovitch, *Plan and Market in Yugoslav Economic Thought* (New Haven, Conn.: Yale University Press, 1971), pp. 178–186. Nicholas R. Lang, "The Dialectics of Decentralization: Economic Reform and Regional Inequality in Yugoslavia," *World Politics* 25, no. 3 (April 1975): 309–335.

58. Dubey, *Yugoslavia,* p. 206.

59. The share of investment in fixed assets financed by the central government declined from 97% in 1953 to less than 20% in 1964. Ibid., p. 35.

60. The share of investment of backward republics in the 1960s, 27%, remains substantially below that of the 1950–1955 period. Ibid., p. 206.

61. Ibid., p. 13.

62. Lang, "Dialectics of Decentralization," p. 315.

63. A. T. Eapen, "Center-State Fiscal Relations in India," unpublished manuscript, p. 4.

64. John M. Echols, "Politics, Budgets, and Regional Equality in Communist and Capitalist Systems," *Comparative Political Studies* 8, no. 3 (October 1975): 272, 277.

65. A. T. Eapen,"Federal-State Fiscal Arrangements in India," in *Revenue Sharing and Its Alternatives: What Future for Fiscal Federalism?* Joint Economic Committee, 90th Congress, 1st sess. (Washington, D.C.: U.S. Government Printing Office, 1967), pp. 469–472.

66. Indian Institute of Public Opinion, "Regional Inequality in Nutrition: A Comparative Study by States and Income Groups," *Quarterly Economic Report* 16, no. 3 (January 1970): 9–18.

6

Choice of Technology and Technological Innovation in China's Economic Development

THOMAS G. RAWSKI

Since 1949 China has achieved significant gains in industrialization, aggregate output, per capita income, and consumption while ameliorating problems of skewed income distribution and idle labor. Growing awareness of these achievements raises many questions about the nature and functioning of China's economic system. In particular, what policies has China adopted in industrial technology, and what shifts have occurred since 1949? To what extent have the Chinese created new resource combinations in industry? How are new ideas absorbed from abroad, and internally, from domestic technical leaders? What can our study of Chinese experience contribute to the economic analysis of technology choice and innovation?

A Model for Technological Advance

Economists have long recognized a positive correlation between experience and productivity in individual activities.[1] A simple extension of the concept of learning by doing is the hypothesis that repetition of particular tasks also lowers the cost of completing other jobs that require the same skills.

The mechanical industries offer fertile ground for elaborating this analysis. The industrial history of many countries shows that the equipment and skills needed to maintain, repair, and manufacture textile machinery, for example, are readily adaptable to the needs of a wide range of engineering goods.[2] Accumulation of experience in one branch of engineering accelerates the pace at which new products and techniques can be mastered and costs reduced elsewhere in this industry. More generally, Kazushi Ohkawa and Henry Rosovsky found that institutional changes as well as experience with new technologies stimulated Japan's "social capability" to import and eventually improve advanced foreign production methods.[3]

These considerations may be formalized as follows. Suppose that a task T requires skill levels $S_{1T}, \ldots, S_{nT}$ in each of n areas. Repetition of T not only lowers its cost but also raises potential in the skill areas to new levels $P_1, P_2, \ldots, P_n$ which may exceed the initial minima required to complete T ($P_i \geq S_i$ for all i). The resulting opportunity to develop previously unattainable skill combinations encourages entrepreneurs to undertake more challenging tasks T^* if they believe that $P_i \geq S_{iT*}$ ($i = 1, 2, \ldots, n$) and that the gains from innovation outweigh the cost of experimentation and the risk of failure.

The initial location and subsequent shifts of industry's skill frontier (characterized by $\{P_i\}$) are influenced by the institutional framework as well as by the quantity and quality of equipment, materials, education, and managerial skills with which the economy is endowed. Recent Chinese developments show that during at least some phases of industrialization, however, production experience may become a key determinant of the level and fungibility of industrial skills. With its focus on externalities and incentives, this model provides a useful vehicle for examining China's economy to the extent that expansion of industry's production frontier can be attributed to the accumulation of skills and the recombination of productive factors rather than to sheer multiplication of human and material resources.

Pre-1949 Period

China's modern mining, manufacturing, and utility output grew rapidly throughout the first three decades of the twentieth century. Because this expansion began from a tiny base, the share of modern industry in gross domestic product amounted to only 3.3% in 1933 and perhaps 4.2% in 1936, the year prior to the outbreak of the Sino-Japanese War. As in other countries, consumer products dominated the manufacturing sector, with textiles, food, drink, and tobacco accounting for 74% of 1933 factory sales.[4]

The development of consumer manufactures, steam and rail transport, mining and modern military strength all stimulated the growth of Chinese suppliers of repair services and spare parts, and later, as domestic skills and demand expanded, of a growing variety of machinery, chemicals, and other intermediate products and capital goods. By the mid 1930s this embryonic producer sector, although small in size and restricted to sectors in which output could develop gradually without block investments, had demonstrated an ability to absorb foreign technology, to respond to shifts in domestic economic conditions, and to compete with foreign suppliers in a growing array of markets, including textile machinery, printing presses, match-making equipment, lathes, soda and acid products, and cement.[5]

The industrial sector inherited by the People's Republic in 1949 included the prewar consumer industries, formerly Japanese- and government-controlled producer goods enterprises that were typically larger in scale but often stripped of key equipment and personnel, and the group of enterprises whose success at producing intermediate and capital goods in the face of foreign competition and domestic instability betokened qualities of initiative and flexibility that proved most important in later years.

1949–1957

The years 1949–1957 witnessed strenuous efforts to bring industrial planning and operations under strong central control. Both the successes and shortcomings of industrial policy in this period bear the stamp of Soviet influence—indeed whole passages from the works of David Granick, Joseph Berliner, and other analysts of Soviet industry may be applied to China without significant modification.

Faced with the impossibility of asserting close control over an industrial sector that soon included ten thousand state enterprises, several million employees, and thousands of construction projects, Peking concentrated its efforts on key commodities, enterprises, and regions. As managerial competence and responsiveness to central direction developed in one area, economic administrators directed their energies elsewhere. Growing control appeared most quickly in ferrous metallurgy, where rationalization was facilitated by the small number of firms and by the key role of a few engineers and technicians in each plant. The machinery industry, with its large number of firms and extreme heterogeneity, was among the most difficult to incorporate into the planning system. Elsewhere, progress toward a Soviet-inspired system fell between these two extremes.

Investment policies emphasized the growth of basic industries, especially mining and metallurgy. Expansion plans in industry centered on a group of about 150 large and modern projects built with

Soviet aid. Together with 143 ancillary projects, these new establishments absorbed half of industrial investment and nearly one-fourth of overall investment under the First Five-Year Plan (table 6–1).

These new enterprises were to form the foundation of a new industrial China. With the exception of the Japanese-built industrial facilities in the Northeast, now to be vastly expanded, the inherited producer sector was not expected to contribute significantly to future development. Regional investment data compiled in table 6–1 show how little was allocated to relatively developed areas, Shanghai, Tientsin, Shantung, and Kwangtung, in contrast to the large sums poured into the development of Northeast (Liaoning, Kirin, Heilungkiang) and Central China.[6]

Neglect of Shanghai, which contributed nearly twenty yuan to the state budget for each yuan received in investment funds, was a most conspicuous aspect of regional policy at this time.[7] Shanghai's investment funds were scattered among small projects: average project size was smaller than in several other provinces and barely larger than in an insignificant municipality such as Hsüchow (Kiangsu).[8]

Production and construction units were supplied with detailed performance plans but were often weak in technical and managerial expertise. Factory chiefs, shop bosses, and shift foremen lacked experience; some could not read technical documents or even make arithmetic calculations. Ex-workers assigned to responsible posts had little scientific knowledge and were unable to adjust to changes in factory routine.[9] At the same time, rapid expansion of output and investment meant that industry's labor force was diluted by a stream of raw recruits.[10]

Faced with a combination of ambitious targets and limited, frequently inadequate resources, managerial personnel at all levels tended to focus their efforts on fulfilling quotas for the volume and value of total output. Quality, cost, assortment, maintenance, and innovation were accorded distinctly secondary importance, a pattern that was strongest in the closing weeks of annual and quarterly plan periods and at other times of intense pressure to raise production. The failure of repeated exhortations to alter this quantity-first approach offered little mystery to Chinese economists: "Since the general indices of our government's plans and statistics are based on quantities, attention has thus been concentrated in these with little or no regard to quality in the distribution of missions and conducting of examinations on the part of responsible organizations on the upper level."[11]

This deliberate policy of emphasizing rapid output growth and import substitution at the expense of quality, cost, and customer service

TABLE 6-1   National and regional investment data and project size, 1953-1957 (millions of current yuan)

Region	1957 share[a] in industrial gross output (%)	Investment outlay, 1953-1957		Industrial average project size
		Overall	Industry	
National total	100.0	55,000[b]	25,030[b]	—
Soviet-aided projects	—	—	11,000[c]	70.512[c]
Support projects	—	—	1,800[c]	12.587[c]
Provincial data				
Shanghai	19.5	1,371[a]	500+[d]	0.200[d]
Liaoning	17.2	7,770[a]		
Shantung	5.1	—	450+[e]	0.960[e]
Kwangtung	4.0	1,438[d]	550[f]	0.835[g]
Kirin	3.3	2,150[a]	1,716[h]	—
Chekiang	3.0	—	276[i]	—
Hupei	2.5	2,210[a]	802[j]	—
Hunan	2.1	1,217[a]	350+[k]	—
Honan	1.9	2,590[a]	654[l]	—

a. Nicholas R. Lardy, "Centralization and Decentralization in China's Fiscal Management," *China Quarterly* 61 (1975): 31, 40. Total 1957 industrial gross output (excluding handicrafts) was 65.02 billion 1952 yuan.

b. *Ten Great Years* (Peking, 1959), translated and published by Western Washington State College, p. 44.

c. *First Five-Year Plan for the Development of the National Economy of the People's Republic of China in 1953-1957* (Peking: Foreign Language Press, 1956), p. 39; these are planned outlays.

d. *Kuang-ming jih-pao* (Kuang-ming daily, Peking), September 24, 1957. Average project outlay is for 600-700 projects undertaken in 1956.

e. *Ta-chung jih-pao* (Mass daily, Chinan), September 30, 1957. Data refer to 1952-1956.

f. *Wen-hui pao* (Wen-hui news, Hong Kong), October 14, 1957.

g. *Ta-kung pao* (Impartial daily, Hong Kong), July 9, 1957; 177 million yuan was to be expended on 212 major units in 1957.

h. Derived by applying 79.8% share of industry in total investment for 1953-1956 reported in *Chi-lin jih-pao* (Kirin daily, Ch'angch'un), August 9, 1957.

i. Data for 1949-1957 reported in *Wen-hui pao* (Wen-hui news, Hong Kong), September 19, 1957.

j. *Hu-pei jih-pao* (Hupei daily, Hankow), December 31, 1957, reported that 36.3% of the provinces First Five-Year Plan investments had gone to industry.

k. *Hsin Hu-nan pao* (New Hunan news, Ch'angsha), September 30, 1957.

l. Figure for 1953-1956 only reported in *Jen-min jih-pao* (People's daily, Peking; hereafter *JMJP*), March 31, 1957.

restricted improvements in workmanship and assortment to what might be termed a "natural" rate flowing from the gradual development of skills from the low levels of the early 1950s; Berliner has referred to this process as "learning by spoiling."[12]

The resulting upward drift in quality, essentially an industrywide Horndal effect, is visible throughout the First Five-Year Plan period.[13] Examples of improvements, some resulting from consultation with Soviet engineers, include a rising share of complex shapes and top-grade products in the steel sector, declining fuel consumption and transmission losses in electric power, reduced waste rates, improved specifications, and new varieties in machine manufacture.

Further signs of technical progress come from achievements in import substitution. The percentage growth in machine production during 1953–1957 was nearly twice that of imports, indicating a sharp rise in the share of domestic machinery in total supply.[14]

In terms of the model, this period may be characterized as one in which rising skills allowed industry to accumulate a substantial but largely unrealized potential for technical advance. The development of skills was not limited to the factory work force. Increased awareness on the part of economic writers of the need to extend their studies of industrial interdependence and future demand patterns beyond the broad aggregates included in the First Five-Year Plan grew from their experience with the practical problems of economic planning. This new economic sophistication was also to become an essential ingredient in future efforts to match output to current requirements.

These changes were accompanied by equally significant developments that created the nucleus of a mechanism for attacking technical difficulties and expanding the flow of technical data among enterprises, administrative and design units, and research groups. In the early 1950s harassed managers often assigned quality control duties to the dregs of the work force. In later years these personnel were supplemented by better-educated young inspectors who began to resist managers' attempts to fill out production quotas with substandard items.[15] Improved supplies of measuring devices also helped to trace quality problems to their sources.

Technical problems uncovered by factory inspectors and visiting investigation teams could now be referred to a growing array of research and design institutes attached to enterprises, industrial ministries, and universities.[16] Lack of experience and equipment initially confined these units to elementary inquiries, and some were attacked as paper organizations existing only "because the Ministry said so." Nevertheless, this was another source of future technical progressiveness.[17] Even during these early years, reports of independent Chinese contributions are not without merit, especially with regard to technical and design modifications needed to operate Soviet processes and equipment in China.[18]

Improved communication provided a final institutional link in China's technological network. In addition to information passed between ministries and enterprises during plan preparations and inspection visits, national technical conferences on design, casting, and machining directed attention to common problems and provided a forum for appraising solutions and popularizing the successes of advanced units. Conferences of factory directors and engineers performed similar functions within individual sectors of industry, as did demonstrations by innovative workers and intervisitation programs organized by regional and local officials.

The proliferation of technical education, the experience imparted by a decade of unprecedented expansion of industrial production and fixed assets, and the lessons learned from efforts to integrate Soviet equipment and methods into the domestic economy all enlarged the skill horizons of individual workers, managers, and planners. Together with the growth of support institutions and the backlog of opportunities arising from industry's one-sided focus on output volume, these changes created a potential for innovation far exceeding the actual gains achieved before 1958. In short, the closing years of the First Five-Year Plan found industry operating well within an expanding skill frontier.

To realize this potential, however, industrial leaders would have to alter the preoccupation with quantity which permeated factory policy at all levels. Strengthening incentives to pursue qualitative objectives was widely advocated during 1957,[19] but major reform was implemented only in response to economic difficulties brought on by the Great Leap Forward of 1958–1960.

The Great Leap Forward

The year 1958 was the first of three years of accelerated pressure to maximize production in the sweeping series of campaigns known as the Great Leap Forward, best remembered for rural collectivization and nationwide efforts to raise iron and steel output from large, medium, and even "backyard" metallurgical enterprises. The Leap was not without its beneficial aspects, particularly in its effort to enhance rural participation in industrialization. But the policies of 1958–1960 accentuated weaknesses inherent in the economy, and their overall impact appears to have been strongly negative, especially in the short run.

The events of this period may be illustrated by developments in the machine tool industry, in which ambitious but attainable 1958 targets were replaced by impossibly high goals. The new targets forced established units to discard normal standards. At the same time, production spilled from the factory sector into newly organized units with no tradition of industrial workmanship or quality control.

Neither the output gains claimed for major plants nor the reported achievements of nonindustrial areas such as Kansu and Fukien could have occurred without drastic erosion of standards. The Shanghai Machine Tool Plant claimed a 1957–58 rise in output of over 400%.[20] The Ta-lien plant, which produced a daily average of seven lathes in August 1958, claimed an output of 471 units in the following month, with daily output reportedly reaching a peak of 55 lathes.[21] Several major plants resorted to using "native" or "simplified" parts during 1958, and one source states that 1958 output of 50,000 machine tools included 35,000 "simplified" tools, implying that output of standard goods was far below the 1957 figure of 28,000 units.[22] The same is probably true of 1959 and 1960, years for which still higher output totals were reported. In small-scale metallurgy there was a similarly radical departure from initial 1958 plans, this time in the form of vast multiplication of small-scale rural enterprises whose products were often useful only as substitutes for iron ore.[23]

In terms of the model, the weakness of the Great Leap was that existing skill potentials often fell short of those required to complete the tasks attempted. Political leaders at all levels supplied an incentive to innovate that was formerly lacking, but skill deficiencies led to costly failures in both urban and rural industry.

The Years since 1960

By 1960 the partial breakdown of normal planning and reporting procedures had greatly increased the need for a policy of industrial consolidation. To this was added the impact of Soviet withdrawal of technical aid, which left key investment projects unfinished, and of consecutive poor harvests. These grave conditions stripped industry of its comfortable reliance on foreign expertise and the passage of time to overcome difficulties. The depressed farm sector required massive injections of machinery, fertilizer, and other manufactured inputs that industry was unprepared to supply. Strained relations with the Soviet Union called for a rapid transition to self-sufficiency in petroleum and other defense-linked commodities.

With foodstuffs suddenly claiming a major share of shrinking foreign exchange supplies, domestic manufacturers were obliged to face a wide range of unforeseen technical problems with only minimal recourse to imports. To meet these difficulties, economic specialists temporarily eclipsed during the Great Leap assumed responsibility for economic affairs. This group instituted reforms that extended far beyond the changes proposed in 1957. The new policies, summarized in the famous and controversial "70 Articles Concerning Industrial Enterprises and Mines" distributed in 1961, included a return to central control over resource allocation, restoration of the authority of professional managers and technical staff within industrial units, and strong emphasis on innovation, cost and quality control, and customer service.[24]

These new priorities, which have been maintained without major change to the present day, were vigorously enforced from the center by a variety of means that included closure of noncompliant enterprises and the return to farming of millions of peasants who had been hastily transferred into the industrial sector during the Great Leap Forward.[25] As the quality-first policies gradually took root, central authorities permitted a modest but growing trend toward provincial and local autonomy in certain policy areas, including investment, research, and supply work.[26] Overall central control is maintained by Peking's final authority over production plans, provincial budgets, and enterprise expenditures.[27]

These administrative shifts have resulted in a substantial redirection of industrial priorities toward previously neglected qualitative considerations. Energies are now focused on removing bottlenecks and expanding linkages within the current economic framework rather than on vaguely formulated future demands. As a result, industry has displayed impressive flexibility and innovative capacity, first in responding to the urgent needs of the early 1960s and later in promoting growth and technical development throughout the economy. Continued expansion of output volume is overshadowed by qualitative gains: creation or expansion of petroleum, fertilizer, electronic, and other new sectors with minimal reliance on imports; integration of foreign technical advances into China's economy, until very recently without substantial contact with foreign factories, machines, and technicians; and growing responsiveness to the requirements of all domestic sectors.

Industry's continuing record of quantitative and qualitative advance owes much to a steady improvement in the degree of integration and cooperation among three types of enterprises: the large and initially isolated projects which dominated the First Five-Year Plan investment efforts; smaller, inherited units which achieved innovative prominence during the 1960s by substituting experience and entrepreneurship for investment; and the revived and expanded rural industries which, since the mid 1960s, have begun to forge increasingly close ties between industry and the rural sector.

Soviet-Assisted Projects

China's First Five-Year Plan sought to implement a balanced-growth strategy of development. Even though paucity of reliable data and of experienced economists necessitated extensive reliance on Soviet technical aid in formulating plans, there was a genuine effort to create a program that, when extended into the 1960s, would endow China with an integrated industrial sector capable of sustaining growth and structural change.[28]

The core of the plan consisted of about 150 Soviet-aided industrial projects. The Soviets provided designs, equipment, engineers, and repayable loans. These projects absorbed about half of 1953–1957 industrial investment and were expected to form the core of China's new modern industrial sector.

These plants were large, integrated, and capital intensive. On the average each of 154 projects was expected to absorb over 70 million yuan during 1953–1957 alone (table 6–1); by way of contrast, outlay on the remaining "above-norm" (large-scale) industrial projects during 1953–1957 averaged only 29.3 million yuan.[29] Several projects were enormous, with investment budgets exceeding aggregate annual capital formation for many provinces (table 6–2). The new plants were often built in anticipation of vaguely defined future demand. Wuhan's Heavy Machinery Plant was designed on the basis of expected 1967 demand.[30] In the automobile and tractor industries, although demand was "large in varieties but small in quantity, we planned for the future and built big integrated plants with many specialized machine tools."[31] Most of the new plants were equipped with ancillary facilities for casting, forging, woodworking, repairs, and parts production. The Loyang Tractor Works was designed to produce 80% of all tractor parts on the premises. Its repair shops were stocked with 743 machine tools (enough, it was said, to equip a plant capable of producing 600 machine tools annually) and were capable of retooling the entire facility for production of new tractor models.[32]

The capital intensity of the new plants is shown in table 6–2, which compares scattered employment and construction cost data for individual projects with sectoral and national data on fixed assets per production worker. The data indicate that capital per worker at the Soviet-aided plants was several times the national average in both machinery and ferrous metallurgy. Scattered reports concerning gross output value per worker also point to a large differential in favor of the new plants.

Gradual completion of these new projects beginning in the mid 1950s led to major expansion of output in a wide range of producer

TABLE 6–2 Capital and gross output per worker, major industrial branches and enterprises, 1952–1956 and 1965 (yuan)

| | Sectoral data | | | Major enterprise data, 1965 | | | |
| | K_f/L | | $GVIO/L_p$ | | | | |
Sector or enterprise	1952	1955	1956	K_c (millions of yuan)	L	K_c/L	$GVIO/L$
All industry	5,656[a]	—	12,172[a]	—	—	—	—
Metal processing	4,750[a]	6,035[a]	12,569[a]	—	—	—	—
Loyang Tractor	—	—	—	400[b]	20,500[c]	19,512	15,244[c]
Wuhan Heavy Machinery	—	—	—	130[d]	7,000[e]	18,571	32,500[c]*
Taiyuan Heavy Machinery	—	—	—	200[e]	7,200[f]	27,778	—
Iron-steel	9,251[a]	13,302[a]	19,625[a]	—	—	—	—
Wuhan Steel	—	—	—	1,800–2,000[b]	35,000[c]	54,285*	28,571[c]
Chemicals	8,120[a]	11,114[a]	—	—	—	—	—
Kirin Fertilizer Plant	—	—	—	220–260[g]	—	—	—

Note: K_f = fixed assets; L = employment; L_p = production workers; $GVIO$ = gross output value; K_c = construction cost.

a. Nai-ruenn Chen, *Chinese Economic Statistics* (Chicago: Aldine, 1967), pp. 260, 485–86.

b. *Chūgoku shiryō geppō* 95 (1956): 17, 21. Entry under Wuhan Steel is the cost of constructing an unspecified 1.5 mmt/year steel facility.

c. Barry M. Richman, *Industrial Society in Communist China* (New York: Random House, 1969), pp. 154, 827–833.

d. Furui Yoshimi, Ide Ichitarō, and Tabayashi Masakichi, *Hōchū shoken* (A visit to China) (Tokyo, 1959), p. 26.

e. *1967 Fei-ch'ing nien-pao* (1967 yearbook of Chinese Communism) (Taipei, 1967), p. 928.

f. Shokoku kagaku gijutsu kenyūkai, "Chūgoku kagaku gijutsu no genjō bunseki" (Analysis of the present state of Chinese science and technology) (1965–66), vol. 1, 64–65.

g. Ma Yin-ch'u, *Ba In-sho rombunshū* (Collected essays of Ma Yin-ch'u) (Tokyo, 1961), p. 31. These data pertain to the mid 1950s.

* Midpoint of data range.

industries.[33] The new plants also manufactured a variety of import substitutes, often at a large cost advantage over foreign substitutes. Domestic electric locomotives cost 39% less than imports even at the trial production stage. Metallurgical equipment carried an average cost only two-thirds of that attached to comparable imports. Railway carriages cost 50%–67% and freight cars 30%–76% less to produce in China than to import. Automatic blast furnaces built with domestic equipment cost only 59% as much as when imported machinery was used. For coke ovens the corresponding figure was 38%. Seamless steel tubes produced at Anshan and delivered to Shanghai cost over one-third less than imports. References to the opposite tendency are rare.[34]

In the sphere of quality and cost, however, performance frequently left much to be desired. Mechanization of casting in machine tool plants, for example, resulted in short-run increases in production costs without offsetting improvements in product quality.[35] Elsewhere, steel costs at the new Anshan works appeared much lower than at the smaller Tientsin plant only because of accounting quirks favoring the larger integrated unit.[36] Even when new plants exceeded the cost and quality standards set by smaller units, Chinese economists began to ask whether the long gestation periods and mass production methods associated with the Soviet facilities were inappropriate in view of the size and short-run variability of domestic demand.[37]

Despite their high priority, the Soviet-aided projects experienced numerous difficulties in construction and operation. Construction managers had to cope with delays, design errors, frequent plan changes, cost overruns, and supply problems. To cite only a few examples: 1000 blueprints drawn up at the Anshan steel complex in the spring of 1952 contained an average of eight errors per page; in the following year, it was discovered that two-thirds of the designs for Anshan's blast furnaces and chemical works contained errors. Soviet blueprints were often not translated. Selection of construction materials based on faulty experiments led to poor results. The expansion of Shenyang's No. 1 Machine Tool Plant cost five times the planned amount. The absence of concrete investment criteria is shown by the odyssey of a plant director whose unsuccessful bid to obtain capital for expansion included a series of plans, calling for sums ranging from 1.9 to 10 million yuan, which he personally took to Peking in search of official sponsorship.[38]

Similar problems obstructed the operation of new plants. Output plans were invariably tardy. Even in 1957, a year of slowdown and consolidation, ministerial directives were not issued on time.[39] Supply plans were set before output targets were determined, and managers were obliged to reconcile supplies and requirements.[40] Unreliable performance by suppliers was the rule rather than the exception, and supply difficulties were exacerbated by a widespread absence of demand planning. Managers at the Loyang Bearing Works discovered that their intended suppliers of special steel were unaware of the new plant's existence and had made no plans to produce the required products.[41] Chemical officials were confused about the demand for soda and sulfuric acid, and they had not determined the mix of nitrogenous, phosphate, and potassium fertilizers that China's agriculture required.[42] Technical suggestions offered by Soviet experts often conflicted with the requirements of current production.[43]

By the end of the First Five-Year Plan period, Chinese economists and planners were keenly aware of the defects in the planning and administration of industrial investment and production. In many cases Soviet-designed plants were too large and too specialized for China. There were other flaws: specifications did not fit domestic raw materials; housing designs were too lavish; there was excessive provision for idle capacity and inadequate allowance for delays in reaching technical norms; integration had been carried to uneconomic extremes.

All these insights, however, became available only with hindsight. Most of the difficulties encountered by the development program of the First Five-Year Plan arose from the failure of Soviet and Chinese planners to anticipate the importance of agricultural progress to the overall economy, the volatility of industrial demand, and the potential contribution of inherited industrial resources to both output growth and technical reforms. It is tempting to argue that planners should have attached higher priority to agricultural investments, but this argument assumes a degree of economic insight unavailable in China or the Soviet Union (or, for that matter, among Western economists) at the time. In fact, any plan that sought to achieve major structural changes in a short time would have encountered these kinds of imbalances and limits to absorptive capacity.

China's First Five-Year Plan investments in large, modern enterprises illustrate an economic strategy that Peking has applied since 1949: decide what needs to be done, do it somehow, then do it right. Chinese leaders consistently chose to solve the "problem of existence or absence" (*yu-wu-wen-t'i*) of some desired product or technique first. Once the product could be manufactured, attention turned to the "problem of advanced or backward," which means improvements in quality, technique, or economic indicators.[44]

This approach assumes that once new activities are begun, managers, technicians, and workers will somehow manage to steer them in desired directions by correcting imbalances and shortcomings. In general, this has been the case, but the adjustment process has proved both costly and time-consuming. When we remember that similar costs occur regularly even in the most advanced economies when rapid expansion of output, capacity, or technical capabilities is attempted, it becomes difficult to argue that China's investment program was unusually inefficient.

Small and Medium Urban Enterprises without High Investment Priority

A very different type of industrial unit has become increasingly prominent since the early 1960s. These are older, smaller enterprises, often part of the legacy of prewar industrial advance in the private sector, which have typically received only modest infusions of investment funds, imported equipment, and external technical assistance since 1949. This type of firm is largely responsible for the flexibility, innovative success, and responsiveness to demand that, in contrast to the experience of the First Five-Year Plan years, seems typical of industry's performance of the past twenty years.

Shanghai's Ta-lung Machinery Works provides a typical example of this type of firm.[45] Ta-lung was established in 1902 as a ship-repair works with eleven workers. In 1906, with the staff enlarged to about fifty, the firm began to specialize in repairing machinery for Shanghai's growing textile industry. After 1911 the business gradually shifted toward manufacture as well as repair of textile equipment. During the 1920s and 1930s Ta-lung gradually developed a full line of cotton spinning machinery which was installed in several highly profitable textile mills. The outbreak of the Sino-Japanese War found the firm preparing to embark on an export promotion drive.

Ta-lung resumed its pattern of varied equipment manufacture after 1949. During 1949–1952 its products included spindles, looms, machine tools, engines, and steel ingots. In 1953 machine tools and mining equipment were the major products. After further shifts the firm was asked in 1955 to specialize in producing formerly imported petroleum equipment. This shift was supported by an investment grant of 3 million yuan, or 1017 yuan per employee, which transformed Ta-lung into Shanghai's largest producer of petroleum equipment. In 1958 further funds were applied to convert the plant to manufacturing chemical fertilizer equipment.[46]

Since 1960, Ta-lung has produced equipment for both the petroleum and the fertilizer industries, experimented with advanced techniques for metallurgy and compressors, and produced equipment for synthesizing diamonds. Employment now stands at forty-three hundred workers, with total output reportedly twenty-three times the 1949 level. As in the prewar years, a substantial segment of the firm's fixed capital is self-supplied.[47]

Old equipment is common in these plants, especially in Shanghai, where the pattern of limited industrial investments observed during the 1950s can be traced to 1965, when Deputy Mayor Ts'ao Ti-ch'iu reported that "much of the existing equipment in Shanghai is outworn and backward."[48] This is confirmed by accounts of skeptical outsiders who assumed that Shanghai's achievements stemmed from a modern equipment base. A Wuhan plant assigned to produce diesel engines responded by demanding several million yuan worth of machinery and several hundred technicians and skilled workers. Instead, some of the Wuhan personnel were sent "to visit the Ch'eng-fu Power Machine Plant of Shanghai, where they discovered that most of their machine tools were old and much specialized equipment was made by workers in the plant. The conditions at the Shanghai plant were not any better than at the Wuhan plant, but the production of diesel engines in the former was progressing rapidly. They also noticed that the Shanghai plant had all the answers to the difficulties bothering them."[49]

Long industrial experience and a history of repair work are also common among this group of firms. The Wuhan plant is a successor to a former private enterprise. When it entered the diesel field, "the leading cadre did not have any experience in organizing the production of diesel engines and none of its technical personnel were specialists in diesel engines . . . Except for a few veteran workers who once repaired some diesel engines, no worker knew anything about diesels."[50]

The primary function of these plants in China's industrial economy is to respond to current domestic demand by providing an appropriate mixture of embodied and disembodied (through training and consulting programs, conferences and the like) technical change drawn from both foreign and domestic sources. This function is particularly significant in the machinery sector, in which the rough measure of self-sufficiency computed in table 6–3 shows the dwindling significance of direct imports in aggregate supply. Chinese sources make it clear that successful fulfillment of this role is the result of reorganizing existing factors, notably human capital, rather than capital widening or deepening.

The contribution of older units to the expansion of fixed capital in China's newer industries may be illustrated by the petroleum and

TABLE 6–3   Production, trade, and self-sufficiency in machinery, 1957–1975

Index	Year				
	1957	1965	1971	1973	1975
1. Machinery imports (includes complete plants), 1957 prices	100	52	74	101	242
2. Machinery production (gross output value), 1952 prices					
A. High series	100	501	1300	1642[a]	2042[a]
B. Low series	100	257	711	930	1156
3. Share of imports in apparent consumption of machinery (%)					
A. Assuming high machinery output	40–45[b]	6–8	4	4–5	7–9
B. Assuming low machinery output	40–45[b]	12–14	7–8	7–8	12–15

Sources: (1) Imports for 1957–1973 in current and 1957 dollars are compiled in U.S. Central Intelligence Agency, *Foreign Trade in Machinery*, pp. 1, 6. Estimated current dollar value of 1975 imports (including machinery, transport equipment, precision instruments and watches and clocks) shown in U.S. Central Intelligence Agency, *China: International Trade, 1976–1977* (Washington, D.C., 1977), p. 13, is converted to 1957 dollars by assuming an 8% annual rate of price increase during 1973–1975. (2A) Based on Chinese statements, from Thomas G. Rawski, "China's Industrial Performance 1949–1973," in *Quantitative Measures of China's Economic Output*, ed. Alexander Eckstein (Ann Arbor, Mich.: University of Michigan Press, 1980), table III-7. (2B) Compiled from estimates of commodity output; from U.S. Central Intelligence Agency, *China: Economic Indicators 1977* (Washington, D.C., 1977), p. 15. (3) Calculated from lines 1 and 2 using the following formula:

$$100a_t = \frac{100M}{M + Q\,((1 - a)/a)}$$

where

a = imports divided by the sum of imports and domestic output during 1957,
a_t = the same quotient for a later year t,
M = imports (in 1957 prices) in t divided by 1957 imports,
Q = domestic machinery output in t divided by 1957 output (all in 1952 prices).

Note that these calculations ignore China's small exports of machinery.

a. Percentage growth during 1971–1975 assumed equal to that of the series shown in line 2B.
b. Chinese statements reported in Chu-yuan Cheng, *The Machine-Building Industry in Communist China* (Chicago: Aldine, 1971), p. 66, and *SCMP* 3392 (1965): p. 21.

chemical fertilizer industries, two sectors that were assigned secondary importance during the First Five-Year Plan years but assumed vital significance after 1960. In both cases output has surged since the mid 1960s, with very limited reliance on equipment imports. The petroleum sector, in which crude oil output rose from 1.5 million tons (mmt) in 1957 to the 1978 level of over 100 mmt, is equipped mainly by converted engineering works, including former textile machine repair shops. Chinese descriptions of the petroleum equipment sector refer mainly to smaller and older plants.[51] The case of chemical fertilizers, in which output grew from 0.8 mmt in 1957 to 29 mmt in 1975 and 44 mmt in 1978, again with little reliance on equipment imports prior to 1975, provides clearer evidence of the role of older firms as equipment suppliers.[52] Domestic fertilizer equipment first appeared in quantity during 1962; Shanghai led the way, supplying 25,000 tons of equipment to one major plant. While expanding output volume, Shanghai firms also enlarged their product line, turning out China's first equipment for urea manufacture in 1965. These achievements were not easy: officials of the Shanghai Boiler Works are now praised for having persevered in efforts to turn out fertilizer equipment despite temporary failure apparently caused by the absence of blueprints.[53]

Small fertilizer plants, which have accounted for the bulk of output growth since 1965, now obtain some machinery from provincial and local sources, but the core of the equipment industry remains in Shanghai, where a group of over four hundred factories supplied three hundred sets of equipment for synthetic ammonia plants between 1970 and 1972. Shanghai's contribution is typified by the case of the first nitrogenous fertilizer plant in remote Tsinghai province, commissioned in 1966: "Some of the equipment of the new plant was manufactured by Tsinghai Province's developing machine building industry. The rest came from Shanghai. Shanghai also trained technical staff for the plant and provided technicians to help install the machinery."[54]

Dependence on technology-bearing products, experience and advice from smaller plants and established industrial centers, notably Shanghai, extends to many other sectors. Producers of machine tools, pumps, bicycles, and transformers all follow Shanghai's technical lead. Even in steel and cable manufacture, sectors with major Soviet-aided plants, older units continue to make innovative contributions.[55]

Visitors flock to Shanghai to "learn new techniques and to exchange knowledge," bringing their technical problems with them. During the first half of 1965 over fifteen thousand visited the metropolis, which also sent out over one thousand personnel to help other places trying to catch up. The visitors "placed emphasis on learning new techniques of recently developed fields, such as electronic spark processing, forge pressing, vacuum casting, iso-ion cutting, argon arc welding, electro-slag welding, hot riveting, chemical and unlined hearths, and many new chemical reaction processes."[56] The general validity of these observations is confirmed by Chinese sources.

> The machine industry departments of every province and
> municipality have . . . achieved outstanding results, and the achievements of

Shanghai are especially outstanding. There has been a big development in technical innovations and the technical revolution, whether in big plants or small ones, and generally speaking, the small factories have done even better.[57]

One of the important factors behind the ability of Shanghai industry to develop . . . is implementation and execution of the policy giving equal priority to the development of large, medium, and small-scale enterprises, and placing medium and small-scale enterprises at the forefront . . . Practice proves that adoption of this method means smaller investments, quicker returns on investment dollars in the process of filling the gaps existing in some enterprises and industries. It also means the rapid development of new products.[58]

How can we explain this pattern of technological dynamism at smaller, older enterprises, a phenomenon that was certainly not anticipated by either the Soviet or the Chinese contributors to China's First Five-Year Plan? Rare Chinese observations on this subject emphasize the role of experience. With their "skilled veteran workers and experienced technical persons, old industrial bases and old enterprises . . . find it easier to tackle . . . complicated technical problems than new enterprises and new industrial bases."[59] Experience alone, however, cannot account for the superior innovative performance of smaller units. Thousands of veteran workers, engineers and managers have been shifted from old to new plants. Even if Shanghai has managed to hoard the cream of the pre-1949 trainees, the favored treatment accorded to new plants in assigning new graduates means at the very least that large newer units at Anshan, Shenyang, Loyang, or Ch'angch'un can match the smaller Shanghai units in terms of technical and engineering skills.

Some of the newer plants received major setbacks from the Soviet technical withdrawal, which may have affected performance over a longer period than is recognized by outsiders. Visitors to Wusih were told that an advanced shop of the Wusih Machine Tool Plant, which was being developed in conjunction with Soviet personnel, did not enter production until 1972![60] The giant Wuhan steel complex, which displayed considerable excess capacity in 1966, may have been similarly affected.[61]

Another possibility is that larger plants may suffer from diseconomies of scale. Smaller firms are said to be relatively "compact and . . . more flexible in adjusting their production." But at Shenyang's No. 1 Machine Tool Plant, organization is "swollen and ineffectual, technical control . . . highly complicated . . . [T]he potentialities of equipment and personnel cannot be fully developed and utilized and production technology is not likely to advance and improve." Innovative activities may be especially difficult under conditions of large-scale production. Ma T'ien-shui, a Shanghai party official, points out that innovations "may seem to work well in small-scale production. But when there is production in bulk, the quality begins to drop." Perhaps in response to this difficulty, "particularly in the case of newly risen industries that require more complex technology, Shanghai follows the principle of going from the small to the large-sized . . . [M]edium and small-sized factories always have to shoulder a greater share of the task of developing new varieties."[62]

A final factor that gives a great advantage to older units is the entrepreneurial opportunism of enterprises that survived the stormy decades of the 1930s and 1940s in the private sector. Particularly in Shanghai, whose functions in China's economy resemble those of New York in America's, there was an abundance of small, modestly capitalized enterprises specializing in what Raymond Vernon calls "producing the unpredictable."[63]

After 1949 these firms were again thrust into a harsh and unpredictable economic climate. Investment and supply planners neglected the inherited private sector, and party propagandists branded established industrial centers as irrational, bourgeois, and parasitic legacies of imperialism. Under these conditions, local pride, patriotism, and self-interest all impelled the staff and workers of these enterprises to show Peking that they too could help build socialism.

When summoned during the 1950s to raise output, older enterprises responded by shattering the performance targets set for them. Their unplanned output caused raw material shortages in 1956 and widespread idle capacity in industry during the following year. After 1960 the authorities demanded quality rather than quantity, and the same enterprises, drawing once again on traditions inherited from the past, responded with competitive supplier behavior appropriate to business downturns: innovation, customer service, and cost reduction.[64] These units provided an essential complement to the large but often inflexible productive capacity of the Soviet-designed industrial projects. Their ability to respond promptly to shifting demand patterns and to fill unexpected gaps between output and current requirements proved to be a key factor in regaining economic momentum following the crisis years of the early 1960s.

The Five Small Industries

The general features of China's small-industry sector require little elaboration.[65] Small rural plants are relatively easy to equip and can use local resources, reduce rural claims on overburdened national transport networks, and cater to local requirements which urban industry tends to overlook. If properly managed, small-scale plants have low capital costs and short gestation periods. By supplying local demand, small industry can reduce the pressure for higher output elsewhere, allowing advanced plants to concentrate on innovation and quality control rather than on output maximization.

Premature expansion of small plants during the Great Leap led to waste and confusion, and many small plants were closed during the retrenchment of 1960–1962. But as agricultural conditions stabilized and the opportunity cost of small-scale industrial ventures declined, official policy began once again to encourage local industrial development. The volume of resources devoted to small factories has expanded steadily since about 1963. Careful attention to pilot projects, cost reduction, and quality control has led to improved results. In 1964, for example, Kwangtung's Hsin-hui Farm Machine Works turned out power tillers at only 55% of the cost of useless models produced in 1960. A Kiangsu pilot project tripled earlier results in ammonia manufacture.[66]

Rural industrial activity can be divided into two segments: the collective and the state-owned sectors. The collective sector includes enterprises owned, financed, and managed by people's communes and their subunits, and consists mainly of handicrafts, processing of agricultural products, repair work, and farm sideline occupations. In 1973 "industry under collective ownership accounted for 3 per cent of the fixed assets, 36.2 per cent of the industrial population, and 14 per cent of the total output value" of all industry.[67]

Available Chinese sources do not discuss the overall size of state-owned small industry, a category including the county-run plants that dominate the so-called five small industries: fertilizer, cement, farm machinery, energy (coal and hydropower), and iron and steel. However, a rough estimate shown in table 6–4 indicates that small plants in these sectors accounted for about 6% of the gross value of 1972 factory output (excluding the handicraft, sideline, and crop-processing activities which are concentrated in the collective sector). Since productivity is low in smaller plants, the share of these enterprises in China's industrial labor force of about 20 million persons is probably larger, perhaps 10%–15%.

Small industry has not spread evenly over China's rural landscape. One Chinese account notes that "local industry has developed on a larger scale and at a faster speed in provinces that have a much better industrial foundation."[68] Hilly districts possessing mineral deposits and hydropower potential, areas with unusually high or rising levels of agricultural yields, and counties maintaining close contact with

TABLE 6–4 Estimated share of the "five small industries" in aggregate factory output for 1972 (billions of 1952 yuan)

| Product or sector | Small-scale share (%) | Gross value of factory output | |
		Total	Small-scale
Chemical fertilizer	60	3.643	2.186
Building materials	50	6.480	3.240
Farm machinery	67	13.009	8.716
Electric power	6	6.589	0.395
Coal	28	4.834	1.353
Iron-steel	10	22.108	2.211
Total	5.8	312.991	18.101

Source: Thomas G. Rawski, "Chinese Economic Planning," *Current Scene* 14, no. 4 (1976): 5. Factory output includes mining, manufacturing, and utilities but excludes handicrafts.

nearby centers of urban industry all appear to enjoy above-average success in expanding local industry.

Collective enterprises are financed mainly by communal savings. The initial financing of state-sector small plants apparently comes from government budgets; many of these units begin operations on an extremely small scale and pay for their own expansion from profits and possibly depreciation funds. Some units receive subsidies in the form of free equipment, low-interest loans, and technical assistance from advanced units.[69]

Does output from small plants make a positive contribution to China's economy? This issue can by investigated in two ways: first, by looking at microeconomic data from the enterprises themselves and, second, by examining the impact of small industry on the rural economy.

Transfer prices for producer goods in China are set substantially below market-clearing levels.[70] This discussion of microeconomic data from rural industry is based on the assumption that current market-clearing prices for small-industry products, while probably below the 1957 equilibrium levels because of intervening industrial growth, remain above the actual transfer prices of 1957. This assumption cannot be verified. However, in view of substantial post-1957 increases in farm-gate prices, rural purchasing power, and stocks of complementary resources, it seems difficult to doubt that rural users would gladly purchase added supplies of fertilizer, machinery, and the like, even if these were made available at 1957 prices rather than the somewhat lower prices now in force.

Under this assumption 1957 costs and prices become a useful standard for evaluating the present contribution of small plants. Tables 6–5 and 6–6 present scattered input and cost data showing that in comparison with large-plant achievements of the mid 1950s, leading enterprises in China's small-scale sector often require less capital per unit of output or capacity and attain lower average cost. These small plants are certainly making a positive contribution to the economy. Since Chinese planners attach positive value to industrial dispersion and rural involvement in industry, and since Chinese cost calculations exclude interest charges, modest excess costs in the small-scale sector are also consistent with this favorable conclusion.

This finding is based on two implicit assumptions: that Chinese prices and costs provide a reasonable reflection of scarcity conditions, and that small-plant products are close substitutes for the 1957 output of larger plants. The first assumption appears valid; in any case, it is beyond the scope of this paper. The second can claim considerable empirical support.[71]

Data in table 6–5 show that small-scale producers of hydroelectricity, synthetic ammonia, and steel products use considerably less capital per unit of product than large plants built during the First Five-Year Plan years. Superior labor productivity at the large K'unming Cement Plant indicates that the same is true in this sector. Small coal mines also require less investment per ton of product than larger ones.[72]

Table 6–6 presents evidence that costs at leading small-scale producers enable their outputs to be sold profitably at prices below those charged in 1957. Fertilizer costs are relatively high in the small-scale sector, but small plants can earn substantial returns even with selling prices that are lower (per ton of nutrient) today than in 1957.[73] Both price and cost fall well below the 1957 price at several small cement plants. The single available citation for steel products shows that a small county plant sells its reinforcing rods at a price below the estimated average 1957 wholesale price for steel products used in construction. Only in the single hydropower observation do we find a large cost excess in the small-scale sector.[74]

Table 6–7 presents data on diesel engine production in 1956–57 and 1975. These figures show that current products of medium and small plants compare favorably with products of the established Peking and Wusih (City) enterprises and are both lighter and cheaper than engines produced by larger firms in the mid 1950s. Even a commune plant just beginning to produce diesels can now match the cost performance of major national enterprises twenty years ago.

These results indicate that especially in the manufacture of fertilizer, cement, and machinery, small-scale, labor-intensive manufacturing methods have demonstrated their usefulness in raising the volume of output without significantly escalating costs. Although average small-plant performance undoubtedly lags well behind the standards achieved by leading units, there is every reason to believe that growing numbers of small factories will succeed in attaining the performance levels described in tables 6–5 to 6–7. Thus direct cost comparisons by themselves point strongly to the conclusion that rural industrialization is an economically viable approach and is making a substantial contribution to China's industrial development.

This positive view of small-scale industry is reinforced by considering the impact of local industrial expansion on China's rural economy. The long-run implications of introducing machine techniques into the work routines of China's rural labor force are enormous. With rural power consumption now in excess of the national 1955 total, machine technology has begun to penetrate the farm sector on a large scale.[75] In 1957 it was hoped that each province could have its own agricultural machinery plant. In 1972 each province manufactured not only farm machinery but also tractors and power machinery as well as fertilizer and cement. Virtually all of China's two thousand or so counties manufacture and repair farm equipment, 70% have cement works, 50% manufacture chemical fertilizers, and over half engage in a whole range of small industry: machinery, fertilizer, cement, iron and steel, and coal mining.[76]

In many regions electricity and machinery are in common use at the lowest level of farm production. In Hopei and Shantung the average production brigade (about 220 households) now operates 81 hp and 50 hp of machinery respectively in 1973.[77] Anhwei province possesses over twice the 1957 national stock of irrigation and drainage equipment, and Kiangsu's annual increments of irrigation equipment are well above the 1957 national stock.[78]

The spread of mechanical technology to regions formerly dependent solely on human and animal power creates requirements similar to those faced by Chinese and foreign entrepreneurs at the turn of the century. Who will operate and repair the new machines? How will users obtain spare parts for machinery that is often not standardized?

The spread of small industry and of its products throughout rural China has initiated a process of skill formation and technical development strongly reminiscent of the prewar industrial history of coastal urban areas. Today, however, resolution of technical difficulties need not await the slow growth of private enterprise. Consultations with expert personnel from government and industry, wintertime technical education campaigns, massive distribution of simple technical hand-

TABLE 6-5 Capital intensity and productivity indicators at large and small plants

Sector and plant	K_c (million yuan)	Q (1000 tons/ yr, or kw)	L	K_c/L (yuan)	K_c/Q (yuan/ton, or yuan/kw)	Q/L (tons/man-yr)
Synthetic ammonia						
Large plants, 1950s						
Kirin Fertilizer Plant	220–260[a]	120[a]	—	—	2,000*	—
A large plant	100[b]	20[b]	—	—	5,000	—
Small plants						
Tanyang (Kiangsu)	7.0[c]	5[c]	—	—	1,400	—
Hsiyang (Shansi)	7.5	10	450	16,667	750	22
Lin (Honan)	6.0	7	520	11,538	857	13
Cement						
K'unming plant (1959)	—	360[d]	1,200[d]	—	—	300
Small plants						
Lin (Honan)	0.3[e]	25	—	—	12	—
Tachai (Shansi)	0.35	20	144	2,430	17.5	139
Hui (Honan)	—	50	500	—	—	100
Nanhai (Kwangtung)	5.0	103	549	9,107	48.5	188
Hydroelectric power						
Large plants						
1953–57	—	—	—	—	1,305[f]	—
1958–62	—	—	—	—	771[f]	—
Small plants						
Huichou (Anhwei, 499 plants)	5.6[g]	7,830 kw[g]	—	—	711	—
Tungcheng (Hupei, 79 plants)	6.6[h]	7,100 kw[h]	—	—	932	—

Iron and steel

Large and medium plants

A large plant	1,000+ᶦ	1,500ᶦ	—	667ᶦ	—
Shoutu (Peking)	—	—	20,000	1,000ʲ	50
18 medium plants	600–700ᶦ	1,100–1,200ᶦ	—	565*	—
Small plants					
A small plant	0.145ᵏ	0.3ᵏ	—	483	—
A small plant	15–16ᶦ	30–40ᶦ	—	443*ᶦ	—
Wusih	10	805	—	—	12
Shanghai Steel Tube	9	814	—	—	11

Source: Unless otherwise noted, data are from interview material recorded by the Rural Small-scale Industries Delegation, June-July 1975.

Note: K_c = construction cost; Q = output or capacity in 1,000 tons/year (or kw for hydropower plants); L = employment.

a. Table 6–2 and Jung-chao Liu, *China's Fertilizer Economy* (Chicago: Aldine, 1971), p. 130; capacity figure is the 1959 output total.

b. Cited in Nai-ruenn Chen and Walter Galenson, *The Chinese Economy under Communism* (Chicago: Aldine, 1972), p. 117. Capacity is given in terms of chemical fertilizer; therefore capital cost per annual ton of ammonia output probably exceeds the figure given here.

c. *JPRS* 31510 (1965): 1–2.

d. Furui, *Hōchū*, p. 19.

e. Jon Sigurdson, "Technology and Employment in China," *World Development* 2 no. 3 (1974): 79.

f. Onoe Etsuzō, "Chūgoku no denryoku kōgyō" (China's electric power industry), in Shigeru Ishikawa, ed., *Chūgoku keizai no chōki tembō* (Long-term prospects for China's economy) (Tokyo: Institute of Developing Economies, 1964), p. 314.

g. *BBC* W804 (1974): A7.
h. *BBC* W895 (1976): A6.
i. *JMJP*, August 19, 1957.
j. *JMJP*, April 14, 1958.
k. *BBC* W686 (1972): A9.
* Midpoint of data range.

TABLE 6–6 Costs and prices for products of large plants, 1957, and small plants, 1975 (in yuan per ton or per kilowatt-hour)

Item and producer	Data for 1957			Data for 1975		
	Production cost	Wholesale price	Retail price	Production cost	Wholesale price	Retail price
Cement						
Li-ch'eng (Shansi)	—	55[a]	—	60[b]	—	80[b]
Tachai (Shansi)	—	—	—	30	38	—
Lin (Honan)-1970 data	—	—	—	36[c]	47[c]	—
Medium plant, 100,000 tons/year	—	—	—	31[c]	—	—
Chemical fertilizers						
Ammonium nitrate	125[d]		310–316[d]	—	—	—
	(625)		(1,550–1,580)			
Hsiyang (Shansi)	—	—	—	200	260–265	300
				(1,000)	(1,300–1,325)	(1,500)
Ammonia bicarbonate						
Lin (Honan)	—	—	—	130	180	—
				(763)	(1,058)	
Hydroelectric power						
Lin (Honan)	.0052[d]	—	—	—	.035	.048
Steel products						
Wusih (Kiangsu)	—	682[a]	—	—	~500	—

Source: Unless otherwise noted, data are from interview material recorded by the Rural Small-Scale Industries Delegation, June-July 1975.

Note: Data in parentheses show costs and prices per ton of nitrogen content.
a. Ian H. MacFarlane, "Construction Trends in China, 1949–74," in U.S. Congress, Joint Economic Committee, *China: A Reassessment of the Economy* (Washington, D.C. 1975), p. 319. The figure for steel is the average 1957 wholesale price of steel products used in construction.
b. Retail price is the price of outside supplies including transport costs.
c. 1956 figures from outside supplies including transport costs.
d. 1956 figures from Nai-ruenn Chen, *Chinese Economic Statistics* (Chicago: Aldine, 1967), p. 280.

TABLE 6-7   Characteristics of Chinese diesel engines, 1956–57 and 1975

Plant	Horsepower	Weight (kg)	Kg/ hp	Production cost (yuan)	Cost/hp (yuan)
Data for 1956–57					
Chinan (Shantung)	—	—	—	—	84[a]
Shanghai Diesel Plant	—	—	—	—	89[a]
Wusih (Kiangsu) Diesel Plant	—	—	—	—	91[a]
Wusih (Kiangsu) Diesel Plant	40[b]	1,202[b]	30[b]	—	—
Weifang (Shantung)	—	—	—	—	117[a]
Weifang (Shantung)	10[b]	260[b]	26[b]	—	—
Nanch'ang (Kiangsi)	12[a]	600[a]	50[a]	—	—
	16[a]	580[a]	36[a]	—	—
Tientsin Engine Plant	small	—	60[b]	—	—
Unspecified	300[c]	1,300[c]	4.3[c]	—	—
Unspecified					
Past	—	—	—	—	200+[d]
Present (1956)	—	—	—	—	150−[d]
Advanced units, 1956	—	—	—	—	110[d]
Data for 1975[e]					
Large plants					
Peking Engine Plant	45–65	—	—	3,200–4,000	60–70
Old model	55	550	10	—	—
New model	60	340	5.7	—	—
Wusih (Kiangsu) Diesel	12	130	10.8	—	—
Medium and small plants					
T'aiyuan (Shansi)	10	126	12.6	—	—
Anyang (Honan)	12	130	10.8	800[f]	67
Hsin-hsiang No. 2 (Honan)	12	150	12.5	700[f]	58
Tzu-ch'i (Chekiang)	3	39	13	—	—
Wusih County Plant (Kiangsu)	4	40	10	—	—
Ch'angchou (Kiangsu)	12	130	10.8	—	—
Shanghai Power Machine Plant	35	310	8.8	—	—
Shanghai Ma-lu Commune	3.5	38–42	11.4*	550	157

* Midpoint of data range.
a. *Chūgoku shiryō geppō* 114 (1957), pp. 17, 42.
b. Wang Hsin-min, "Opinions on Developing Our Country's Production of Diesel and Coal-Gas Engines," *CHKY* 5 (1957): 5.
c. *JMJP*, October 30, 1956.
d. *JMJP*, May 13, 1956.
e. Collected by Rural Small-Scale Industries Delegation.
f. Prices paid by purchasers.

books, and transfer of educated urban youth to rural areas all can hasten the process of skill accumulation. At the same time, Peking's emphasis on self-reliance and bland acceptance of periodic reports of wasteful mistakes reveal considerable sophistication and understanding of the inescapable trial-and-error nature of technical advance.

The small-scale sector has already shown its ability to contribute to industrial expansion. Small plants provide a source of industrial growth that economizes on several scarce resources: foreign exchange, highly skilled technicians, long-distance rail and truck transport, and government financing. Rural industrialization raises investment without increasing taxes, provides a constructive outlet for local pride, and allows localities to remedy some of the errors and oversights of an inevitably heavy-handed system of economic planning.

In the short term, however, the greatest impact of small industry is on farming itself. In the absence of path-breaking technological innovation or of massive investment in waterworks, further intensification of an already highly developed farming cycle is the chief means of raising agricultural production. Small industry has contributed to agricultural intensification by providing fertilizers, construction materials, water control, processing, and transport equipment. In addition, the spread of electrification and machinery has released large quantities of labor to fill rising rural demand which is partly a result of increased use of fertilizer, pumps, and other products of small industry.

China has now made significant headway in building up a capacity to analyze, select, mold, and in some instances originate industrial technologies. Domestic engineering firms incorporate a growing range of techniques into their products, and these in turn provide the technical foundation for modernization in all sectors of the economy. An extensive communications network carries foreign and domestic technical data and engineering know-how to all economic units. Administrative structures and methods have been modified to facilitate the mastery and absorption of new production methods. These developments are central aspects of any large nation's transition to modern economic growth.

These advances originated before 1949 in China's small private industrial sector. They appear closely linked to the accumulation of experience in investment, production, and administration rather than to increases in the stock of capital and formal education. Sharp divergence between the loci of post-1949 industrial investment and of innovative leadership, which is most marked in the case of Shanghai, strongly supports the emphasis that this essay has placed on experience as a determinant of the location and evolution of industry's production frontier. If this approach is valid, one should expect a multiplication of innovative poles within China's industrial sector, first in firms and regions that benefited from massive investments during the 1950s and eventually from the rural industries now in the early stages of development.

The contribution of prewar developments to industry's subsequent achievements underlines the long-term nature of the industrialization process. The Chinese case offers little support for the optimistic view that industrial latecomers can utilize the advances of others to leapfrog into higher stages of development or to quickly establish a wide range of technologies keyed to local factor proportions. With significant exceptions, of which the small-scale fertilizer industry is the best example, deviations from international technologies are broadly confined to the sort of "improvement engineering" familiar from the industrial history of Japan and other countries. Even in the small-scale sector, substantial capital requirements ensure that productivity of factory workers will remain far above the national average.[79]

China's present industrial situation also bears the imprint of shifts that began only after 1949. The massive expansion of large-scale industry begun during the 1950s continues, but with a substantially reduced, but still significant, import component. The rising rate of industrial capital formation constitutes a sharp break with the past; it has transformed industry from the smallest to the largest contributor to aggregate output.

Since 1960, the expanding scale of industrial activity has been accompanied by increasingly effective efforts to improve cohesion within industry by shortening lines of communication between producers and users, among planners, managers, and blue-collar workers, and between industrial plants and the growing array of support institutions. The enlarged role of provincial and local planning agencies in setting patterns of resource allocation, extended national campaigns aimed at improving product designs and increasing the degree of industrial specialization and interenterprise cooperation, and efforts to overcome "inert areas" within enterprises by the joint efforts of managers, technicians, and workers—all are measures that have contributed to industry's growing flexibility and responsiveness to changes in demand as well as increased the output derived from available resources.[80]

If investment policy has expanded the scale of industry, these administrative and institutional shifts have allowed planners to take advantage of the special features of various groups of industrial producers. They have also contributed to a redirection of incentives which has reduced earlier overemphasis on output volume and has spurred Chinese industry toward levels of efficiency that now appear to be substantially higher than those attained in the planned economies of the Soviet Union and Eastern Europe.

In studying the evolution of China's industrial sector, one is struck by the developmental significance of implementation rather than planning and of incentives rather than sheer skills. Externalities appear to be a ubiquitous and vital aspect of industrial activity, whether in the form of skill accumulation, regional development, or interaction between rural industry and the farm sector. These features appear to justify China's policy of early and widespread national and regional import substitution despite the extensive short-run costs imposed on both producers and consumers of import substitutes.

Chinese planners are well aware of these costs. In seeking to capture the benefits of international or interregional trade as well as those of import substitution, they now appear to advocate the mixture of contact and isolation first imposed on an unwilling China by the vagaries of European politics, Japanese aggression, and the Sino-Soviet dispute. External contact allows domestic producers to draw in both embodied and disembodied techniques from foreign sources (or in the case of rural industry, from advanced domestic enterprises), while isolation spurs producers to extract the maximum potential from available material and human resources.

Published materials and visitor accounts do little to explain how Chinese economists and planners deal with these issues. We do not know, for example, the criteria or methods used to determine the extent to which particular commodities will be obtained from foreign, national, provincial, or local suppliers. This omission is doubly unfortunate because it matches a gap in our own understanding. How should investment decisions be made in economies in which the future is obscured by volatile demand conditions and in which major externalities complicate the assessment of cost and productivity? In the analysis of such situations, it seems obvious that conventional forms of investment programming must be supplemented with approaches associated with the work of Albert Hirschmann, with emphasis on administration, on the impact of imbalances and bottlenecks in problem-solving capabilities, and on the general absence of durable optimum solutions to basic policy issues.[81]

Notes

The author gratefully acknowledges comments by the participants at the conference, especially C. Peter Timmer and Shigeru Ishikawa. A revised and extended treatment of the topics discussed in this essay is presented in Thomas G. Rawski, *China's Transition to Industrialism:*

Producer Goods and Economic Development in the Twentieth Century (Ann Arbor: University of Michigan Press, 1980).

1. "The division of labor, by reducing every man's business to some one simple operation, and by making this operation the sole employment of his life, necessarily increases very much the dexterity of the workman," Adam Smith, *The Wealth of Nations,* book 1, chap. 1; Kenneth Arrow, "The Economic Implications of Learning by Doing," *Review of Economic Studies* (June 1962): 155–173.

2. Edward Ames and Nathan Rosenberg, "The Progressive Division and Specialization of Industries," *Journal of Development Studies* 1, no. 3 (1965): 373; Thomas R. Navin, *The Whitin Machine Works since 1831* (Cambridge, Mass.: Harvard University Press, 1950), especially pp. 421–423.

3. Kazushi Ohkawa and Henry Rosovsky, *Japanese Economic Growth* (Stanford, Calif.: Stanford University Press, 1973), especially pp. 213–215 and 218–228.

4. Figure for 1933 calculated from Ta-chung Liu and Kung-chai Yeh, *The Economy of the Chinese Mainland* (Princeton: Princeton University Press, 1965), pp. 66, 426–428. Estimated 1936 industrial net value added was 35% above the 1933 level, but GDP rose by only 4.8% during 1933–1936; see John K. Chang, *Industrial Development in Pre-Communist China* (Chicago: Aldine, 1969), p. 61, and K. C. Yeh, "Capital Formation," in Alexander Eckstein, Walter Galenson, and Ta-chung Liu, eds., *Economic Trends in Communist China* (Chicago: Aldine, 1968), p. 510.

5. These developments are discussed in greater detail in Thomas G. Rawski, "The Growth of Producer Industries, 1900–1971," in Dwight H. Perkins, ed., *China's Modern Economy in Historical Perspective* (Stanford: Stanford University Press, 1975), pp. 203–221.

6. *T'ien-chin jih pao* (Tientsin daily), October 4, 1957, reported that only 7.02% of the machine tools in Tientsin's machinery and electrical industries had been newly added during the First Five-Year Plan years.

7. Shanghai budget and investment data are from Nicholas R. Lardy, "Economic Planning in the People's Republic of China: Central-Provincial Fiscal Relations," in U.S. Congress, Joint Economic Committee, *China: A Reassessment of the Economy* (Washington, D.C., 1975), p. 104.

8. In 1957 Hsüchou planned to carry out 58 basic construction projects totaling 9.03 million yuan, an average of 155,690 yuan per project. *Hsin-hua jih-pao* (New China daily, Nanking), August 3, 1957.

9. Typical discussions appear in Hsü Yen, "Factories and Mines Must Strengthen Technical Analysis and Research," *Chung-kung-yeh t'ung-hsün* (Heavy industry bulletin) 21 (1954): 9–10, and "Strength-

ening the Training of Basic Level Production Leaders Is an Important Current Task," ibid., 29 (1954): pp. 17–23.

10. Nationwide year-end employment in industry and construction rose from 3.26 million in 1949 to 6.31 million in 1952 and 10.66 million in 1956. Nai-ruenn Chen, *Chinese Economic Statistics* (Chicago: Aldine, 1967), pp. 476–477.

11. *Survey of the China Mainland Press* (hereafter *SCMP*) 1446 (1957), p. 15.

12. Joseph S. Berliner, *Factory and Manager in the USSR* (Cambridge, Mass.: Harvard University Press, 1957), p. 139. Numerous instances of waste and damage caused by exposing machinery to the elements, improper installation, neglect of lubrication or other elementary maintenance measures, workers' refusal to use measuring tools, and other blunders reported in Chinese publications verify the applicability of Berliner's phrase to Chinese industry in this period.

13. Charles Kennedy and A. P. Thirlwall, "Surveys in Applied Economics: Technical Progress," *Economic Journal* 82, no. 1 (1972): 39, discuss the case of the Horndal iron works in Sweden which "experienced no new investment for fifteen years yet output per man hour rose steadily by 2% per annum."

14. China's imports of machinery and transport equipment rose by 193% in terms of current U.S. dollars and by 190% in terms of 1957 U.S. dollars between 1952 and 1957; U.S. Central Intelligence Agency, *Foreign Trade in Machinery and Equipment since 1952* (Washington, D.C.: CIA, 1975), pp. 1, 6. During the same years, officially estimated machinery output in terms of constant 1952 prices rose from 1404 to 6177 million yuan, an increase of 340%; Chen, *Chinese Economic Statistics*, pp. 222–223.

15. Typical reports appear in *T'ien-chin jih-pao,* June 6, 1953; *Jen-min jih-pao* (hereafter *JMJP*), September 20, 1953, and March 15, 1955; *Tung-pei jih-pao (Northeast daily, Shenyang), April 8, 1954; Kung-jen jih-pao* (Daily worker, Peking), July 19, 1955.

16. By 1958 the industrial and communication sectors had established a total of 415 research institutes with 59,200 employees (*Ten Great Years*, p. 140).

17. Criticism of enterprise research facilities may be found in Chiang Li, "Several Problems as Seen from Four Chinan Plants," *Chi-hsieh kung-yeh* (Machinery industry; hereafter *CHKY*) 1 (1957): 30; Ti Yun-ch'ing, "Discussion of Several Problems of Current Enterprise Technical Work," *CHKY* 16 (1957): 21–23. A 1957 article on the chemical industry's "Directive for Strengthening Scientific Research Work" commented that "in the past few years, although our ministry's research work . . . has achieved certain results . . . generally

speaking our country's research work is still at the stage of building strength and completing a few small-scale tasks." *Hua-hsüeh kung-yeh* (Chemical industry, hereafter *HHKY*) 9 (1957): 1.

18. M. Gardner Clark, *The Development of China's Steel Industry and Soviet Technical Aid* (Ithaca, N.Y.: N.Y. State School of Industrial and Labor Relations, 1973), pp. 33–38.

19. Many of these proposals are described in Jan S. Prybyla, *The Political Economy of Communist China* (Scranton, Pa.: International Textbook, 1970), chap. 7.

20. *Shin Chūgoku no kikai kōgyō* (New China's machinery industry) (Tokyo: Tōā keizai kenkyūkai, 1960), p. 57; *Wen-hui pao* (Wen-hui news, Shanghai), January 1, 1959.

21. *Lü-ta jih-pao* (Lüta daily), September 28 and October 12, 1958.

22. Plant data from *JMJP*, November 6, 1958, and *Liao-ning jih-pao* (Liaoning daily, Shenyang), January 17, 1959. Total number of "simplified" tools from *Ta-kung pao* (Impartial daily, Peking), September 27, 1959.

23. A lengthy report in the May 1959 issue of *Foundry* magazine found that to produce machine castings, "not a single plant which does not use an alkaline, hot-blast iron furnace can profitably use native iron in its regular production" (translated in *Joint Publications Research Service*—hereafter *JPRS*—1048-D, pp. 1–12).

24. A preliminary version of the unpublished "70 Articles" appears in *Documents of Chinese Communist Party Central Committee, September 1956–April 1969* (Hong Kong: Union Research Institute, 1971), I, 689–693.

25. Enforcement and continuity are discussed in Thomas G. Rawski, "China's Industrial System," in *China: A Reassessment*, pp. 186–192.

26. Ibid., pp. 188–189; Carl Riskin, "China's Rural Industries: Self-Reliant Systems or Independent Kingdoms?" *China Quarterly* 73 (1978): 77–98; Bruce L. Reynolds, "Central Planning in China: The Significance of Material Allocation Conferences," *Bulletin of the Association for Comparative Economic Studies* 17, no. 1 (1975): 3–14.

27. Evidence of strong central authority appears in Lardy, "Economic Planning," and in visitor accounts cited in Rawski, "China's Industrial System," pp. 190–192.

28. Soviet economic coefficients were adopted at both the national and enterprise levels. See Shigeru Ishikawa, "A Note on the Choice of Technology in China," *Journal of Development Studies* 9, no. 1 (1972): 179, and Chiang Cheng, "Problems and Weak Points in Technical Work," *CHKY* 12 (1957): 25.

29. The 490 above-norm projects received about five-sixths of total

First Five-Year Plan industrial investment outlays (K. C. Yeh, "Capital Formation," p. 522). Subtracting the 11,000 million yuan planned expenditure on 154 Soviet-aided projects from five-sixths of the 1953–1957 investment total shown in table 6–1 leaves 9,858 million yuan to be shared among 336 remaining projects.

30. Hsiang Lin, "How to Implement the Principle of 'Frugal National Construction' in Basic Construction," *CHKY* 11 (1957): 18. Hsiang also remarked that "in the past, when we determined the scale of new plant designs, it was usually according to planned national demand in the Third Five-Year Plan period."

31. Pai Ou, "Brief Discussion of the Direction and Tasks of the Machinery Industry during the First and Second Five-Year Plans," *CHKY* 12 (1957): 2.

32. Pai, "Brief Discussion," p. 6; Giga Sōichirō, *Chūgoku no shakai-shugi kigyō* (China's socialist enterprises) (Tokyo: Minerva, 1965), p. 257.

33. Much of the growth in commodity output during 1957–1965 shown in Robert M. Field, "Civilian Industrial Production in the People's Republic of China, 1949–74," in *China: A Reassessment,* pp. 166–167, can be attributed to completion of these facilities.

34. Hsü Pao-min, "Economic Significance of Using General Technical Equipment," *Yeh-chin pao* (Metallurgy) 19 (1957): 28; *Chung-kuo hsin-wen* (China news), February 7, 1958; *JMJP,* June 7, 1957; *Kuang-hsi jih-pao* (Kwangsi daily, Nanning), January 1, 1954. For high-priced import substitutes, see Fan Jo-i, "More on Price Policy for Heavy Industrial Products," *Ching-chi yen-chiu* (Economic research; hereafter *CCYC*) 3 (1957): 62 and Kang Chao, *Capital Formation in Mainland China, 1952–1965* (Berkeley: University of California Press, 1974), p. 40. Opinion on the appropriateness of exchange rates is divided: Frederick M. Cone, *Chinese Industrial Growth: Brief Studies of Selected Investment Areas* (Santa Monica, Calif.: Rand Corp., 1969), p. 59, claims that the yuan was overvalued during the 1950s, particularly with regard to machinery. Chao, *Capital Formation,* pp. 31–37, maintains the opposite view.

35. Meng Chih-chien, "On the Mechanization of Casting Shops," *CHKY* 13 (1957): 7.

36. Hsü I, "On Several Problems of Economic Accounting," *CCYC* 4 (1958): 64, 72–73.

37. Hsiang, "How to Implement the Principle" p. 19, provides a typical example.

38. *JMJP,* January 31 and March 13, 1953; April 1 and 24, 1954; Pai, "Brief Discussion," p. 5; Hu Kang, "Do Not Overlook the Utility of Screws," *CHKY* 20 (1956): 32–33.

39. February 1957 was described as "the time when many of the industrial, building and transportation enterprises are planning production goals for 1957" (*SCMP* 1481 (1957): 5). Factories had not received their 1957 plans by the end of February, and it was not until late March that "the State Economic Commission has completed its plans for the year to be submitted to the State Council" (*SCMP* 1494 (1957): 7, and 1503 (1957): 14).

40. Hsü, "Economic Accounting," p. 69. The First Ministry of Machine-Building Industry admitted in 1957 that its previous supply work had been marred by "a certain amount of chaos"; "Directive for 1957," *CHKY* 9 (1957): 7.

41. Wang Te-yuan, "Perceive the Conditions of Steel Supply," *CHKY* 9 (1957): 29.

42. Chang Chen (vice-minister of chemicals), "For Better Fulfillment of the Second Five-Year Plan Tasks for Chemical Construction," *HHKY* 11 (1957): 12; P'an Kuang-chi, "Opinions on the Development Path of the Basic Chemicals Sector," *HHKY* 8 (1957): 33.

43. In one instance plant officials were accused of reverting to the original routine the moment the Soviet advisers left the premises! "Why Are Newly Expanded Workshops Unable to Fulfill State Plans?" *CHKY* 11 (1956): 28.

44. This approach is drawn out with extraordinary clarity in Chang, "For Better Fulfillment," p. 13, and P'eng T'ao (minister of chemicals), "Fully Implement the Principle of 'Frugal National Construction,'" *HHKY* 1 (1958): 3.

45. Historical information from Chung-kuo k'o-hsüeh yuan Shang-hai ching-chi yen-chiu so and Shang-hai she-hui k'o-hsüeh yuan ching-chi yen-chiu so, *Ta-lung chi-ch'i-ch'ang ti fa-sheng fa-chan yü kai-tsao* (Birth, development, and reform of Ta-lung Machinery Works) (Shanghai: Shang-hai jen-min ch'u-pan she, 1959). Some of the material is summarized in Rawski, "Growth of Producer Industries," pp. 207–213.

46. *Kuang-ming jih-pao*, September 24, 1957; 1956 investment was 1.68 million yuan; *Chieh-fang jih-pao* (Liberation daily, Shanghai), October 1, 1957; *Wen-hui pao* (Shanghai), January 16, 1958. Ta-lung employed 2950 workers in 1956 (*Ta-lung*, p. 119).

47. Information about Ta-lung from the following sources: Hu Kuang, "The Developing Petroleum Equipment Industry," *CHKY* 20 (1964): 15; *JPRS* 29598 (1965): 18, and 29685 (1965): 12–31; *SCMP* 5289 (1973): 124–125; British Broadcasting Corporation, Summary of World Broadcasts, Part III: The Far East, *Weekly Economic Report* (hereafter *BBC*) W759 (1974): A5. Technical articles written by Ta-lung personnel appear in the following issues of *Shang-hai chi-hsieh*

(Shanghai machinery): 11(1965): 18; 12(1965): 34–35; 1(1966): 36–37, 43.

48. *SCMP* Supplement 131 (1965): 26. Vice-Mayor Ts'ao also stated that "in 1961 the [basic economic policy of] readjustment consisted mainly in shortening the front of capital construction" and his list of tasks for 1962 made no mention of investment activities (ibid., 101 (1962): 6–7). In December 1965, Ts'ao reported that "no big industrial construction and expansion projects were undertaken in Shanghai over the past two years; in most cases, technological transformation was effected on the original foundation of the enterprise" (ibid., 150 (1966): 8).

49. *JPRS* 33603 (1966): 11.

50. Ibid. Examples of firms making transitions from repair work to manufacturing are common in Chinese press and radio reports.

51. Estimates of crude oil output are from U.S. Central Intelligence Agency, *China: A Statistical Compendium* (Washington, D.C., 1979), p. 9; for the equipment industry, see Chu-yuan Cheng, *China's Petroleum Industry* (New York: Praeger, 1976), chap. 5.

52. Fertilizer output estimates in terms of product weight are from CIA, *Statistical Compendium*, p. 13.

53. *Yang-ch'eng wen-pao* (Canton evening news), January 9, 1964; *SCMP* 3422 (1965): 24–25, and 4814 (1971): 190–191.

54. *SCMP* 5317 (1973): 29–30; *JPRS* 35070 (1966): 25.

55. Examples of Shanghai's technical leadership appear in *BBC*, W804 (1974): A11; *JPRS* 31658 (1965): 19; *CHKY* 7 (1962): 11; Joan Robinson, *Economic Management in China* (London: Anglo-Chinese Educational Institute, 1973), pp. 23–24; *JPRS* 29021 (1965): 58–59; 28876 (1965): 2; 29937 (1965): 26–32; 33835 (1966): 8–9.

56. *JPRS* 30743 (1965): 23–25.

57. Ibid., 32222 (1965): 10.

58. Ibid., 31758 (1965): 2.

59. *SCMP* 3275 (1964): 4–5.

60. Author's notes while a member of the Rural Small-Scale Industries Delegation sponsored by the Committee on Scholarly Communication with the People's Republic of China, June 30, 1975.

61. Richman, *Industrial Society*, p. 470.

62. I am indebted to Alexander Eckstein for the suggestion concerning economies of scale. Quotations are from *SCMP* 4392 (1965): 3; *JPRS* 31671 (1965): pp. 2, 23; and *SCMP* 3492 (1965), p. 3.

63. Raymond Vernon, *Metropolis 1985* (New York: Doubleday, 1963), pp. 100 ff. Arthur L. Stinchcombe called my attention to this similarity between the two cities.

64. Compare the following U.S. example: "Indeed, one of the compensations of slack business for the engineer-entrepreneur . . . was

the chance of devoting more time to innovations. It is not surprising . . . that the automatics, the universals, the gear shapers, and the grinding machines were developed most rapidly during the depressions of the 1870's and the 1890's. The relatively prosperous 1880's were years of quantitative rather than qualitative progress. Depressions tended to shift the attention of businessmen to ways of cutting costs." W. Paul Strassmann, *Risk and Technological Innovation* (Ithaca, N.Y.: Cornell University Press, 1959), p. 154.

65. Carl Riskin, "Small Industry and the Chinese Model of Development," *China Quarterly* 46 (1971): 245–273; Jon Sigurdson, "Rural Industrialization in China," in *China: A Reassessment*, pp. 411–435; Dwight H. Perkins et al., *Rural Small-Scale Industry in the People's Republic of China* (Berkeley: University of California Press, 1977).

66. *Nan-fang jih-pao* (Southern daily, Canton), April 18, 1965; *SCMP* 3534 (1975): 22–23.

67. Chang Chun-chiao, "On Exercising All-Round Dictatorship over the Bourgeoisie," *Peking Review* 14 (1975): 6. Since collective industries often use part-time labor and typically collect processing fees rather than buying, processing, and then reselling grain and other farm produce, these figures cannot be directly compared with data for state-owned industries.

68. "Local Industry in China," *Peking Review*, 39 (1971): 9.

69. Rural Small-Scale Industries Delegation, trip notes; John K. Galbraith, *A China Passage* (Boston: Houghton Mifflin, 1973), p. 127.

70. To take chemical fertilizer as an example, the Ta-ts'ai-yuan (great vegetable garden) Brigade of Ch'eng-kuan Commune, Lin County, Honan, reports that overfulfillment of its grain sales quota enables it to purchase additional supplies of chemical fertilizer from the state (Rural Small-Scale Industries Delegation, trip notes). More generally, Shigeru Ishikawa estimates that the 1972 equilibrium price of ammonium sulfate fertilizer was approximately double the actual transfer price; see his "Chūgoku ni okeru gijutsu hatten no ichi kenkyū," in Shigeru Ishikawa et al., *Chūgoku no kagaku gijutsu ni kansuru ichi kenkyū* (Studies on China's science and technology) (Tokyo: Nihon Keizai Kenkyū sentā, 1974), p. 22.

71. On the technical characteristics of small factory output, see Perkins et al., *Rural Industry,* and table 6–7.

72. Investment costs reportedly ranged from 18 yuan per ton of capacity for mines producing under 15,000 tons annually to 28 yuan per ton for mines producing over 90,000 tons per year (*JMJP*, March 3, 1958). Production cost is inversely related to scale, ranging from 11.70 yuan per ton for small mines to 11.17 and 9.75 yuan per ton at medium and large mines. *Chūgoku shiryō geppō* 130 (1958): 21.

73. Data for two fertilizer plants visited by the Rural Small-Scale

Industries Delegation indicate annual rates of return to construction cost of 17% and 33% respectively. The profit figures presumably are net of depreciation but gross of allowances for interest on fixed capital.

74. In this particular case, generation of power is part of a multi-purpose project designed primarily to provide water for irrigation.

75. Rural power consumption has risen from 3.2 billion kilowatt-hours in 1965 to 4.3 times that figure, or 13.76 billion kilowatt-hours in 1973. National power output in 1955 was 12.28 billion kilowatt-hours. See Kang Chao, *Agricultural Production in Communist China* (Madison, Wis.: University of Wisconsin Press, 1970), p. 139; *SCMP* 5529 (1974): 57; Chen, "For Better Fulfillment" p. 187.

76. *Chūgoku shiryō geppō* 109 (1957): 39; *SCMP* 4992 (1971): 28; *BBC* W716 (1973): A9; Rural Small-Scale Industries Delegation, trip notes, June 13, 1975.

77. Frederick W. Crook, "The Commune System in the People's Republic of China, 1963–74," in *China: A Reassessment,* p. 388; *SCMP* 5453 (1973): 75; *BBC* W714 (1973): A10.

78. Thomas G. Rawski, "Recent Trends in the Chinese Economy," *China Quarterly* 53 (1973): 27; Chu-yuan Cheng, *The Machine-Building Industry in Communist China* (Chicago: Aldine, 1971), p. 257.

79. Data in tables 6–2 and 6–5, for example, show that despite substantial reductions in equipment prices, capital per worker in recently constructed small fertilizer plants exceeds the 1955 average for the entire chemical sector.

80. Some of these changes are discussed in Lardy, "Economic Planning"; Reynolds, "Central Planning"; and Ishikawa, "Choice of Technology." Additional analysis may be found in Carl Riskin, "Workers' Incentives in Chinese Industry," in *China: A Reassessment,* pp. 199–224; Kojima Reiitsu, *Chūgoku no keizai to gijutsu* (China's economy and technology) (Tokyo: Keisō shobō, 1975), part 2; and Rawski, "China's Industrial Performance."

81. Albert O. Hirschman, *The Strategy of Economic Development* (New Haven, Conn.: Yale University Press, 1958) and *A Bias for Hope* (New Haven, Conn.: Yale University Press, 1971).

7

Health Care Services in China's Economic Development

TEH-WEI HU

Health care services can be considered both an end and a means in economic development. In economic terms, health care services are both consumption and investment goods. The consumption aspects include the amount of satisfaction engendered by being healthy compared with the social and psychological costs of poor health. These satisfaction levels can be measured in terms of the reduction in the mortality rate, lowered incidence of mass infectious diseases, and the sense of security provided by easy access to health services. Thus better health services can be considered an end in themselves. Economists also consider health services an investment contribution to individuals and to society as a whole. This investment aspect is defined as the relationship between health status and labor productivity, which is measured in terms of output. Health services are therefore a means of economic development.

The government of the People's Republic of China (PRC) is well aware of these economic implications of health services. For instance, officials of the Ministry of Health indicated that production and health work must be closely coordinated and planned.[1] They suggested a direct relationship between health and productivity. The official newspapers have also occasionally stated that agricultural productivity and health care are mutually dependent, so one should not ignore health care.[2] In fact, health services have been used in the PRC not only to further economic development but also to facilitate ideological or political strategies, especially during the period following the Cultural Revolution. It is well known that the People's Republic of China has made impressive strides in its public health programs, particularly in primary health care, during the past two decades.

Principles of Health Care

The Chinese government has emphasized four basic principles in delivering health care services to its people: (1) Put prevention first. (2) Unite Western and traditional medicine. (3) Combine health with mass movements. (4) Concentrate on the rural areas. These are perhaps the unique features of health policy in China compared with other developing countries.

By the mid 1960s the Chinese government had already carried out many "patriotic" health campaigns involving millions of people and aimed at getting rid of the "four pests" (flies, mosquitoes, bed bugs, rats), improving environmental sanitation, preventing parasitic diseases (schistosomiasis), and eliminating venereal disease. However, the government had failed to extend curative services and to provide medical insurance coverage to over 80% of the rural population. In retrospect, Chairman Mao's June 26, 1965, directive, issued on the eve of the Cultural Revolution, marks the turning point toward emphasis on rural health care. In it he said, "In medical and health work, put the stress on the rural areas," and he called for the modification of health care delivery and medical education. This directive had a broader impact on health care services than did earlier policies. This chapter therefore focuses on health care services in China since 1965 and it examines how resources are allocated in the provision of health care services for the majority of people. Resource allocation here means not only the distribution and financing of health services but also the economic impact of health services and the alternative uses of resources in economic development.

Organization of China's Health Care System

The People's Republic of China comprises twenty-one provinces, five autonomous regions, and three centrally administered metropolitan areas (Peking, Shanghai, and Tientsin). Within each of these provincial-level administrative units, a health department (or bureau) operates under guidelines from the Ministry of Health in Peking, which has primary responsibility for formulating health care policies and supervising health research institutions throughout the country. The provincial department (or bureau) is in charge of medical schools in the province, oversees the provincial hospital system, works out annual plans at provincial health conferences, and supervises the activities of lower units, but it does not directly manage the local hospitals or health activities. The major tasks of delivering and financing health services are left to the local political units.

The subprovincial political unit in rural areas is the *hsien,* or county; in urban areas it is the city. The political structure and health care organization within counties are shown in figure 7–1. The average size of a county is about 300,000 people, although the larger counties may have populations of close to 1 million. The organizational levels descend from county to commune to production brigade to production

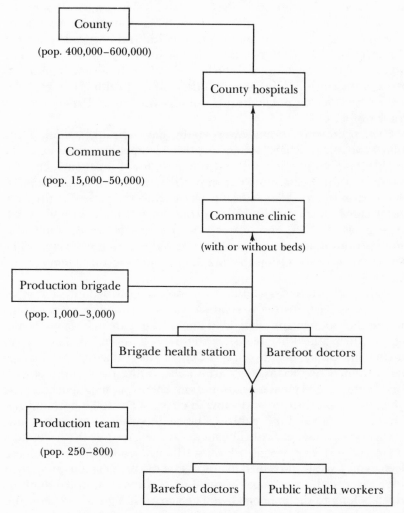

FIGURE 7–1 Rural health care and its referral system in China

team. The commune is the basic political unit. Production brigades or teams are not parts of the governmental hierarchy; they serve mainly as accounting units for production and management, and their leaders do not draw salaries from the government but earn work points as do other peasants. A commune has a population of 15,000–50,000 persons, although the largest of them may have as many as 60,000–70,000 persons. A commune contains 10 to 25 production brigades. Each production brigade is in turn divided into 5 to 20 production teams with populations of 250 to 800. A production team (or several teams, depending on the population) shares a barefoot doctor and a number of public health workers. A barefoot doctor is a peasant who receives three to six months of medical training and returns to the farm to treat "light diseases": minor injuries, gastrointestinal illnesses, colds, bronchitis, and the like. He also administers immunizations, birth control, and oversees other public health activities which are carried out by public health workers trained and supervised by the barefoot doctor.

Each production brigade reportedly has a health station within which two or three barefoot doctors provide health care services. The health station also has a referral function, for if a patient's illness is too serious for the barefoot doctor to treat, the health station requests the services of a mobile medical team or sends the patient to the commune clinic, which usually includes traditional Chinese doctors, Western-trained doctors, and nurses who perform minor operations. A more serious illnes may be further referred to a county hospital. The arrows in figure 7–1 show the direction of the referral system in rural China.

In the PRC cities of over 100,000 people are divided into a number of districts. Each district is subdivided into a number of neighborhoods; they in turn are subdivided into resident areas, or lanes. In the Chinese urban health care system (figure 7–2), each lane has a street doctor and public health workers. These street doctors are not formally trained physicians; they are similar to the rural barefoot doctors. Within each lane is a health station, and every neighborhood has a health station with street doctors in charge. The neighborhood station serves as a unit for organizing the neighborhood outpatient clinic or small hospitals. Seriously ill patients are referred by the street doctor to the district hospital, whose staff includes traditional Chinese doctors and Western-trained doctors. The district hospital can in turn refer cases to the municipal hospital or specialized hospital, both of which belong to the municipality. The arrows in figure 7–2 show the direction of the referral system in the urban area.

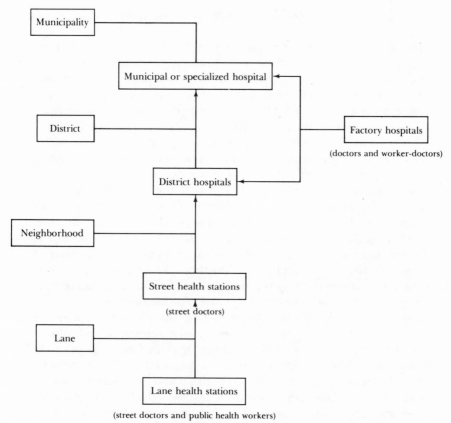

FIGURE 7–2 Urban health care and its referral system in China

The street doctors usually take care of workers' dependents, while the workers, during the working period, are treated by their fellow worker doctors in the factory. Again, the duties and training of a worker doctor are similar to those of a barefoot or street doctor. Depending on the size of the factory, it may have a clinic or hospital from which a seriously ill patient can be transferred to a district or municipal hospital.

The available descriptions of county and municipality health care systems indicate extensive autonomy within each local political unit. From local news reports it is apparent that administrative coordination among the various levels is effected by periodic regional and national conferences attended by various health administrators. Indeed, the health care system is not a centralized system.

Medical Manpower Redistribution

Most developing countries have shortages of physicians. The physician-population ratio is about 1 : 5200 in East Asia (excluding Japan) and 1 : 1800 in Latin America.[3] China is no exception. Although there are no official statistics, estimates of the physician-population ratio range from 1 : 5000[4] to 1 : 2500.[5] Either estimate represents an inadequate supply of doctors by Western standards. The distribution of physicians in rural China was worse before 1966, when 60%–80% of the physicians were located in urban areas, where only 15%–20% of the total population resided. In other words, the estimated physician-population ratio was 1 : 8000 to 1 : 15,400 in the rural areas and 1 : 680 to 1 : 890 in the urban areas.[6] This uneven medical manpower distribution was Chairman Mao's major concern when he issued his directive urging medical personnel to go to the rural areas. To overcome the shortage and imbalance of medical manpower, China chose to train barefoot doctors and public health workers rather than concentrate resources on training regular doctors. This strategy can be interpreted as China's adaptation to its particular factor endowments. The training of regular doctors requires large numbers of experienced physicians, medical capital equipment, and extended periods of time. China has a scarcity of capital and highly skilled medical personnel but an abundance of labor and know-how of traditional medicine. The Chinese strategy, therefore, is to distribute their scarce resources as widely as possible and to substitute less skilled labor for capital and more advanced skills. This strategy has apparently improved the accessibility of primary health care to China's rural majority.

Several approaches to increasing the availability of health care services in rural areas have been adopted in China. First, urban medical personnel have been relocated to rural areas, either by permanent settlement or in mobile teams for periods of six months to one year. The decision on resettlement is made either by the urban hospital revolutionary committee or on a voluntary basis. In general, one-third of an urban hospital's personnel are on the road in the mobile medical services. The central government encourages direct subsidies (or transfers of medical manpower and facilities) from one urban area to a rural or autonomous region, the so-called division of area responsibility. For instance, the city of Shanghai sent its medical personnel to Tibet and Heilungkiang;[7] the city of Tientsin sent its medical personnel to Kwangsi;[8] and the city of Peking sent its medical personnel to Kansu. Travel expenses are paid by the respective city governments.

By 1973 China had dispatched 800,000 medical personnel to rural areas.[9] This redistribution approach increases health care services and trains barefoot doctors in the rural areas. The Chinese Communist party argued that the reallocation of urban medical personnel would improve the doctors' ideological education and induce them to learn about disease problems in rural China and to adopt or modify medical technology so that rural peasants would benefit from their services.

The redistribution of medical personnel from urban to rural areas, however, has affected health services in urban areas. Physicians in urban areas have increased their work loads, resulting in increased rotation of night shifts in hospitals, less time for outpatient treatment, fewer surgeries, and longer waiting times for patients in need of treatment.[10]

The second means used to increase the availability of health care in rural areas is to integrate Western and traditional Chinese approaches to medicine. The Chinese traditional physician complements the Western-trained physician. China has built special hospitals and clinics for traditional medicine and has created special wards for it in existing hospitals. Many rural Chinese are used to traditional medicine, and their openness to this treatment, along with the government's promotion of it, can increase health services to rural areas in a short period, given the relatively large number of traditional physicians already available. Despite the availability of Western medicine, the Chinese often look to traditional medicine as an alternative, and when Western medicine has failed, they look to traditional medicine as a last resort. A large majority of patients, especially in rural areas, are treated by traditional medicine.[11]

A third step was to shorten the medical college curriculum from five or six years to three so that more graduates could be trained. Furthermore, three-year medical colleges have been created within major hospitals (such as Shanghai First Hospital, Peking Worker-Peasant-Soldier Hospital). This approach can be considered a trade-off between quantity and quality, given the same resource constraints. Obviously, it will affect future medical research in the PRC. (The Chinese are now planning to extend medical training to four years.)

The fourth and most important source of greater health care in rural areas is the expansion of the training of barefoot doctors, who are trained locally by mobile team urban doctors or sent to urban areas for training. Experienced barefoot doctors, especially those in northwestern China, train new barefoot doctors. Thus the quality of training that barefoot doctors receive varies greatly among regions.

A national barefoot-doctor–to-population ratio, by provinces, has been compiled from Chinese news reports and travelers' reports (table 7–1). The figures reported are for the period from July 1969 to

August 1974, but most were obtained in 1972 and 1973 and were reported in approximate numbers, with no size of population mentioned. Therefore, in order to estimate the 1970 ratio of barefoot doctors to population by province, population figures were obtained from a report by John Aird.[12] Theodore Shabad and Leo Orleans have also made separate population estimates for the PRC, ranging from 765 million to 800 million. In view of the less rigid birth control in rural than in urban areas and the decrease in mortality rate in the PRC,[13] Aird's estimate of 828.8 million appears to be more realistic. Table 7–1 summarizes the distribution of barefoot doctors in the PRC by province. The estimated total number of barefoot doctors in China is 1.08 million, an estimate very close to that provided by the PRC Health Ministry.[14]

The estimated average barefoot-doctor–population ratio, as shown

TABLE 7–1 Distribution of barefoot doctors in the People's Republic of China by province, 1970–1973

Province or region	Population (in millions)	Barefoot doctor	
		Total	Population per barefoot doctor
East			
Anhwei (1)	41.4	36,700	1,128
Chekiang[a]	31.8	41,678	763
Fukien (2)	18.7	22,000	850
Kiangsu (3)	65.6	60,000	1,093
Shantung (4)	69.8	120,000	581
Central south			
Honan[a]	60.3	79,030	763
Hunan (5)	44.3	50,000	886
Hupeh (5)	38.9	50,000	778
Kiangsi (6)	23.6	70,000	337
Kwangsi (7)	26.9	30,000	896
Kwangtung (8)	46.2	51,000	905
Southwest			
Kweichow (9)	21.9	62,600	350
Szechwan (10)[b]	89.6	125,000	716
Yunnan (11)	23.5	30,000	783
North			
Hopeh (12)	61.8	53,000	1,166
Shansi[a]	20.4	26,736	763

Health Care Services

TABLE 7-1 (*continued*)

Province or region	Population (in millions)	Barefoot doctor Total	Population per barefoot doctor
Northwest			
Kansu (13)	17.0	30,500	557
Ninghsia (14)	2.5	4,050	617
Shensi (15)	24.2	50,000	484
Sinkiang (16)	7.7	10,000	770
Tsinghai (17)	3.0	5,800	517
Northeast			
Heilungkiang (18)	24.3	15,000	1,620
Kirin (19)	18.4	21,674	849
Liaoning (20)	36.8	38,000	968
Inner Mongolia (21)	6.7	11,500	582
Tibet (22)	1.5	4,085	367
Total	826.8	1,083,353	763 (average)

Sources: Population figures are from John S. Aird, *Population Estimates for the Provinces of the People's Republic of China, 1953 to 1974* (Washington, D.C.: U.S. Department of Commerce, 1974), Series P-95, no. 73, appendix table 1, p. 22, calendar year 1971. (1) *Foreign Broadcast Information Service, Daily Report: People's Republic of China* (FBIS) September 25, 1973. (2) *Ta-Kung Pao*, Hong Kong, October 24, 1973. (3) *FBIS*, May 28, 1971. (4) *FBIS*, September 6, 1972. (5) *China News Analysis*, Hong Kong, No. 889, August 4, 1972. (6) *FBIS*, July 3, 1969. (7) *FBIS*, July 17, 1974. (8) *Ta-Kung Pao*, Hong Kong, October 12, 1972. (9) *FBIS*, August 16, 1974. (10) *FBIS*, February 17, 1972. (11) *FBIS*, September 21, 1970. (12) *FBIS*, June 29, 1971. (13) *Ta-Kung Pao*, Hong Kong, November 27, 1972. (14) *Ta-Kung Pao*, Hong Kong, October 23, 1973. It reports that the Ningsia area of 1 million population has 1620 barefoot doctors; thus with a 2.5 million population in the province, it should have 4050 barefoot doctors. (15) *FBIS*, October 5, 1973. (16) *Peking Review*, no. 43, October 26, 1973. (17) *FBIS*, June 25, 1974. (18) *FBIS*, June 24, 1970. (19) *FBIS*, October 29, 1973. (20) Letter from Peter K. New, October 29, 1973. (21) *Ta-Kung Pao*, Hong Kong, February 7, 1973. (22) *FBIS*, July 23, 1973.

a. Figures are estimated from the assumption of 763 persons to each barefoot doctor, a known average relevant to the other 23 provinces or regions.
b. The report indicates that the estimate of 50,000 barefoot doctors is based on a 1:3 ratio between barefoot doctors and public health workers.

in table 7-1, is 1:760. This ratio certainly represents an impressive improvement in health manpower. The pre–Cultural Revolution physician-to-population ratio was 1:5000 in general, and 1:8000 for rural China. The quality and level of training that a barefoot doctor receives is not as good as that of a medically trained physician, and the barefoot doctor is a half-time peasant. The barefoot-doctor–population ratio of 1:760 therefore is not comparable to a similar physician-population ratio; however, this ratio indicates that patients have access to basic health care, since barefoot doctors provide a minimum standard of care for common illnesses and serve as referral agents. The Chinese have claimed that 95% of illnesses can be treated at the local commune without further referral.[15] The services provided by the barefoot doctor are seen as an important factor in solving the physician shortage problem in China.

On the tenth anniversary of Mao's directive, China claimed to have trained 1.3 million barefoot doctors and 3.6 million public health workers.[16] Given the PRC population estimate of about 850 million in 1975, the doctor-population ratio becomes 1:650, indicating that the PRC has further improved the accessibility of paramedical health care.

As table 7–1 indicates, barefoot doctors are not equally distributed among provinces. The doctor-population ratio ranges from 1:340 in Kiangsi to about 1:1600 in Heilungkiang. On the average, the population-doctor ratio is lower in the Northwest, Inner Mongolia, and Tibet than it is in the East and the Northeast. Presumably the need for physicians in the Northwest, Inner Mongolia, and Tibet is more urgent than in the more urbanized eastern region where more physicians are available or in central south and southwestern China, which have an average ratio of barefoot doctors to population. The incidence of barefoot doctors trained by other barefoot doctors (rather than by physicians) is reported to be greater in the Northwest, Inner Mongolia, and Tibet regions than in other areas, so that health care quality may vary greatly among regions.

In the hierarchy of medical services, public health workers are supervised by barefoot doctors. Thirteen provinces or regions have reported their number of public health workers by means of newsprint or radio. Based on these figures, the ratio of public health workers to population is estimated to be 1:265, as shown in table 7–2. Assuming a total population of 828.8 million in 1970, we can then estimate the number of public health workers at about 3.1 million. Again, this independent estimate, based on reports from individual provinces, is consistent with the national figure provided by the Ministry of Health in 1974. Thus the average ratio between barefoot doctors and public health workers is now about 1:3. Table 7–2 indicates that there are relatively more public health workers per capita in the East, Kwangtung, and Kwangsi than in the southwest or northwest regions. The differences can be explained by the nation's important schistosomiasis control program, launched in the past decade, since this program's massive public health campaigns have been concentrated in the schistosomiasis epidemic areas of the east and southeast regions. No figures relating to public health workers in the northwestern and part of the central south regions of China are available.

TABLE 7–2   Distribution of public health workers in the People's Republic of China's thirteen provinces, 1970–1972

| Province or region | Population (in millions) | Public health workers | |
		Total	Population per worker
East			
Anhwei	41.4	189,000	219
Fukien	18.7	63,000	296
Kiangsu	65.6	290,000	226
Shantung	69.8	200,000	349
South central			
Kwangsi	26.9	190,000	141
Kwangtung	46.2	200,000	231
Southwest			
Szechwan	89.6	375,000[a]	238
Yunnan	23.5	60,000	392
North			
Hopeh	61.8	200,000	309
Northeast			
Heilungkiang	24.3	50,000	486
Kirin	18.4	83,392	220
Liaoning	36.8	13,000	541
Inner Mongolia	6.7	13,000	515
Estimated national total	826.8	3,120,000	265[b]

Sources: Population figures are from John S. Aird, *Population Estimates for the Provinces of the People's Republic of China*, 1953 to 1954, Washington, D.C., U.S. Department of Commerce, Series p-95, No. 73, 1974, Appendix Table 1, P. 22, calendar year 1971. The numbers of public health workers are from the following sources (listed in same order as provinces): *Foreign Broadcast Information Service, Daily Report: People's Republic of China (FBIS)*, September 25, 1973; *Ta-Kung Pao*, Hong Kong, October 24, 1973; *FBIS*, May 28, 1971; *FBIS*, September 6, 1973; *FBIS*, July 17, 1974; *Ta-Kung Pao*, Hong Kong, October 12, 1972; *FBIS*, February 17, 1972; *FBIS*, September 21, 1970; *FBIS*, June 29, 1971; *FBIS*, June 24, 1970; *FBIS*, October 29, 1973; Letter from Peter K. M. New, October 29, 1973; *Ta-Kung Pao*, Hong Kong, February 7, 1973.

a. The report indicates 500,000 barefoot doctors and public health workers. The public health worker estimate is based on 3:1 ratio between barefoot doctors and public health workers.

b. The figure 265 is the weighted average among 13 provinces. The total figure is obtained from the total population figure divided by 265.

These estimates of barefoot doctors and public health workers lend credence to the claim that there is at least one public health worker in each production team and an average of two or three barefoot doctors in each production brigade in rural China. The great increase in the number of barefoot doctors and public health workers over a period of ten years is indeed an impressive achievement, but questions about the possible trade-off between quantity and quality in the training of medical personnel, the costs and effectiveness of medical services provided by barefoot doctors instead of trained physicians, and the impact of redistribution of medical manpower on health services in urban and rural areas are difficult to answer, especially when this system's political implications may outweigh its economic considerations.

It can be argued that the redistribution of medical manpower from urban to rural areas reflects a type of income redistribution. That the central government requires many urban areas to take up the financial and manpower supply responsibility for relocating urban medical personnel is an urban-rural income redistribution approach. This relocation has some negative effects on urban health services, but what is the outcome for the rural population as a result of these efforts during the past decade? The severe scarcity of data prevents an investigation of the medical manpower redistribution on a national scale. A few examples from individual communes have been reported during the past few years, but it would be very difficult to examine the validity of those claims or to determine the net impact of medical manpower redistribution without considering other environmental, sociodemographic, and economic factors. Thus the reports outlined here serve only as gross indications of the improvement of health status in rural areas.

1. Wei-tsin Commune, Liao-yuan Hsien, Kirin Province, reported a 50% reduction in incidence of common illnesses in 1972 compared with 1970.
2. Man-sa Brigade in Yunnan Province reported that its disease rate was reduced from 30% in 1968 to 4% of the population in 1972.
3. Lin-hsa Hsien, Kansu Province, reported a reduction in the disease rate from 30% to 7% over a seven-year period.
4. Chien-hu Commune, Kiangsu Province, reported a 70% reduction in the incidence of intestinal infectious diseases in 1972 compared with a few years ago.[17]

Other reports cite increases in infant and child weights and decreases in mortality rates in many rural areas of China. Several current crude death rates in various communes or rural areas are available: 7.3 per thousand for Sha-chiao Commune, Sun-te Hsien, Kwangtung; 5.2 per thousand for Chi-yi Commune in the Shanghai area; 5 per thousand for Tung-ting Commune, Wu Hsien, Kiangsu; 4 per thousand for Nan-ying, Shanghai area; 6 per thousand for the Nanking area.[18] Comparing these rates with those of other countries indicates that China's health status is well above that of many other countries, granted that the crude death rate is only one of many indicators of a nation's health status. For example, India has a crude death rate of 16.3 per thousand; the Philippines' rate is 10.5 per thousand; the rates are 9.4 per thousand for the United States, 7.9 per thousand for the Soviet Union, and 6.6 per thousand for Japan.[19]

Health officials in the PRC now claim that the leading causes of death are no longer infectious diseases and malnutrition but cancer, cardiovascular disease, cerebrovascular disease, and respiratory disease. In fact, the current leading causes of death are the same as those in the United States and other developed countries. Although there are no hard statistics to empirically measure the net impact of redistribution of medical manpower to rural China, the fragmentary reports suggest that rural China has received substantial benefits from this redistribution.

The Financing of Health Care Services

It would be misleading to say that health care services in the PRC are free or vitually free to all people.[20] Health care insurance is neither a uniform nor a well-planned system. A delegation of the Canadian Medical Association visited the PRC in 1973 and reported that the health care system is not centralized. The Canadians claimed that the PRC system is even less socialized than the Canadian System.[21] The Canadian delegation presumably implied that the Chinese health care system is not financed by the central or provincial government, as is the Canadian system in which almost 100% of the population is covered by medical and hospital insurance.[22] A large portion of Chinese have to pay part of their medical expenses from their own pockets.

There are three major types of health care insurance coverage in the PRC. The first, introduced in 1951 and called "public expenses medical insurance" (*kung-fei yi-liau*), covers the state cadres and students, or about 2% of the population.[23] All their medical expenses are covered by the insurance scheme without any contribution to the insurance premium. The coverage includes visits to clinics and costs incurred during hospitalization but excludes meal costs in the hospital. Family members of state cadres are not covered under this government-financed insurance plan.

The second type covers the workers or staff members in factories and state-owned firms. Introduced in 1951 and revised in 1953, it is called "labor medical insurance" (*lao-pao yi-liau*). The labor medical insurance fund takes in contributions from factory employers and represents about 2%–3% of the total income of the factory before the salaries are distributed to workers. (These percentages vary among factories and over time.) In general, these percentages are mandated by the province through the same process that approves the factory's annual production plan. Factory workers receive medical services at no charge to them. Thus the labor medical insurance is seen as a non-coinsurance system, since the employer's contributions to the insurance premium are not considered a reduction of salaries or wages. It is estimated that about 10% of the population in the country, mostly in urban areas, is covered by the labor medical insurance, including the dependents of these factory workers.[24] However, this insurance provides comprehensive coverage only to the workers, not to their dependents. Dependents must pay about 50% of the medical expenses under the labor medical insurance system.

A third program covers the rural agricultural areas, where about 80% of the country's 800 million people reside. To implement its planned expansion of rural health care services to these people, the Chinese government needed large financial resources, and although the central government could reallocate health care expenditures from urban to rural or from rich to poor provinces, it was still difficult for the central government to finance the total amount required. It was therefore decided that decentralized health care was the most economical approach. As a result, the "cooperative medical services"(*ho-tso yi-liau*) concept was actively advocated and promoted at the commune level, beginning in 1966. It was claimed that 70% of China's 50,000 communes have now adopted this self-reliance approach to financing.[25]

A typical cooperative medical service works as follows. Participation is voluntary. The main forces for establishing cooperative services are poor and lower-middle-class peasants. In the early period of the service all commune members had the option to join or not to join the system. In recent years, however, if a commune decides collectively to join, then everyone in the commune must participate.

The annual membership fee varies among communes and within communes over time. The fee is calculated from the previous year's expenditures for treatment and medicine within a commune. For instance, Pu-chiang Commune, Chekiang Province, had fewer serious illnesses in 1972 than ever before, and since they had used rather inexpensive herbal medicine extensively, the annual membership fee was reduced from 1 yuan (equivalent to U.S. $0.45) in 1972 to 0.35 yuan in 1973.[26] About fifteen communes across the country reported their annual membership fees as ranging from 0.35 to 3.60 yuan per person in 1973.[27] The average is about 1.50 yuan per person per year, so for the average family of five annual membership fees are about 7.5 yuan. Annual take-home income ranges from 150 to 350 yuan per worker. If a figure of 250 yuan is assumed for an average worker, then a family with two workers (husband and wife) has an income of 500 yuan per year. Thus the financial burden of the medical services premium is about 1.5% of the family's disposable income. Medical services premiums and income vary considerably among communes. A survey of eight communes reveals that the ratio of premium to disposable personal income varies from 0.6% to 3% in different parts of the country; thus an average estimate of 1.5% of the family's disposable income is reasonable.[28] A lump sum payment of 7.5 yuan in a given month represents about one-fifth to one-sixth of a family's monthly income. Thus 1.5% of the annual disposable income is not an insignificant figure for poor and lower-middle-income peasants, as most visitors to the PRC have claimed.[29] In fact, one of the reasons that 30% of communes in the country still do not have cooperative medical services is the financial burden that payment of medical services premiums places on commune members.

Once an individual or an entire family joins the cooperative medical service, they pay an additional fee of 0.05–0.10 yuan for each visit to the health station. This fee helps pay the station's maintenance expenses (excluding the salaries of barefoot doctors and public health workers, who are paid from production team funds). The registration or visit fee also discourages indiscriminate use of available services. During the early days of cooperative medical services, when registration fees were not charged, some communes reported that there were unnecessary visits and requests for tonic herbs. Several commune cooperative medical services in the earlier period had to be discontinued because of their large deficits.

One of the mechanisms for controlling health costs in the brigade is the use of barefoot doctors for referring patients to county or city hospitals. If a patient seeks care at these hospitals on his own, he cannot receive reimbursement from the brigade health funds. On the other hand, if the barefoot doctor refers a patient to these hospitals, part of the patient's medical expense is paid by the brigade health fund. Some communes pay 50% of the costs; others pay fixed amounts of 30 or 40 yuan, while the rest of the expenses, including food costs, are paid by the patients themselves.[30] These examples indicate that free medical services or unlimited medical financing are not feasible even in a socialized country. Limits must be set to minimize medical expenses.

Another modification of the medical payment system illustrates concern for controlling medical expenses. During the early period of cooperative medical services, accounts were set up by communes at the county or city hospital, and treatment of their members was charged against the commune account. However, this system led to unnecessary expenses to communes. The hospitals now require patients to pay all expenses while they receive medical services. No credit is allowed for the commune, and individual patients must request reimbursement for medical expenses from the commune. Such refund requests are reviewed by a peer group in the commune. The commune believes that this modification reduces their medical expenses for county or city hospitals.

Hospital charges vary with the location of the hospital and the type of illness. The average daily room charge is 0.60 yuan for Dalien Second Hospital, 1 yuan for Peking Worker-Peasant-Soldier Hospital, 1.5 yuan at the Norman Bethune International Peace Hospital. On the average, it is about 1 yuan a day, excluding meals. Surgery fees range from 8 yuan to 30 yuan in Peking and Shanghai. Tonsillectomy costs 8 yuan while chest surgery is about 30 yuan. The average length of stay per admission is about two weeks. Thus a serious illness may cost a patient more than 45 yuan—more than one month's income for a poor or lower-middle-income peasant. Obviously these charges relative to income are not low as some U.S. travelers or news reporters have thought, although they are low by U.S. standards. In recognition that hospital expenses are not inexpensive for Chinese peasants, some hospitals in Peking, Dalien, and Shanghai have offered a lower room rate (about 50% less) for poor and lower-middle-income peasants by putting more beds in a ward.

One important aspect of the campaign to reduce and finance local cooperative medical services is the promotion of herbal medicine and acupuncture. Most herbal medicines can be grown locally and processed by the grower, thus minimizing costs. Local surplus herbs are sold to other communes or to the province, and the proceeds go to the local cooperative medical funds. Costs reductions have been in the form of either a reduction in state subsidies to the local communes or a reduction in the registration of membership fees of the local cooperative medical services. A few examples follow:

1. The Langtsun production brigade in Hopei Province reported a saving of 1400 yuan in a year through the use of herbal medicine.
2. The Hsiangtun People's Commune in Kiangsi Province reported that its use of herbal medicine for 70% of the prescriptions in 1970 reduced imports of Western medicines 53% from the previous year's level. As a result, the province was able to reduce its medical subsidies to the commune.
3. A commune in Shantung Province reported that in 1969, before cooperative medicine, the commune spent 91,000 yuan. In 1973, after it had adopted the barefoot doctor system and herbal medicine, the total medical expenses for the commune amounted to 36,715 yuan—a year's saving of 54,585 yuan.[31]

Yet these reported savings do not represent net savings for the commune, even if the reported figures are accurate. Other costs are involved in using self-produced herbal medicine, such as the opportunity costs of labor and land used to cultivate herbs that could be used for other purposes.

Herbal medicine and acupuncture have a long history in Chinese medicine. The vast majority of rural Chinese people prefer traditional practices to modern medicine even when modern medicine is physically and financially possible. Thus, in expanding health care services, the Chinese government had to consider not only economic cost and manpower resources but also the attitudes of the population. In view of many reports that most illnesses in a brigade were of the common type, which could effectively be treated by traditional medicine, the use of traditional medicine in China is a logical alternative.[32]

Although commune members pay membership and registration fees, the contributions of the production team, commune, and county government are also important in financing local health care services. Each production team pays a certain amount of money from its collective welfare fund for each member subscribing to the medical services. The production team contributes from 0.10 yuan to 1 yuan per member, depending on agricultural production during the year and utilization of the service by team members. Each commune has a "public accumulated fund" contributed by production teams, which comprises a reserve fund and a welfare fund. The reserve fund (about 7%–10% of gross income) may be used to buy farm equipment or to finance hospital construction, supplemented by state funds. The welfare fund (about 2%–3% of the gross income) is used to pay for education costs, cooperative medical services, and social welfare assistance.[33] Under the self-reliance principle, high-income communes that accumulate larger public welfare funds share larger amounts of health costs and can reduce medical service premiums paid by individual members. On the other hand, low-income communes do not have large public welfare funds, so individuals have to pay higher premiums.

To the extent that poor rural areas are financially unable to carry out cooperative medical services, the central government has a national policy for providing additional resources to the relatively poor and rural area. This policy is implemented in two ways: through direct subsidies from the central government, and through subsidies from urban to rural areas.

Since the Cultural Revolution, the central government is reported to have allocated about 60% of government health expenditures to rural areas, compared with 20%–30% before 1965.[34] Although the redistribution of health funds is initiated by the central government, the actual implementation takes place at the provincial and county levels. The national budget is a unified fiscal plan that includes the revenue and expenditures of central, provincial, and local governments. The simultaneous determination of national and provincial financial budgets enables the central government to influence the geographic distribution of health care resources. Once the province receives its revenue, it allocates the resources to counties and municipalities; the counties in turn allocate funds to communes.

It is difficult to discuss the share that various levels of government have in financing local health care services. State funds for local services are used mainly for capital expenditures of local health hospitals or clinics. In many instances the state contributes about 50% of total construction funds.[35] The balance of construction costs is paid from brigade health station funds or cooperative medical services funds. These funds represent surplus revenue from local health services, after the maintenance costs of the health station are paid. Therefore it can be safely argued that the largest share of health care services expenses is paid at the household, brigade, and commune levels. The higher levels of government (county, province, and central government) merely provide portions of funds for capital expenditures. Only during a poor harvest or in the case of the depletion of commune welfare funds does the state provide additional support for local health services.

The second way of financing rural health care services involves subsidies from urban areas to rural areas or poor regions. The central government encourages direct subsidies, in the form of manpower or facilities, from urban to rural areas. In the relocation of manpower the urban area pays all the travel expenses as well as the salaries of urban medical personnel while they are stationed in a rural region. Therefore one can conclude that the central and provincial governments play important roles in formulating redistribution policy but relatively minor roles in financing health services. The implementation of policy is left to the local government, which uses local manpower and financing. This decentralization approach is intended to maximize community participation and investment in health services and to reduce the financial burden on the central government to cover wider areas without increasing their budgets.

Cost-Effectiveness and Economic Development

The central government has been placing its budgetary priorities on defense and heavy industry,[36] but even with a rather small percentage of the government budget earmarked for health services, the PRC has made impressive strides in developing such services.

There are two major difficulties in undertaking a cost-benefit study of a health program. First, unlike a physical or educational investment, it is difficult to identify all the costs and benefits of health services. Second, even if all elements could be identified, it is difficult to assess their monetary value. Especially in China, the political considerations and the value system (public interest–"serve the people" versus self-interest–maximization of personal gain) render any attempt at a cost-benefit assessment problematical at best. Because of data limitations and the emphasis on political and social considerations in the PRC, this analysis is focused on effectiveness more than on a direct cost-benefit comparison of barefoot doctor service.

The economic benefits expected as a result of improved health services are (1) reduction of days lost due to illness (working days devoted to production), (2) improved productivity due to improvement in the health of the labor force, (3) savings of time previously spent in traveling and waiting for treatment (more time for production), and (4) a decrease in mortality rate, resulting in longer participation in the labor force.

The Chinese press has recently released reports of increases in productivity and in days worked as a result of the services provided by barefoot doctors. However, it would be difficult to calculate the net economic effects of these services on agricultural productivity based solely on these news reports. The ideal method of measuring the net effect of health care services on agricultural productivity is to estimate a production function using agricultural output as a dependent variable and labor input, acreage, rainfall, and population per barefoot doctor as independent variables. The regression coefficient of the barefoot doctors' variable provides a net relation between the distribution of barefoot doctors and agricultural output, with other production factors held constant. An attempt has been made to estimate an agricultural production function by including health services variables in the equation based on macro data, but because of data limitations, the economic implications are not discussed in this chapter.[37] Instead, this chapter analyzes the micro data based on news reports of economic gains attributed to the services of barefoot doctors and compares these gains with service costs.

For the cost-effectiveness of barefoot doctor services, two sources of information are used: (1) the reported reduction in lost working days as a result of treatment by barefoot doctors and (2) the amount of traveling and waiting time saved because of the immediate availability of the barefoot doctor. Thus the quantified effectiveness represents only part of the overall economic benefit provided by barefoot doctors. A few examples of the measurement of effectiveness as individual commune and production brigade levels follow.

Chunshing brigade, Kukong Hsien, Kwangtung Province has a population of 2900, with 1139 members of the labor force.[38] If the barefoot doctors were not in the brigade, the population would have to go to communes for treatment. The distance between brigade and commune, about 10 li (3.1 miles) would be a one-day round trip, and a patient making the journey to the commune would normally be accompanied by a healthy adult. Since 95% of the illnesses are of the common type, treatment can be provided by the barefoot doctors within the brigade. Medical services at the brigade level were reported to have saved 6000 man-days during 1968.[39] Thus the net gain would be 5700 man-days (95% × 6000). With the assumption of 300 workdays per peasant during a year, 5700 workdays are equivalent to 19 man-years.

The brigade also claimed that the aggregate labor productivity in the brigade was 14% higher than before as a result of improved health services. However, this increase in productivity cannot be attributed solely to the improvement in health services, without controlling for changes in other factors of production.

Other benefits that may result from services provided by the barefoot doctors are increases in infant and child weights, reduction in the incidence of common illnesses, and a decrease in the mortality rate, which in turn may increase brigade output. Another benefit is that the preventive health care may reduce major illnesses. Barefoot doctor services can also reduce costs for the brigade health fund, since only major illnesses are treated at the county or city hospital level.

In Shantung Province a brigade reported that it saved 3000 man-days in 1973 as a result of the availability of barefoot doctors. It reported that 50 man-days is the time taken to cultivate 1 acre of land to a full harvest; thus the equivalent of 60 additional acres was cultivated as a result of the barefoot doctor's services.[40] Since the productivity per acre in the brigade is unknown, 3000 man-days are assumed to be equivalent to 10 man-years.

In Kiangsu Province the Tao-Ling Commune reported that 450 man-years of labor were saved as a result of the services of its 70 barefoot doctors during 1971. Another brigade, in Hwo-An county, reported that due to the services of barefoot doctors, 28 man-years were gained in production during 1972.[41]

The cost of barefoot doctor services includes the cost of providing training, the cost of receiving training, and the cost of providing the services. Since barefoot doctors are trained by urban medical personnel, the time and services devoted by urban medical personnel to treating patients while concurrently training barefoot doctors are part of the cost of training. There are reports that the "downward movement" of urban medical personnel in training barefoot doctors has reduced by one-third the number of urban medical personnel available in the city. Thus services and major operations in urban hospitals have been reduced.[42] Furthermore, research and development activities formerly carried out by some urban medical personnel have probably been reduced as a result of the time spent training barefoot doctors. There is no way of directly measuring these costs, but the direct cost of providing training is the cost of urban doctors' time. Since this type of training is more labor intensive than capital intensive, only labor costs are accounted for. The types of training and class sizes vary among regions. A county hospital in Shanghai requires 13 doctors to teach 274 students for a period of three months, or 1 doctor trains about 20 barefoot doctors in three months.[43]

The second type of cost is the cost of receiving training. The average training period for a barefoot doctor ranges from three to six months. The training period may take place during the agricultural slack season, so that the cost of surplus labor is not as high as during the working season. On the other hand, the marginal productivity of barefoot doctors is not counted as zero.[44] Barefoot doctors always find other productive activities during a slack season (not to mention the value of leisure itself). In other words, the production brigade subsidizes six man-months for each barefoot doctor during the training period.

The cost of providing services by barefoot doctors is the production time lost due to their services. On the average, a barefoot doctor is required to work on the farm at least 100 days per year. Three news reports indicated that one barefoot doctor worked 250 days, one worked 200 days, and the other worked 140 days on the farm.[45] Those who worked more than 200 days may be exceptions; most likely barefoot doctors work about 150 days. If there are 3 barefoot doctors in each brigade, then the annual cost of providing barefoot doctor services in the brigade is 450 man-days, or 15 man-months.

Needless to say, there are other nonmeasurable costs of introducing barefoot doctors, such as the trade-off between the quality and quantity of services.[46] Barefoot doctors have more uneven training than medical school graduates, so that cases of inadequate treatment may occur more often than previously, and patients have also been reported to lose confidence in barefoot doctors.[47] However, the sense of security and access to health care that the barefoot doctor can provide may well offset these nonmeasurable costs. A comparison of cost-effectiveness based purely on man-year productivity gains or losses suggests that the introduction of barefoot doctors in the commune is not only socially significant but also economically worthwhile.

A simple illustration of the net contribution of the barefoot doctors to the national economy can be estimated from these economic benefits and costs of the barefoot doctor services.[48] For instance, the labor savings (reduction of workdays lost and savings in traveling and waiting time) per barefoot doctor of the four sample brigades ranges from 3.3 man-years to 9.3 man-years, an average of 6.3 man-years. However, it may take about one year to defray the cost of barefoot doctor services, considering their six months of training (an upper estimate) and half-time medical services. Therefore the net labor savings per barefoot doctor is about 5 man-years. Given the estimated number of 1.083 million barefoot doctors in the PRC during the early 1970s, a total of 5.415 million man-years was saved.

Farm workers are paid according to their work points, which are determined by their labor productivity. The average peasant income of 250 yuan per year can therefore be considered the annual productivity of rural labor. Under the assumption that the marginal productivity of labor is equal to the average productivity of labor, the average wages of peasants can be applied to these saved man-years. The total monetary value of the net labor savings is about 1353 million yuan (250 yuan × 5.415 million man-years).

The magnitude of these net contributions of the barefoot doctor services can be compared with the PRC's gross domestic product (GDP) as well as with the total value of agricultural output (VAO). Based on Perkin's estimates,[49] the PRC's 1974 GDP and VAO, at the 1971 price level, are 256 billion yuan and 67 billion yuan, respectively.

Thus the estimated net contribution of the barefoot doctor's services is about 0.5% (1.353 ÷ 256) of the GDP, or about 2% (1.353 ÷ 67) of the total VAO. The estimated magnitude of the barefoot doctor's services to the national economy and agricultural sector may not seem very impressive, but like many other human investments, some of the returns are intangible or only indirectly related to the national output. The rural health services may need to operate for a much longer time before their actual impact on agricultural output is realized. Furthermore, health services may relate more directly to labor and other inputs, so that the net effect of health services on agricultural production becomes less obvious. This analysis simply attempts to assess the short-run contributions of the barefoot doctor's services to the PRC's economy, based on rather crude data and simplified assumptions.

Overall, it can be concluded that health care services in the PRC during the past decade have been both a means and an end in China's economic development. Based on these empirical data and my personal impressions, the PRC may have achieved more in terms of consumption (such as reducing disease and mortality rates—ends of economic development) than in terms of investment (increases in productivity—means of economic development) through implementation of health care services. Health care services have a positive impact on agricultural productivity, an investment aspect, but the influence is not significant when compared with production factors. Considering both consumption and investment benefits of health care services, the redistribution policy and medical manpower training approaches that the PRC has chosen are an economical and effective strategy.

The Chinese solutions to the shortage of medical manpower, however, can be considered successful only in the short run. If training resources are shifted from high-level to paramedical training, will the PRC in the long run be forced to import medical techniques? Will such dependency conflict with the ideals of self-reliance or self-sufficiency? To what extent do people in the PRC allow trade-offs in medical resources between quality and quantity and curative and preventive medicine? These and many other questions remain unanswered.

Can the Chinese System Be Applied Elsewhere?

Before 1966 China urgently needed health care services for its people, especially in the vast rural areas. It is a costly task, however, for a central government to implement local health services. Within China's agricultural economic framework, the adoption of barefoot doctor services and the promotion of herbal medicine (under the co-operative medical system) are cost minimization approaches that enable local political units to operate financially self-supporting medical services. The major theme of cooperative medicine is self-reliance, which implies decentralization of medical services. The decentralization approach in China is not unique to health care services. It is China's strategy for economic development in many other areas as well, such as industrialization and agricultural development.

Discussions and debates about the transferability of the PRC health system to other developing countries, or even to minority areas of the United States, have appeared in many studies.[50] Because of differing economic incentives, political systems, and cultural backgrounds, the PRC system cannot be exported as a whole to other countries. What other countries, especially the developing countries, can learn from the PRC does not necessarily depend on the effectiveness of the Chinese health care system but on some of the issues that implementation of that system has underscored and solved to greater or lesser degrees.

There is a serious shortage of physicians, and an imbalanced distribution of physicians between urban and rural areas in many developing countries. For instance, ratios of population to medical doctors are 1:3700 for urban and 1:24,200 for rural areas in Pakistan, 1:800 for urban and 1:50,000 for rural areas in Kenya, 1:1500 for urban and 1:10,000 for rural areas in the Philippines, 1:2275 for urban and 1:10,000 for rural areas in Iran.[51] An effective way to improve the shortage and imbalanced distribution of medical manpower is to rely on local resources to train paramedical workers. These paramedical workers should be well respected and integrated into the local society, as are the barefoot doctors in the PRC, so that they can identify diseases even without patient-initiated contacts at the local health station.

Public health and primary health care services are as important as curative health services. China has put a major emphasis on the former type, a logical and effective approach to improving health care in a developing country. Sophisticated health care training such as that provided by medical schools in the developed countries is too expensive and unnecessary for treating common illnesses or parasitic diseases. In fact, once physicians in underdeveloped countries complete their training, they usually either practice in the urban areas of their home countries or emigrate to the developed world.[52] Thus health care services in rural areas can be more effectively improved by emphasizing paramedical health personnel.

China is not unique, nor is it the pioneer in training paramedics.

Many developing countries, such as India and some African countries, and developed countries such as the United States (in Indian reservation programs) have taken similar approaches. China has had marked success in developing paramedical services. Two factors in addition to the political and social reasons have contributed to its success. First, there are economic and noneconomic incentives to become barefoot doctors. For instance, barefoot doctors are relatively well paid among the peasants. The wage rate for peasants ranges from one to ten work points. Barefoot doctors are paid between eight and ten points. Furthermore, an accomplished barefoot doctor can be nominated to medical school, be nominated to the Communist party, or be promoted to cadre in the political system. Second, well-organized referral system from barefoot doctor to commune health stations, county hospitals, and district hospitals insures easy access to health care services. China's system of financial incentives encourages patients to follow the referral scheme and thus reduces the load on urban health services. No matter what the political and social systems of other developing countries, the economic and related noneconomic incentives for paramedics and efficient use of referral systems seem to be key elements for incorporation into any country's paramedical services.

To correct the imbalanced distribution of health services between urban and rural areas, the governments of developing countries should reduce the funds for construction of urban hospitals. When urban areas do not increase the number of hospital beds, they may absorb fewer physicians, and the funds saved can be used to improve the outpatient health stations in rural areas.

The financial redistribution between urban and rural health services is not a guarantee of the success of a health care delivery system. Such a plan relies not only on central government enforcement but also on effective execution and management on the part of local or regional governments. In fact, the example of the PRC indicates that decentralization is an effective and economical approach to health care. Developing countries without adequate central government–financed resources for improving their health care delivery systems should promote local participation by utilizing local manpower to train paramedics and by absorbing local resources to finance and insure health care expenses. The theme of self-reliance as exemplified by the PRC may be considered by these developing countries.

Experiences in the PRC suggest that even in a socialized country, free medical services can lead to the overutilization or abuse of health services. Modifying a free medical services system into a copayment system may reduce overutilization.

China's unique political system, incentive system, and the virtual lack of licensing and regulation of medical professions in the PRC makes direct transfer of the Chinese health care services system to other developing countries difficult. Even Chinese health professionals admit that each society must develop solutions to its problem based on its own social, economic, and cultural background. Nevertheless, the general experiences of the PRC in promoting primary and preventive medicine indicates that reliance on local resources, mass involvement in health care delivery, and an effective medical referral system are all useful concepts for developing countries.

Notes

The Social Science Research Council and Pennsylvania State University provided previous financial support. A large portion of this paper was prepared in 1974–75 while I was a Visiting Research Professor at the Fogarty International Center for Advanced Study in the Health Sciences, National Institutes of Health. However, I am solely responsible for the contents of this paper, which do not necessarily represent the official opinions of the sponsoring institutions. I am grateful for help from and discussions with Parris Chang, Pi-Chao Chen, Charles Y. Liu, Joseph R. Quinn, and for comments and suggestions from participants at the conference.

1. Hsu Yun-Pei, "Advance the Great Work of Protecting the People's Health," *Chinese Medical Journal,* May 1960, p. 409.

2. *Jen-min jih-pao,* Peking, January 16, 1973.

3. Agency for International Development, *Proposed Foreign Aid Program* (FY 1968), (Washington, D.C.: U.S. Government Printing Office, 1967), table 3.

4. Leo A. Orleans, "Medical Education and Manpower in Communist China," *Comparative Education Review,* February 1969.

5. C. Y. Chen, "Health Manpower: Growth and Distribution," in M. Wegman, T. Y. Lin, and E. F. Purcell, eds., *Public Health in the People's Republic of China* (New York: Josiah Macy, Jr., Foundation, 1973) pp. 139–157.

6. Ibid.

7. *Foreign Broadcast Information Services Daily Report (FBIS),* People's Republic of China, Washington, D.C., U.S. Department of Commerce, June 11, 1974.

8. *Jen-min jih-pao,* Peking, June 27, 1973.

9. *Peking Review,* Peking, February 1975.

10. These negative impacts were revealed by Chinese physicians who recently left the PRC and were interviewed in Hong Kong.

11. Ralph C. Croizier, "Traditional Medicine as a Basis for Chinese

Medical Practice," in Joseph R. Quinn, ed., *Medicine and Public Health in the People's Republic of China* (Washington, D.C.: National Institutes of Health, U.S. Department of Health, Education, and Welfare, 1972), DHEW (NIH) Publication 72-67, pp. 3–17.

12. John S. Aird, *Population Estimates for Provinces of People's Republic of China, 1953 to 1974* (Washington, D.C.: U.S. Department of Commerce, 1974), Series P-95, no. 73.

13. Pi-chao Chen, "The Barefoot Doctors in the People's Republic of China," *Famille et Développement* 1, no. 1 (1975): 1–15.

14. *FBIS*, June 18, 1974.

15. *Red Flag* (in Chinese), Peking, January 1969.

16. *Kuang-ming jih-pao*, Peking, June 26, 1975.

17. *Jen-min jih-pao*, January 18, July 25, June 26, June 4, 1973.

18. Pi-chao Chen, *Public Health Development and Birth Planning Programs in the PRC* (Washington, D.C.: Smithsonian Institution, 1976); Nanking rate obtained in a personal interview in Nanking.

19. World Bank, *Health: Sector Policy Paper* (Washington, D.C., 1975).

20. Lloyd G. Reynolds, "China as a Less Developed Economy," *American Economic Review* 65 (June 1975): 418–428.

21. Canadian Medical Association, *China Report: Health Care in the World's Most Populous Country* (Ottawa, 1973).

22. Marc Lalonde, *A New Perspective of the Health of Canadians* (Ottawa: Department of National Health and Welfare, 1974), p. 27.

23. Chen, *Public Health Development*.

24. This estimate was obtained from health officials whom I interviewed in Peking.

25. *FBIS* 122, 1973, p. B7.

26. *Jen-min jih-pao*, February 26, 1973.

27. Fees reported in *China Reconstructs*, *FBIS*, *Kuang-ming jih-pao*, and *Jen-min jih-pao*.

28. Chen, *Public Health Development*.

29. It would be interesting to compare the financial burden of similar medical services premiums in other countries. However, the lack of data makes such a comparison impossible.

30. Chang-wei Administrative Region Revolutionary Committee (CARRC), "Thriving Cooperative Medical Services," *Chinese Medical Journal* (June 1974): 328–332.

31. *FBIS*, September 10, 1970; September 22, 1970; *CARRC*, "Thriving Cooperative Medical Services."

32. *Red Flag*, Peking, January 1969.

33. Jeoffrey B. Gordon, "The Organization and Financing of Health Services," in Joseph Quinn, ed., *China Medicine as We Saw It*

(Bethesda, Md.: Fogarty International Center, 1974), DHEW (NIH) Publication 75-684, pp. 63–93. The percentages vary among communes.

34. Mark Seldon, "The Chinese Health System," *Health PAC Bulletin* (December 1973): 1–18.

35. Jack Geiger, "China Part 2: A Pragmatic Approach to Medicine," *Medical World News* (June 1, 1976), pp. 22–29.

36. Audrey Donnithorne, *The Budget Plans in China: Central, Local, Economic Relations* (Australia National Amity Press, 1972).

37. Agricultural production function based on 1973 and 1974 PRC provincial data was estimated with and without health services variables:

$$Q = -0.345 + 0.481S + 0.661L + 0.069H, \qquad R^2 = 0.97, N = 52;$$
$$(0.084) \quad (0.078) \quad (0.089)$$

$$Q = -0.324 + 0.473S + 0.655L, \qquad\qquad R^2 = 0.97, N = 52.$$
$$(0.083) \quad (0.078)$$

Q is grain output in millions of tons, S is grain crop acreage in millions of hectares, L is population in millions, and H is the number of barefoot doctors per million population. Both equations are in the double-log form. Inclusion of the health services variable leads to a slight increase in values of the land and labor shares of the total output. Thus the health services variable may have certain indirect effects on the improvement of labor quality and on qualities and quantities of other inputs which in turn increase the agricultural output. For more detailed discussions, see Teh-wei Hu and Charles Liu, "The Role of Health Services in the Agricultural Productivity in the People's Republic of China," paper presented at the Western Economic Association, San Diego, California, June 1975.

38. *Red Flag,* January 1, 1969.

39. Ibid.

40. *CARRC,* "Thriving Cooperative Medical Services."

41. *Jen-min jih-pao,* November 10, 1972; July 25, 1973.

42. *Current Science,* Hong Kong, U.S. Information Services, 1969.

43. V. W. Sidel and Ruth Sidel, *Serve the People: Observations on Medicine in the People's Republic of China* (New York: Josiah Macy, Jr., Foundation, 1973), p. 82.

44. Peter S. Heller, "The Strategy of Health Sector Planning," in Wegman, Lin, and Purcell, eds., *Public Health in the People's Republic,* pp. 62–108.

45. *Jen-min jih-pao,* February 20, 1973; *Red Flag,* December 1972; *Jen-min jih-pao,* August 21, 1973.

46. Heller, "Strategy of Health Sector Planning"; Robert C. Hsu,

"The Barefoot Doctors of the People's Republic of China—Some Problems," *New England Journal of Medicine* (July 18, 1974): 124–127.

47. *Red Flag,* December 1972, December 1973; *Jen-min jih-pao,* June 10, 1971.

48. The author has benefited from the suggestions of Robert Dernberger.

49. Dwight H. Perkins, "The Central Features of China's Economic Development," chapter 4, table 4–1. The figures in this chapter are converted to the 1971 price level from the 1957 price level. The conversion rate is 5.96% higher than the 1957 price, based on another paper by Perkins, "Growth and Changing Structure of China's Twentieth-Century Economy," in D. H. Perkins, ed., *China's Modern Economy in Historical Perspective,* (Stanford, Calif.: Stanford University Press, 1975), table 6, p. 134.

50. Sidel and Sidel, *Serve the People;* Heller, "Strategy of Health Sector Planning"; Johnson Foundation, *Wingspread Report: Health Care in the People's Republic of China* (Racine, Wis.: Johnson Foundation, 1973); Christian Medical Commission, *Health Care in China: An Introduction* (Geneva, 1974).

51. World Bank, *Health: Sector Policy Paper.*

52. Ibid.

Three

THE RELEVANCE OF CHINA'S EXPERIENCE TO THE OTHER DEVELOPING COUNTRIES

8

Characteristics of the Chinese Economic Model Specific to the Chinese Environment
ALBERT FEUERWERKER

There are few well-established empirical generalizations about economic development, but certainly most would agree that it may be measured, at least minimally, by the expansion of per capita national product, by a decline in the output share of the primary sector, and by the adoption or adaptation of new technological possibilities. The performance of the economy of the People's Republic of China along these dimensions since the early 1950s has been a moderately good one. To what extent have these economic results been dependent on complementarities—in the broad sense of inputs and outputs exchanged between the economy and other parts of the social system—in the environment of the PRC in the past quarter of a century? In particular, what are the contemporary links between the Chinese economy and the characteristics of its wider society?[1]

The contemporary Chinese economic model is shaped by technical, political, intellectual, and social parameters characteristic of the Chinese environment. None of these linkages is unique to China; each can probably be found in some recognizable form in other national settings. What is distinctively Chinese—at least before the world enters that utopian state of "great harmony" (ta-t'ung) announced by Chinese thinkers from K'ang Yu-wei to Mao Tse-tung—is the totality of these noneconomic complementarities. This essay suggests that their interrelatedness within their domestic history and habitat is such that the successful replication of the Chinese experience by other nations must remain problematic, at best.

What might the "Chinese model" be if we took Taiwan rather than the PRC as our starting point?[2] For simplicity let us look only at the agricultural sector. Taiwan's agricultural growth relied heavily on the utilization of new plant varieties and animal breeds developed by basic research abroad but adapted to local conditions by high-quality applied research in Taiwan. This new technology was effectively diffused through the farmers' associations, which combine extension work with the provision of production requisites and credit. The required infrastructure of irrigation, flood control, and drainage was undertaken by government agencies, with costs recovered through taxation on increased production. Individual farmers significantly increased purchases of fertilizers, pesticides, tools, and equipment from nonfarm sources; these capital inputs were combined with additional labor to increase output per hectare. Land reform increased the farmer's incentives to add purchased nonfarm inputs. While prices and markets, together with agricultural taxation, served to transfer much of the economic gains from increased agricultural output to the nonagricultural sectors, real increments to farmers' incomes were significant enough to prevent backward-sloping supply curves and perverse responses to price. Various levels of government provided strong leadership and control, through the farmers' associations, the Provincial Food Bureau, and the government monopoly enterprises. Foreign financial and technical assistance was successfully channeled through the Sino-American Joint Commission on Rural Reconstruction.[3]

This is, of course, a conventional description of the growth of agricultural output in Taiwan from the point of view of neoclassical economics. The implied "model" suggests that in the abstract there is no secret about how economic development occurs: it is the product of increases in factors of production—land (including qualitative improvements), labor (including levels of health, skill, and managerial competence), and capital (including embodied technology). At this level of analysis there is little to differentiate a Chinese model derived from the Taiwan experience from one that takes the PRC as its benchmark. The primary economic variables interact in a predicted manner, once they are incorporated into a production function, regardless of the broader societal context.

Sources-of-growth analysis, following from Robert Solow's pathbreaking paper,[4] has gone somewhat further to disaggregate current factor inputs in order to specify with greater precision the contribution of increased inputs and technological change to output growth. This work has claimed, for example, that only a small proportion of the growth of national product in advanced countries is accounted for by increases in inputs of labor or capital. The "unexplained residual" ("noninput" growth factors such as technological change, education of the labor force, and motivational efficiency) may be responsible for

50%–80% of growth.[5] The sources-of-growth methodology has been criticized for ignoring cumulative feedbacks endogenous to the economy as the structure of economic activity is altered over time, for assuming a disembodied and neutral technical progress, and for its typical use of the Cobb-Douglas production function.[6] Its applicability to less developed countries, in which perfectly competitive product and factor markets are not to be assumed, is also problematic. But it has the unquestioned virtue of calling attention, perhaps unintentionally, to the boundaries between the economic system, narrowly conceived, and the noneconomic complementarities that distinguish the two Chinese models of economic development. For, if abstractly there is no secret about how development occurs once the inputs are in place in a given structure, then the quantity and quality of human and material inputs, the goals and organization of the production and distribution systems within which they are employed, management and work styles, and the subjective "meaning" of work are all substantially supplied to the economy by the other societal subsystems, which thus indirectly but inexorably affect the outcome of productive activity. It is problematic indeed that any required set of complementarities will be forthcoming just because it is assumed in a neoclassical growth model.

In part what I am discussing here has been described by Harvey Liebenstein as X-efficiency, that is, that portion of the unexplained residual not accounted for by embodied technological change or labor force skills.[7] The data examined by Liebenstein suggest that "the amount to be gained by increasing X-efficiency is frequently significant" in contrast to the usually "trivial" gains from movement "along a production surface towards greater allocative efficiency."[8] The existence of X-efficiency implies of course the possibility of a corresponding X-inefficiency. None of the complementarities to be considered here have invariably contributed to maximizing either per capita output or subjective welfare in the PRC, however measured. Ambiguity of outcomes is frequently the name of the game; but why should we expect anything else?

For much of the Ch'ing dynasty, Taiwan and the mainland provinces of the People's Republic of China shared a common historical heritage. Yet except at the most abstract level their respective economic development models diverge greatly. The reason is clear: their twentieth-century histories differ radically. The moral is that one should be most cautious about assuming pandemic and enduring Chinese traits—except perhaps, with some fairly major qualifications, for language and food—on the basis of the evidence of the millenia before 1949. Only when these have been embodied, as many have, in the values and institutions of the PRC can they be said still to affect the Chinese economic model.

The Economy and the Natural Environment: Size and Factor Endowment

Nothing is more specific to the Chinese environment than the country's large size and a factor endowment characterized by a surplus of labor and a shortage of land. These more strictly technical parameters will be reviewed before considering the effects of the political, ideological, and social complementarities to which this paper is primarily addressed.

Dwight Perkins argues that "accelerated industrialization and slowed pace of agricultural development" in the PRC, compared with other large developing countries, is not the consequence of a policy decision by the Chinese government to emulate the Soviet pattern of development but reflects China's great difficulty in achieving "easy and rapid breakthroughs in farm technology that would in turn make possible an accelerated agricultural rate of growth."[9] If the Soviet model influenced Chinese planners during the First Five-Year Plan (1953–1957), in the 1960s and early 1970s even annual investments in agriculture of state funds in the amount of 5 billion yuan (to which must be added an equivalent investment by rural communes from their own funds) resulted in a rate of growth of only about 2% a year. In fact, the share of agriculture fell more rapidly after 1957 than between 1952 and 1957. Using the Kelley-Williamson-Cheetham computational formula and Perkins's data on sectoral shares, one can estimate the annual rate of decline of the relative share of China's agricultural sector at an astounding 2.29% from 1957 to 1971—four times the rate of the "typical" less developed country and twice that of Japan in the late Meiji period.[10]

Perkins tentatively attributes this rapid diminution in the relative importance of the agricultural sector to the fact "that China was a labor-surplus, land-short economy," whose stock of cultivated acreage could be extended only at prohibitive costs and in which yields per hectare were approaching the limits achievable with the existing technology. What are the implications of this "contradiction" for the distinctiveness of the Chinese developmental model? The much remarked linkage of industrial investment to agriculture is reflected in the slogan "Taking agriculture as the foundation and industry as the leading factor," in the promotion of small-scale rural industry intended primarily to supply agriculture with production requisites, and in the large share accounted for by chemical plants in the rapid increase since 1972 of complete industrial plants purchased from abroad.[11] Rather than the consequence of some ideological preference for the uncorrupted Arcadia as against the profligacy of modern urban living, this may be more a pragmatic response to the overriding necessity to make a major effort just to keep agricultural output abreast of population growth, industrial expansion, and export requirements.

The canonical precepts are also present of course, as in the frequently stated intent to overcome "the three major differences between workers and peasants, between town and country, and between manual and physical labor." For the moment my contention is that China's factor endowment introduces an ambiguity in the definition of the Chinese model. To describe it as realistically rural oriented as opposed to delusively urban oriented, as is sometimes done, misses the point. No "agricultural revolution" releasing manpower for industry has yet occurred in China, nor is it inevitable that the European or Japanese paths will be followed. It is the industrial sector of the Chinese economy that is now growing most rapidly, and within that sector the overwhelming share of state investment is directed to heavy industry, especially iron and steel, hydrocarbons, and chemical fertilizers. A secondary allocation is made to light industry closely linked to agriculture, but the funds for the expansion of small-scale rural enterprises (which includes a resurgence of handicraft production) are for the most part generated locally.[12] In other words, the Fourth Five-Year Plan (1971–1975)—we must speak of it symbolically since planning for all practical purposes appears to be on an annual basis—suggests that one aspect of *the* Chinese model, from the mid 1960s to the present at least, is a reasonable effort to fit economic development efforts to the specific realities of the Chinese environment, which themselves are complex and therefore generate a multifaceted approach. Not all who govern the PRC are satisfied with this pragmatic line.[13]

To turn now from the shortage of land, which includes the attributes of fertility that form the basis of the Ricardian theory of land rent, to China's surplus of labor, the first problem is to determine the precise size of the current population of the PRC, a figure perhaps unknown even to the Peking government. The latest U.S. government estimate for 1974 is an almost unbelievable 920 million.[14] A large and growing population is an ambiguous asset for economic development. Simon Kuznets has suggested that for the developed countries, population growth (strictly speaking, modern demographic patterns) may have contributed directly to the rise in product per capita. But that relationship is inverted in the less developed countries, in part because advances in public health and medicine (at the cost of a relatively small proportion of total domestic product) have made possible "far more rapid reductions in death rates, unrelated to the much slower process of economic growth."[15] Indeed, the unusually rapid development of Japan—a labor-surplus, land-short, late but successful starter—is attributable in part to the circumstance that population growth before 1915 was fairly stable at about 0.9% per annum,[16] compared with 2.5% or more for the typical developing country.

Changes in the contours of the Chinese model in the past twenty-five years have probably been influenced substantially by the demographic profile. It can safely be assumed that during the war and civil war from 1937 to 1949 China's annual population growth was less than 1%. The return of peace, improved living standards, and the notable success of public health campaigns in the 1950s probably led to an annual net increment of births over deaths somewhat in excess of 2%, although there may have been a temporary drop during the depression years 1960–1962. For most of the 1960s the rate was 2% or more again, but it may have fallen now to less than 2% as a result of the family planning efforts of the last few years. If entry into the labor force occurs somewhere between the ages of fourteen and eighteen, until about 1965 only those born before 1949—a relatively small cohort—would have been seeking employment. But since the mid 1960s that number would have increased sharply, perhaps pushing against or beyond the trend line of production growth, and would not level off unless or until the effects of family planning came into play.

The smaller cohort of pre-1949 births by the early 1960s already occupied the many new positions in the state and industrial structure that opened as political penetration and economic development occurred after 1949.[17] It is plausible to regard the emphasis on small-scale rural industry at the commune level, which began in the 1960s and accelerated in the 1970s, in part as an effort to provide employment for new entrants into the labor market who cannot be absorbed in the capital-intensive heavy industry sector and who are redundant in agriculture except at peak periods. Many of these are "educated youth", products of the much-expanded post-1949 educational system whose lack of a secure place in the occupational structure was much evident during the Cultural Revolution. In a more direct fashion the rural sector has been asked to absorb these new workers under the banner of "going to the mountains or rural areas" (shang-shan hsia-hsiang). The relatively small state farm sector, for example, about which we know very little except that it is concentrated in areas bordering the Soviet Union such as Heilungkiang, Sinkiang, and the Mongolian Autonomous Region,[18] has incorporated a large number of secondary school graduates since 1969. More commonly now, educated urban youth are settled in groups in communes at reasonable distances from their homes; or, if they are of rural origin, they return to their native villages. The problems connected with absorbing educated youth into the countryside are complex. For many at least, the "higher cultural level" that they bring to the peasant village seems to find its outlet in an enlarged overhead structure of educational, medical and public health, cultural, and technical facilities, thus contributing to modernization of the countryside. The Chinese model of labor allocation since the mid 1960s—for example, control over urban growth by limiting the permanent urban labor force, promotion of labor-intensive local industries, the rustication of educated but supernumerary urban youth—fits very well the specific Chinese labor-surplus condition.

Broadly stated, the task of the agricultural sector in a developing country is not only to produce food and fiber but also to provide sheer subsistence opportunities for people who are not really needed anywhere. To repeat the well-known fact: the improved technology which has been effectively diffused throughout China's agricultural sector since 1949 has been predominantly labor intensive. Better soil preparation, close planting and interplanting, improved cultivation practices, double and triple cropping, increased applications of fertilizers and insecticides, extensive water control, irrigation, and drainage projects constructed with mass labor inputs, and the like, have significantly increased output per hectare although probably not productivity per unit of labor, given the population increment that has had to be absorbed. For the near future, mechanization of agriculture except in the forms of electrification, water pumps, farm machinery's contribution to a more rapid turnaround between harvests, and improved local transport and storage would move the Chinese model away from that pragmatic fit to its factor endowment, which I have suggested is one of its specific characteristics.

China's size influences the Chinese model of development in a number of ways. The growth patterns of small and large countries may be quite different in contour; a necessary but not sufficient condition, according to Kuznets, is that smaller countries must rely more heavily than larger countries on foreign trade in order to attain economic growth.[19] China's importation of technology, particularly as embodied in machinery and equipment since 1950, has made a large contribution to increased production. But the PRC's total foreign trade, until five years ago when an increase in real terms began, has ranged only between 6% and 9% of annual national product.[20] Obviously, with the qualifications already made, the Chinese model eschews major reliance on foreign trade or aid and, after the rupture with the Soviet Union, dependence on too limited a number of suppliers or customers. China's size is also ultimately responsible for the continuing transportation bottleneck which has constrained the growth of production. Decentralization of industry, efforts to develop provincial or lower-level self-sufficiency in basic foodstuffs, probably the pattern of importing some grains to supply the coastal cities (which goes back to the Kuomintang era)—these are aspects of the Chinese model that respond to the present inadequacies of the national transport network. Finally, the difficulty of implementing the noneconomic complementarities is amplified by great distances and the remoteness of large rural areas not served by the existing transportation facilities.

The Economy and the Polity: "Put Politics in Command"

There is always the problem of a lack of specificity, of "suggesting types or variables which need somehow to be taken into account, rather than clear, verifiable statements of relationships between specified variables,"[21] when one attempts to characterize the values of a society and their relationship to observable social structures and processes. With trepidation but also with considerable support from the relevant literature, one can suggest that the dominant values in the PRC, even with respect to the economy, are political ones. This summary statement does not imply that the degree to which politics should be in command is not itself a continuing political issue, that generally dominant values are effectively implemented in every instance; nor does it imply that values are not subject to change. The salience of political values, however, is reflected in an ambiguity about the extent to which the growth of national product is the unqualified primary goal of the Chinese model of development. Other observers have noted this uncertainty in more or less approving terms.[22] There should be no question about the commitment of the PRC leadership to the ideals of egalitarianism, the development of human potential, and the making of "Communist man," indeed for some to a strong strand of belief identified with Mao Tse-tung that rapid economic development in China's circumstances can be achieved only through such an emphasis.

Even bourgeois economists should have little difficulty in discerning the appropriateness to China's situation in 1949 of at least some aspects of the "proletarian world view" with which Maoism seeks to replace deeply imbedded values inherited from the *ancien régime:* struggle, the active effort to control and harness nature in man's interest in contrast to the age-old belief in a harmony of the human and natural spheres which led to a passive fatalism and limited aspirations;[23] selflessness, the development of a commitment to the national community in place of the narrow family- and locality-centered horizons of old China;[24] active participation, politicization of the populace in place of the relegation of decision making and administration to a circumscribed elite, the traditional "gentry";[25] and nonspecialization, the diffusion among a population largely peasant in origin—even the augmented working class—with, as the Chinese put it, a "low cultural level" of a broad acquaintance with alternative societal roles, basic applied science, and a do-it-yourself orientation.[26] It is much more problematic that there still exists in the PRC today a bourgeoisie against whom a fierce class struggle must be directed; that the elimination of all individual incentives is either possible or, for a socialist or even a communist society, desirable; that participatory democracy, its virtues acknowledged, is either as a matter of morality or efficiency the only appropriate means for decision making; or that "experts" are always narrow and "all round reds" will overcome every obstacle. But emphasizing the political development of Chinese man equally with, or even at the expense of, current economic output cannot gainsay the necessity, rationality, and apparent effectiveness of this aspect of the Chinese model.[27]

A second aspect of the dominance of politics over economics in the PRC development model may be considered under the rubric efficiency economics versus developmental economics. The former, of course, consists of adjustments, say of a production function, within a given equilibrium system. If anything is manifest about pre-1949 China, it is that no feasible amount of tinkering with the economy could have brought on modern economic growth.[28] It was not, as Carl Riskin has shown, that the economy as a whole operated so close to the subsistence level that no economic surplus was being produced. On the contrary, in 1933 the actual surplus above essential consumption exceeded one-quarter of net domestic product. But that surplus was neutralized so far as economic development is concerned by economic and political institutions that allocated it to luxury consumption and other nonproductive expenditures.[29] Economic development in China required development economics, which means institutional change toward a new equilibrium system which then may be (so economists hope) tuned via efficiency economics. The redistribution of the actual surplus after 1949 and the concomitant realization of a potential surplus attributable to unemployed or underutilized resources required, above all, the exercise of effective political power. This no Chinese government had possessed for more than half a century. The usual picture of the Nanking regime, for example, as the active tool of local landlord interests is a fiction, before the start of the Sino-Japanese War at least; its true nemesis was the failure of its feeble attempts to penetrate and control local society in the interest, among other things, of economic development.[30]

Alexander Gerschenkron's generalization from the experience of European economic history seems valid for the Chinese case. The greater the degree of "backwardness" at the beginning of industrialization and the later in the sequence among developing nations the process of modern economic growth is begun, the larger is the required quantum of "political" coordination and leadership (banking cartels in Germany, the state in Russia and the Soviet Union) and the more necessary is the role of mobilization ideology (Marxism).[31] No model of development would have been appropriate to the Chinese environment in 1949 that did not specify the structural basis of the "lost" surplus, institutionalize organization and ideology with the resources and powers to do something about it, and continue to allocate political resources and powers sufficient to effect a solution. In the actual course of restructuring the economy—in any case a lengthy process of evaluation and feedback that inevitably brings errors—the PRC leadership's perceptions of the causes of China's backwardness introduced into the Chinese model a distorting element that was not expelled until the 1960s.

Both the economic historians and the political leadership believed that the old economy, which was brought crashing to the ground in 1945–1949, suffered under the double oppression and exploitation of domestic feudalists and foreign imperialists who together blocked development. China's stagnation was not the consequence of any significant divergence of its society and economy from the universal evolutionary stages of Marxism (the Asiatic mode of production theory is untenable in the PRC). All that was required to accelerate the "normal" development from feudalism through capitalism to socialism—indeed it would even be possible to leapfrog over the capitalists stage—was liberation from the feudal-imperialist yoke. Once the Kuomintang excrescence was removed, the new Peking government faced a *tabula rasa*.[32]

The implications of this overview of China's economic history were particularly profound for agricultural policy in the initial post-1949 Chinese model. It assumed, first and correctly, the validity of the redistributionist analysis. A second but partially erroneous assumption followed from the first: that the revolutionary civil war of 1945–1949 entirely removed the obstacles to development. The correctness of the redistributionist diagnosis of China's pre-1949 economic stagnation—even if one acknowledges that it is more basic than the alternative technological analysis—does not negate the technological approach, with its emphasis on the adverse man-land ratio and the limitations of current agricultural technology; rather it places the technological approach in a more adequate theoretical and empirical context. Thus an outlook that largely ignored existing technological constraints contributed importantly to the immense optimism and self-confidence—unaccompanied by significant new economic investment as opposed to organizational and ideological inputs—with which the PRC economic model approached agricultural development during the first decade. Only in the aftermath of the Great Leap Forward was there a reorientation of agricultural policy acknowledging that organization and enthusiasm require complementary economic and technical inputs before their potential contributions to increased production can be realized.

Thus the precedence of politics over economics narrowly defined, which is one feature of the Chinese development model, is related in two contexts to the problem of restructuring the values and institutions inherited by the PRC in 1949. There was a compelling need to modernize the outlook of Chinese man before human physical and psychological energy could be joined to economic inputs for the purpose of enhancing the material welfare of the populace, and this need was recognized and met by the political leadership.[33] Similarly, the implementation of a genuine developmental economics required profound social changes, a revolution led by political forces which for the first time in China's long history penetrated to the underlying society. The politicization of society, including the economic system, may be an irreversible process, but it is precisely the continued salience of doubts about that permanence that suggests a third context in which this aspect of the Chinese model is specifically rooted in the Chinese environment.

Repeated allusions in Chinese publications to the "basic line for the entire historical period of socialism" may sometimes be puzzling to foreign readers even if they have in mind the statement by Mao Tsetung to which reference is being made:

> Socialist society covers a considerably long historical period. In the historical period of socialism, there are still classes, class contradictions and class struggle, there is the struggle between the socialist road and the capi-

talist road, and there is the danger of capitalist restoration. We must recognize the protracted and complex nature of this struggle. We must heighten our vigilance. We must conduct socialist education. We must correctly understand and handle class contradictions and class struggle, distinguish the contradiction between ourselves and the enemy from those among the people and handle them correctly. Otherwise a socialist country like ours will turn into its opposite and degenerate, and a capitalist restoration will take place. From now on we must remind ourselves of this every year, every month and every day so that we can retain a rather sober understanding of this problem and have a Marxist-Leninist line.[34]

In a formal sense this warning about the danger of capitalist restoration can be traced to the late summer and autumn of 1962, when Mao launched a counterattack against the adjustments in the economy and the loosening of controls over intellectuals brought on by the crisis following the Great Leap Forward of 1958–59. For the rural population the winter of 1961–62 marked the low point of the depression. In an effort to restore production, Teng Tzu-hui who headed the party's rural work department, backed apparently by Ch'en Yun, Teng Hsiao-p'ing and Liu Shao-ch'i, proposed the nationwide fixing of output quotas by household units, in effect dismantling the commune system. The two previous years had already seen both a substantial retreat from the policies of the Great Leap Forward and a loosening of party control in the countryside marked by the spread of a "tide of individual production." By a possibly narrow margin Mao and his supporters at the Tenth Plenum of the Eighth Central Committee in September 1962 and the Central Committee Work Conference which preceded it in August were able to draw a line against any further subversion of the collective economy. However, the Socialist Education Movement, which the plenum unanimously initiated for the purpose of reestablishing control over the rural population and cadres, became a battleground between, on one side, the party functionaries and economic managers whose policies had by 1962 restored the economy to 1957 levels and, on the other, the more ideological followers of Mao Tse-tung. How these conflicts led to the Cultural Revolution of 1966–1969 is well known.

The point here is that the issue in 1962 was more than a matter of alternative economic policies. It had escalated for Mao to a question of the degree of revolutionary commitment not only of leading party bureaucrats like Liu Shao-ch'i but also of society at large. The intellectuals attacked him in scarcely veiled writings set in the T'ang or Ming dynasties or in Aesopian essays, the local cadres had retreated into passivity after the exertions of the Great Leap, and even the peasants responded more enthusiastically to the *san-tzu i-pao* ("three self, one guarantee," that is, the extension of private plots, free markets, and small enterprises with sole responsibility for their own profit and loss, and production quotas based on the individual household) than to the slogan of the "Three Red Banners." Adjustments, compromise, trial and error in the economy in response to the crisis created by poor weather, the withdrawal of Soviet technicians, and incredibly bad management during the Great Leap—these were necessary and acceptable within limits. But the entire "superstructure" was experiencing tremors. The political revolution that had transformed China's relations of production and begun the process of economic development seemed to be in danger. This was not acceptable and had to be met head on with ever greater infusions of political ideology and a refurbished organization.[35]

We cannot ignore the ideas of Mao Tse-tung in looking for the source of the particular mixture of politics and economics that forms the Chinese model; like the nation's factor endowment, he is quintessentially Chinese.[36] That Mao views economic problems on a very broad canvas may be a decisive contribution to the emphasis on cultural change and political mobilization as conditions and concomitants of increased output. In the present instance Mao's attention to cracks in the superstructure, to the central importance of shared (revolutionary) values, reflects simultaneously the whole tenor of his thought and personality and his apprehension of the reality of twentieth-century Chinese history. From these sources arise that extraordinary infusion of politics into society, including the economy, during the 1960s (the Cultural Revolution in particular) and only to a lesser degree during the 1970s.

There is a broad but basic difference between a developed country and a less developed one. In the more successful (as measured by GNP per capita) of the modern states, if one compares (using Marxist terminology) the respective strengths of the economic base and the superstructure, it appears that the economy is more vulnerable to recession, depression, inflation, international monetary instability, and so forth, than the bourgeois cultural integument that propagates the basic values and shields the characteristic institutions of that society from question and attack. As recent Harris polls bear out, Watergate and Vietnam have not undermined the commitment of the majority of Americans to the positive, decent, and humanitarian values of their society, notwithstanding the manifest deficiencies of many of its political leaders.[37] The political system may be troubled, but the likelihood of a fascist reaction or a communist revolution is nil. In less developed nations the situation is reversed. While so much of a modern economic sector can be easily destroyed, say by the bombs of an external aggressor, the underlying agrarian sector resists being "bombed into the stone age." The horror and tragedy of Vietnam provide some proof. Nor are the contradictions between the productive forces and the relations of production in a less developed (agrarian) economy such that, without an external contingency that subverts the superstructure, a peasant revolution can seize power. Rather, it is the superstructure that is vulnerable, in substantial measure because contact with the more advanced powers in the past two centuries, as a consequence of inperialism, we can say, has disrupted the existing integration of values, ideology, and institutions, weakened the ability of the social and intellectual elites to justify the status quo and insufficiently diffused and internalized the quasi-Western accretions to the traditional cultural integument to provide a viable substitute and shield for the *ancien régime*. Revolution takes place in the superstructure, and once power is seized and new relations of production established, a major item on the new regime's agenda is to develop the productive forces of the new society. But its power is as tenuous as that of the decrepit *ancien régime* until it has developed a new cultural integument to justify and protect its institutions.

Mao Tse-tung would agree with this formulation, as evidenced by the following excerpt from his "Notes on Reading the Soviet Text *Political Economy*."

Lenin said: "The more backward a country is, the more difficult is the transition from capitalism to socialism." At present this formulation seems not to be correct. In fact, the more backward the economy, the easier the transition from capitalism to socialism, not more difficult. The more deprived men are, the more they want revolution. In Western capitalist countries the rate of employment and the level of wages are both relatively high, and the workers have been deeply influenced by the bourgeoisie. When you look at it, it wouldn't be that easy to carry out socialist transformation in these countries. The level of mechanization in these countries is very high, so that after the victory of the revolution the question of further increasing mechanization would not be a major one. The important question is the transformation of human beings.

. . . The history of all revolutions proves that it is not necessary that new productive forces be fully developed before it is possible to transform backward relations of production. Our revolution began by propagating Marxism-Leninism with the aim of creating new public opinion in order to give impetus to the revolution. In the course of the revolution, after we overthrew the backward superstructure, it was then possible to wipe out the old relations of production. Once the old relations of production were wiped out, new relations of production were established. This then opened the way for the development of the new productive forces of society. At this point it was possible to carry out a major technological revolution and massively develop society's produc-

274

tive forces. Simultaneously with the development of the productive forces, we must still continuously carry out the transformation of the relations of production and the transformation of consciousness.[38]

Before the intrusion of the West, late-imperial China was characterized by a remarkable degree of integration. At least among the literate elite there were few dissenters or "Sunday Confucians." Though the premodern Chinese intellectual might sometimes have been hard pressed to earn his livelihood, he was rarely alienated and never deracinated. The source of this integration was a broad commitment to a single social and political ideology that historians call Confucianism. These social values were firmly based in a philosophical and religious system that itself commanded intense belief. Together, the operational values of the society (which shaped its institutions, in generic terms its constitution, laws, and so forth) and their philosophical-religious justification formed a total system that claimed to comprehend the real meaning of life and humanity, a totality that was both prerational and far more comprehensive than what modern rationalism can devise. Here was a genuine conservatism committed to continuity, not in reaction to modernist challenges, not from a sense of previous loss and a vague hope that the restoration of a homogeneous and organic society would remove the symptoms of decay. Its beliefs and values were not just relative things, but the root of morality itself. Basic beliefs, operational values, and social institutions were highly integrated and mutually reinforcing. Through the eighteenth century the system indeed worked, for the political and social elites in any case, to nourish mind and body generously in a society as glorious as that of any previous Chinese imperial age, despite those who hold that Chinese civilization was sterile after the T'ang or, more generously, the Sung dynasty.

Medieval Christian Europe was just such an integrated and unified society, even into the eighteenth century, although probably not to the degree achieved in China. In Western society this integration succumbed to an internally generated secularist attack on the metaphysical and mythological grounds on which the social values were based. When its philosophical and religious justifications were undermined, the *ancien régime* itself could not long endure. In China the process of change in the nineteenth and twentieth centuries was different. It was not the basic social values that crumbled before a rationalist onslaught; rather the political institutions of society showed themselves unable to cope with the external threat of foreign imperialism. While the political system of China's *ancien régime* was partially dismantled (the establishment of the republic in 1911), and new institutional forms (modern education, political parties and politicians, the new professions, popular journalism, a sprinkling of industrial plants) sprouted here and there on the horizon, the old values persisted for a longer time among the elites and the peasant masses and obstructed the reintegration of Chinese society on a new and more just basis. In other words, no fundamental social revolution took place.

The cultural revolution of the early 1920s, known as the May Fourth Movement, weakened these values among large numbers of the political and intellectual elites, but it only incompletely replaced them with any genuine commitment to the hodgepodge of Western alternatives with which many toyed in these years. Conservative values persisted side by side with a frequently shallow and deracinated Westernism, until war and civil war in the 1930s and 1940s exhausted and discredited this semitraditional superstructure and replaced it with the state and society of the People's Republic.[39]

Mao Tse-tung, of course, was a central participant in the intellectual and political drama of these decades. His writings reflect an acute awareness of both the critical necessity and the extreme difficulty of establishing once more an autonomous Chinese society in which basic beliefs, political ideology, and empirical institutions would be tightly integrated, in which there would be no "Sunday Maoists."[40] The fecklessness of the twentieth-century intellectuals, which of course in the Chinese context means every graduate of a middle school and hence almost anybody in any position of responsibility, continued to preoccupy him as did the perception of his own experience that the critical struggle was in the superstructure, for men's minds. We may also speak of Mao's "volunteerism";[41] this is the departure from Marxist materialism for which his Soviet critics call him to task. But above all, I believe, it is his personal experience of China's twentieth-century history that focuses his apprehension on the fragility of the superstructure established after 1949. How could it be otherwise after less than a generation and in view of the partially compromised character, the Western origin, of the Marxism-Leninism with which the new China has sought to reintegrate itself?

We may use somewhat more Weberian language. The transition from imperial China, when the power and privilege of the dynasty and the bureaucracy were the regime's uppermost considerations, to a modern state dedicated to developmental and welfare goals may include a phase in which developmental goals are enunciated by a regulatory administration as much preoccupied with securing a high level of noncontingent support as with increasing output. This is because it is inherently more difficult to establish a new generalized value commitment than to increase the output of coal or grain. The economy, in brief, remains imbedded in the polity. To give it free rein before a new cultural integument is constructed which is genuinely national and sufficiently internalized may have short-run payoffs but risks the revolution that opened the possibilities for economic development.

The Economy and the Value System: "Transforming Consciousness"

The question of style rather than the content as it affects the Chinese economy is an important one. If politics are in command—that is, if economic goals such as maximizing output and efficiency may be subordinated to political needs—then the command style employed in the PRC is rooted in an identifiably Chinese concept of man. This in turn is a product of Marxism in its sinicized form reinforced by reverberations from China's philosophical heritage.[42]

In place of an exclusive concentration on the "best" allocation of material resources and labor, the Chinese developmental model assumes that higher productivity and greater output in the long run will result from a labor force possessing technical skills, high motivation stemming from knowing the "meaning" of one's work, political discipline, a group-oriented outlook, initiative, a role in decision making, and a commitment to status equality. The diffusion of some of these attributes is the province of the educational system of the PRC. Educational activities in the broad sense, as carried on in schools at all levels, in study sessions in work organizations and neighborhoods, in the press, through the arts and the entertainment media, and in the course of campaigns (*yün-tung*), are the loci of unending efforts to transform consciousness (*kai-tsao ssu-hsiang*).[43] Their aim is twofold: to impart the skills required for productive activity and to inculcate the values that support the social system of the PRC—that is, to internalize the Maoist superstructure in the individual consciousness. The fusion of knowledge and values in the educational process, of course, is not as an abstraction exclusively Chinese or Maoist. But the relative weights given to these two components, the constraints placed on which values are acceptable, and the active (even directive) role of the polity in education are based on specifically Chinese concepts of the nature of man and the role of the state.

As it affects education in the PRC, the operative Chinese concept of man has two basic premises: first, that man's essential nature is social and, second, that the conscious mind that incarnates his nature is malleable. The first premise stands in contrast to the mainstream of liberal Western thought, which stresses the self-regarding nature of the individual and addresses itself to the isolated "natural" man. This premise rejects any sharp distinction between public acts and a domain private to the individual person and denies that each person can be the best judge of what is in his interest. While accepting some biological limitations, this premise minimizes the saliency of any innate shortcomings in natural endowment (intellectual or emotional) and therefore provides support for reliance on altering the conduct of man through education as a means of resolving social issues, including increasing production.

The belief that man is not motivated primarily by self-interest can be traced as far back as Mencius, who argued for the inherent altruism of human nature, although it might be stunted or distorted by the absence of education or by an inadequate livelihood.

> Man's nature is naturally good just as water naturally flows downward. There is no man without this good nature; neither is there water that does not flow downward. Now you can strike water and cause it to splash upward over your forehead, and by damming and leading it, you can force it uphill. Is this the nature of water? It is the forced circumstances that makes it do so. Man can be made to do evil, for his nature can be treated the same way.[44]

In another place Mencius specified the five critical social relationships that framed human existence.

> According to the way of man, if they are well fed, warmly clothed, and comfortably lodged but without education, they will become almost like animals. The sage (emperor Shun) worried about it and he appointed Hsieh to be minister of education and to teach the people human relations, that between father and son, there should be affection; between ruler and minister, there should be righteousness; between husband and wife, there should be attention to their separate functions; between old and young, there should be a proper order; and between friends, there should be faithfulness. Emperor Yao said, "Encourage them, lead them on, rectify them, straighten them, help them, aid them, so they will discover for themselves [their moral nature], and in addition, stimulate them and confer kindness on them." When sages were so much concerned with their people, had they the time for farming?[45]

I do not mean to imply, of course, that the Mencian view was unchallenged; it was challenged in the theories of Hsun Tzu, for example. But the mainstream of Confucianism, especially Neo-Confucianism, never departed far from Mencius' view of man. Nor is Confucianism's positing man as without innate defects and defining him by his natural social obligations (that is, by the "Five Relations") the cause of the contemporary Chinese rejection of self-interest as a defining human characteristic. The Confucian concepts were utilized to justify a sharply hierarchical and rigid social system which is anathema to contemporary Chinese thought. What I do suggest is that the Chinese acceptance in the twentieth century of the Marxist doctrine of man's social nature as opposed to the atomistic individualism of classical liberalism was made easier by persisting resonances from tradition.[46]

The second premise, that man's social nature is malleable, finds little support in Confucianism. It is a Marxist importation into Chinese thought. It rejects any idea of panhumanism, any hint that there might be a universal human nature devoid of specific class content.[47] It denies that there is anything unalterable either in human capacities (for example, intelligence) or in the personality (for example, the unconscious psychostructure). Compared with classical Marxism and with current Soviet philosophy and psychology, however, the Chinese faith in human plasticity has a special flavor, springing from the belief that revolution takes place first in the superstructure.

For Marx, changing human nature depended ultimately on developments in the economic base; the growing forces of production would come into conflict with existing relations of production. Change could therefore be expected to be a very slow process. The Maoist emphasis on will rather than history, on the direct accessibility of human nature to manipulation via the superstructure, independent of constraints from the economic base, offers the prospect of a much more rapid transformation of human consciousness. It is also a source of the apparently unbounded optimism with which educators (and political leaders) in the PRC approach the transformation of consciousness. Pavlovian psychology in the Soviet Union affirms the malleability of the psychological nervous system and thus introduces an additional step from the point of view of social change; in contrast, the direct object of transformation in China is the conscious mind.

In the PRC, as in traditional Chinese thought, knowledge or beliefs have closely linked consequences in action. As a result, the state is accorded a legitimate role in shaping the factual and value content of consciousness. This is again as in premodern China; the legendary instruction of the people by the government recounted in the second quotation from Mencius was repeated in actuality over two millenia of recorded history. This intervention by the polity in the substance of the educational process is further supported by reference to the malleability of man. One purpose of what Donald Munro calls state "fosterage" is to prevent possible negative societal influences flowing from bad thoughts. Education, in other words, is constantly subject to measurement against a prescribed orthodoxy—Munro's "legitimacy criterion"—which establishes what is to be taught and learned. There is no moral problem about the role of outside agents of change, as there might be in a Western liberal society. The resonances from imperial Confucianism that also disdained value-free instruction are obvious and require no comment.

Even in the natural sciences there is no such thing as value-neutral education in the PRC, and the mix in lower-school textbooks at least seems heavily to favor the inculcation of values. Here the model of wartime education in Yenan and the other base areas remains very much an inspiration.[48] At higher educational levels, more immediately concerned with the knowledge and skills required for production, the explicit value content may be less, but the presence of an orthodoxy that cannot be exceeded (or questioned) finds its expression in an emphasis on applied studies rather than theory.[49] Max Weber drew a distinction between what he called exemplary prophecy, to be found in Chinese and Indian religions, and emissary prophecy, characteristic of the transcendental religions of the West. Exemplary prophets of religions that have no gods or only immanent gods influence others by their deeds, in contrast with the emissary prophets who persuade others by their "truths," by the principles they expound.[50] The distinction among proponents of religious knowledge may also be usefully extended to the realm of the natural sciences. Indigenous science in premodern China tended to be applied science, and the scientists tended to be "doers," who exerted their influence by the example of their works. Modern Western science has been increasingly theoretical science, and the great scientists have been theoreticians, "pure" scientists, who claimed their special qualities from Science in the same manner as the emissary prophets asserted their ordination from God. Theoretical science in twentieth-century China was an importation from the West that came to China largely in the heads of the thousands of Chinese who acquired their scientific educations in Europe, America, or (indirectly) in Japan. Thus to emphasize theory is possibly thrice suspect in the PRC: it has no indigenous roots, it is the province of unreliable "bourgeois" intellectuals carried over from the *ancien régime,* and its payoffs are of indeterminate social utility in what is still a poor society.

With respect to economic performance, the primary context within which to consider the educational process characteristic of the PRC is that of incentives for greater and better-quality production. William Skinner and Edwin Winckler have suggested a cycling of mobilization and normalization phases in the Chinese countryside in which normative, coercive, and remunerative incentives are in turn used to obtain compliance with the system goals as established by the political leadership.[51] I shall not discuss their model, but I want to use their terminology. Official policy may be summarized as avoiding the use of material incentives as a primary means to motivate work performance or to allocate labor. It is not the actual degree of deemphasis on remunerative incentives in the PRC that is of concern, although this too has been exaggerated by some writers. Rather, the dominance of normative incentives and ultimately the question of the degree to which coercion disappeared after the bitter years of land reform in the early 1950s are worthy of attention.

Normative incentives may, of course, include an appeal to one's patriotism or group or class identification. However, this is better regarded as background noise in the press and other media than as the specific form in which normative incentives are applied in a particular work group. The message of the media is only one aspect of the characteristic manipulation of the culture's symbolic elements, by means of which regulatory or authoritarian regimes tend to maintain themselves. Research has concluded that the mass media may be more effective in transmitting cognitive ideas, but that face-to-face communication is essential for attitude change.[52] Studies of the diffusion of agricultural innovations to peasants in Brazil, Nigeria, and India, in fact, indicate that the degree of "change agent" contact with villagers was more highly correlated with program success than any other variable tested.[53]

The social context of the PRC is far different from that of the countries in which this research was conducted. "Transformation" in China, while it overlaps in part with the rural sociologist's emphasis on inducing desirable individual decisions, of course, differs in critical ways: in the range of choices to be effected, in the means employed, in the degree of explicit politicization, and in the desired integration of any particular change with all other aspects of life. Yet it remains the case in China, as elsewhere, that the teaching of both skills and values is more difficult when there are many decision makers than when there are only a few. The adoption of new technology and desirable attitudes is more easily effected in the armed forces or in a large state-owned industrial plant, for example, than it is in the agricultural or rural small-scale industry sectors where the decision makers, even in a collective economy, are much more numerous. It is also easier to change people's attitudes when the change agent knows what these attitudes are and when people are in organized groups rather than isolated, in part because the group provides a forum for expressing dissonant attitudes, a precondition for attitude change not limited to the Maoist theory of contradictions. Thus the typical Chinese use of the small group (*hsiao-tsu*), either in the place of work or the neighborhood, as the locus for "transforming consciousness" is a reasonable approach in the circumstances of the PRC.[54]

Substantively, there are two components to the normative incentives which, as aspects of the transformation of consciousness, are applied in the small group. The first has to do with learning the "meaning" of one's job; the second invokes the sanction of peer respect to change attitudes. Persuasion through face-to-face discussion is facilitated by frequent reference to real or quasimythical personalities such as the famous Lei Feng, who has recently reemerged as an object of emulation, or to model enterprises such as Tachai brigade and Taching oil field, models of successful individual transformation and the pursuant social results.[55] True exemplars of the ideal Confucian man were, of course, also widely used in traditional education.

Learning the meaning of one's job in part implies what is already familiar from discussions and experiments in the United States and elsewhere directed to overcoming the worker dissatisfaction and alienation that stems from the fragmented nature of work on the assembly line. To have a team of workers assemble an automobile rather than individuals performing repetitive jobs presumably raises morale and product quality and perhaps even output without affecting the wage bill significantly. In the Chinese case, however, understanding the importance of one's functional role in the production process and deriving some pride in a quality product is only an intermediate goal. What is additionally sought is not merely the cognitive apprehension of society's values but the internalization of a comprehensive and consistent world view that provides a rationale for subordinating some present individual (material) interests to the claims of the future general interest of the working class.

This form of didacticism is derived primarily from Marxism, but it can also draw support from the Chinese political tradition that the ruler and his officials systematically undertake to instruct the people about the basis of government and social order and the relation of specific administrative acts to the larger picture. Central directives sent to local officials, who in turn were obliged to proselytize them among the population, typically contained elaborate rationales constructed from basic value statements and illustrative historical (or mythical) examples. Whether the rationales were true or false—they were frequently misleading—the emperor's directives were rarely mindless orders or peremptory decrees. One consequence was a much higher order of value consensus in premodern China, than, for example, in India.[56]

Peer approval or disapproval as a source of attitude change is hardly unique to China. What is specific to the Chinese model is the degree to which this process is formalized in the small group context. If indeed a sensitivity to "shame" before others rather than internalized "guilt" is, as some anthropologists suggest, a primary means of childhood socialization in Chinese culture, the effectiveness of peer pressure in bringing about a transformation of consciousness (and its phenomenological correlate, approved behavior, such as a greater and more disciplined work effort) may be partially explained. The discussion of models that epitomize desirable traits within the peer group should be most effective (have the highest marginal return) in social contexts characterized by relatively low cultural and technical levels and in which it is therefore more difficult to communicate the scientific-technical or philosophical-ideological justification for actions or beliefs. Such a social setting is, of course, the countryside. But in actual practice, efforts to introduce small group political rituals into rural villages met with many difficulties, at least before the Cultural Revolution, and they were neither so endemic nor so stable among the rural population as among urban workers, students, and cadres. Since the Cultural Revolution, rural life has probably undergone greater formal politicization, paradoxically coupled with widespread emphasis on improving the material level of life.[57]

In the absence of any commitment to the concept of an autonomous individual, the Chinese may not be troubled by the manipulative process of transforming consciousness (with the object, among other goals, of increasing the quantity of output). The effectiveness of peer respect, learning from models, and understanding the purpose of one's work in motivating achievement and releasing individual energy cannot be gainsaid. But to imply that this aspect of the PRC's development model is wholly normative and involves no coercion is misleading. Do or can other less developed societies share the Chinese concept of man? Munro has suggested that the use of the stick (negative examples with implied threats) as well as the carrot in the process of persuasion is explicitly coercive. While implied threats may not be so blatant as direct administrative sanctions or naked force, the effects are the same. He has asked, from the standpoint of liberal thought, why are the needs and values of the actual pretransformation individual less legitimate than hypothetical, future, generalized interests? Is it acceptable for the group to have the right to persuade an individual to work for the group interest without informing that individual of the process of transformation that he will undergo and of the possible outcomes (personality changes, for example), without permitting him to choose among outcomes or to reject the whole process? Above all, there is a substantial difference between a few political leaders' deciding to use certain tools or to produce more fertilizer, and that same restricted and self-perpetuating leadership's determining the true interests of the great majority and the values they may legitimately hold. In what sense can this be egalitarianism?[58] In a developing society, where despite many important changes both vertical and horizontal communication are anemic, the "mass line" may provide some of the linkage between ruler and ruled, between center and periphery which (with equally imperfect results) characterizes a developed, democratic society. But however much it may act to prevent immoral disparities of income and wealth, the mass line remains a notably unstable means of guaranteeing genuine status equality, which should include the power to command as well as to spend.

The Economy and the Social System: Experience in Complex Organizations

The ability of China's government to put politics in command by employing manipulative techniques in response to the constraints of its factor endowment and size is a product not only of its Marxist-Leninist-Maoist authoritarianism but also of its recent historical experience. The tremendous revolutionary changes that came after 1949 used or adapted the underlying strengths of the Chinese social system rather than discarded them mindlessly. The worst features of the *ancien régime* were wiped out, including irrational and obstructive differentials in property, consumption, life-style, and patterns of deference that had immobilized society's "surplus" and impeded the release of human energy. Agriculture was reorganized on a cooperative basis, and industry nationalized. But at least some of the positive aspects of the 1949 inheritance were incorporated into the renovated social system.

Perkins has argued that in comparison with many other less developed countries premodern Chinese society was characterized by values and traits conducive to modern economic growth once other real barriers to development were dismantled. Perkins summarizes the favorable inheritance from pre-1949 China as "a prior accumulation of experience with complex organizations or institutions." His list of key features includes an economy highly developed in relation to the available indigenous technology (complex farm technology and associated institutional arrangements, a high degree of agricultural commercialization, an elaborate premodern monetary and banking system); extensive urbanization served by large and intricate commercial networks and by complex noneconomic institutions;[59] and high esteem for education and literacy, probably more widespread than in any contemporary Asian society except Japan and closely linked to political power.[60] In the context of this premodern development, Perkins continues, there were "created values and traits that made the Chinese people on the average effective entrepreneurs, workers, and organization men when given the opportunity . . . Thus China on the eve of its post-1949 push on the economic front had a hardworking, readily trainable population already experienced in the operation of or participation in a commercial economy." His claim for the adaptability of these values and traits to modern economic growth rests on two kinds of evidence: first, the ability of the PRC to implement centralized planning and control of the modern sector, to overcome the withdrawal of Soviet technical assistance with only minor economic losses, and to promote extensive small-scale labor-intensive industries without apparent problems of management or control of the labor force; second, "the undisputed fact that the Chinese populations of Southeast Asia and Taiwan succeeded in engineering a rapid increase in their gross national product in the 1960s and 1970s."[61]

In contrast to certain African and Southeast Asian nations the revolutionary power that came to rule in China did not have to create a state from tribalism, or transform a subsistence economy in which man against nature wrests a living from the soil into an integrated economy. These differences might be usefully examined in the light of Gunnar Myrdal's well-known thesis of the "soft state" as the principal obstacle to economic development in South Asia. Myrdal's soft state is one in which "policies decided on are often not enforced, if they are enacted at all," and "the authorities, even when framing policies, are unwilling to place obligations on people. This reluctance . . . derives from economic, social, and political structure of the South Asian countries as they have emerged under the impact of colonialism and the fight for independence."[62] In Western Europe there was a long-term trend toward the elaboration and institutionalization of civic and community obligations and controls; colonialism in South Asia, Myrdal suggests, led to a decay of traditional village organization without creating a viable substitute. The precolonial authoritarian tradition was strengthened by colonial rule and transformed into paternalism; people became accustomed to being ordered about but also to getting away with as much as they could. This breakdown of social discipline was reinforced by the liberation movements of the last decades of colonial rule which encouraged disobedience to authority and noncooperation with the colonial power structure. As a result, the newly independent governments faced a legacy of anarchic attitudes with which their weak administrations, shot through by corruption, have been unable to cope. The late-imperial and modern history of China were different and presented the new Chinese government with a distinctive array of problems and assets.

No South Asian state possessed so effective a polity as that of imperial China before the nineteenth century. This was both a reflection and a cause of a degree of national cultural identity (even if not of modern nationalism before the twentieth century) unmatched, for example, in India with its multiple and frequently conflicting regional traditions. The formal writ of the imperial government never penetrated local society; imperially appointed officials were not usually to be found beneath the *hsien* or *chou* level (county or department, of which there were approximately 1500 in the Ch'ing period). And the economic resources of the local community were only minimally available for national purposes. In theory, however, every important aspect of rural life was under the surveillance and direction of the state (as perhaps was also the case in those South Asian countries with more authoritarian traditions), and great but only partially effective efforts were made by the Ch'ing rulers to implement the theory.[63] The premodern political fabric was tough and extensive and not so easily accessible to subversion and conquest by foreign imperialists as the fragmented Indian polity or the island kingdoms of Southeast Asia.

In contrast to Myrdal's characterization of the South Asian rural community, the villages, markets, and towns of late-imperial China were integrated by more than *Gemeinschaft* relations, although these were also important. Private ownership of land, with minor exceptions, was the norm in imperial China, and land was sold, mortgaged, and rented by means of formal written contracts. The percentage of agricultural produce that was marketed before recent times is difficult to calculate—Perkins suggests 30%–40% in the twentieth century—but the level of interprovincial trade in Ming and Ch'ing China, if one may judge from the accounts of foreign observers, was on a per capita basis at least equal to that of Europe as late as 1800, and the absolute amount, of course, was much greater.[64] The commerce in agricultural produce was carried on in the channels of an elaborate and sophisticated marketing system linking the villages of rural China economically and culturally to the market towns, and these in turn were linked to higher levels in the commercial hierarchy.[65] The self-sufficient village of late-imperial China is a myth, and within the village or marketing community some important bundles of impersonal *Gesellschaft* relations were interwoven with ties of family and lineage. All this was true before any foreign political or economic incursions into China and was hardly changed by the foreign presence which became sizable along China's eastern and southern littorals after the mid-nineteenth century. Local society, moreover, was indeed a stratified community, with wealth, power, and prestige un-equally held by the local elite (the "gentry" of so much Sinological writings); but the leadership of that elite also provided it with commu-nity institutions—village walls and militia for self-defense, for exam-ple—that were clearly not always in the interest of only the upper strata.[66] Even stratification within the lineage, the archetypical *Ge-meinschaft* institution which in much of southern China might be co-terminous with the political community, did not preclude the exis-tence of effective pan-lineage interests which could be the source of armed conflict with other communities or the state.[67] Again, these forms of local integration were little affected by imperialism in the nineteenth and twentieth centuries.

The outcomes of the Western impact were so profoundly different in India and in China that at times it is difficult to believe that the treaty ports of China were a historical and geographical extension of the earlier foreign expansion into South and Southeast Asia.[68] China never lost its sovereignty, and although the imperial political system showed many signs of decay in the nineteenth century, it remained effective enough to limit most foreigners (the missionaries with their right of inland residence were an exception) to the treaty ports. Ex-cept for Thailand, all of South and Southeast Asia had come under European political control by the mid-nineteenth century. Where they did not resort to indirect rule as in Indonesia, the foreigners dis-patched their colonial administrators even into the rural areas and from the port cities began a transformation of their colonies that sig-nificantly undermined not just the traditional polity and economy but also the cultural commitment of the colonial elites.

The eighteenth century saw a progressive ruin of most traditional Indian merchant groups as English and European traders and entre-preneurs engulfed the fragmented indigenous commercial sector from the coastal towns that had grown up around the English forts. The Indian merchants who survived did so in partnership with the British and by shifting their activities from traditional trade bases at Surat, Calicut, or Hughli to the new European-founded port cities. Rhoads Murphey summarizes the ensuing process of change in the economy.

Commercial success in India was followed in the nineteenth century by the spread of British-built rail lines linking the foreign-founded port cities with their hinterlands, draining goods to them from all parts of the country, and diffusing in return not merely imported goods and the products of new India-based factories but also new foreign-style ideas. Finally British sovereignty made possible massive British investment in the production pro-

cess: a plantation sector, mines, new and greatly increased production of commercial crops for export (jute, cotton, wheat, tobacco), and the dissemination
of steam and electric power. Traditional inland cities were transformed into
growing industrial centers, using power-driven machinery and Western
methods in both production and organization . . . More and more of India
was being drawn into the pattern of development set by the Western-founded
colonial ports.[69]

Few Indians saw British rule as something to be resisted until well into
the nineteenth century, and many of the elite became enthusiastic collaborators in an effort to adapt the treaty port model as the basis for
what they identified as the strengthening and rebuilding of India.
Even the twentieth-century independence movement was led by "con-
verts to the British model who were asking for their freedom" and not
by "rejectors of an alien system." What first took form in the colonial
ports, Murphey concludes, spread and shaped virtually all social
change and created "virtually de novo the people, groups, institutions, and ideas" of an independent India.

Unlike the ports of South and Southeast Asia, which were usually
new cities founded by Europeans, the Chinese treaty ports grew up
beside the walls of existing major trade centers. These were the loca-
tions that the foreigners themselves sought and from which they
tapped the China market. Although the Cohong monopoly at Canton
was destroyed, foreign traders at China's ports never achieved the
penetration and displacement of the indigenous commercial sector
that occurred in India. The inland distribution of foreign goods, and
to a lesser extent the assembly of exports, was dominated by Chinese
merchants and operated through the traditional channels of trade. In
the 1860s and 1870s branches of foreign firms, especially British,
handled much of the importation of cotton goods into such ports as
Hankow, which were the urban markets for large regional trading
areas. But these branches were unable to develop permanent direct
ties with rural Chinese distributors even at the central market level,
not to mention intermediate or basic markets. The Chinese firms with
whom the foreigners dealt at Chungking or Hankow were located at
the apex of the traditional marketing structure and had the advantage of local know-how and long-standing connections with lower-
level markets. Increasingly, inland Chinese firms preferred to buy
directly in Shanghai or Hong Kong, where the selection of goods was
larger and where they might benefit from competition among importers and frequent auction sales. Chinese and foreign steamship
companies on the Yangtze were highly competitive and offered terms
as favorable to Chinese merchants as to foreign ones. Moreover, the

Chefoo Convention of 1876 formalized the right of Chinese shippers to obtain transit passes and thus to obtain nominal equality of taxation with the foreigner. It is perhaps only a small exaggeration, with respect to the importation and distribution of the major staples of commerce, to describe the foreign trading firms in China as having been gradually transformed into Shanghai and Hong Kong commission agents serving the established Chinese commercial network. For some proprietary goods or those representing an advanced technology, networks of Chinese agents under direct foreign supervision were established from about the turn of the century. Some of the increasing Japanese trade after the Sino-Japanese War of 1894–1895 was also distributed by direct methods. But the bulk of the distribution of imports remained in Chinese hands.[70]

In fact, as Murphey shows,[71] the importance of foreign trade in the Chinese economy has frequently been exaggerated, perhaps because the marvelous volumes of Maritime Customs statistics stand as one of the few apparently comprehensive sources of quantitative data for the study of China's economic history. Unlike Southeast Asia and India, China did not undergo a major shift in the traditional economy toward increased production of crops for export, and there was no corresponding foreign economic, political, or cultural penetration into its villages with the consequent disruption of the traditional village social structure. As central power crumbled in the twentieth century, there is fragmentary evidence that the local elite leadership tightened its domination of rural society, increasing both its political power vis-à-vis successive ineffectual central governments and its prodigal control of the economic surplus.[72] The 1920s and 1930s probably saw a decline in popular "welfare" as a consequence—except for the Taiping period, this was not the case in secular terms in the nineteenth century—but the fabric of local society remained insulated from Western influence, either direct or as mediated by Westernizing Chinese reformers and centralizers.[73] Even into the twentieth century the railroad network remained very much underdeveloped; the sparseness of rail transport continues to be major problem for the economy of the PRC. And modern industry spread only in a most limited degree from the treaty ports, where it was fitfully inaugurated by both foreign and Chinese interests, to the vast interior beyond the coastal littorals. In other words, very little of China was drawn into the pattern of development set by the Western-dominated treaty ports.

The tenacity of the traditional economy and society, which reflected strength and integration within the constraints of the indigenous technology, that is, "development," left no vacuum for the foreigners to fill. The polity before 1949 was too weak to withstand foreign demands for special privileges derogatory of China's sovereignty; and intellectually, organizationally, and financially, it was incapable of undertaking the reforms demanded by twentieth-century conditions. But even in the treaty ports very few Chinese ever sought to strengthen and rebuild China on an exclusively foreign model, and the handful who did were soon left behind. Contact with the West in the treaty ports heightened the Chinese sense of indentity rather than undermined it, in contrast to the frequent experience in India and Southeast Asia. For Mao Tse-tung, as for Chang Chih-tung and Chiang Kai-shek—yes, also Chiang Kai-shek and the mainstream of the Kuomintang, if not for the few "total Westernizers" among them—the problem of maintaining the Chinese "essence" while making use of Western "practical knowledge" has been a central one.

Thus when it established its government in 1949, the Chinese Communist party inherited a society that had suffered years of war and civil war and severe economic hardship. But, in Myrdal's terms, China's society had not experienced a major breakdown of discipline and subversion by foreign power and influence of the social institutions that contained the lives of the vast majority of its population. Central political power at Peking and Nanking and Chungking had suffered disastrously at the hands of warlords, Japanese invaders, and Communist armies and cadres, but the presence or absence of effective organization at this level had been very distant from the immediate needs and concerns of most of the populace. From Yenan, of course, the Party had encouraged disobedience to the Kuomintang government, but always in a context of substituting a new ideological and organizational discipline for that promoted by its rivals. Anarchic mass "noncooperation" à la Gandhi was not the Chinese political style. In fact, the process of Communist "takeover" at the micro level consisted precisely in lopping off the traditional local elite and replacing it almost village by village and organization by organization with a new Marxist-Maoist–trained leadership who in a sense became the legatees of a highly disciplined and integrated society.[74]

City and countryside present somewhat different viewpoints. Rural China is organized in many important aspects along lines that analytically show a direct continuity with the "natural" social units of the past. Feudal landlords, usurers, local bullies, secret societies, religious sects are gone. But the cooperative sector, both spatially and structurally in agricultural production, is able to draw on the experience of centuries during which certain patterns of interdependence ("essential form and function," Skinner terms it) have evolved which make efficient use of rural China's land and labor endowments. Skinner has shown how, except for the abortive and self-destructive attempt of the Great Leap Forward to dispense with the traditional institutions of peasant marketing, the PRC has accepted and utilized rural periodic markets as a significant component of the system of commodity distribution, expecting only gradually to reform (modernize) these institutions.[75] Similarly, he suggests a correspondence between the rural people's commune and the traditional marketing community. The number of agricultural communes in 1959 was 21,600; in the course of the trying years, 1959–1961, and along with other adjustments in rural organization, the average commune was much reduced in size and the total number increased to 74,000. Skinner's analysis of the contemporary data concludes that the prototype of the commune was evolved in areas where agrarian modernization was relatively advanced, and in the first stages of the Great Leap the Party leadership and cadres attempted to organize all of rural China into collective administrative units of a size corresponding to the modernized marketing community (three times as large as the traditional marketing area) that operated in these advanced areas. But in the three-quarters of rural China that was still largely traditional and dependent on basic-level marketing systems (Skinner's "standard marketing community"), " 'local particularism' at first hampered, then frustrated, and finally defeated the efforts of Communist cadremen to organize collectivized units at a level above that of basic marketing systems. By the winter of 1960–61, Communist planners and cadremen alike had gained new respect for the enduring significance of natural social systems, and were seeking ways to use traditional solidarities for their own organizational ends . . . Thus with collectivization as with marketing, the Communists have been constrained to accept traditional structures as given, to build on their inert strength, and to work through them toward the institutions of a socialist society."[76]

In the south of China at least, where single-surname villagers are more common, the production team (*sheng-ch'an tui*) may coincide with the very small lineage, and the brigade (*ta-tui*) with the moderately large lineage. But the large lineage as a focus of local political power and all higher-order lineage organization were quickly dismantled after 1949. Therefore one can no longer think of rural China as organized politically along kinship lines with the potential of effective resistance to the state. Key aspects of the kinship system remain operative, however, and regional variations suggest that in the villages of north China (subject to Party penetration and organization since the 1940s) and in more prosperous areas the influence of kinship ties may be less salient than elsewhere. The persistence of lineage exogamy and patrilocal residence and the strict controls since the late 1950s on migration to the cities have maintained the existence of the local agnatic kinship group. The family, as William Parish points out, retains its importance not because of the baneful survival of "feudal customs" or the reluctance of the government to employ coercion to curtail its influence but because it is an essential organizational element in making the present system of collective agricultural production work in the interest of its peasant members.

Parish notes that despite the increased security for the average peasant provided by the commune system, the returns from agriculture are still variable, the greatly improved rural health conditions have not eliminated chronic disease, and daughters continue to be lost to the family when they marry. Therefore male children and relatively large families early in life are valued. "The more able-bodied workers a family has—particularly male laborers—the more it will earn." The existence of a private or household sector separate from collective work, moreover, makes "the work of the young and the old valuable, or at least . . . less of a burden than they would be in a setting where all production took place outside the home." It is the household sector—private plots, the raising of pigs and chickens, minor handicrafts—that provides the peasant family with cash throughout the year, in the intervals between the twice yearly distribution of collective earnings. The indirect contribution of child care provided by grandparents, which enables young mothers to work in the fields, is also of significance. "In sum," Parish concludes, "the household is a differentiated production unit" which is "most efficient when it includes a moderate number of people all doing their separate kind of work." Further strengthening the family, by making grown children more dependent on their parents, is the private ownership of rural housing. "When a son decides to marry, . . . he may request a small plot of land on which to build a new house, but the building expense must come out of his own or his family's pocket." As a result, most sons live close to their parents, either in their parents' house or in rooms newly added to that structure. Finally, welfare in rural China, maintenance in old age in particular, "still depends almost entirely upon the family," except for those old people without children who are supported by the production team (itself frequently the small lineage of which the family is a part).[77]

The basic configuration of cooperative agriculture, while allowing some degree of autonomy at each level, incorporates the traditional natural social units of rural China. Township (*hsiang,* centered on the basic market town), village, and neighborhood are now renamed commune, brigade, and team. The family remains essential to the structure of production. Ownership of land and capital and distribution of the product have been radically altered, but peasant identification with and desire for the increased welfare of his family and the wider but still familiar social network in which it is nested have been powerful motivating forces in eliciting physical and psychic energy for technical change and increased output. In some distant and perhaps hypothetical future, when the technical basis of China's agriculture is transformed by advanced seed types, chemical fertilizers, and mechanization, the direct contribution to production traceable to the survival of these traditional social units may become marginal. Their need is of the present and perhaps cannot be expected to persist unchanged into the communist stage of "ownership by the whole people," which is envisaged as ultimately replacing collective ownership even in rural China. The problems arising from the existence side by side of state-owned and cooperative sectors—especially a continuation of "distribution according to work and exchange through money," to cite a statement by Chairman Mao much quoted recently —have been the focus in 1975 of a plethora of articles and broadcasts on the necessity of strengthening the "dictatorship of the proletariat." While these certainly reflect unhappiness in very orthodox circles with the pragmatic post–Great Leap agricultural policies, the verbal campaign was not accompanied up to mid 1975 by very much organizational input or mobilizational activity. It is perhaps only a restatement, a reminder, of the basic path to the Chinese utopia that will require "a fairly long time" to traverse.[78]

The urban scene is something else. As Murphey's *Outsiders* graphically recounts, the Chinese revolution rejected the treaty port inheritance which was the leading edge in independent India. On what model should the newly entered cities, in which the Communists had last stood in 1927, be organized? The traditional Chinese city, dominated politically and economically by "transients, migrants, and outsiders,"[79] offered few institutions adaptable to the needs of the rapid industrialization that the PRC sought. The city of the mid-twentieth century as an actuality, "between two worlds," was the natural domicile of the "comprador capitalists," "imperialist lackies," and "vacillating bourgeoisie" whose brief hour in the limelight was now over. Cities, any large cities, with their teeming populations, wretched slums, decaying public services, and characteristic anonymity, could not easily be infused with a sense of community comparable to that provided by the long-lived natural social units of the countryside. It is in the cities that the problems of discipline, organization, and community have most plagued the PRC. The oscillation between local autonomy and central direction, between popular participation and pyramiding bureaucracy which characterized the administration of urban

China; the conflict between a "proletariat" privileged in ideology and divided in actuality into permanent and less favored temporary workers, between the needs for technical and administrative expertise and the claims of political reliability, exploded in the Cultural Revolution of 1966–1969 which affected rural China hardly at all.[80] Visitors to the PRC have been struck by the contrast between the opening phrases of the inevitable briefings heard in both the city and the countryside—"Since the Cultural Revolution" in the first case; "Since Liberation" in the latter.

New urban patterns are evolving with apparently larger citizen participation than before 1966 but also with a continuing tension that no visitor to Shanghai in recent years can have missed. One thing seems certain: urban living standards are higher. In the attempt to narrow the "three major differences between workers and peasants, between town and country, and between manual and mental labor," it is rural life that will be urbanized, not city life ruralized. The promotion of rural small-scale industry and rustication of educated urban youth are steps to that end, although they have other purposes as well. The consequences for the social organization that now supports agricultural production are, of course, still unknowable.

The Economy and the External World

Before the withdrawal of Soviet technicians in 1960, some eleven thousand Soviet scientists and specialists were sent to China for varying periods of time. Perhaps one-half were associated with the large number of complete industrial plants sold to China by the Soviet Union. An equal number served as advisers or instructors in government offices, educational institutions, military units, hospitals, railroads, and other economic enterprises. A smaller cohort of technicians from the socialist countries of Eastern Europe filled similar roles. In sum, a massive face-to-face transfer of specialized knowledge by foreigners resident in China took place in the decade from 1950 to 1960, much greater in scope and intensity than any earlier experience with the reception of foreign technology by China.[81] The presence of a large number of foreigners in China in relatively intimate, long-lasting contact with the major economic, political, and cultural institutions ended abruptly in 1960, not to be revived. Large-scale importation of technology embodied in commodities was resumed in the 1970s, but foreigners in China have since 1960 been tightly controlled as to numbers, length of stay, and above all access to Chinese society.

Is there something specifically Chinese about this virtual exclusion of the foreigner (or the even more restricted access by citizens of the PRC to the external world)? It seems a reasonable response to the problems raised by the "demonstration effect" as these have been experienced in other developing countries. The regulatory character of the PRC political system—that it is a "hard" rather than a "soft" state à la Myrdal—makes the imposition of such restrictions possible, undoubtedly helping to reduce the pressure for immediate increases in consumption. Yet this "exclusiveness" probably represents something more than avoidance of the demonstration effect.

Foreigners in the main are not parties to the integrating myths of contemporary Chinese society and, innocently or not, question discrepancies between ideology and practice. Through constant repetition such questioning may subvert the credulity of those whose function is to supply answers. Of course, every society is open to tough questioning; but not every society is so troubled in its superstructure, perhaps because not every society demands of its people such a degree of explicit commitment in return for such hopeful promises. The problem is how to obtain foreign technology without foreign contamination. The best answer so far is to import it in the form of high-technology machinery and equipment along with a comprehensive array of the leading foreign scientific and engineering publications. Resident foreign experts may sometimes be necessary, but only as a temporary measure in each case and always as far as possible in a context that insulates them from the living China.

The experience with Russian advisers and technicians, moreover, though unquestionably of great importance for China's material development, had two drawbacks apart from any doubts about the Chinese model expressed by Soviet citizens in China. First, it exacerbated sensitivities about dependence on the foreigner, even the Russian "big brother," that were never very deeply hidden beneath the skin of every Chinese nationalist. Second, that experience provided adequate evidence that many of the characteristics of the Soviet economic model were intimately bound up with the Russian "environment" and were not transferable to China. Machinery, equipment, scientific formulas, some kinds of blueprints are all permeable at national borders. But manner, mode, style, mood—the intangibles that live men add to the diagram and the printed word—why should foreign versions of these take root in China which has a plethora of her own? Memories of a century of imperialist intrusions and humiliation combine with flashbacks to a consummate older past to produce contemporary Chinese commitment and pride. Modern Chinese nationalism attained its intensity by incorporating the culturalist xenophobia of Confucian tradition.

From the end of the nineteenth century until 1949 nationalist strivings to combine domestic reform (to achieve the political and material basis for ending foreign special privileges) with an attack on the imperialist prerogatives have constituted the main content of China's history. Each of the successive centralizing efforts in the first half of the twentieth century—the late-Ch'ing reform program, the brief rule of Yuan Shih-k'ai in the first years after the republican revolution of 1911, the nationalist revolution of the 1920s from which the Kuomintang emerged victorious and established its government at Nanking, and the rise to power of the Chinese Communist party—has been a response to this two-pronged nationalist program of domestic reform, in particular, economic development, and anti-imperialism. After the brief and conditional successes but ultimate failure of their predecessors, the Chinese Communists came to rule China as the legitimate and authoritative inheritors of the leadership of this nationalist revolution. For the PRC ultimately to seek anything other than to limit its dependence on foreign trade or aid to a level that was indispensable, to exclude the foreigners themselves from China except as approving tourists, and to seek a Chinese way to "wealth and power" would be to contravene the lessons of China's modern history.

From a sufficient distance, all societies appear to be smoothly functioning equilibrium systems. This impression is reinforced if observations are made at a single point in time. The more abstract the analysis and the more cross-sectional the data, the greater is the likelihood that discordancies will be missed, that the first small signs of eventual large changes will be ignored. One is struck by how much straining is necessary to assemble all the parts of the Chinese development story into something that for the moment is quintessentially Chinese. What has been omitted, of course, is amplification of the essential qualifying statement: "This summary statement does not imply that the degree to which politics should be in command is not itself a continuing political issue, that generally dominant values are effectively implemented in every instance; nor does it imply that values are not subject to change." This disclaimer was made with specific reference to the politicization of economic decisions, but it is applicable as well to all the generalities offered.

The People's Republic of China has a history—a longer one now than the history of Kuomintang China which preceded it—and a future. It is a society characterized by political struggles about the shape of that future as intense as those that shaped its history, although they may not be so visible as the politics of a more "open" society. The backward and forward linkage effects of the remarkable degree of industrialization have not yet worked themselves into the economy or society as a whole. It is questionable, for example, that the sectoral and geographic unevenness of economic development of the present is a sure guide to the future. Nor do we escape the quicksands of our ignorance by assuming casually that the imperatives of modern technology, in agriculture as well as in industry, are compatible with the Maoist vision in its pristine form. What happens after everyone has a bicycle is not a trivial or abusive question. And that vision, too, is far from timeless. The "thought of Mao Tse-tung," which is the object of so much exegesis, assumed its present form only in the 1960s. To be sure, there are intimations that can be traced as far back as the May Fourth period, responses to China's painful history in the previous century, but much that is central is directly a product of the experience of the first two decades of the PRC. Mao has died and is no longer able to amend his thought, although the experiences, of course, extend beyond the lifetime of any leader.

What I propose is that the economic development "model" of the People's Republic of China up to the time of Mao's death had been deeply conditioned by China's natural environment, by the saliency of the issue of political integration in modern China, by a specifically Chinese view of the nature of man, by the possibility for the PRC government to work through some enduring traditional institutions in establishing its socialist society, and by the imperatives of modern Chinese nationalism.

Notes

1. This chapter is not another attempt to discuss the question of origins. I am satisfied with John Fairbank's rendering of *Jen-min Chung-kuo* as the "People's Middle Kingdom" [John K. Fairbank, *China: The People's Middle Kingdom and the United States* (Cambridge, Mass.: Harvard University Press, 1967), p. 44]. China today is inevitably a product of all of its past—the imperial Confucian tradition, the turbulent twentieth century including the history of the Communist movement from its founding in 1921, and the shifting tides in the People's Republic since 1949. It is probably only of secondary importance that these attributes are of earlier or later origin, although it is frequently of substantial interest to observe both continuities with the past and changes from older patterns.

2. Taiwan's economic development since the early 1950s has in many ways been no less impressive than that of the provinces on the Chinese mainland. See Mo-huan Hsing, "Taiwan," in *The Philippines*

and Taiwan: Industrialization and Trade Policies (Published for the Development Center of the OECD by Oxford University Press, 1971), pp. 135–309.

3. U.S. Department of Agriculture, Economic Research Service, *Taiwan's Agricultural Development: Its Relevance for Developing Countries Today.* Foreign Agricultural Economic Report No. 39 (Washington, D.C.: U.S. Government Printing Office, 1968), pp. 84–91.

4. R. M. Solow, "Technical Change and the Aggregate Production Function," *Review of Economics and Statistics* 39 (August 1957): 312–320.

5. Harvey Liebenstein, "Allocative Efficiency vs. 'X-Efficiency,'" *American Economic Review* 56, no. 3 (June 1966): 404.

6. See, for example, Allen C. Kelley, Jeffrey G. Williamson, and Russell J. Cheetham, *Dualistic Economic Development: Theory and History* (Chicago: University of Chicago Press, 1972), pp. 3–4, 111–113, 178, 216–217, 320–321.

7. Liebenstein, "Allocative Efficiency vs. 'X-Efficiency,'" pp. 406–415.

8. Ibid., p. 413.

9. Dwight H. Perkins, "Growth and Changing Structure of China's Twentieth-Century Economy," in Dwight H. Perkins, ed., *China's Modern Economy in Historical Perspective* (Stanford, Calif.: Stanford University Press, 1975), pp. 143, 147.

10. Kelley, Williamson, and Cheetham, *Dualistic Economic Development,* p. 109.

11. Robert F. Dernberger, "The Resurgence of 'Chung-hsueh wei-t'i, Hsi-hsueh wei-yung' (Chinese learning for the fundamental principles, Western learning for practical application) in Contemporary China: The Transfer of Technology to the PRC," May 1975, table A5.

12. See, for example, Chi Yen, "Going in for Agriculture in a Big Way," *Peking Review,* June 6, 1975, on the experience of Hopei province.

13. See, for example, two recent "orthodox" jeremiads which remind one of Jonathan Edwards dolorously lamenting the falling away from Calvinism of the eighteenth-century Puritans: Yao Wen-yuan, "Lun Lin Piao fan-tang chi-t'uan ti she-hui chi-ch'u" (On the social basis of Lin Piao's anti-party clique), *Hung-ch'i* (Red flag), no. 3, 1975, pp. 20–29; and Chang Ch'un-ch'iao, "Lun tui tzu-ch'an-chieh-chi ti ch'uan-mien chuan-cheng" (On exercising all-round dictatorship over the bourgeoisie), *Hung-ch'i,* no. 4, 1975, pp. 3–12. These two pieces are translated in *Peking Review,* March 7, 1975, and April 4, 1975.

14. Central Intelligence Agency, Office of Economic Research, "People's Republic of China: Economic Indicators," June 1975.

15. Simon Kuznets, *Modern Economic Growth: Rate, Structure, and Spread* (New Haven, Conn.: Yale University Press, 1966), pp. 34–63.

16. Kazushi Ohkawa, *The Growth Rate of the Japanese Economy since 1878* (Tokyo: Kinokuniya, 1957), p. 27.

17. On pre–Cultural Revolution blockages to advancement by younger aspirants to Party and state positions, see A. Doak Barnett, *Cadres, Bureaucracy, and Political Power in Communist China* (New York: Columbia University Press, 1967), pp. 54–60; Michel Oksenberg, "Local Leaders in Rural China, 1962–65: Individual Attributes, Bureaucratic Positions, and Political Recruitment," in A. Doak Barnett, ed., *Chinese Communist Politics in Action* (Seattle, Wash.: University of Washington Press, 1969), pp. 155–215; and Michel Oksenberg, "Getting Ahead and Along in Communist China: The Ladder of Success on the Eve of the Cultural Revolution," in John Wilson Lewis, ed., *Party Leadership and Revolutionary Power in China* (Cambridge: Cambridge University Press, 1970), pp. 304–347. The distinction between industrial workers with tenure and temporary and contract workers who move in and out of industry from the agricultural or urban household sectors, a matter that added some fuel to the fires of the Cultural Revolution in urban areas, is treated in Christopher Howe, *Wage Patterns and Wage Policy in Modern China, 1919–1972* (Cambridge: Cambridge University Press, 1973), pp. 107–108, pp. 127–129. All pre-1960 entrants to the labor force who were included in the 1963 labor plan were made permanent. Thereafter a considerable preference was shown for temporary labor. The temporary system is still in use, although there have been some improvements in payment practices. "Economism"?

18. H. V. Henle, *Report on China's Agriculture* (Rome: Food and Agricultural Organization of the United Nations, 1974), pp. 210–211, mentions a 1971 estimate which he obtained in China of 1,500 state farms with a total area of 1.2 million hectares, a considerable drop from the early 1960s if the figure is not in error, suggesting that successful state farms that have opened new areas to cultivation may later be converted into communes.

19. Kuznets, *Modern Economic Growth*, pp. 300–304.

20. Alexander Eckstein, *Communist China's Economic Growth and Foreign Trade* (New York: McGraw-Hill, 1966), pp. 117–134, 292–300, indicates the difficulty of making reliable estimates of the ratio of foreign trade to GNP.

21. Robert K. Merton, *Social Theory and Social Structure* (Glencoe, Ill.: Free Press, 1949), p. 9.

22. As an example, see John G. Gurley, "Capitalist and Maoist Economic Development," in Edward Friedman and Mark Selden, eds.,

America's Asia: Dissenting Essays on Asian-American Relations (New York: Vintage Books, 1971), pp. 324–356: "Finally, Maoists seem perfectly willing to pursue the goal of transforming man even though it is temporarily at the expense of some economic growth" (p. 333).

23. See Derk Bodde, "Harmony and Conflict in Chinese Philosophy," in Arthur F. Wright, ed., *Studies in Chinese Thought* (Chicago: University of Chicago Press, 1953), pp. 19–80.

24. The literature on Chinese familism is very extensive; Maurice Freedman, *Chinese Lineage and Chinese Society: Fukien and Kwantung* (London: Athlone Press, 1966), and Maurice Freedman, ed., *Family and Kinship in Chinese Society* (Stanford, Calif.: Stanford University Press, 1970) may be noted.

25. See Chung-li Chang, *The Chinese Gentry: Studies on Their Role in Nineteenth-Century Chinese Society* (Seattle, Wash.: University of Washington Press, 1955), and Ping-ti Ho, *The Ladder of Success in Imperial China: Aspects of Social Mobility, 1368–1911* (New York: Columbia University Press, 1962).

26. Donald J. Munro, *The Concept of Man in Contemporary China* (Ann Arbor, Mich.: University of Michigan Press, 1977), chap. 7, treats this matter of "red" or "expert" with considerable skill.

27. It is perhaps outside the scope of this paper, but the bourgeois economists—and even nonbourgeois economists—who acknowledge the morphological consistency with the Chinese environment in 1949 of an emphasis on man rather than "things" may yet have some hesitation about the long run when, rather than the form alone, they consider the full range of the intended content of the minds and emotions of "Communist man." Apart from the severely limited opportunities for communication which visiting delegations have had, this can be inferred only from Chinese newspapers, magazines, radio broadcasts, books, theater, art, music, and film.

28. For a general account, see Albert Feuerwerker, *The Chinese Economy, 1912–1949*, Michigan Papers in Chinese Studies No. 1 (Ann Arbor, Mich.: Center for Chinese Studies, 1968).

29. Carl Riskin, "Surplus and Stagnation in Modern China," in Dwight H. Perkins, ed., *China's Modern Economy in Historical Perspective* (Stanford, Calif.: Stanford University Press, 1975), pp. 49–84.

30. See Hung-mao Tien, *Government and Politics in Kuomintang China, 1927–1937* (Stanford, Calif.: Stanford University Press, 1972), pp. 129–150; and Lloyd E. Eastman, *The Abortive Revolution: China under Nationalist Rule, 1927–1937* (Cambridge, Mass.: Harvard University Press, 1974), pp. 181–243.

31. Alexander Gerschenkron, *Economic Backwardness in Historical Perspective* (Cambridge, Mass.: Harvard University Press, 1962), pp. 5–30.

32. Albert Feuerwerker, "China's Modern Economic History in Chinese Communist Historiography," in Albert Feuerwerker, ed., *History in Communist China* (Cambridge, Mass.: MIT Press, 1968), pp. 216–246.

33. On the critical problem of "becoming modern" in other societies, see Alex Inkeles and David Horton Smith, *Becoming Modern: Individual Change in Six Developing Countries* (Cambridge, Mass.: Harvard University Press, 1974), and Everett M. Rogers, *Modernization among Peasants: The Impact of Communication* (New York: Holt, Rinehart, and Winston, 1969).

34. This quotation appears, for example, in Chang Ch'un-ch'iao's "Report on the Revision of the Constitution" to the Fourth National People's Congress on January 13, 1975, but without any indication as to when or where Mao uttered it. A shortened version is incorporated in chapter 1 of the "Constitution of the Communist Party of China" adopted by the Tenth National Congress on August 28, 1973. References to the Party's "basic line" occur frequently in the press between 1969 and 1975 with full or partial citation of Mao's words but without, so far as I am aware, giving any date or source. The one exception, and this may be a giveaway, is Lin Piao's, "Report to the Ninth National Congress of the Communist Party of China" on April 1, 1969: "At the working conference of the Central Committee at Peitaho in August 1962 and at the Tenth Plenary Session of the Eighth Central Committee of the Party in September of the same year, Chairman Mao put forward more comprehensively the basic line of our Party for the whole historical period of socialism. Chairman Mao pointed out"—and here the entire quotation follows. Texts, probably only partial records, of Mao's speeches at these two meetings are available in *Mao Tse-tung ssu-hsiang wan-sui* (Long live the thought of Mao Tse-tung), August 1969, a 716-page collection issued in the PRC by unknown compilers and reprinted photographically by the Institute of International Relations, Taipei, in June 1973, pp. 423–429, 430–436. From these I would judge that the quotation as cited by Chang Ch'un-ch'iao and others is a polished composite derived from preliminary remarks at the two Central Committee meetings. See Stuart Schram's review of *Mao Tse-tung ssu-hsiang wan-sui* in *China Quarterly*, no. 57 (January–March 1974), pp. 156–165, on the reliability of these texts.

35. On these events, see Jürgen Domes, *The Internal Politics of China, 1949–1972* (New York: Praeger, 1973), pp. 123–147; Richard C. Thornton, *China: The Struggle for Power, 1917–1972* (Bloomington, Ind.: Indiana University Press, 1973), pp. 244–268; Byung-joon Ahn, "Adjustments to the Great Leap Forward and Their Ideological Legacy," in Chalmers Johnson, ed., *Ideology and Politics in Contemporary China* (Seattle, Wash.: University of Washington Press, 1973), pp.

257–300; and Merle Goldman, "Party Policies towards the Intellectuals: The Unique Blooming and Contending of 1961–62," in John Wilson Lewis, ed., *Party Leadership and Revolutionary Power in China* (Cambridge: Cambridge University Press, 1970), pp. 268–303.

36. Stuart Schram, ed., *Mao Tse-tung Unrehearsed: Talks and Letters, 1956–1971* (London: Penguin Books, 1974) reveals an earthy pungency and verve in Mao that no living national leader can match, in texts filled with numberless topical and frequently droll references to China's history past and present. *Mao Tse-tung ssu-hsiang wan-sui* has even more of the same. The American edition of Schram's anthology, by the way, which adopted the title *Chairman Mao Talks to the People: Talks and Letters, 1956–1971* (New York: Pantheon, 1974) for a collection of speeches and writings not generally accessible within China is a fine example of what Schram elsewhere describes as the phenomenon of "the plaster saint worshipped by some of his self-appointed disciples."

37. On these values see Robert N. Bellah, *The Broken Covenant: American Civil Religion in Time of Trial* (New York: Seabury Press, 1975).

38. *Mao Tse-tung ssu-hsiang wan-sui,* pp. 333–334. These notes are dated 1961–1962.

39. On the durability of conservative thought, see Charlotte Furth, ed., *The Limits of Change: Essays on Conservative Alternatives in Republican China* (Cambridge, Mass.: Harvard University Press, 1976).

40. The best biography is Stuart Schram, *Mao Tse-tung* (Harmondsworth: Penguin Books, 1967); see also Schram's magistral essay, "Introduction: The Cultural Revolution in Historical Perspective," in Stuart R. Schram, ed., *Authority, Participation, and Cultural Change in China* (Cambridge: Cambridge University Press, 1973).

41. See Frederic Wakeman, Jr., *History and Will: Philosophical Perspectives of Mao Tse-tung's Thought* (Berkeley: University of California Press, 1973).

42. For much of the contents of this section I am indebted to many conversations with Donald J. Munro whose *The Concept of Man in Contemporary China* provides a brilliant analysis of values and education in the PRC.

43. *Ssu-hsiang* is literally "thought." This conscious content of the mind is seen by current Chinese educational philosophy and psychology as the central attribute of man's social nature and therefore as the proper focus for transformation.

44. *The Book of Mencius,* translated by Wing-tsit Chan, *A Source Book in Chinese Philosophy* (Princeton, N.J.: Princeton University Press, 1963), p. 52.

45. Ibid., pp. 69–70.

46. See Jerome B. Grieder, "The Question of 'Politics' in the May Fourth Era," in Benjamin I. Schwartz, ed., *Reflections on the May Fourth Movement: A Symposium* (Cambridge, Mass.: Harvard University Press, 1973), pp. 95–101. Early twentieth-century attempts to "renovate the people" (*hsin-min,* a term that carries a connotation similar to "transforming consciousness") by Liang Ch'i-ch'ao, for example, also rejected individualism as a basis for reintegrating Chinese society. See Hao Chang, *Liang Ch'i-ch'ao and Intellectual Transition in China, 1890–1907* (Cambridge, Mass.: Harvard University Press, 1971).

47. See, for example, *Jen-min jih-pao,* June 18, 1963, which contains an attack on one Liu Chieh of the Department of History at Chungshan University who ventured to suggest that Confucian *jen* ("humanity, benevolence") was an "abstract ethical concept" which "has been induced from all kinds of concrete happenings in human society from ancient times till the present."

48. See Peter J. Seybolt, "Yenan Education and the Chinese Revolution, 1937–1945" (Ph.D. thesis, Harvard University, 1970).

49. On the situation of the biological sciences, a field critical to the future development of agriculture, see *Plant Studies in the People's Republic of China: A Trip Report of the American Plant Studies Delegation* (Washington, D.C.: National Academy of Sciences, 1975).

50. "The Social Psychology of the World Religions," in H. H. Gerth and C. Wright Mills, trans. and eds., *From Max Weber: Essays in Sociology* (New York: Oxford University Press, 1946), pp. 276–301.

51. G. William Skinner and Edwin A. Winckler, "Compliance Succession in Rural Communist China: A Cyclical Theory," in Amitai Etzioni, ed., *Complex Organizations: A Sociological Reader,* 2nd ed. (New York: Holt, Rinehart and Winston, 1969), pp. 410–438.

52. Rogers, *Modernization among Peasants,* pp. 96–145.

53. William A. Herzog, Jr., "Diffusion of Innovations to Peasants in Brazil, Nigeria, and India," in Robert A. Solo and Everett M. Rogers, eds., *Inducing Technological Change for Economic Growth and Development* (East Lansing, Mich.: Michigan State University Press, 1972), pp. 116–117.

54. On the small group, see Martin King Whyte, *Small Groups and Political Rituals in China* (Berkeley: University of California Press, 1974).

55. Lei Feng was a young soldier (whether or not he ever existed as depicted is unimportant) who was posthumously extolled as a symbol of the revolutionary virtues of selflessness, simplicity, struggle, and sacrifice. A campaign to "learn from Lei Feng" emerged in the People's Liberation Army in early 1963 and was quickly extended to

the whole nation under the slogan "Learn from Lei Feng and the PLA." The context is that which I have described earlier of Mao Tse-tung's attempt to renovate the superstructure in the wake of the Great Leap Forward. Lei Feng's resurrection, reported by recent visitors to the PRC, appears related to the reassertion of "orthodox" values, possibly in response to the "normalization" implied by the state constitution adopted by the Fourth National People's Congress in January 1975, in the articles by Chang Ch'un-ch'iao and Yao Wen-yuan cited in note 13.

56. The system of village lectures (*hsiang-yüeh*) in the Ch'ing period is a good example of this type of popular indoctrination. See Kung-chuan Hsiao, *Rural China: Imperial Control in the Nineteenth Century* (Seattle, Wash.: University of Washington Press, 1960), pp. 184–205.

57. Whyte, *Small Groups and Political Rituals in China,* pp. 165–166.

58. Munro, *The Concept of Man in Contemporary China,* chap. 8.

59. As of 1800 approximately 4% of the world's population of 900 million to 1 billion lived in cities with more than 10,000 inhabitants. One-third of these urban dwellers were in China. Gilbert Rozman, *Urban Networks in Ch'ing China and Tokugawa Japan* (Princeton, N.J.: Princeton University Press, 1973), p. 6.

60. Evelyn Sakakida Rawski, *Education and Popular Literacy in Ch'ing China* (Ann Arbor, Mich.: University of Michigan Press, 1979), indicates a much higher level of literacy in premodern China than most students have hitherto suggested.

61. Dwight H. Perkins, "Introduction: The Persistence of the Past," in Perkins, *China's Modern Economy,* pp. 3, 5, 7, 10.

62. Gunnar Myrdal, *Asian Drama: An Inquiry into the Poverty of Nations,* 3 vols. (New York: Pantheon, 1968), p. 66. The "soft state" theme runs throughout *Asian Drama;* for a briefer statement see Myrdal, "The 'Soft State' in Underdeveloped Countries," in Paul Streeten, ed., *Unfashionable Economics: Essays in Honour of Lord Balogh* (London: Weidenfield and Nicolson, 1970), pp. 227–243.

63. Hsiao, *Rural China,* pp. 43–258, describes in great detail the Ch'ing police (*pao-chia*), tax collection (*li-chia*), famine prevention, and ideological control institutions.

64. Rhoads Murphey, *The Outsiders: The Western Experience in India and China* (Ann Arbor, Mich.: University of Michigan Press, 1977), provides an excellent summary of dozens of firsthand foreign accounts of the traditional economy.

65. G. William Skinner, "Marketing and Social Structure in Rural China," *Journal of Asian Studies* 24, no. 1 (November 1964): 3–43; 24, no. 2 (February 1965): 195–228; 24, no. 3 (May 1965): 363–399.

66. See Philip A. Kuhn, *Rebellion and Its Enemies in Late Imperial China: Militarization and Social Structure, 1796–1864* (Cambridge, Mass.: Harvard University Press, 1970).

67. See Maurice Freedman, *Lineage Organization in Southeastern China* (London: Athlone Press, 1958); and Freedman, *Chinese Lineage and Chinese Society.*

68. I am indebted for much of what follows to many conversations with Rhoads Murphey and to his provocatively revisionist work, *The Outsiders.*

69. *The Outsiders,* pp. 64–65. The quotations that follow are from pp. 71, 73 of the same work.

70. See Albert Feuerwerker, *The Chinese Economy, ca. 1870–1911,* Michigan Papers in Chinese Studies No. 5 (Ann Arbor, Mich.: Center for Chinese Studies, 1969), pp. 44–61.

71. *The Outsiders,* chap. 11.

72. Kuhn, *Rebellion and Its Enemies in Late Imperial China,* pp. 211–225.

73. For a marvelously graphic account of "traditional" Szechwan in 1948, see A. Doak Barnett, *China on the Eve of Communist Takeover* (New York: Praeger, 1963), pp. 103–154.

74. Franz Schurmann, *Ideology and Organization in Communist China,* 2nd ed. (Berkeley: University of California Press, 1968), pp. 365–380, pp. 402–442, describes this process both in the cities and the countryside.

75. "Marketing and Social Structure in Rural China," pp. 371–376.

76. Ibid., pp. 382–399.

77. For this discussion of the rural family I have relied on William L. Parish, Jr., "Socialism and the Chinese Peasant Family," *Journal of Asian Studies* 34, no. 3 (May 1975): 613–630.

78. See the articles cited in note 13.

79. Mark Elvin, "Introduction," in Mark Elvin and G. William Skinner, eds., *The Chinese City between Two Worlds* (Stanford, Calif.: Stanford University Press, 1974), p. 3.

80. See John Wilson Lewis, ed., *The City in Communist China* (Stanford, Calif.: Stanford University Press, 1971), especially Lewis' "Introduction: Order and Modernization in the Chinese City," pp. 1–26.

81. Dernberger, "The Transfer of Technology to the PRC," pp. 18–20.

9

Is the Chinese Model Transferable?

ROBERT F. DERNBERGER AND FRANÇOISE LE GALL

Various arguments have been presented in the preceding chapters to explain why China's development experience over the past twenty-five years might be relevant to other developing countries. These explanations include the relative success of the Chinese in achieving a social transformation and other nonquantitative objectives according to the ideals of socialism (Maoism), in addition to a relatively high rate of growth in material output; the extent to which China's economic development has relied on the initiative and involvement of the masses and lower-level political and economic units, while the upper-level political leadership has retained considerable control over the allocation of resources; and the spirit of self-reliance that underlies much of China's economic development program. As the previous chapters have made clear, there have been both successes and failures in China's economic development program, and the Chinese leadership has often exaggerated the success of its programs and institutions.[1] Nonetheless, the question is a matter of degree, and in this regard the relative success and the characteristics of China's economic development program explain its appeal and the belief in its importance in the search for solutions to the economic development problem throughout the Third World.

Even if it were not for these considerations, China's development experience would still merit attention as a possible source of solutions. China's economic development program is one of the most complete and inclusive of such programs in the world today. Among its specific ingredients are attempts to reduce the rate of population growth through birth control programs; to control urbanization and redistribute population, to make distribution of necessities more equitable and less dependent on the distribution of income; to institute a public health system in which the training of personnel and the distribution of services better fit the needs of the population; to develop an education system that produces people in the numbers and with the qualifications to meet the needs of the society and the economy and in which the distribution of educational opportunities is more equitable; to obtain the full employment of the potential labor force and its allocation to the employment needs of economic development; to maximize the rate of savings and to allocate those savings to investment in a way that achieves the desired restructuring of the economy and maximizes the rate of growth; to develop an incentive system that does not include large quasi-rents to scarce labor yet maximizes their efforts by means of nonmaterial rewards, to develop a modern, large-scale industrial sector while rationing the scarce holdings of foreign exchange to necessary imports; to increase the output of industrial products in the modern sector by developing a rural, small-scale industrial sector that relies on local resources and capabilities—the list could go on and on, but the point has been made. For almost any problem encountered in a textbook on economic development or in the actual process in a developing country in the Third World, the Chinese have tried in one way or another to solve it. The question raised in this chapter is whether the Chinese solution is transferable to the other developing countries.

The study of China's development experience raises the question, What *is* the Chinese model? Use of the term *the* Chinese model implies a conception of Chinese development as a complete, integrated, and consistent package of economic institutions and policies. In reality the Chinese over the past twenty-five years have adopted and implemented many different and frequently inconsistent economic institutions and policies, a distinction that has important implications for the problem of transferability.

The notion of transferability can be discussed in two ways. One approach considers that the Chinese model as a whole owes much to the particular geographic, economic, political, and social environment inherited by the Chinese Communists in 1949 and to several important complementarities between some of the characteristics common to the different models. A somewhat different wholistic view suggests that before borrowing the Maoist model of economic development, developing countries must first carry out a Communist revolution. Any wholistic approach implies that it is improbable that *the* Chinese economic model could be successfully transferred elsewhere. A second approach that considers the essential aspects of the model leads to the more interesting and relevant question: Can any particular economic institution or policy implemented in China since 1949 be successfully transferred to other countries?

Limits to the Analysis

The institutions and policies implemented by the Chinese over the past twenty-five years include the collectivization of agriculture, the rural, small-scale industries, and the allocation and full employment of labor within the framework of a more equitable distribution of income and noninflationary wages. These three are not only representative of the whole range of economic institutions and policies in the Chinese model; they are among the key elements of that model. Our study of these elements is an attempt to determine the extent to which their contribution to China's economic development has been related to and dependent on the characteristics of the Chinese environment. In this way more evidence may be obtained to judge the validity of the answer suggested by most of the contributors to the question of transferability: the particular economic institutions and policies of China depend on one another and on unique characteristics of the Chinese environment, thereby making the successful transfer of the model in whole or in part most unlikely.

Little attention is devoted to determining exactly how successful these specific economic institutions and policies have been in China, and only several qualifications of their "success" are presented in this chapter. The basic premise is that these economic institutions and policies have been successful, and the purpose is to determine why and how, that is, to what extent features of the Chinese environment have been responsible for this success. If they have been a major factor, this lends support to the wholistic hypothesis: that individual elements of the Chinese model or versions of that model are unlikely to be successfully transferred to the other developing countries. This approach to the question of transferability, however, overlooks a whole range of important questions.

Some of the other developing countries have also been quite successful in their economic development and have implemented their own models or sets of economic institutions and policies. Perhaps those economic institutions and policies are better suited to the environments and needs of the less successful developing countries than those implemented in China. Furthermore, some of the other developing countries have adopted institutions and policies similar to the three elements of the Chinese model to be analyzed in this chapter. In those cases two questions arise: How have the institutions and policies been adapted to fit the environments of the other developing countries? And how successful have these economic institutions and policies been in non-Chinese environments?

There is a long list of developing countries that have not been able to make much progress in solving their economic problems and for which the adoption of successful features of China's system would suggest itself. Such a conclusion depends on the nature of the decision-making groups, the political, economic, and social environment and heritage in the potential borrowing country.

Finally, what are the long-run consequences on a country's environment once an element of the Chinese model has been successfully transferred? This problem has received considerable attention in the literature and has been of particular concern to the socialist countries in their borrowing from the industrialized countries of the West.[2] Because of China's historical experience and the dictates of Maoist ideology, the Chinese development model with its emphasis on self-reliance is an explicit recognition of the danger involved in the mechanical absorption of foreign material.

All these questions on the need and desire for and the results of the transfer of individual elements of China's development model, in addition to the feasibility of and methods used in such a transfer, are relevant in offering a complete answer to the question whether the Chinese model is transferable.

The Collectivization of Agriculture

It has been argued that the collectivization of agriculture is one of the four principal characteristics of a Soviet model economy. Most socialist economies have retained this institution, and China is no exception.[3] However, the Chinese collectivization of agricultural production contrasts sharply with that of most other socialist economies. Its divergence resides in the relatively smooth and rapid transition to collectivization, in the tri-level organization of the collective unit (communes, brigades, teams), in the acceptance and support of this structure by the political leadership and the peasants and in its contribution to the increase in the level of agricultural production. To the degree that China has accomplished these results, the Chinese agricultural model is readily identifiable as a special case of "successful" collectivized agriculture. More important for the argument in this chapter, these successes have in large part been achieved within the context of the unique features of China's environment.

Both Benjamin Ward and Dwight Perkins contend that one such

feature is the attitude of the Chinese Communist party and its leaders. Unlike other socialist leaders, the Chinese leaders have retained their allegiance to the rural poor, the major source of their political support. This somewhat atypical effort of the Chinese government and in particular of Mao Tse-tung to "put the poor in command," to quote Perkins, explains in part the relatively smooth and rapid transition to collectivized agriculture in China.

For comparative purposes, the most important characteristics that distinguish China's experience of collectivization from that in other socialist countries can be summarized under three headings: institutional organization, relations between collective units and the state, and government objectives. In each case the orientation of China's political evolution to the peasants and other factors peculiar to China are responsible for the distinctive characteristics of Chinese collectivized agriculture.

Several features of the institutional organization of the three-level collective unit (commune, brigade, production team) deserve attention. First, the three levels of the collective unit were organized in sequence from the lowest level to the highest. Second, the size of each unit was determined by the characteristics of China's traditional agricultural production, with significant variance in unit size from one part of rural China to another. Third, the transition from the earning of income on the basis of land, capital, and labor effort contributed to the earning of a share of the income on the basis of work effort alone followed the same sequence. Finally, and most important, despite repeated attempts by the Maoists to elevate production decisions and income distribution to the higher levels, the basic decision-making level has remained the team (a group of twenty-five to fifty households in the traditional village). The post-Mao leadership has assured the peasants that it will remain at that level for the near future. These features go a long way in explaining the success of collectivization in China.

Moreover, the transition to collectivized agriculture in China was relatively smooth and rapid. The successful transition can be explained quite simply. By the mid twentieth century major problems had emerged in the pattern of ownership and use of land. Inequity in ownership can be overemphasized by citing differences in the holdings of absentee landlords compared with those of the landless peasant laborers. Land use, however, was more equitable because the majority of China's peasant households were owner-operators who worked their own land along with rented land. Nonetheless, population pressure had rendered the average size of the farm worked by the Chinese peasant household very small. In addition, China's agriculture was very labor intensive.

The land reform carried out by the Chinese Communists immediately following their "liberation" of a rural area resulted in the significant redistribution of land ownership and income from the rich to the poor but did not alter the traditional labor-intensive methods of production. Private property rights remained in force, and the poorer peasants—the majority—faced the same dismal prospect of having to sell their land or labor to others to earn a living. Thus the prospect of joining an elementary producers' cooperative would appeal to and benefit the majority of the peasant households. The economies of scale that result from combining the small plots of land, labor, and capital owned by a group of twenty-five to fifty individual households and the pooling of risks were obvious to most of the members of the elementary producers' cooperatives.

The transition from the elementary to the advance producers' cooperatives a few years later also appealed to a majority of the members. This was because the advanced producers' cooperatives redistributed income from the former owners of larger-than-average units of land and capital to those who derived their income mainly from labor. Furthermore, the cadres were instructed to ensure that the majority of members in the new advanced producers' cooperatives received an increase in income as a result of this transition. The available evidence indicates that this promise was kept.[4] In addition, some obvious economies of scale are associated with the larger units of production in Chinese agriculture, but initially these advantages may not have been as obvious as the income redistribution effects.

The transition from the advanced producers' cooperatives to the communes was certainly rapid, but neither smooth nor successful. As a result of the ensuing agricultural crises in 1959–1961, the basic production decision-making and income distribution functions were restored to the team (the former elementary producers' cooperative). The commune and the brigade have remained parts of the collectivized unit, largely for the performance of activities in which economies of scale warrant their retention. The combination of a labor-intensive agriculture and a large rural population in relation to cultivable land in China, both inherited characteristics of the Chinese environment, are important in explaining the relatively rapid and smooth transition to collectivized agriculture in China. These conditions are replicable only in countries in which a more equitable redistribution of land to the agrarian households would result in holdings per household for a large portion of the rural population that were too inefficient to maintain a sufficient standard of living.[5]

The relations between the collectivized units of production and the state in China differ from those in most other socialist countries. These relations emphasize formalized negotiated compromises rather than bureaucratic or administrative orders handed down by the state. As in other socialist countries, tax "norms," output delivery "quotas," and labor requisition "quotas" are established within the state bureaucracy and broken down as they descend the bureaucratic hierarchy. However, unlike a more typical Soviet model of agriculture, there is substantial variability in the norms and quotas among the collective units in China's rural economy. Of course, one should not overestimate the bargaining power of the collective units in China's agriculture.

Finally, the objectives of the Chinese leadership have been a major factor in the relative success of the transition from household to collectivized agriculture. Throughout China's political evolution its leaders have been faithful to the cause and the interests of the rural poor. The leaders, especially Mao, firmly believed—as do most socialists—in the economies of scale in agricultural production. Collectivization of agriculture was to generate an increase in output and, therefore, an increase in the surplus that could be obtained by the state for investment in economic development. In the case of China the unification of scattered plots into larger fields, the use of limited supplies of agricultural machinery and capital available over a larger area, and the pooling of labor for irrigation and capital construction projects gave the collectives a yield potential not available within the confines of household farming.

The leadership maintained that these increases in output and the surplus transferred to the state would occur only if the majority of peasants shared in the increased output. To this end, several measures were enacted. The tax rates for the commune have been relatively low and have declined over time. The prices paid by the state for contracted grain deliveries have not deviated from market prices nearly as much as they did in the Soviet Union before the reforms of 1956. Also, once the collective unit has agreed to the negotiated tax payment and deliveries to the state, both of which can be thought of as fixed costs in the short run, the increase in output goes to the collective and its members. Although industrial workers still enjoy significantly higher income than peasants, the majority of peasants have witnessed an improved standard of living.

It can be argued that these features of Chinese collectivized agriculture had little to do with the leadership's desire to serve the interests of the peasants. One could interpret the step-by-step transition process and the retention of the team as the decision-making and income allocation unit as a clever attempt by the leadership to avoid many of the problems encountered by other socialist countries in their collectivization movements and to gain the naive acceptance of the peasants.

The actual outcome in China may also have been a compromise between the Maoists, who wanted to proceed rapidly in favor of the commune, and the "moderates" backing Liu Shao-ch'i, who favored the team as the decision-making unit. The relative independence granted the collectives does not prove that this aspect of China's collectivization is due to the leadership's concern for the peasants. One can argue that the atypical relations between the collective units and the state merely reflect the leadership's desire to maximize the peasants' incentive to increase output, thereby avoiding the counterproductive results of excessive state control and bureaucratic administration that occurred in other countries. The leadership's ojective, however, is still the same: to maximize the agricultural surplus obtained by the state for investment in other sectors. The motive of greater agricultural surplus, rather than interest in the welfare of the rural poor, could also underlie the policies allowing the peasants to benefit from the collective's increased output.

At some point, however, the argument becomes circular. The argument states that collectivized agriculture has been relatively successful in China and that this success is explained, in part, by its unique characteristics: institutional organization, relations with the state, and objectives. These characteristics are said to be part of the fallout of China's socialist revolution, what Ward refers to as the political leadership's institution of a "humane agrarian" regime or what Perkins refers to as "putting the poor in command." Whether the leadership's real motive was to extract a larger agricultural surplus or to serve the masses is difficult to determine. Why argue? Whatever the reason, the results are the same.

It is conceivable that, whatever their motive, the political leaders of another developing country with a very high ratio of peasant households per unit of arable land could replicate the exceptional features of China's collectivized agriculture and achieve a rapid and smooth transition from peasant household to collectivized farming. Yet would collectivized agriculture in these other countries increase agricultural output, even if collectivization were supported by the peasants? Herein lies the major question raised in this chapter. Although the unique characteristics of China's collectivized agriculture have facilitated and may even have been necessary for the success of collectivization in contemporary China, an equally significant explanation of that success is to be found in the structure of the rural economy inherited by the Chinese Communists in 1949.

Development economists have devoted considerable attention to a question crucial to countries whose circumstances are similar to those found in China in the early 1950s. That question is the process by which an expanding modern industrial sector absorbs labor from a rural sector with "surplus" labor. The essential question posed by development economists is the following: If capital accumulation and industrial growth are not rapid enough to absorb all the surplus labor in the rural sector, how can the remaining surplus rural labor force be most effectively employed? Nicholas Georgescu-Roegen contends that the capitalist-market agriculture would not work because the landowners-operators would hire farm laborers only until their marginal productivity equaled the wage rate, which because of the surplus rural population would be driven to the subsistence level. Such a process would leave part of the rural population unemployed.[6] Georgescu-Roegen has argued that land reform resulting in "roughly equal size" holdings per household would work as a means of assuring full employment and larger total output, only if these holdings were large enough to provide at least a subsistence standard of living to each household. Given the land owned by the family, employment and output would be maximized because each family member has to be fed and would be put to work as long as his marginal productivity, his contribution to output, was positive.

We argue, as does V. M. Dandekar, that Georgescu-Roegen's reasoning is not valid when the rural population pressure is so large that land reform produces household holdings of less than efficient or optimal size.[7] Household holdings too small to maintain a subsistence standard of living characterized China in the early 1950s. For Dandekar the answer was clear. Collectivization of agriculture would not only allow for maximum employment and output but also—because of economies of scale in production—provide at least a subsistence standard of living. The results of collectivization in several socialist countries could be offered as evidence for the lack of economies of scale. However, matters of incentives and income distribution may account in good measure for the problems that materialized. Nonetheless, empirical estimates for farm-level production functions in nonsocialist countries indicate the existence of decreasing or constant returns to scale; that is, economies of scale do not render collectivized agriculture superior to household farming in a labor-intensive or traditional technology if the household's holdings are sufficient to maintain a subsistence standard of living per household member.[8]

While this may be true for the agriculture of most developing countries, two distinctive aspects of China's traditional agriculture suggest that this conclusion did not hold over the past twenty-five years in China. Quite the contrary, within the context of a traditional, labor-intensive agriculture, collectivization took advantage of the existence of economies of scale and allowed the Chinese to obtain yields greater than those possible from household farming. Traditional Chinese agriculture in the pre-1949 period relied to a much greater extent than the agriculture of other developing countries on irrigation and multiple cropping to achieve relatively high yields.[9] The economies of scale derived from the mobilization of labor (associated with the collective units) for construction of irrigation projects and for control of the storage and distribution of water are significant in comparison with the undertakings of individual households.

Equally important are the economies of scale due to the mobilization of labor in the growing of crops itself.[10] In the pre-1949 period China's multiple cropping index was already at a remarkably high level, and shortages of labor were experienced during the periods when one crop was being harvested, the land prepared, and the next crop planted.[11] Given the evolution of China's traditional agriculture, which grew as many different crops as possible in an agricultural year, the timing and intensity of labor during the peak periods of activity were critical. The Chinese agricultural development program since 1949 has also emphasized increases in multiple cropping as a source of increasing yields. To the extent that the land per household and the labor per household differed, the collectivization of both labor and crops in order to better schedule and coordinate the multiple cropping activities and alleviate the constraint on yields due to labor shortages offered significant economies of scale.[12]

There are, of course, diseconomies of scale in the organization and management of labor in agricultural activities. This is undoubtedly one reason that the team has remained the basic unit of production while the larger units, the communes and brigades, have assumed responsibility for constructing and operating irrigation projects. In the agriculture of China these larger-scale units offer economies of scale in other respects as well. The operation of mechanized facilities for food processing and other former household activities frees household labor to engage in production and thus further reduces the constraint of labor shortages. Finally, these larger units can effectively operate machine shops that produce agricultural machinery for labor-intensive tasks and thus further alleviate the labor shortages of the production teams.

In light of these arguments, it appears reasonable to conclude that the economic environment of China's traditional agriculture—too little cultivated land per rural household to allow for efficient farm operation and heavy reliance on irrigation and multiple cropping— can go a long way in explaining the smooth transition from individual household farming to collectivized agriculture and its success. This is true whether institutional organization, relations with the state, and objectives of China's collectivized agriculture reflected the Communist leaders' self-interest or their desire to serve the masses. The motives of the leadership and the corresponding characteristics of China's collectivized agriculture could conceivably be duplicated in other developing countries with similar rural population densities per unit of arable land, thereby achieving the peasants' support of collectivized agriculture. It is most unlikely that this is also true for the unique characteristics of China's traditional agriculture.

Rural, Small-Scale Industry

In the industrial sector the Chinese over the past twenty-five years have achieved exceptional rates of growth for a developing country; these growth rates are high, relatively stable, and cover a period of considerable duration.[13] Such rates of industrial growth have also been achieved in other socialist countries by means of nationalized industries that operate according to planned output and supply allocation targets and by means of a centralized budget process that channels a high rate of savings into investment for the creation and expansion of a large-scale, capital-intensive, modern industrial sector. The degree of decentralization in the Chinese model is considerable, but the most novel aspect of China's industrial development over the past twenty-five years is the role of the rural, small-scale industries.[14]

Chapter 6 details the stages of China's industrial development from the large, modern, capital-intensive plants that were based on the Soviet model and prevailed during the First Five-Year Plan to the rural, small-scale industries that were greatly expanded during the 1960s. Rawski also describes the activities of the small-scale workshops owned by the commune and the brigade and of the county-owned enterprises that concentrated on the "five small industries": cement, iron and steel, agricultural machinery, chemical fertilizer, and electric power. As a result of this program, by the early 1970s the rural, small-scale industries accounted for half or more of China's total industrial production of chemical fertilizer, agricultural machinery, and building materials, a fourth of coal production, a fifth of iron and steel output, and between 5% and 10% of the electric power generated in China.[15] All these products are important industrial inputs for the expansion and modernization of China's agriculture. The basic ideological and economic rationale of China's rural, small-scale industry program is that the rural areas need not wait for the development of the modern industrial and transportation sector; they can rely on their own initiative, savings, and resources to develop small-scale industries and on the use of labor-intensive, native technology to produce their own industrial products.

Much of the capital for the rural industries is not self-provided. Rather it is produced in modern sector industries at the provincial or central government level, although each of the small-scale industries has its own machine shop. These machine shops are an important source of new equipment for the planned increase in mechanization and capital intensity of the existing plant and for the increase in capacity. The dual source of investment is related to two important aspects of China's rural, small-scale industry program. First, the rural, small-scale industries, especially the county-owned and operated industries, depend on the modern industrial sector for some of their equipment, inputs, and expertise; they are not the result of local self-reliance. Second, their objective is to maximize the output of industrial products for local use in the development and modernization of China's agriculture, not to provide employment for surplus rural labor (as advocated by the Chinese, in a view similar to that of Ragnar Nurkse, during the Great Leap Forward). Given the alternatives, a relatively capital intensive technology has been chosen; and these plants, once established, attempt to increase the capital intensity of their production process on their own.

Of course, when compared with the modern, large-scale sector, the rural industries are more labor intensive, have lower labor productivity, use more traditional technology and poorer-grade inputs, and produce poorer-quality output.[16] The Chinese do not question the desirability—in terms of input productivity and quality of output—of producing these products in the modern, large-scale industrial sector by means of modern technology, as soon as sufficient capital is available.

When we seek explanations for the success of this program, we again find that China's environment suggests an answer. The guarantee of infant industry protection has enabled the counties and communes to use local investment funds and resources to produce industrial products. Isolation from the competitive tests of costs, efficiency, and prices in the modern, large-scale industrial sector is provided by China's vast area and limited modern transportation network in addition to the state's control over the allocation and distribution of the industrial products produced in the modern sector. Local units undertaking the development of these industries also receive implicit subsidies and crucial assistance from the state.

Unlike some of the more primitive rural plants of the late fifties and early sixties, the rural, small-scale industries now use relatively standard, although dated, equipment. This equipment is produced in the modern, large-scale industrial sector. Despite the capacity of the modern sector to produce large quantities of multipurpose machine tools and simple equipment regarded as fixed capital in the rural industries, the demand for equipment in the rural industries exceeds the supply. Due to the administered pricing system used for the transfer of industrial products in China, the allocation of supply is rationed by decisions at various levels of the state's allocative administration, not by increased prices of the equipment and machinery.

What all this means is that the investment costs are kept low, (subsidized by the state) for the local units that obtain an allocation of the desired machinery and equipment from the state. The equipment allocated to these small rural industries includes that for a well-equipped machine shop. These machine shops then produce additional machinery and equipment according to plans provided by the state. The machinery and equipment provided by these local machine shops enable the rural industries to supplement or expand the capacity made possible by the initial allocation of machinery and equipment from the large-scale sector.

Finally, and very important for the success of the program, the rural, small-scale industry policy is adopted and supported by both the government and the party. Within the context of state ownership and control over industry, the rural industries are urged to seek the assistance of "fraternal" plants in both the modern and the rural sectors for solutions to their problems. This has resulted in the creation of an informal network of personal visits, exchanges of technology, and even allocations of vital inputs among industrial plants. This type of cooperation may not be in the best interest of the plants in the modern industrial sector. Moreover, the nonmarket allocation of machinery and equipment from the modern to the rural sector undoubtedly results in inefficient allocation and a reduction in the profits of state enterprises. Yet this system of implicit subsidies merely reflects a cost that the Chinese have been willing to pay to make the rural, small-scale industries "successful."

Most of the plants in the rural sector, especially those owned and operated by the counties, are independent accounting units, buying their inputs, labor and capital included, and selling their output at administered prices. Thus despite their infant industry protection and the implicit subsidies provided by the state, the need to be "profitable" would force a sort of efficiency test on their operations, depending on the appropriateness of the administerial prices used. In China, however, such an enterprise is not a completely independent economic entity but one of the many income-earning activities of the unit (county, commune, brigade, or team) to which it belongs. Its expenditures are part of a larger budget. If the local unit deems an enterprise profitable in the sense of being necessary or advantageous, it will undertake such a project, whatever the use of administered prices may show concerning its financial profitability. Any inefficiencies are subsidized by the unit through the spreading of waste and risk among many economic activities. Thus the criterion for judging the value of the output is its use value. These susidies can be justified as economically rational if the inefficiencies of the rural industries constitute initial, short-run costs that are eliminated in the long run by means of learning by doing. However, despite some evidence that input productivity of these small plants increases rapidly during the first few years of operation, it is doubtful that the local owning unit decides to invest in them on the basis of efficiency criteria (comparative rates of profits) or opportunity costs. The reason is simple. The small-scale industries are viewed by the local unit as very profitable—in terms of both economic rationality and financial profitability.

The economic rationality of the rural industries is viewed in terms of the most important objective of the local unit: an increase in crop yields. The many campaigns to raise agricultural output call for local producers to increase inputs of chemical fertilizer, cement, electric power, agricultural machinery, and the like. Although the independent marginal contribution of each input to increased output in the local areas may not be estimated, all inputs are considered a joint package that leads to significantly higher yields. The rural industry program also provides for significant qualitative change in the increased familiarity of the rural labor force with industrial technology. This change facilitates the economic development of the local unit or area and of the economy as a whole. Criteria for financial profitability suggest that given the administered prices for the inputs and outputs, most of the rural, small-scale industries are very profitable and return the initial investment costs in a fairly short period of time.[17]

In addition to the characteristics of China's economic and political environment, the success of the small rural industries has been facilitated by the character of China's resource endowment. A necessary condition for the success of this program (despite China's widespread agricultural area) has been the existence of poorer-grade deposits of coal, limestone, and iron ore and extensive irrigation networks that are fairly abundant throughout much of the agricultural area, providing the necessary inputs to the local units. China's abundant labor supply and its "relatively" low productivity in the agricultural sector have made it relatively easy to provide for the approximately 15 million workers employed in the rural industrial sector: the very large absolute level of employment has required less than 5% of the rural labor force.[18]

This combination of geographic, economic, and political facets is unlikely to be replicated in any of the other developing countries. This conclusion does not imply that a different type of rural, small-scale industry program cannot be successfully launched in any of the other developing countries with a system of taxes and subsidies to protect the rural industry from outside competition and insure its profitability. Within the context of private ownership of industry and noncollective units of production in agriculture, however, the explicit subsidies involved to both the producers and the users of the products of the rural industrial sector represent an important drain on the central government's budget and a large transfer of income from urban to rural areas. These changes represent a major reorientation of priorities in the economic development programs for many of the developing countries. This argument has pointed out that a rural, small-scale industry program would require not only a major change in economic objectives but also the political ability to carry it out, along with the necessary industrial capacity in the modern sector and distribution of resources in the rural areas.

The Allocation of Labor and the Distribution of Income

In addition to the collectivization of agriculture and the rural, small-scale industry program, the simultaneous achievement of full employment, a more equitable distribution of income, and stable prices is frequently cited as an indicator of the relative success of China's development efforts. China does not bear the telltale marks of a dual economy. The urban centers are not crowded with a reserve army of unemployed, and throughout the economy everyone has a job. Moreover, while incomes vary considerably both within and among occupations, and between and among rural and urban areas, the worst excesses of an inequitable income distribution have been eliminated.[19]

Much of China's success in achieving full employment and a more equitable distribution of income can be attributed to the adoption of a socialist economic system. However, the mere adoption of such a system does not explain fully the extent to which the Chinese have been able to achieve a level of employment and an income distribution that compare favorably with the accomplishments of other socialist economies, especially when China's economic development and large population are taken into account. Once again, unique features of China's economic, social, and political heritage in 1949 significantly contribute to an explanation of its success.

In the urban, industrial sector China, like other socialist economies, has used the unified state budget process to mobilize a high rate of savings under the control of the central government. A large share of those savings has been invested in state industrial enterprises in urban areas. Despite the large urban population and the existing industrial base in 1949, the urban population was a relatively small share of the total population. The industrial labor force was an even smaller proportion of the total labor force.[20] The relatively large and growing infusion of industrial investment in the urban areas—attributable in part to the "big-push" policy of the Soviet model—resulted in a rapid increase in industrial employment, not only in absolute terms, but also as a percentage of the total labor force.

This outcome might appear surprising at first given the type of investment undertaken. In their desire to maximize the growth rate of output instead of creating employment from their investment in industry, the Chinese adopted a capital-intensive, modern technology for the urban industrial sector. Yet many of the ancillary processes in the modern industries used very labor intensive methods of production. Furthermore, rather than assign workers to specialized tasks, the Chinese utilized work gangs even for the production processes that relied on relatively modern, capital-intensive technology. This work gang approach was traditional of factory work in China in the pre-1949 period.

To complement this employment in the urban industrial sector, China's large land mass, underdeveloped modern transportation network, and limited urban social overhead capital for industry generated rapid increases in employment in the service sectors: construction, transportation, and trade. Even after twenty-five years of large-scale investment and rapid growth, the service sectors continue to be labor intensive in China because, compared with industry, these sectors have been given low priority in the allocation of investment.

There is no reason that any of these means of generating employment cannot be adopted by any other developing country, as long as it can achieve a high rate of savings and can divert a significant share of savings to investment in industry. The adaptation of modern capital-intensive industry to better fit an abundant labor supply is not unique to China. The service sectors are also relatively labor intensive in the developing countries.

The distinctive feature of China's experience, however, was its ability to accomplish a rapid growth in employment in the modern sector without a wage or price inflation, all the while implementing a more equitable distribution of income. Although the role of normative and ideological appeals in China has been given much publicity, material incentives have remained the basic mechanism for rewarding the workers and peasants for their work since 1949. Like several other socialist countries, China has adopted the Soviet eight-grade wage system for industrial workers. These wages are set by the state. The resulting wage structure is not very different from the distribution of wages among blue-collar industrial workers in the West.[21] China is unique in its severe limitation of the bonuses, piece rates, fringe benefits, and the like, that cause industrial labor incomes to become considerably more inequitable than indicated by wage differentials in these other socialist economies.

This limitation has been accomplished in part through reliance on Maoist ideology and normative appeals. These appeals are made more effective by the traditional use of social pressure and peer approval and by the example of Chinese government and party officials who receive much lower incomes than their counterparts elsewhere. Yet even without these pressures the inability to use higher money incomes for buying luxury goods—private cars, fancy housing, imports for private consumption, foreign travel—would limit the incentive for earning a higher income. Indeed, before the death of Mao, incomes or standards of living considered excessive by "the masses" were undoubtedly more trouble than they were worth, perhaps explaining why many families with above-average incomes are reported to have accumulated large "savings" deposited in the state's banking system. The state's direct control over the assignment and allocation of labor, especially skilled labor and plant managers, the lack of alternative employment, and the job security that goes with job assignments also explain the state's ability to limit incomes and salaries in the modern industrial sector in China.

Finally, as in many other socialist economies, industrial workers at all wage levels in China receive many important fringe benefits —health plans, retirement plans, a standard work day and week, subsidized housing. These fringe benefits are probably a significant portion of industrial labor income and are more equitably distributed than money wage income. In addition, unlike most other socialist economies, China has introduced the rationing of basic necessities at relatively low prices, and the rations favor those performing the most strenuous work. The security of a stable real income somewhat divorced from the level of the worker's money income not only reduces the incentive attached to higher money incomes but also makes the distribution of real incomes even more equal than is indicated by the relatively equitable distribution of money incomes.

An obvious feature of China's economic environment also helps explain the ability of the Chinese over the past twenty-five years to secure a rapid increase in employment in the urban sector without important increases in wages. Although income distribution may be more equitable in China than in the other developing countries, a significant inequity in urban-rural incomes remains. This is especially true when the fringe benefits and amenities of urban living associated with jobs in the state sector are taken into account. Compared with workers in other sectors, industrial workers have had relatively stable money wages and have lagged far behind increases in labor productivity and profits. Yet despite the rapid increase in industrial employment, material benefits associated with employment in the urban and industrial sector have remained a strong incentive in the recruitment of new workers. On the supply side, the increase in the labor force due to the natural increase in China's population supplied more than enough labor to meet the rapidly growing demand for nonagricultural workers.

Apart from its rate of growth, the absorption of labor by the growing nonagricultural sectors is not specific to the Chinese economy. What is unusual about China's experience is the absence of significant urban unemployment and the full employment of the large residual labor force in the rural areas. To explain this result, it is again necessary to identify features peculiar—even among socialist economies—to China's economic system, environment, and tradition. Not only does the state control the recruitment and allocation of labor within the state sector of the economy; it also strictly controls the distribution and movement of the population. If this does not stem the flow of those who want a job in the urban sector, the identifiable unemployed in the urban areas are periodically rounded up and sent back to the rural areas. In addition, even those who are legitimate urban residents—middle school graduates, skilled laborers—may be assigned work in the rural areas.

This extensive control and reallocation of the urban population is not merely a device to keep the cities free of rampant unemployment by hiding the unemployment problem in the countryside but serves many positive purposes as well. It supports the radical objective of making every Chinese a worker-peasant-soldier; its more significant economic benefits are the restriction, in the absence of sufficient social overhead capital, of the uncontrolled urbanization that has accompanied economic development in the other developing countries and has resulted in cities such as Cairo and Calcutta; the reduction of urban-rural income differences by redistributing skilled labor and public services from the urban to the rural areas; and the redistribution of the surplus or unemployed labor force so that the burden of creating employment opportunities for the potentially unemployed falls on the collective not on the state sector of the economy.

This last result is a unique facet of China's development experience and is, I believe, the major explanation for China's solution of the problem of full employment of the labor force. Approximately three-fourths of China's very large labor force are members of rural communes, brigades, and teams; and the large increase in the labor force for which jobs are not available in the urban, nonagricultural sector is reallocated to these collective units. To the extent that these collective units are responsible for providing for the income of their members, much as a family farm must support the members of the family, they have an incentive to find work for their members as long as their contribution to the collective's output is positive. This has not been a serious problem in the rural collective sector of China's economy due to the somewhat distinctive characteristics of the inherited agricultural economy in 1949 and the existence of traditionally labor-intensive farming activities in Chinese agriculture. Furthermore, the Communists' continued emphasis on such programs as irrigation, the use of organic fertilizers, the spread of multiple cropping, and farmland reconstruction has meant not only employment for China's surplus labor force but also an increase in the labor force participation rate in rural areas and more work days per laborer to satisfy the greater demands for labor.[22]

Again, material incentives supplemented by normative and ideological appeals and campaigns have been relied on to increase employment and labor effort in China's countryside. In the countryside the collective was not required to pay money wages for this effort but was able to print its own money. As in many other socialist countries with collectivized agriculture, the collective issued work points for the peasant's labor, and these points were good only as a claim on a share of the collective unit's net income. In other words, the incomes distributed for obtaining a significant increase in labor effort in the agricultural sector were noninflationary by definition because the incomes paid out as work points were only convertible into purchasing power equal in value to the net income of the collective unit itself. In this manner, the collective was able to find employment for its members, and the members had an incentive to increase the income of the collective unit while bearing the risk and uncertainty of the collective's economic activities. Individual families were allocated small private plots to earn income or raise products for their own use as a hedge on the risks associated with their share of the collective's income.

Although this institutional organization of the rural economy provided the means for achieving full employment without inflation, the resulting burden on the collective unit did little to promote the more equitable distribution of income in the Chinese countryside. The average standard of living in rural China has obviously increased, and a large class of destitute peasants without land and without employment opportunities has been eliminated. The distribution of income among families within the same collective unit is more equitable than it would be in a system of private farming. However, the income of its members is determined largely by the net income of the collective unit itself, which in turn is determined largely by the location of the collective unit—nearness to an urban center, access to water, access to transportation routes, the fertility of the soil. As a result there is a significant inequality in the distribution of income among collective units in the rural areas. Insofar as the collective units are not part of the state's budget, there is little direct redistribution of income among collective units. As a result of government policies to increase agricultural output, members of a suburban commune can earn more than a factory worker, while members of a collective in the dry and hilly areas of Shansi who are urged to develop their unit without the benefit of state aid can be earning very low incomes.

Much of this argument, of course, relies on impressionistic evidence, logical deductions, and scattered bits of quantitative information. Few would argue, however, with the conclusion that although urban-rural and interregional rural differences in income remain a serious problem, income distribution in China appears to be more equitable than in any of the other developing countries. The simultaneous attainment of full employment without wage inflation is a more obvious achievement of the Chinese Communists.

The achievement of these economic goals can be explained, as shown before, by the interaction of a host of features in China's environment. Some of the institutions and policies can easily be found in other socialist economies, and these could be adopted in the other developing countries. Of crucial importance, however, are the aspects of China's environment not readily found in combination in the other developing countries: a large population, effective control over the geographical distribution and movement of the population, the labor-intensive nature of the traditional agriculture, and the even more labor-intensive means by which the Chinese are attempting to modernize and solve their agricultural problem.

We have attempted to show that attributing the success of the economic institutions and programs introduced by the Chinese Communists solely to unique features of the Communist Revolution and ideology is too simple. Features of China's economic, social, and political environment and history have been important determinants of that success. On the other hand, the combination of features that are peculiar to the Chinese environment and help explain the success of these institutions and programs in China is not likely to be found in the other developing countries, considerably limiting the possibility of successfully transfering China's development experience to these countries. Thus our answer to the question of transferability agrees with that suggested by most of the participants at the conference.

Before concluding on this somewhat negative note, we must add two important qualifications. First, we have generously labeled the institutions and programs analyzed as "successes" merely as a working hypothesis to carry out our analysis; however, that hypothesis may be a misleading and inappropriate one. Second, our negative conclusion concerning the transfer of either specific institutions and programs of the Chinese model or the model itself does not imply that China's development experience over the past twenty-five years is without lessons for the other developing countries.

Have These Programs Been Successful?

The collectivization of agriculture, rural, small-scale industries, and the allocation of labor and distribution of income were chosen to determine the transferability of the Chinese development model, for several reasons. Each of these programs was important in China's attempt to solve its economic development problems; each has been part of the Chinese development model for most of the past twenty-five years and will probably remain so in the near future; and each has been widely publicized outside China as an example of or reason for China's success in achieving the objectives of economic development. Uncritical acceptance of the success of these programs can be questioned, however, not only on the basis of the more pessimistic evaluations published outside China, but also on the basis of the ever-growing negative review by the post-Mao Chinese leadership itself. In light of these more pessimistic evaluations, how can we justify our use of the word "success" to describe the three programs?

The Chinese Communists inherited an agricultural sector described by knowledgeable experts as caught in a "high-level equilibrium trap."[23] A major source of increased agricultural output over the previous four centuries, more land brought under cultivation, was being exhausted by the middle of the twentieth century. With the rise in the population growth rate in the twentieth century, the balance between increases in food supplies and population was precarious. Chinese agricultural output has always been subject to the whims of nature, and famines were a common phenomena in the life of every Chinese peasant. Famines were becoming more and more severe during the nineteenth and twentieth centuries as the economy became increasingly commercialized. Against this background, the Chinese Communists introduced the collectivization of agriculture and were able to maintain a rate of growth of agricultural production above 2% while providing a more equitable distribution of food to the peasants at a fairly stable level somewhat above the level recommended by the United Nations for the developing countries.

Bad weather and inappropriate policy implementation still created agricultural crises, such as the crisis after the Great Leap Forward in 1958. Nonetheless, the general institutional and policy framework introduced by the Chinese Communists helped prevent the widespread famines that traditionally followed these disasters. In addition, the growth of agricultural production achieved in China over the past twenty-five years, while not exceptional, has provided for and supported a program of industrialization and economic development that has been among the most successful undertaken by the developing countries. Perhaps the most important reason for regarding China's collectivized agriculture as successful is that interviews with refugees from China and statements by China's leaders indicate that these institutions and policies are supported by the peasants and political leaders alike.[24]

However, collectivized agriculture has obviously not solved China's agricultural problem. Indeed, compared with the record of other developing countries during the past quarter of a century, China's growth rate in agricultural production has been below average. More important, while the growth rate during this period displays neither an upward nor a downward trend in terms of gross output, it reveals a downward trend in terms of net output; it has taken more and more inputs per unit of output to maintain the average rate of growth.[25] Although the level of output in most years has allowed the maintenance of a minimum standard of living with no evidence of serious famines, the output level has continued to follow the traditional cyclical pattern, with some troughs of near-crisis proportions. China's reorganization of agricultural production has been very successful with regard to the mobilization of labor effort and a more equitable distribution of income, but the historical record of the superior output growth of private agriculture has continued to hold true in the developing countries.[26]

On the basis of these arguments, some will conclude that household farming, even within the context of a socialist economy, could have done better. This is a nontestable hypothesis.[27] It is also possible that collectivized agriculture in China could have done better if the weather had been more favorable, or if Mao had not unleashed local cadres and radical followers to build communes in a rush to achieve full communism, or if Mao had not sided with Ch'en Yung-kuei and his experiment at the Ta-chai brigade against Liu Shao-ch'i, who supported the development of key communes, and so on. These questions are unsolvable and not of concern here. In any event the attempt to promote economic development by means of household farming would only have resulted in the replication of many of the conditions that fostered and guaranteed the success of the Communist Revolution in the first place.

Our assertion that rural, small-scale industries in China have been successful was based primarily on the following argument. Given the constraints of China's transportation network, the small-scale industries were able to mobilize local, lower-grade inputs for the widespread production of lower-quality, but useful, industrial products that were necessary inputs in China's rural economic development, or agricultural transformation. In addition, rural industrial development served as a large-scale training program in industrial technology for China's dominant rural population and avoided the unconstrained growth of urban, industrial centers with their corresponding social, economic, and environmental problems. However, the post-Mao leadership, while not abandoning the program, has been quick to emphasize the serious inefficiencies and wastes involved.

The large-scale creation of a decentralized industrial sector at the lowest levels actually created an industrial sector which, by means of decentralized negotiations and deals with plants in the modern industrial sector, relied on supplies of key inputs and capital goods from the modern sector and utilized modern transportation facilities for that purpose. The ability of the rural, small-scale industrial sector to rely on this assistance from the modern industrial sector was one of the principle reasons that the rural program achieved the success that it did. That success, however, weakened the central planner's control over the allocation of industrial raw materials and output and reduced the potential growth of the modern sector.[28] Moreover, the considerable emphasis on the use value and not the profitability of their activities, the pooling of risks and costs of these industrial undertakings at the local level, and poor bookkeeping practices (even though the use of administerial prices made most of the rural, small-scale industries "profitable"), the low output quality and inefficiencies in their operation made possible by the lack of competition or isolation from outside suppliers meant that many of these enterprises, rather than learning by doing, continued to waste resources, both local and those supplied by the modern sector.

As the new leadership has made clear, all this is to be changed in the near future with the elimination of the most inefficient of the rural industries and the extension of the state's economic administrative and supply allocation control over the activities of the remaining enterprises. Labor discipline and specialization are to be enforced, and there is to be stricter adherence to proper cost accounting, with "profitability" assuming considerable importance. Nonetheless, these comments, now openly expressed by the Chinese themselves, are only meant as an important qualification to a general assessment that China's rural, small-scale industry program has been successful.

As with collectivization in agriculture, the appeal of China's experience in the development of rural, small-scale industries depends on the mix of objectives and their importance in the other developing countries. As a short-run means, China's rural program has increased the supply of industrial products, technology, and skills available to the peasants in a large rural economy without a well-developed transportation network. But the program has not been very efficient. More important, the new Chinese leadership makes clear that this program is a short-run policy and not the long-run solution to industrialization or modernization of agriculture in China.

Finally, our assertion concerning the success of the Chinese in mobilizing labor, its allocation, and full employment and in distributing income is related to the state's control over the individual's freedom to choose his place of residence and his employment. Few other developing countries would be able to implement such a system of extensive controls; few of the "democratic" ones would have the desire to do so. As for the Chinese success in achieving full employment and a more equitable distribution of income, the land reform, rationing system, collectivization of agricultural production, state control over the allocation of labor, and the nationalization of industry are all important institutional changes that made this result possible. Again this institutional reorganization of the economy may be precluded by the objectives of a nonsocialist society. Furthermore, although China's income distribution is undoubtedly more equitable than those of most other developing countries, considerable inequities remain. The recent emphasis on the need for material incentives based on skill and productivity differences indicates that these inequities will continue and may increase in the near future.

This discussion is not meant to serve as a counterargument to the significant achievements of the Chinese. The apparent success of these economic institutions and policies in attaining a particular set of economic development objectives accounts for their popular appeal and the widespread interest of the other developing countries. The purpose here has been to point out that despite this success and the possibility of replicating aspects of China's environment and heritage that facilitated the Chinese accomplishments, these institutions and policies may involve costs and changes unacceptable to the other developing countries. This latter consideration further supports our conclusion that China's experience is not transferable to the other developing countries.[29]

The "Lessons" from China

The negative conclusion concerning the transfer of China's experience does not imply that China's experience is of limited relevance to the other developing countries or to those studying the problem of economic development. Quite the contrary, this conclusion pertains solely to the evaluation of the transferability of the Chinese model in its entirety or of the particular economic programs, institutions, and policies that make up the Chinese model of the past twenty-five years. If, however, the Chinese development experience is interpreted as a model that includes a myriad of techniques in a range of fields and, more generally, low-level technological experiments in cause and effect that are free of the influence of cultural, political, and economic systems, then China's development experience provides a treasure house of empirical evidence. Such evidence could be of great use to the other developing countries, especially true of the great scale and variance among economic activities in China and because of China's emphasis on nontraditional attempts to solve economic problems.

Until now, only selected and seriously biased bits and pieces of data on China's development experience accumulated at the micro level have been made available to those outside (and inside) China. Yet the opening of China to outsiders and the changes resulting from the new Chinese leadership's belief that borrowing Western technology is more rapid and less costly than self-reliance offer the hope of greater access to China's immense empirical record. Access to this micro-data bank on China's development is still only a hope, but recent technical delegations to China have obtained some of the data and, in conjunction with their impressions, have published a growing number of reports.[30]

Our conclusion, then, is a bit ironic. Although China's development experience over the past three decades has been cited by many as a successful model for the other developing countries, the dramatic events in China since the death of Mao have seen the Chinese leaders hold forth Western science, technology, and even economic principles and methods as a necessary solution to their development problem. These Western "lessons," of course, have always been available to the other developing countries. The new opportunities to obtain a greater understanding of the successes and failures in the wide variety of experiments in low-level technology and production methods may well provide the other developing countries with the most useful lessons from China's development experience.

Notes

1. The new post-Mao leadership has called into question many of these exaggerated claims of the past.

2. See the papers and sources cited in Fredric J. Fleron, Jr., ed., *Technology and Communist Culture, the Socio-Cultural Impact of Technology under Socialism* (New York: Praeger Publishers, 1977).

3. Detailed discussions of the institutional organization, functioning, and results of collectivized agriculture in China can be found in Kenneth R. Walker, "Organization of Agricultural Production," in Alexander Eckstein, Walter Galenson, and Ta-chung Liu, eds., *Economic Trends in Communist China* (Chicago: Aldine Publishing Company, 1968), pp. 397–458.

4. This argument and the evidence to support it are presented in David Ladd Denny, "Rural Policies and the Distribution of Agricultural Products in China: 1950–1959," Ph.D. dissertation, University of Michigan, 1971, especially pp. 255–264.

5. Private household farming could be equally efficient, and some would argue even more efficient, in these circumstances only with serious inequality in land ownership, that is, only if a group of land holders owned land on a scale at which production would be efficient and hired agricultural laborers to work the land as wage laborers. The latter possibility, of course, was ruled out in China by the ideological objectives of the Chinese Communist leaders, the Chinese Revolution, and the majority of the peasants. This institutional organization of farming would also result in rural unemployment, a problem analyzed later in this chapter.

6. Nicholas Georgescu-Roegen, "Economic Theory and Agrarian Economics," *Oxford Economic Papers* 12 (1960): 1–40. For the theoreti-

cal model and analysis commonly used to explain the existence of a dual economy with redundant labor in the rural sector in developing economies, see John C. Fei and Gustav Ranis, *Development of the Labor Surplus Economy* (New Haven, Conn.: Yale University Press, 1964).

7. V. M. Dandekar, "Economic Theory and Agrarian Reform," *Oxford Economic Papers* 14, no. 1 (1962): 69–80.

8. See P. K. Bardhan, "Size, Productivity, and Returns to Scale: An Analysis of Farm-Level Data in Indian Agriculture," *Journal of Political Economy* 81 (November/December 1973): 1370–1386; and D. L. Chinn, "Rural Poverty and the Structure of Farm Household Income in Developing Countries: Evidence from Taiwan," *Economic Development and Cultural Change* 27, No. 2 (January, 1979): 283–301. Production functions estimated at a more aggregated level for some regions of mainland China exhibit increasing returns to scale. See D. L. Chinn, "Land Utilization and Productivity in Prewar Chinese Agriculture: Preconditions for Collectivization," *American Journal of Agricultural Economics* 59, no. 3 (August 1977): 559–564.

9. See the good quantitative description of China's traditional agriculture in H. V. Henle, *Report on China's Agriculture,* Food and Agricultural Organization, United Nations, 1974, pp. 82–126 (withdrawn from circulation shortly after it was published because of protest by a member country of Food and Agricultural Organization).

10. The following argument draws extensively from Dennis L. Chinn, "Cooperative Farming in North China," *Quarterly Journal of Economics* 94, no. 2 (March 1980): 279–297.

11. Buck's survey of 260 localities in 1929–1933 showed that despite a national average of 1.7 idle months a year for each able-bodied rural male, over three-fourths of the localities surveyed experienced labor shortages at some period during the cropping cycle, most often at harvest time. See Thomas G. Rawski, "Industrialization, Technology, and Employment in the People's Republic of China," Studies in Employment and Rural Development No. 41, Development Policy Staff, International Bank for Reconstruction and Development, 1977 (mimeographed), pp. 84–87. Rawski's analysis reproduces and relies on the basic data presented by John L. Buck, *Land Utilization in China* (Nanking: University of Nanking Press, 1937), pp. 296, 301.

12. Using Buck's data for two representative farms with different ratios of labor to cultivated area and, therefore, different cropping patterns, Chinn shows how combining the two farms and reallocating the labor and crops, even with no change in yields per crop (no economies of scale), leads to an increase in total output and incomes per member because of the relaxation of the labor constraint for the higher-yield crops. See Chinn, "Land Utilization," pp. 6–23.

13. According to one set of estimates for a continuous time series of the gross value of industrial production in China, 1949–1976, the average annual rate of growth was 13%. National Foreign Assessment Center, CIA, *China: Economic Indicators,* ER77-10508, October 1977 (Photoduplication Service, Library of Congress, Washington, D.C.), p. 3.

14. For a much more detailed discussion and analysis of China's rural, small-scale industry program, see American Rural Small-Scale Industry Delegation, *Rural Small-Scale Industry in the People's Republic of China* (Berkeley: University of California Press, 1977); Jon Sigurdson, *Rural Industrialization in China* (Cambridge, Mass.: Harvard University Press, 1977); and Carl Riskin, "Small Industry and the Chinese Model of Development," *China Quarterly* no. 46 (1971): 245–273; idem, "China's Rural Industry: Self-Reliant Systems or Independent Kingdoms?" *China Quarterly,* no. 73 (1978): 77–98.

15. Rawski, *Industrialization, Technology, and Employment,* table 3.8, p. 67.

16. Using data for a sample of firms in both the urban, large-scale industry and rural, small-scale industry sectors, Rawski argues that by the mid 1970s some plants in the latter sector were able to achieve the level of input productivity and efficiency that had been attained by plants in the former sector in the mid 1950s. Rawski, *Industrialization, Technology, and Employment* pp. 78–79.

17. To cite a few examples for which the necessary data are available from the plants visited by the American Rural Small-Scale Industry Delegation, a cement plant constructed in the late 1960s with an investment of 350,000 yuan had an output with a gross value of 760,-000 yuan and annual profits of 160,000 yuan. An ammonia bicarbonate chemical fertilizer plant had an annual rate of return to construction costs of 33%, while an ammonium nitrate chemical fertilizer plant had an annual rate of return to construction cost of 17%. American Rural Small-Scale Industry Delegation, *Rural Small-Scale Industry,* pp. 99, 181–182. The income provided by these rural, small-scale industries is an important explanation for the increase in the commune's income relative to that of the lower-level units in the 1970s, although the team continues to account for the dominant share. For a discussion of this argument, see Frederick W. Crook, "The Commune System in the People's Republic of China, 1963–1974," in U.S. Congress, Joint Economic Committee, *China: A Reassessment of the Economy* (Washington, D.C.: U.S. Government Printing Office, 1975) p. 377. Examples from the report of the American Rural Small-Scale Industries Delegation illustrate the importance of these industries to the commune as an economic unit, vis-à-vis the team. In one commune

seven enterprises accounted for one-third of the total grain and industrial output value produced at the commune and brigade level; in
another, commune-owned industries accounted for one-fifth of the
total grain and industry income at the commune, brigade, and team
levels; in one county commune- and brigade-run industries accounted for over one-third of the county's total income. As the report
of the delegation concludes, "The significance of the commune as
an economic unit is heightened by the greater profitability of commune enterprises as compared with brigade enterprises and the
greater profit in industry as compared to agriculture" (p. 244). The
operations of these rural, small-scale industries, of course, vary
greatly as one moves from the larger, single-product plants owned
and operated by districts and municipalities down to the repair shops
operated by the brigades and the teams. For example, the financial
transactions, accounting of costs and revenues, allocation of inputs
and outputs for those plants at the higher levels—districts and municipalities—are similar to those in modern, large-scale industrial sector. The output of these plants is distributed over a fairly wide area by
the state's supply allocation network, they have a permanent work
force paid wages according to the eight-grade wage scale, and so on.
The same is true of the county-owned plants, although the distribution of the output of these plants is controlled by the county supply
authorities and restricted to local users. In the cooperative sector,
however, these plants utilize part-time and seasonal labor to a much
greater extent; the workers are paid work points for a share of their
team's total income, and the output is produced for the use of the unit
owning and operating the plant. Operated more as a workshop or repair station, these commune-run shops produce several types of agricultural machinery and equipment, turning from the production of
one type to another as their local needs are met. Finally, in many cases
the finances of these cooperatively owned plants may not even be an
independent item in the cooperative unit's budget, using inputs and
labor available within the commune and distributing the resulting
output within the commune with no financial transaction. In cases
where a small-scale enterprise owned and operated by the commune
performs services or produces current inputs for the production
teams, a processing fee or service charge may be paid, but these fees
are usually nominal and represent significant savings for the team
compared with the alternatives available.

18. Rawski, *Industrialization, Technology, and Employment,* pp. 70–71.

19. While the statistics necessary to support the argument are not
available, it is quite probable that China has one of the world's lowest
levels of unemployment, especially when the large size of the total

population and high labor force participation rate are taken into account, and one of the most equitable size distributions of income, especially in comparing ratios of the top 10% to the lowest 10% of income earners. For an analysis of this question, using the available data, see Alexander Eckstein, *China's Economic Revolution* (New York: Cambridge University Press, 1977), pp. 298–309, and Christopher Howe, *China's Economy* (New York: Basic Books, 1978), chap. 6.

20. In 1953 the urban population was 13.5% of the total population. The share of urban population in the total had increased to 14.6% by 1957; but despite the rapid industrialization that had taken place during the early 1950s, employment in industry was still less than 5% of the total labor force.

21. See Eckstein, *China's Economic Revolution*, pp. 299–300. For an excellent discussion of the structure of wages in China's industries, see Carl Riskin, "Worker's Incentives in Chinese Industry," in *China: A Reassessment*, pp. 199–224.

22. See Rawski, *Industrialization, Technology, and Employment*, especially pp. 133–135.

23. The use of the "high-level equilibrium trap" model to analyze China's economic evolution between the fifteenth and the twentieth centuries was made popular by Mark Elvin. See his *Pattern of the Chinese Past* (Stanford, Calif.: Stanford University Press, 1973), pp. 298–315; idem, "The High-Level Equilibrium Trap: The Causes of the Decline of Invention in the Traditional Chinese Textile Industries," in W. E. Willmott, ed., *Economic Organization in Chinese Society* (Stanford, Calif.: Stanford University Press, 1972), pp. 137–172; and my brief summary of that model in "The Role of the Foreigner in China's Economic Development," in Dwight H. Perkins, ed., *China's Modern Economy in Historical Perspective* (Stanford, Calif.: Stanford University Press, 1975), pp. 24–27. The most recent use of that model for analyzing China's economic history is by John C. H. Fei and Tsui-jung Liu, "Population Dynamics of Agrarianism in Traditional China," in *Conference on Modern Chinese Economic History* (Taipei: Institute of Economics, Academia Sinica, 1978), pp. 53–83.

24. See William Parrish and Martin King Whyte, *Village and Family in Contemporary China* (Chicago: University of Chicago Press, 1978).

25. These conclusions are presented and defended in Robert F. Dernberger, "The Program for Agricultural Transformation in the People's Republic of China," paper presented at the Seventh Sino-American Conference on Mainland China, Taipei, June 1978, and published in *Mainland China in the Post-Mao Period* (Taipei: Institute of International Relations, 1978), sec.II-2, pp. 1–42. These conclusions are derived on the basis of the Anthony Tang–Thomas Gottschang

data bank of agricultural statistics for the People's Republic of China, prepared as part of the Mellon Project on China's Economy, Center for Chinese Studies, University of Michigan.

26. For a biased but empirically based series of articles to support the second half of the assertion made in the text, see the collection of conference papers in W. A. Douglas Jackson, ed., *Agrarian Policies and Problems in Communist and Non-Communist Countries* (Seattle, Wash.: University of Washington Press, 1971). According to one contributor, this favorable comparison of private farming with cooperative agriculture continues to exist in the Soviet Union today. "It is of special interest to compare the yields of collective farms with those of the private sector, which still exists today in the Soviet Union in the form of the small subsidiary holdings of the kolkhoz farmers and some other groups. This comparison is quite favorable to the private sector." Otto Schiller, "The Agrarian Question: Communist Experience and Its Implications for Developing Countries," in Jackson, *Agrarian Policies and Problems*, p. 236.

27. For a humorous and most interesting illustration of this point see Alec Nove, *Economic Rationality and Soviet Politics* (New York: Frederick A. Praeger, 1964), chap. 1 ("Was Stalin Really Necessary?" reprinted from *Encounter*, April 1962). "Before his assassination in 1911, the last intelligent Tsarist Prime Minister, Stolypin, expressed the belief that his land reform measures would create in about twenty years a prosperous peasantry which would provide a stable foundation for society and the throne. No one will know if he would have been right, if he had not been murdered, if the Tsar had been wise, if Rasputin had not existed, if the war had not broken out . . . But of what use is it to indulge in such speculations? . . . In assessing the choices open to the Bolsheviks in, say 1926, the events before that date must be taken as given. The real question, surely, is to consider the practical alternatives which Stalin and his colleagues had before them" (p. 14).

28. See Bruce L. Reynolds, "Decentralized Planning and Agricultural Development in the People's Republic of China, 1952–1977," paper presented at the Annual Meeting of the American Economics Association, New York, December 1977.

29. The irony of present developments in China must be noted for readers who are not familiar with them. The feasibility of transferring elements of China's development experience to the other developing countries was a question of widespread interest during the twenty-five years of China's development policies based on self-reliance. Now, just as this question of transfer is being investigated, the post-Mao leadership has rejected self-reliance as a major principle of their de-

velopment policies and is actively negotiating with the developed countries to create an enormous transfer process from those countries to China. Nonetheless, there is no indication that the new leadership has rejected the three economic institutions or programs selected for analysis in this chapter.

30. For a rather complete list of these delegations and the citations for their trip reports, see *China Exchange Newsletter,* published by the Committee on Scholarly Communication with the People's Republic of China, National Academy of Sciences, Washington, D.C.

Contributors

Robert F. Dernberger is a professor of economics at the University of Michigan and chairman of the Social Science Research Council's Subcommittee for Research on the Chinese Economy.

Albert Feuerwerker is director of the Center for Chinese Studies at the University of Michigan and author of *The Chinese Economy, ca. 1870–1911* and *Economic Trends in the Republic of China, 1912–1949*.

Teh-wei Hu is a professor of economics at Pennsylvania State University and author of *An Economic Analysis of the Cooperative Medical Services in the People's Republic of China*.

Nicholas Lardy is an associate professor of economics at Yale University and author of *Economic Growth and Distribution in China*.

Françoise Le Gall is in the Asian Department of the International Monetary Fund in Washington and a former graduate student in the Chinese Economics Program at the University of Michigan.

Dwight H. Perkins is director of the Harvard Institute for International Development and chairman of the Department of Economics at Harvard University. He is the author of *Agricultural Development in China, 1368–1968* and *Market Control and Planning in Communist China*.

Thomas G. Rawski is a professor of economics at the University of Toronto and author of *Economic Growth and Employment in China*.

Amartya Sen is a professor of economics at Nuffield College, Oxford University, and author of *Collective Choice and Social Welfare*.

Benjamin Ward is a professor of economics at the University of California, Berkeley, and author of *The Socialist Economy*.

Thomas E. Weisskopf is a professor of economics at the University of Michigan and a co-author of *Studies in Development Planning*.

Index

HARVARD EAST ASIAN SERIES

30. *Politics in the Tokugawa Bakufu, 1600–1843.* Conrad Totman.
31. *Hara Kei in the Politics of Compromise, 1905–1915.* Tetsuo Najita.
32. *The Chinese World Order: Traditional China's Foreign Relations.* Ed. John K. Fairbank.
33. *The Buddhist Revival in China.* Holmes Welch.
34. *Traditional Medicine in Modern China: Science, Nationalism, and the Tensions of Cultural Change.* Ralph C. Croizier.
35. *Party Rivalry and Political Change in Taishō Japan.* Peter Duus.
36. *The Rhetoric of Empire: American China Policy, 1895–1901.* Marilyn B. Young.
37. *Radical Nationalist in Japan: Kita Ikki, 1883–1937.* George M. Wilson.
38. *While China Faced West: American Reformers in Nationalist China, 1928–1937.* James C. Thomson, Jr.
39. *The Failure of Freedom: A Portrait of Modern Japanese Intellectuals.* Tatsuo Arima.
40. *Asian Ideas of East and West: Tagore and His Critics in Japan, China, and India.* Stephen N. Hay.
41. *Canton under Communism: Programs and Politics in a Provincial Capital, 1949–1968.* Ezra F. Vogel.
42. *Ting Wen-chiang: Science and China's New Culture.* Charlotte Furth.
43. *The Manchurian Frontier in Ch'ing History.* Robert H. G. Lee.
44. *Motoori Norinage, 1730–1801.* Shigeru Matsumoto.
45. *The Comprador in Nineteenth Century China: Bridge between East and West.* Yen-p'ing Hao.
46. *Hu Shih and the Chinese Renaissance: Liberalism in the Chinese Revolution, 1917–1937.* Jerome B. Grieder.
47. *The Chinese Peasant Economy: Agricultural Development in Hopei and Shantung, 1890–1949.* Ramon H. Myers.
48. *Japanese Tradition and Western Law: Emperor, State, and Law in the Thought of Hozumi Yatsuka.* Richard H. Minear.
49. *Rebellion and Its Enemies in Late Imperial China: Militarization and Social Structure, 1796–1864.* Philip A. Kuhn.
50. *Early Chinese Revolutionaries: Radical Intellectuals in Shanghai and Chekiang, 1902–1911.* Mary Backus Rankin.
51. *Communication and Imperial Control in China: Evolution of the Palace Memorial System, 1693–1735.* Silas H. L. Wu.
52. *Vietnam and the Chinese Model: A Comparative Sudy of Ngugen and Ch'ing Civil Government in the First Half of the Nineteenth Century.* Alexander Barton Woodside.
53. *The Modernization of the Chinese Salt Administration, 1900–1920.* S. A. M. Adshead.
54. *Chang Chih-tung and Educational Reform in China.* William Ayers.
55. *Kuo Mo-jo: The Early Years.* David Tod Roy.
56. *Social Reformers in Urban China: The Chinese Y.M.C.A., 1895–1926.* Shirley S. Garrett.
57. *Biographic Dictionary of Chinese Communism, 1921–1965.* Donald W. Klein and Anne B. Clark.

58. *Imperialism and Chinese Nationalism: Germany in Shantung.* John E. Shrecker.
59. *Monarchy in the Emperor's Eyes: Image and Reality in the Ch'ien-lung Reign.* Harold L. Kahn.
60. *Yamagata Aritomo in the Rise of Modern Japan, 1838–1922.* Roger F. Hackett.
61. *Russia and China: Their Diplomatic Relations to 1728.* Mark Mancall.
62. *The Yenan Way in Revolutionary China.* Mark Selden.
63. *The Mississippi Chinese: Between Black and White.* James W. Loewen.
64. *Liang Ch'i-ch'ao and Intellectual Transition in China, 1890–1907.* Hao Chang.
65. *A Korean Village: Between Farm and Sea.* Vincent S. R. Brandt.
66. *Agricultural Change and the Peasant Economy of South China.* Evelyn S. Rawski.
67. *The Peace Conspiracy: Wang Ching-wei and the China War, 1937–1941.* Gerald Bunker.
68. *Mori Arinori.* Ivan Hall.
69. *Buddhism under Mao.* Holmes Welch.
70. *Student Radicals in Prewar Japan.* Henry Smith.
71. *The Romantic Generation of Modern Chinese Writers.* Leo Ou-fan Lee.
72. *Deus Destroyed: The Image of Christianity in Early Modern Japan.* George Elison.
73. *Land Taxation in Imperial China, 1750–1911.* Yeh-chien Wang.
74. *Chinese Ways in Warfare.* Ed. Frank A. Kierman, Jr., and John K. Fairbank.
75. *Pepper, Guns, and Parleys: The Dutch East India Company and China, 1662–1681.* John E. Wills, Jr.
76. *A Study of Samurai Income and Entrepreneurship: Quantitative Analyses of Economic and Social Aspects of the Samurai in Tokugawa and Meiji Japan.* Kozo Yamamura.
77. *Between Tradition and Modernity: Wang T'ao and Reform in Late Ch'ing China.* Paul A. Cohen.
78. *The Abortive Revolution: China under Nationalist Rule, 1927–1937.* Lloyd E. Eastman.
79. *Russia and the Roots of the Chinese Revolution, 1896–1911.* Don C. Price.
80. *Toward Industrial Democracy: Management and Workers in Modern Japan.* Kunio Odaka.
81. *China's Republican Revolution: The Case of Kwangtung, 1895–1913.* Edward J. M. Rhoads.
82. *Politics and Policy in Traditional Korea.* James B. Palais.
83. *Folk Buddhist Religion: Dissenting Sects in Late Traditional China.* Daniel L. Overmyer.
84. *The Limits of Change: Essays on Conservative Alternatives in Republican China.* Ed. Charlotte Furth.
85. *Yenching University and Sino-Western Relations, 1916–1952.* Philip West.
86. *Japanese Marxist: A Portrait of Kawakami Hajime, 1876–1946.* Gail Lee Bernstein.
87. *China's Forty Millions: Minority Nationalities and National Integration in the People's Republic of China.* June Teufel Dreyer.

88. *Japanese Colonial Education in Taiwan, 1895–1945*. E. Patricia Tsurumi.
89. *Modern Chinese Literature in the May Fourth Era*. Ed. Merle Goldman.
90. *The Broken Wave: The Chinese Communist Peasant Movement, 1922–1928*. Roy Hofheinz, Jr.
91. *Passage to Power: K'ang-hsi and His Heir Apparent, 1661–1722*. Silas H. L. Wu.
92. *Chinese Communism and the Rise of Mao*. Benjamin I. Schwartz.
93. *China's Development Experience in Comparative Perspective*. Ed. Robert F. Dernberger.

(Some of these titles may be out of print in a given year. Write to Harvard University Press for information and ordering.)